LONELY PLANET
BLUE
LIST.

THE BEST IN TRAVEL 2007

MELBOURNE ✪ OAKLAND ✪ LONDON

CONTENTS »

The original idea for Bluelist was but a twinkle in an avid Lonely Planet staffer's eye some 18 months ago. It was loosely formed back then. We wanted to share what we know is happening in travel now and stimulate discussion on the subject among people who love travel as much as we do. In the time it's taken for this copy of Bluelist 2007 to reach you, the idea has really taken hold at Lonely Planet and within our travel community. It's become a catch cry for anything to do with recommending and sharing ideas on the best travel experiences of the moment.

Bluelist has been even more fun to work on this year as we've refined the focus, responded to all your feedback on the first edition, and added lots more ideas and information including lists from our travellers via the Bluelist website. The site is an adventure all of its own, with more than 5000 lists submitted in its first year, ranging in subject matter from the best airports for dishevelled travellers to the best places to be stung by nonlethal jellyfish.

Take a look for yourself, post your own Bluelists and comment on other people's.

Bluelist 2007 kicks off with the 'Top 11' countries to visit, as voted by travellers in our annual Travellers' Pulse survey. You won't find many surprises in the list of countries, but we hope you'll find something new in the suggestions we offer for exploring these classic travel destinations.

Next up are the much-loved Bluelists, which this year amalgamate travellers' postings on our website with our own recommendations. In this section, you'll find the old faithful categories, such as best value destinations and cities on the rise, but also a whole load of stuff that you might not even have thought of: paranormal travel, slow travel, Eurovision repeat offenders, spinning out in Japan, dining on the wild side, to name but a few.

The third part of the book constitutes an interlude of sorts, where we feature a theme that we reckon is about to hit the travel landscape. This year we are

By Roz Hopkins
Publisher, Lonely Planet

BLUELIST [2] (blu‚list) *v.* »
To recommend a travel experience.

profiling dark tourism. I won't try to explain; flip to p122 to find out more.

Last year, we profiled every country in the world one way or another, but this year we wanted to be more focused. In the GoLists (p140), you'll find a range of 30 countries, cities or regions that have been recommended by our travel-expert commissioning editors. These guys will tell you where to go, whether it be Madagascar, Turkmenistan, Brooklyn or southern Laos.

Last but not least, in the final section of the book we review the state of travel and forecast new directions and events for places that aren't covered elsewhere in the book, in a series of short, snappy, news-style reports. Want to know where the next Rock Paper Scissors Championship is being held? You'll find out here.

Although we might like to pretend to people at dinner parties that we Lonely Planeteers are constantly on the road or up the mountain (and whenever we can, we are!), like any company, we have to endure our share of meetings and marker pens. Many a whiteboard moment has been spent deliberating over the 'key value proposition' of Bluelist. Last year, it was all about recommending travel experiences. This year, I think it's even simpler. Bluelist 2007 is a conversation about travel. We know you've got something to say... www.lonelyplanet.com/bluelist.

Surprisingly I did manage to cover most of the territory I mapped out last year, except I fell down badly on the big trip that has sat at the top of my must-do list for far too long – the Trans-Siberian Railway. I didn't find the time to do it last year and it looks like the big-red-railway-ride is going to stay at the top of my list for another try.

The idea of a road circuit of the Scandinavian countries also stayed that way, just an idea, but having a go at the Plymouth–Banjul Challenge is still on the agenda. No, not the Paris–Dakar Rally, that's big money. This one is decisively small change, and anyway it goes further. The finishing point is Banjul, Gambia, the next capital down the West Africa coast after Dakar. There have been Lonely Planet competitors in the last two Plymouth–Banjul runs and Maureen and I have our names down to be at the starting line in February 2007. Now all we need is to find a suitable car, which the organisers insist 'should ideally cost less than UK£100'. Yes, you read that right, just two zeros. It's a nice contrast with the Paris–Dakar, where UK£100,000 would hardly get you to the start line. Well, it is supposed to be a challenge.

The country that headed up my 'Places to Go' Bluelist last year was Afghanistan and I not only went back to that difficult destination, but I also managed to see a fair amount of the country including forays into central Afghanistan to visit the Bamiyan Valley, the beautiful lakes of Band-e Amir and the mysterious and impossibly remote Minaret of Jam. I was able to sneak into Iraq for a week, not the disaster area of the centre and south of course, but the reasonably secure Kurdistan region in the north. Albania, on the other hand, may still have a 'bad land' reputation, but definitely no longer deserves it. I found Albania easy to travel around, surprisingly bright and forward looking and, apart from some slightly nutty road behaviour, quite safe.

My travels over the last year also took me to some African destinations that are well off the regular routes, such as Angola and the Central African Republic, and included the evocative African place name, Timbuktu. If you're reaching for your atlas, it's in the centre of Mali, an extraordinarily exotic country that will definitely be attracting more visitors in the years to come. Pakistan is not an everyday destination either and my reason for going there was certainly unplanned; I dropped in to visit an aid organisation working in Kashmir after the disastrous October 2005 earthquake. But, of course, it's tempted me to think about a return visit!

I'm sure other weird and wonderful destinations will find there way onto my Bluelist for the next 12 months, but one that's definitely planned is Mongolia. Over the past year I've been to a number of places where Genghis Khan, that most famous Mongolian, dropped by, so it seems entirely appropriate to be pursuing him home next year. At the other extreme I've also got some very civilised travel lined up on book promotion tours, where you run from city to city to talk about your book, and after a week or two become totally confused about where you are. Book tours will take me to Italy, the UK, the USA and even to China.

Every year I try to do at least one long walk. Since the past year's only real walk was a short if spectacular stroll along the recently opened Great Ocean Walk in the Australian state of Victoria, I'm planning to make up

By Tony Wheeler
Cofounder of Lonely Planet

SO WHAT'S NEXT? »

How did my personal Bluelist for last year fare? And what do I have lined up for the next 12 months?

for it during the next year. In Australia I'm going to walk for the second time the Overland Track in the island state of Tasmania, and in England I've got the classic coast-to-coast walk known as the Wainwright Way lined up. It's a two-week trek that kicks off in the Lake District and ends up in the Yorkshire Dales.

The technology trends we've witnessed in travel for years seem to have accelerated in the past 12 months. Mobile-phone coverage now reaches the most unlikely places. I popped a Roshan (Afghani mobile-phone company) SIM card into my phone in Kabul and instantly I had phone connections in the backest backblocks of Afghanistan. Internet cafés are equally geographically diverse (yes, I tried a few out in Iraq); it's amazing how you can get online in the places you least expect.

The continuing boom in cheap flights through the airline segment now known as LCCs (low-cost carriers) also seems to know no bounds, but I suspect the most important travel trend in the years to come will be how to make this boom work in a sustainable fashion. The global warming nonbelievers are becoming fewer and fewer. If we want to keep on seeing the world (and having a world to keep on seeing), we're going to have to find ways to make travel more environmentally positive.

I've always said I like travel at the extremes. My sleeping bag was a necessity at some of the places I stayed in Afghanistan, but the year's hostelries also included a stay at the luxurious Banyan Tree Resort in Thailand and a stay in a castle in Ireland. Nevertheless, the most contrasting travel extremes I encountered were on a little bar crawl in Washington DC. I hit the town with Stelios Haji-Ioannou, the creator of the pioneering European low-cost airline EasyJet, and Eric Anderson, the creator of Space Adventures. Here's travel at polar opposites, I thought, in one Georgetown bar: I'm having a beer with the guy who will take you anywhere in Europe for 10 quid and the guy who will take you up to the International Space Station for 10 million.

I've been creating personal Bluelists for more than 10 years and gradually ticking them off, but here are 10 things to do and places to go I really should get around to:

- ✪ Take the Trans-Siberian Railway train trip. The big-red-railway-ride has been on my must-do list for far too long.

- ✪ Travel up the Karakoram Highway from Islamabad in Pakistan to Kashgar in China.

- ✪ Voyage by ship along the Inside Passage to Alaska.

- ✪ Head to Taiwan. Over the years I've managed to see most countries in Asia, but this one has always evaded me.

- ✪ Tramp the Tongariro Circuit in New Zealand.

- ✪ Dive with the whale sharks at Ningaloo Reef off Western Australia.

- ✪ Walk the Kokoda Trail in Papua New Guinea.

- ✪ Travel to the Pacific nation of Vanuatu and check out those amazing volcanoes.

- ✪ Journey to Kakadu in Australia's Northern Territory. For some reason I've never managed to visit one of the country's most spectacular national parks.

- ✪ Explore Yemen, one of the most interesting countries in the Middle East.

TRAVEL PLANNER

JANUARY

- Brahmaputra Beach Festival in Guwahati, India
- Celebrations for Sigulda's 800th year, Latvia
- Chinese New Year, Hong Kong
- Coney Island Polar Bears First Dip on New Year's Day, Brooklyn, USA
- Minstrel (aka Coon) Carnival in Cape Town, South Africa
- Feria Taurina bullfighting season in Cartagena, Colombia
- Festival in the Desert, Mali
- Hogmanay, Scotland
- International Circus Festival, Monaco
- La Tamborrada (St Sebastián's Day), San Sebastián, Spain
- Monte Carlo Rally, Monaco
- Nagaur Cattle Fair in Rajasthan, India
- Niramekko Obisha festival, Ichikawa, Japan
- Palena Rodeo in Patagonia, Chile
- Stay at the Snow Hotel, Finland
- Sugar Bowl at the New Orleans Superdome, USA

FEBRUARY

- Al Jenadriyah in Riyadh, Saudi Arabia
- Bob Marley's Birthday, Jamaica
- Carnaval in San Sebastián, Spain
- Carnival, Trinidad
- Festival of Dance in Madhya Pradesh, India
- Fiesta de Nuestra Senora de la Candelaria in Cartagena, Colombia
- Mardi Gras in New Orleans, USA
- Mas Domnik & Miss Dominica competition, Dominica
- Pan-African Film Festival in Ouagadougou, Burkina Faso
- Portland International Film Festival, USA
- Pre-Easter celebrations in Barcelona, Spain
- Sunrise at the Great Temple of Ramses II in Abu Simbel, Egypt

MARCH

- Ay Noruz in Xinjiang, China
- Belfast Film Festival, Northern Ireland
- Bun Wat Phu Champasak, Laos
- Chapchar Kut in Mizoram, India
- Festival Internacional de Cine in Cartagena, Colombia
- Formula One Grand Prix, Bahrain
- Hina Matsuri, Japan
- Maitisong Festival in Gaborone, Botswana
- Pasifika Festival in Auckland, New Zealand
- Phnom Penh Arts Festival, Cambodia
- St Patrick's Day in Boston, USA
- Start of the International Polar Year 2007–2008, Antarctica
- World Music Awards, Monaco

APRIL

- 2007 Cricket World Cup finals, Barbados
- Antigua Sailing Week, Antigua & Barbuda
- Anzac Day at Gallipoli, Turkey
- Ashokastami Mela in Unakoti, India
- Drop of Water is a Nugget of Gold Day, Turkmenistan
- Fireworks Festival in Valletta, Malta

Flame Tree Festival, Guam &
Northern Mariana Islands

French Quarter Festival in
New Orleans, USA

Gathering of Nations Powwow
in Albuquerque, USA

Hanami in Tokyo, Japan

Horse Day, Turkmenistan

Jazz & Heritage Festival in
New Orleans, USA

Land-diving ceremonies on
Pentecost Island,Vanuatu

Rite of Spring Festival, Iceland

Shad Sukmynsiem in Khasi
Hills, India

Spring Arts Festival, Monaco

Tennis Masters Series in
Monte Carlo, Monaco

MAY

Billabong Pro Tahiti Surf
Festival, Tahiti

Bird-watching on Ramsey
Island, Wales

Carpet Day, Turkmenistan

Chonta Festival in Shuar
villages, Ecuador

Diving in Myanmar (Burma)

Eurovision Song Contest Final
in Helsinki, Finland

Festa di San Nicola in Bari, Italy

Forumla One Grand Prix, Monaco

Helston Furry Dance in
Cornwall, England

Hot-air ballooning over Serengeti
National Park, Tanzania

Jongmyo Daeje ceremony,
South Korea

Prague Symphony Orchestra
concert season, Czech Republic

Re-enactment of 1876
April Uprising in
Koprivshtitsa, Bulgaria

Watson Lake Music Festival
in Yukon, Canada

Welcome spring in
London, England

JUNE

America's Cup in Valencia, Spain

Amsterdam Roots Festival,
Netherlands

Blues Festival in Chicago, USA

Bun Bang Fai, Laos

Fisherman's Birthday
Celebrations, Grenada

Gay Pride Month in
New York, USA

Gay Pride Parade,
Portland, USA

Golowan Festival in
Penzance, England

Homowo Festival, Ghana

Junkanoo Summer
Festival, Bahamas

Kluane Chilkat International
Bike Relay in Haines
Junction, Canada

Matariki celebrations,
New Zealand

Mermaid Parade on Coney
Island, Brooklyn, USA

Midnight sun in
Reykjavík, Iceland

Portland Rose Festival
in Oregon, USA

Salmon season in
Anchorage, USA

Springtime festivals in
New York, USA

Wife-Carrying World
Championships in
Sonkajärvi, Finland

Xinjiang Grape Festival
in Turpan, China

TRAVEL PLANNER

JULY

Asian Cup football finals in Hanoi, Vietnam

Celtic Fusion International Musical Arts Festival in Castlewellan, Northern Ireland

Climb Mt Fuji, Japan

Golden Days in Fairbanks, USA

Great Texas Mosquito Festival in Clute, USA

Heilala Festival & Miss Galaxy Pageant, Tonga

Independence celebrations, Kiribati

International Folklore Festival in Zagreb, Croatia

Jerash festival in Jerash, Jordan

Melon Day, Turkmenistan

Nanaimo World Championship Bathtub Race, Canada

Nathan's Famous Hot Dog Eating Contest on Coney Island, Brooklyn, USA

Nine-day festival of music & theatre in Ghent, Belgium

Oregon Brewers Festival in Portland, USA

Pan American Games in Rio, Brazil

Rath Yatra in Puri, India

Refugee Film Festival in Phnom Penh, Cambodia

Rome, Italy is at its best

Sagra della Madonna della Bruna in Matera, Italy

Savonlinna Opera Festival, Finland

Summer Restaurant Week in New York, USA

Watch 4 July fireworks from Brooklyn waterfront, USA

World BodyPainting Festival in Seeboden, Austria

World Eskimo Indian Olympics in Fairbanks, USA

World Masters Orienteering Championships in Kuusamo, Finland

AUGUST

All-Ireland Road Bowls Championship, Northern Ireland

Carriacou Regatta Festival, Grenada

Cornwall Folk Festival, England

Earth Celebration on Sado Island, Japan

Folklore Days Festival in Koprivshtitsa, Bulgaria

Hillsborough International Oyster Festival & World Oyster-Eating Championship, Northern Ireland

Independence celebrations, Gabon

International Folk Festival of Danubian Countries in Tulcea, Romania

Kantō Matsuri in Akita, Japan

Mass Games in Pyongyang, North Korea

Nebuta Matsuri in Aomori, Japan

Nehru Trophy Snake Boat Race, Kerala, India

Neputa Matsuri in Hirosaki, Japan

Pageant of the Golden Tree in Bruges, Belgium

Red Stripe Reggage Sumfest, Jamaica

Santa Fe Indian Market, USA

Semana Grande in San Sebastián, Spain

Sfântu Gheorghe Film Festival, Romania

South Pacific Games, Samoa

Tanabata Matsuri in Sendai, Japan

Whitehorse's Yukon International Storytelling Festival, Canada

Places to go, things to do

SEPTEMBER

- Air Guitar World Championships in Oulu, Finland
- Atlantic Antic street fair in Brooklyn, USA
- Bungy jumping at Verzasca Dam, Switzerland
- Deni Ute Muster in Deniliquin, Australia
- Festival Week in Kosrae, Micronesia
- Highland show in Goroka, Papua New Guinea
- International Film Festival in San Sebastián, Spain
- International Symposium on Antarctic Earth Science (ISAES) in Santa Barbara, USA
- Jazz in Puglia Festival in Lecce, Italy
- Southern Decadence in New Orleans, USA
- St Ives September Festival in Cornwall, England
- Week-long Alele festivities & fishing competitions, Marshall Islands
- Whale-watching, Tonga
- Zozobra in Santa Fe, USA

OCTOBER

- Albuquerque International Balloon Fiesta, USA
- Amsterdam Dance Event, Netherlands
- Belang Races in Dullah, Kei Islands
- Bird-watching in the Danube Delta
- Buddha Mahotsav in Tawang Gompa, India
- Bun Nam, Laos
- Celebrations for the annual rice harvest, Cambodia
- Diwali, India
- Enjoy fewer crowds in Goa, India
- Festival Kreol, Seychelles
- Iceland Airwaves, Iceland
- October Wine Festival in Chişinău, Moldova
- Oktoberfest in Windhoek, Namibia
- Pushkar Camel Fair, India
- Voodoo Music Experience in City Park, New Orleans, USA
- Watch red crabs emerge on Christmas Island, Australia
- World Creole Music Festival, Dominica

NOVEMBER

- Cannabis Cup in Amsterdam, Netherlands
- Celebrations for founding day of Tena, Ecuador
- Hawaiki Nui Canoe Race, Tahiti & French Polynesia
- Loy Krathong in Santichaiprakan Park, Bangkok, Thailand
- Reinado Nacional de Bellaza, Cartagena, Colombia
- Sasi Lompa Festival in Haruku, Maluku
- Sonepur Mela in Bihar, India
- Tiare Festival, Cook Islands

DECEMBER

- Celebrate Christmas in Dublin, Ireland
- Festival of Carnatic Music & Dance in Tamil Nadu, India
- Festival of the Oases, Tunisia
- Good Neighbourliness Day, Turkmenistan
- Hornbill Festival in Kohima, India
- Tramp the Milford Track, New Zealand
- Tulcea Winter Carnival, Romania

SO HOW DID WE COME UP WITH THIS YEAR'S LIST OF TOP DESTINATIONS?

Well, we didn't – you did! For the past few years Lonely Planet has been running an online travel survey named Travellers' Pulse. It's grown significantly since we kicked it off in 2003, and this year 33,000 people from 170 countries responded, which makes it the world's biggest survey of its kind.

Destinations are a key focus of Travellers' Pulse; we explore where travellers have been, where they're going and their favourite places. This allows our passionate, well-travelled audience to give us insights as to 'what's hot' and helps us develop better and more targeted products for the travel community.

So what did travellers say this year? Europe is again the number-one region to visit. This is not surprising given the wealth of travel opportunities the continent offers and its easy and increasingly cheap accessibility. City breaks and short escapes are continuing to rise, with Barcelona voted the preferred short-escape destination. Interestingly, Melbourne was ranked number three (well ahead of its perennial rival Sydney), which may be due to the Commonwealth Games being held in the city around the time of this survey. A surprising result was that no Asian city made the top 10 list.

In terms of most popular countries, the traditional favourites headed the list again. Is this surprising? Are travellers becoming less intrepid? Are we resorting to visiting only mainstream destinations? Not at all. On the contrary, we're now more inquisitive and adventurous than ever.

What the survey tells us is that there's an increased focus on pick-and-mix trips. While travellers are still picking the well-known places to visit (for very valid reasons), they're also mixing the iconic tourist draws with new, out of the way regions and activities (such as visiting Paris then riding white Camargue horses in the swamplands of southeastern France), or they're experiencing traditional places in different ways (like taking a graffiti tour of Brooklyn).

Travellers will continue to want to fall under the romantic charm of the Taj Mahal at sunset, stroll among the many groups of locals doing Pilates in Tiananmen Sq or eat gelato at the Trevi Fountain, because these are timeless experiences.

It's the emerging desire to get under the skin of a place and hunt out unique experiences through direct interactions that makes the most hardened traveller return to Tokyo or Florence or Sydney again and again.

So if you're thinking of heading to perennial ports of call like France, Thailand and India, then sift through this section to read what our expert authors have to say about these classic destinations, visit Bluelist at www.lonelyplanet.com and hit the road!

AUSTRALIA »

to experience way more of this vast country by staying put. See a place's big-ticket attraction, and then go where Australians go, and find the extraordinary in the ordinary.

Everyday events and activities are often the most memorable occasions for visitors. Interacting with Australia at a local level offers up remarkable insights into this complex country. Simply playing golf here can lead to encounters with inhabitants, such as crocs in a course's water hole and roos on the green. And why stop at poking at a chop on a barbecue? Taste a sugar ant or – worse for some – Vegemite.

Australia's eco-operators and indigenous-run tours are a quick way in under the country's skin. These small-group excursions offer a specialised focus on unique aspects of Australia. The best are

BEYOND THE STEREOTYPE

Australia is whatever you want it to be. Annually, more than 5.6 million people jettison their working weeks, and choose the vast brown land in the south to spend some quality time. Australia's highways carry grey-haired nomads and their caravans to a string of seaside townships with a lawn-bowls club in every port. The country's wineries, produce markets, bars, cafés and restaurants sate culinary types. Backpackers bound from beach to bar to bed and back. Adventurers rock climb, raft, snorkel, hike and cycle their way around. For others, the chance to cheer at a Melbourne Cup or the World Lizard Racing Championships provides motive enough. For arty types, Australia presents sophisticated cities with exhibitions and performances aplenty, plus less-populated places with rock-art galleries and Dreamtime meanings.

Whatever the focus of an Australian holiday, the majority of visitors will taste the city, the coast and the countryside. They'll catch a glimpse of the sails of the Sydney Opera House billowing above the glistening harbour; they'll drop into the ocean, preferably the Pacific to swim among the fishes and corals of the Great Barrier Reef; and they'll see red, via the sea of red dirt surrounding Uluru.

A DEEPER LOOK

Australia's essence is revealed with time. It's not necessary to plan a longer holiday to get a whiff of it, just spend more time in one place. It's possible

also carefully managed to minimise impacts on the environment and maximise benefits to the community where they're based. Volunteering opportunities provide backstage passes to some of the country's more interesting elements. Be a dragon for the day, by carrying a Chinese dragon through clouds of incense, crowds and clatter during New Year celebrations. Track the hairy-nosed wombat or help to save the threatened purple-wing butterfly by spending a week with a conservation organisation.

HOT FOR 2007

Football (soccer) is the new Australian Rules footy – almost. Soccer has seen a surge in popularity since Australia's 2006 relative success in the World Cup.

NINGALOO REEF OFFERS A CHANCE TO PUT A LITTLE PERSPECTIVE ON HOW WE FIT INTO THE LANDSCAPE DOWNUNDER.

Australia's essence is revealed with time...it's possible to experience way more of this vast country by staying put.

Melbourne has emerged as the country's coolest city. It's shirked the dowdy shroud, and come out as the edgy, understated leader in arts, food, sport and festivals.

2007 sees Australia's next legislative elections, with the opposition Labor Party challenging the incumbent Coalition and Prime Minister Howard's third term (that's a decade, folks).

SIGHTS UNSEEN

The world knows Australia's northeast coast for its extraordinary Great Barrier Reef. But few have a clue about the exceptionally gorgeous Ningaloo Reef on the west coast. Ningaloo is distinguished by its hard corals, which take a great variety of shapes and sizes. It's possible to snorkel off the beach over Ningaloo (no requisite boat rides, as with reaching the GBR), but it's also worth touring to the outer reef: glide quietly through the turtle nursery to reach the stuff of divers' dreams. Each season brings a passing parade of marine life, including whale sharks, manta rays and whales.

REGION OF CHOICE

Tasmania's isolation has fostered a truly unique landscape and way of life. The world is wising up to Tasmanians. For decades, they've been telling ghoulish tales of two-headed locals and a flesh-eating mammal, the Tasmanian devil, to scare off visitors and keep their island paradise a secret. Tasmania's wilderness areas are some of the country's best, and are complemented by excellent visitor facilities. An appreciation for the finer things in life has also given rise to bundles of boutique food producers and a healthy arts industry.

– *Simone Egger*

To push the iconic NZ experience even further, spend some time in Auckland or Wellington immersing yourself in Pacific Island cultures, watching Samoan cricket, shopping with Tongan, Niuean and Fijian families at the markets, or enjoying Tokelauan dancing. This is an aspect of NZ travel as yet unexplored by travellers and unexploited by the tourism industry, so you'll be forging your own Pacific path.

HOT FOR 2007

The round of celebrations that mark Mataraki, the Maori New Year, run through June and July and include Maori dance, foods, arts and fashions, and music from traditional *waiata* (songs) to contemporary chartbusters, such as Katchafire.

NEW ZEALAND

BEYOND THE STEREOTYPE

Most people come to New Zealand for the great outdoors – those mountains, glaciers and forests. And of course those three hobbit films, featuring spectacular landscapes aplenty, haven't hurt one little bit. The country's greatest tourist hot spots are those that allow travellers to immerse themselves in the fantastic environment: skiing or jetboating in the stunning mountains and ravines around Queenstown, or trekking and zorbing the thermal wonderlands of the Rotorua region.

There's fabulous scenery sufficient to fill any photo album, but for a holiday that sticks in your memory, you have to experience the people who live here. And alongside them, NZ's decision to stay out of the War on Terror reminded the world that here sits a safe, sane country.

A DEEPER LOOK

New Zealanders are a fascinating bunch. They're politically stroppy, fresh, innovative and extremely fond of travellers (they love any intrepid soul who's made the effort to come visit). In particular, the country's Maori culture is unique. It's something you can encounter only here, and travellers are starting to insist that it's an element of their NZ trip. Maori tourism is no longer just traditional dance shows at arms' length; you can now canoe rivers with Maori guides retelling their tribal legends, or wander the streets of Auckland to discover urban Maori.

For those interested in the country's Pacific Island cultures, you can't do better than to time a visit around Auckland's Pasifika festival in March 2007, the world's largest celebration of Pacific culture. At the other end of the North Island, Wellington also boasts a strong Pacific culture. NZ's funkiest, prettiest, most compact little city is fast becoming a destination in its own right rather than a stopover between the North and South Islands.

SIGHTS UNSEEN

Instead of spending another week in Queenstown, with its busy schedule of bungy jumping, jetboating and bar hopping, consider heading a couple of hours east to the Pacific coast and the secluded hills of the windswept Catlins Forest Park.

There's fabulous scenery sufficient to fill any photo album, but for a holiday that sticks in your memory, you have to experience the people who live here.

The area's relative lack of infrastructure reflects its position as slightly off the tourist trail, but it's not exactly the wilderness. If you don't want to pitch a tent, there are comfy rental houses with roaring fires. And if you don't fancy dinner from a can, there are cafés by the dozen with espresso machines to keep the caffeine junkies happy.

REGIONS OF CHOICE

New Zealand's two opposing 'coasts' form captivating bookends to the country.

The South Island's West Coast hemmed in by high surf and the Southern Alps, is unique and offers one of NZ's greatest road trips. Coasters boast of their descent from gold miners and exhibit a healthy disdain for 'the rules'. The wind off the Tasman Sea might be bitingly cold, but for the handful of travellers who get here, a West Coast welcome is legendarily warm.

The East Coast, an isolated, craggy corner of the North Island, sees even fewer travellers. The area's small population is predominantly Maori, and tiny colourful *marae* (meeting houses) dot the hills. A single road winds from Opotiki to Gisborne but carries little traffic. When an intrepid traveller's pack hits the dusty floor of any small East Coast pub, they're guaranteed almost celebrity status.

Choose a coast, or better yet, spend some time in each, and compare the charms of NZ's two 'frontier' regions.

– Errol Hunt

INTENSITY PERMEATES THE NEW ZEALAND TRAVEL EXPERIENCE, WHETHER IT'S NATURAL GRANDEUR OR CULTURAL ICONS. THE HAKA'S CERTAINLY NOT FOR THE FAINT-HEARTED.

TOP 11 HOT PICKS • TRAVELLER'S PULSE 2007 • FAVOURITE COUNTRY

3

USA

Travelling by public transport in the USA is not impossible, but it is slow and often expensive. However, there are some great train routes, and deals on tickets are available if you book online in advance. Greyhound buses often get a bad rap, but they can work out just fine for independent travellers who don't want to drive between major cities. For those travelling by car you can now rent hybrid cars or get into the 'drive-away car' scene. And don't forget the trusty bike for some 21st-century rawhide; cycling is growing in popularity in the USA and it's almost possible to stay entirely on quiet back roads, so get pedalling.

BEYOND THE STEREOTYPE

Stripping away preconceptions, the USA is overwhelmingly alluring and it's not just a fake, well-spun image. In fact, what attracts tourists the most isn't based on hype at all – it's simply how things are. New York is gritty and cool, the Grand Canyon is vast and impressive, the open road is liberating. Finding the real, although sometimes unusual, USA makes for the best trips whether you're hiking in the Alaskan wilderness, slurping milkshakes in retro diners, clubbing in Los Angeles or gaping at wacky Americana on Route 66. It's the simple pleasures, amid a backdrop of prairies, mountains, lakes, forests, oceans, deserts and cities, that continue to give the country appeal – and dedicated followers still want in.

A DEEPER LOOK

It isn't easy to get jazzed about ecotourism in the USA, when every other person is driving a gas-guzzling SUV. However, there are opportunities to make a difference: from bringing tourism back to New Orleans or rooting out quieter national parks, to taking the pressure off overtouristed sites or buying from independent shops instead of big chains. In fact, by doing these things you're already having a unique American experience and getting a deeper look at the country. To peer in even further, listen to the locals – you'll be eating the town's best slice of pizza and drinking the cheapest happy-hour beer before you know it.

HOT FOR 2007

In a bid to build better relations with the international community, the USA is looking towards travel and tourism to help improve its image. It's hoping that a more positive, welcoming attitude towards tourists will impress them, and the good word will spread. So, 2007 is the year to get to know the real America and not just the image.

SIGHTS UNSEEN

A trip to the Grand Canyon National Park is an iconic American experience that leaves even jaded visitors amazed and all who witness it somehow changed. However, if you want to have a similar experience further off the tourist trail, head to Bryce Canyon

THERE'S LESS COMPETITION FOR SPACE AT BRYCE CANYON NATIONAL PARK – FIND YOUR OWN PERCH AND ENJOY THE VIEW.

It's the simple pleasures, amid a backdrop of prairies, mountains, lakes, forests, oceans, deserts and cities, that continue to give the country appeal...

and Zion National Parks in Utah. You can whisk in and out of the parks in a few hours but numerous trails will take you deeper into the heart of rocks and landscape. Other national parks and monuments around Bryce Canyon, such as Grand Staircase-Escalante National Monument, are for the even more adventurous.

City-lovers should try Portland (p186) instead of Seattle, or San Diego instead of Los Angeles. They're on the tourist map but not completely overrun.

REGION OF CHOICE

Southern states, baby! Beginning in New Orleans (p178), Louisiana, take a trip west to French-speaking Cajun country. Next, hit the road in the direction of hip Austin and Big Bend National Park in Texas, the incredible Carlsbad Caverns National Park and Gila Cliff Dwellings National Monument in New Mexico. Finally, stop for a while to draw breath in Tucson, Arizona.

This trip will take you two to three weeks, and will give you cultural insights that go far beyond the clichés of swampy bayous, honky-tonk and crawfish. And, because the southern states are a less-explored part of the country, they will offer you a more personal adventure. It's approximately 3200km of mind-opening travel.

– Heather Dickson

island-hopping in Sicily. If you're going to get the most out of Italy, the trick is to focus on the details or you'll be overwhelmed by the whole. Italy is as much in the languid lines of the Boy of Mòzia statue in Sicily as it is in the Colosseum. Picking your highlights carefully will give you room to savour them, while adopting a slightly nonchalant attitude to the other splendours around you will make you feel ever-so Italian. Courses in painting, cooking, wine-making, frescoes, marbling and mosaics will also give you a rewarding entrée into Italy, enabling you to engage with expats, chefs, artists and artisans who will enthusiastically share their version of Italy with you and enable you to make a connection with the country, by placing it within a meaningful context.

ITALY

BEYOND THE STEREOTYPE

Italy is a moveable feast of endless courses. No matter how much you gorge yourself on its splendours, you always feel you haven't made it past the antipasti. Few countries offer such variety and few visitors leave without a fervent desire to return. The treasures of Rome, Venice and Florence draw tourists to them like moths to an incandescent flame, but Italy is not just an urban adventure. The northern wall of the Alps, the Dolomites, the Lucanian Apennines and the towering volcanoes of Vesuvius, Etna and Stromboli invite you to indulge in the whole gamut of mountain sports. It may be 'Old Europe', but Italy is the soul of Western civilisation, embodying some of its most refined achievements as well as its most venal failings. As such, it is endlessly compelling, unpredictable and engaging.

A DEEPER LOOK

United only in 1870, Italy has a history that's more a storybook of histories than a single, linear tome. And as the modern world succumbs to a bland homogeneity, Italy obstinately clings to its regional distinctions – there isn't one single idea of Italy, but a multitude of regional landscapes, characters and cuisines. This regionality is what sets Italy apart from the rest of Europe. A wine holiday in Umbria couldn't be more different to a romantic weekend on the Venetian lagoons or a week's

HOT FOR 2007

Following the drop in tourist figures and the elections in 2006, Italy is undergoing a period of serious self-reflection, especially in the tourist heartlands as travellers turn their focus from traditional hot spots to more off-the-beaten-track experiences. Verona, Ravenna, Mantua, Turin, Bologna and Palermo are growing quietly in popularity; and the southern half of the country continues to steal a march on the traditional provinces north of Rome. Sicily, in particular, is wildly popular and this season sights will be set on the emerging destination of Puglia and Basilicata (p188). Sardinia, too, is developing into something of an adventure mecca, offering some

Italy obstinately clings to its regional distinctions – there isn't one single idea of Italy, but a multitude of regional landscapes, characters and cuisines.

of the most challenging trekking, climbing and canyoning in Europe, as well as some spectacular diving.

SIGHTS UNSEEN

Italy is justifiably famous for its ancient sites; the granddaddy of them all being the relics of Rome and the ash-covered city of Pompeii. Closer to Naples, though, tucked in the lee of the coast is Herculaneum with its extraordinary stash of wooden artefacts. Beds, lintels and household shrines were so blackened and charred by the pyroclastic surge that they were instantly transformed to carbon.

It's an extraordinary archive of everyday Roman life. Other lesser known archaeological sites well worth the visit are the spectacular archaeological park in Syracuse and the dramatically tumbled temples of Selinunte, both in Sicily, and the romantic setting of pretty Paestum, south of Pompeii.

REGION OF CHOICE

Sardinia may lack the Italian mainland's suave glamour, but its untamed natural beauty and rugged rural scenery make it a maverick among Med islands. What's more, Sardinians are slowly waking up to their island's potential as an adventure destination. Few experiences can beat trekking down the Gola Su Gorruppu gorge or the windy heights of the Supramonte. Sardinia also harbours some of Europe's most challenging rock climbing and kitesurfing. The stunning multiday Selvaggio Blu trek scales the cliffs along the sparkling blue seaboards, while windsurfers and kitesurfers flock to the northeastern coastline around Porto Pollo. Adventure aside, rural Sardinia is utterly authentic, an endearing flashback to an Italy of an earlier era.

– Paula Hardy

BEEP BEEP! STREET CHIC IS ON EVERY ITALIAN ITINERARY.

TOP 11 HOT PICKS · TRAVELLER'S PULSE 2007 · FAVOURITE COUNTRY

5

Thailand is an entrepreneurial hot spot. 'In the sun' Teaching English as a Foreign Language (TEFL) courses and the city's proliferation of English-language schools attract many well-dressed 20-something teachers from around the world. And, as a regional hub for the UN and other international organisations, Bangkok is a volunteering magnet too; 'volunteering training' aimed at gap-year escapees is starting to emerge (for example, check out www.volunteerabroad.com, www.starfishventures.co.uk and www.thai-dragonfly.com).

HOT FOR 2007

Major trends for 2007 will include culture propagated to tourists, 'We Love the King' merchandise, concrete infrastructure,

THAILAND »

BEYOND THE STEREOTYPE

Thailand remains Southeast Asia's most visited country, with its well-travelled trail leading more than 15 million international tourists annually to dazzling islands and beaches, the northern cultural capital of Chiang Mai and other hot spots. Lush and balmy, Thailand is the kind of place northern-hemisphere types dream about for at least nine months of the year. Few countries possess such an unbeatable combination of fine weather and gracious hospitality. It's been called the France of Asia – staunchly independent, big on classic sights and proud of its revered cuisine traditions.

The stopover of choice, Thailand is blessed with a heady mix of postcard-perfect locations and natural attractions. Thai kitsch meets serenity in this kingdom of contradictions. But for such a popular destination, there are still relatively unexplored places such as Songkhla, Ko Tarutao and the provinces of Mae Hong Son, Khon Kaen and Roi Et.

A DEEPER LOOK

Led by glammed-up Bangkokians and flashy travellers, Thailand's tourism scene is cranking up a notch, and everywhere seems to be going modern, or 'dern' as the locals say. VIP connections and seamless service make it all too easy to travel here. But for a more genuine dose of Thailand, use local buses; your fellow passengers will make the trip far more interesting. Similarly, opt to eat streetside fare to see what flavours really turn on the Thais.

underwater marriages for dive-mad couples and local variations of international fast food.

Medical tourism is fast becoming Thailand's newest franchise. Leading the pack is Bangkok's Bumrungrad International hospital, famed for its standard of care and medical merit. No wonder people feel comfortable coming here for a face lift, or major heart surgery, en route to Ko Samui for a recovery aided by beachside cocktails.

With ever-increasing low-cost carriers and special price deals, Thailand remains a favourite spot for Scandinavians, Germans, Australians – just about everyone – and it's now also attracting the booming middle class from India and China. The new Suvarnabhumi Airport, completed in late 2006, is a seven-storey steel and glass marvel

It's been called the France of Asia – staunchly independent, big on classic sights and proud of its revered cuisine traditions.

30km east of Bangkok operating as many as 76 flights per hour on two simultaneous runways. Plans to extend the state-of-the-art Bangkok Mass Transit System Skytrain (BTS), which whizzes 300,000 passengers per day over traffic bottlenecks, are on the table and will make the capital more accessible than ever.

New retail megaplexes, the banning of Bangkok's child sellers and the continued activity of truckloads of construction workers indicate where the city is heading. But it all comes to a grinding halt in mid-April for Songkran, the nonstop three-day waterworks festival celebrating the Thai New Year. It's reason alone to visit.

SIGHTS UNSEEN

Only 86km north of Bangkok, Ayuthaya, the Thai capital from 1350 to 1767, attracts its fair share of visitors, but equally impressive ruins can be found a further 364km north at photogenic Sukhothai, a largely overlooked Unesco World Heritage site. Without the bus loads of day-trippers often present at other sites, Sukhothai feels so calm that you can almost inhale its timelessness.

REGION OF CHOICE

Thailand's northeastern Isan (or *isǎan*) region is not why most people buy their airline ticket, but those who stumble into the country's forgotten backyard discover quintessential Thai living. One thousand years ago Isan was part of the ancient Khmer empire centred on Angkor. These days, savvy travellers are savouring the serenity at Khmer temple complexes such as Phanom Rung, feasting on the region's fiery food in sleepy villages and meeting some of the country's most loveable locals.

– Sarah Wintle

Staying in a restored manor house or mill, cottage or castle, owned by the Landmark Trust or National Trust, helps preserve unique buildings for the future and provides a great backdrop for a trip. After treading Britain's national parks, it's easy to leave your own footprint on the landscape in a positive way, seeing new parts of the country and meeting like-minded folk. Learn dry-stone walling in Yorkshire, plant trees for your grandkids to use when recreating Robin Hood legends, plant flower borders in historic gardens with groups such as the British Trust for Conservation Volunteers, for a day, a week or more.

BRITAIN

BEYOND THE STEREOTYPE

For such a small island, Britain has packed a big punch for centuries. Ideas of cream teas in picture-postcard villages, playing kings and queens in crumbling castles, tracking down sights of literary legends or supping a pint by a roaring log fire after a day wandering rolling dales keep visitors coming back in their millions, whether or not they have ancestry here. Ancient Stonehenge, Roman footsteps on Hadrian's Wall, legends of King Arthur and Robin Hood, gracious and graceful Georgian Edinburgh and Bath are a tiny part of the attractions for history buffs, while still-buzzing Soho, the Beatles' Liverpool, clubbing in newly revitalised Newcastle and Leeds, and Glasgow's music scene span decades of contemporary culture.

A DEEPER LOOK

Bored of expensive treks to 'regional' airports (the 1p flight suddenly seems less of a bargain and cheap flights seem even less of an environmental bargain), Brits are looking again at what they have at home and making the most of it. Being jostled by dawdling crowds in Oxford, Stratford-upon-Avon or London's West End, it's easy to wonder how there can be room in these pint-sized isles to find something new. But niche, individual holidays, concentrating on quality and sustainability, are becoming increasingly popular.

HOT FOR 2007

The British holidays of youth – slightly bored car journeys lit up by that first glimpse of the sea – are back in a big way as the nostalgia trip continues. Years of grumpy guesthouse owners, greasy food and questionable things floating past swimmers are in decline as the nation relearns to like to be beside the sea. It's not all boutique B&Bs and slick marketing, but that's half the fun. Cornwall's blue-flag beaches, the biomes of the Eden Project, the Lost Gardens of Heligan, Rick Stein's seafood, the Tate gallery at St Ives and a newly opened branch of Jamie Oliver's Fifteen restaurant more than make up for the 'attractions' at Land's End (as covered in Cornwall, p152), and it's a similar story throughout Britain. Alternative music at Camber

Bored of expensive treks to 'regional' airports...Brits are looking again at what they have at home and making the most of it.

Sands, Whitby's Goth festival or decent surfing in Scotland provide alternatives to bucket-and-spade wielding toddlers.

SIGHTS UNSEEN

Millions visit Stonehenge each year, many feeling cheated by the roaring traffic as it whizzes by just inches away. Much more satisfying is Avebury, an archetypal English village built within a stone circle, which ticks all the village-cricket and traditional-pub boxes. In a dash to Bath, Oxford and the Cotswolds, it's easy to miss the thatched-cottage villages dotted around Wiltshire, complete with highly favourable gastropubs.

CITY OF CHOICE

Mention Birmingham (aka Brum) to many and you can still expect a sniggered response, but Brummies are having the last laugh. Architectural renewal has transformed previously run-down parts of the city into a confident and energetic hub. The Bullring shopping complex, the futuristic new Selfridges building and the Jewellery Quarter mean world-class shopping, and the city's thriving restaurant scene goes beyond the famous but much-loved balti. The world is listening to local bands The Streets and The Editors, and buzzing bars and clubs mean legendary nights out. International flights connect Brum with the rest of the world, and decent rail and road links mean it's easy to reach vast swathes of countryside for lazy days of walking and cosy pubs.

– Sam Trafford

BE LED DOWN BRITAIN'S GARDEN PATH, LINED WITH CULTURAL CHARM AND UNEXPECTED ADVENTURES.

TOP 11 HOT PICKS · TRAVELLER'S PULSE 2007 · FAVOURITE COUNTRY · 7

CANADA

and New Brunswick, and uncover Canada's beating cultural heart. Linger in the cities soaking up the culture, strolling the cobblestone streets of Old Montréal and honing your linguistic skills. From there take to the provincial back roads and discover why maple syrup is not just a syrup in Canada, it's an institution.

Step back in time and immerse yourself in the history of the Maritime provinces. Settle down in a pub in St John's, one of North America's oldest cities, and watch as the mist curls in off the ocean, creeping its way up the narrow streets. Visit the red shores of Prince Edward Island and share a lobster plate with the locals (bibs provided), and get acquainted with the brews of Nova Scotia.

If it's space you're after, Canada has national parks covered and

BEYOND THE STEREOTYPE

Breathtaking coastline, majestic mountains, remote tundras, cosmopolitan cities and rolling plains – is it any wonder Canada is consistently one of the world's top-10 travel destinations? The only wonder is why some people choose to visit the other nine instead.

Stretching from the Pacific Ocean to the Atlantic, sharing its southern border with the United States and reaching north right up into the Arctic Circle, Canada is a nation of captivating beauty and stunning contrasts. This land beckons city-slickers with fine dining, galleries, bars, museums, architecture, theatre and sports; it tempts adventure travellers with promises of hiking, skiing, kayaking and mountain biking; and it lures wildlife enthusiasts with visions of mountain lions, moose, beavers, whales, elk and – wait for it – three species of bear.

Canada is so vast and complex, a lifetime simply isn't long enough to uncover all its secrets.

A DEEPER LOOK

This is a big country (the world's second largest, in fact) so barrelling across it in three days is not a good idea. Slow it down. Take your time. See if you can't discover your own reasons for flying the maple-leaf flag. One of the first things you'll notice about Canada is that it's decidedly bilingual. Spend time in the proudly French-Canadian provinces of Québec

ecotourism is the name of the game. Sign yourself up for a tour and gain insider knowledge of the landscape and wildlife. If it's solitude you seek head up to Nunavut, Canada's newest territory, where caribou outnumber people 30 to one.

HOT FOR 2007

Canada has been gripped by football fever despite the sport's decided lack of ice or sticks. In July, Canada will host the FIFA U-20 World Cup with games held in Montréal, Ottawa, Toronto, Edmonton, Vancouver and Victoria.

Canadians love a good festival and 2007 is shaping up to be a pretty good year. Take in the Toronto International Film Festival and the Montreal Jazz Festival for starters, then ask around for what else is on while you're there.

Slow it down. Take your time. See if you can't discover your own reasons for flying the maple-leaf flag.

And why not visit Alberta? Home to Banff in the Rocky Mountains, the incredible Calgary Stampede, North America's largest shopping mall and a whole lot of prairies, it's all happening in Alberta.

SIGHTS UNSEEN

For ski fiends in Canada, it doesn't get better than Whistler – or does it? Whistler has world-class skiing amid jaw-dropping scenery, but it also has huge crowds and prices likely to induce heart failure, increasingly so as the nation gears up to host the 2010 Winter Olympics. Enter Fernie Alpine Resort, in the southeast corner of British Columbia. With more than 100 alpine trails, snowboarding, snowcat skiing and eye-popping views, Fernie is a gift from the winter gods and the good people who first strapped pieces of wood to their feet and threw themselves off a mountain.

REGION OF CHOICE

Coastal British Columbia is a region of unparalleled beauty, diverse wildlife, old-world towns and outdoor adventures. Some come to take high tea in Victoria, others seek close encounters of the wildlife kind. Vancouver Island boasts colonial architecture, fine dining, shops, galleries and a thriving pub culture. The coastal mainland has long been renowned for its stunning rainforests and is now home to the newest (and largest) protected area in North America, the Great Bear Rainforest. It has bears aplenty – grizzlies, black and rare white Kermodes – as well as eagles, wolves, orca and 1000-year-old cedars. Hiking, sailing, wind surfing, kayaking, skiing and whale-watching are regional highlights if you feel like getting active.

– Lauren Rollheiser

You might not get your hands dirty but you'll witness the production of local-style wine, which is matured for six years before drinking, as well as dairy farming and cheese-making. Munch on Comté, the famous Jurassien cheese with a hazelnut flavour, as well as Morbier, Bleu de Gex and the supersoft, nutty Mont d'Or, made with unpasteurised milk and wrapped in spruce bark – reputedly a favourite of King Louis XV. Some farms run snails and will cook them up for you, while others keep wily boar, feisty goats and gentle horses.

The serene mountains beckon cyclists, hikers and cross-country skiers, and you can sate yourself at the end of the day on homemade goats' cheese, jam, yoghurt, bread, cake, and goat and boar meat. Your hosts will make you welcome as

FRANCE

BEYOND THE STEREOTYPE

France is a beacon for travellers. Paris, a famous centre for romance, art, fashion and culture, is often the top attraction – who could ignore its atmospheric streets and the river Seine, incredible art collections, icons such as the Tour Eiffel and the mouthwatering marvels of French cuisine and wine.

Of course, the pleasures of travel in France aren't limited to the capital. Provence is known for its warm, fertile countryside, the Alps for world-class ski slopes, Rheims and Chartres for their intricate cathedrals, Brittany for its Celtic celebrations and Champagne for its top-notch bubbly.

The list of highlights paints the picture of what makes France a truly great destination. France's regions give local produce its flavour and community life its savour. Boeuf bourguignon, calvados from Normandy, quiche Lorraine and Champagne all do their regions proud. This is where French life is lived, and where travellers love to visit and long to return to.

A DEEPER LOOK

Be welcomed into rural life on a farmstay in the Jura and you might start to get ideas. The wine is yellow in this quiet mountain range, the cheese so soft it's eaten with a spoon, and the smoked Jésus sausage delicious. Better yet, you can see how it's all made.

you experience what might well be a different way of living, and enjoying, life.

HOT FOR 2007

Marseille has a spunk and sparkle as strident as the French national anthem 'La Marseillaise', with all of the attitude and none of the pomp. France's second-largest city is a cosmopolitan port totally unlike the rest of Provence or the Côte d'Azur. Its clubbing beach scene and postmodern housing developments, along with its openness to North African culture and thriving bazaars, have revitalised the working-class city. New low-cost flights will soon connect Marseille with about 10 other European cities, adding air travellers to those who already pass through this long-established port city.

France's regions give local produce its flavour...this is where French life is lived, and where travellers love to visit and long to return to.

SIGHTS UNSEEN

Lope through the Alps in spring or summer to get the most out of the alpine national parks. Parc National des Écrins, spectacular home to lynx, ibex, chamois, bearded vultures and marmots, offers opportunities for kayaking, climbing, hang-gliding and scrambling along age-old smugglers' paths. Resorts also offer kitesurfing, paragliding and skydiving. Mountainous Parc National de la Vanoise is a forested sanctuary for chamois, ibex, marmots, golden eagles and intrepid mountain-bikers. Both parks also have incredible glaciers. Glacial skiing is available nearby – and even in summer, depending on snow conditions.

REGION OF CHOICE

Far from typically French, Alsace is unquestionably Alsatian, known for its elegant storks and distinctive, half-timbered houses. With its strong Germanic influence, France's smallest *département* (administrative division) attracts many visitors with its historic atmosphere, wonderful pubs, vineyards and breweries, cosy eateries and unique culture. Cathedrals at Strasbourg and Metz are masterpieces of gothic architecture, and the wooded mountains offer walking, snow-shoeing, cycling and skiing. Idle in the Unesco World Heritage site of central Strasbourg and dip into the industrial museums of Mulhouse. Your taste of Alsace is guaranteed to linger.

– Laura Gibb

JOIN A *VIGNERON* FOR A GLASS OR TWO OF HIS BEST IN THE CHAMPAGNE TOWN OF REUIL.

China's train network is extensive and affordable and, though they can be achingly slow, trains are still a fairly efficient way to get across the country. They're also a good opportunity to swap stories with the locals.

But why not cycle? Well-pedalled routes include Guangxi's Yangshuo and the Dragon's Backbone Rice Terraces, near Longsheng, as well as Beijing to the Great Wall. At least one person has taken her unicycle from Guangzhou to Kunming, while others have cycled the 3000km stretch from Heilongjiang to Sichuan. Cycling in Tibet is another option.

HOT FOR 2007

The famed Qinghai–Tibet Railway, the most elevated railway in the world reaching 5072m above sea

CHINA

BEYOND THE STEREOTYPE

One trip to China and you're hooked, clambering along the Great Wall, flying kites at Tiananmen Square and wandering through Shanghai back streets. And like all great addictions, you're always coming back for more: cruising down the Yangtze, picnicking atop Guangxi's karst peaks, perhaps a few karaoke- and casino-fuelled nights in Macau. In a land so vast and varied – and one that's transforming at a cracking pace – it seems there's a lifetime's worth of adventures to be had. Yet it's not long before one thing becomes clear: the people are the real highlight. Inquisitive, proud, generous and gregarious, the Chinese people are where the story begins.

A DEEPER LOOK

When you turn up early in the morning to marvel at Beijing's Summer Palace, you find that a thousand others have thought to do the same. And it sure can take a while to climb up Tai Shan when you're behind a team of tourists, blocking the track at their own steady pace. China is full of blockbuster sights and everybody wants the best view.

However, it's all too easy to step off the beaten track and find yourself the only traveller in town. Places such as western Guizhou, pockets of the Xishuangbanna region and much of Gansu may not be at the top of most visitors' agendas, but any time spent in a quiet ancient village, talking to locals, will soon become your own China adventure.

level, is up and running. Dogged by controversy – many claim it will bring employment and security problems into Lhasa, changing life in Tibet for the worse – it will nonetheless be a huge source of interest for trainspotters and travellers alike.

Hainan Island, in southern China, has long been an open secret among the Chinese. But now the island's tropical beaches and well-developed tourism scene has piqued the interest of Western travellers and low-cost carriers. It's a good time to explore the island ahead of the pack.

Travellers will be piling in to check out new-look Beijing. With PTW Architect's 'Water Cube' National Swimming Centre, Herzog and de Meuron's 'Bird's Nest' stadium and Ram Koolhass's CCTV Tower underway, 2007 marks the

FOR A WELL-BALANCED TRIP IN CHINA, MIX SOME MULTICULTURAL EXPLORATION, BIG CITIES AND OPEN SPACES.

Inquisitive, proud, generous and gregarious, the Chinese people are where the story begins.

moment to witness the capital's unprecedented transformation. Unless you're already assured tickets to the 2008 Olympics, that is.

SIGHTS UNSEEN

The Army of Terracotta Warriors is one of China's iconic sights. Though hugely impressive, the enormous grounds are surrounded by coaches and overly competent touts. Few are aware that, just 40km away, lies the tomb of Emperor Han Jing (Han dynasty). Though part of the appeal of Han Jing's tomb is its obscurity, it is archaeologically fascinating in its own right. Only partially excavated, the tomb stands in marked contrast to the Terracotta Warriors for its humility: the warriors here are smaller and less grandiose, and far more is revealed of daily life than martial preoccupations. Glass covers parts of the tomb, allowing you to walk over the ongoing excavations below, and giant windows reveal close-up cross sections of the pits. If you're lucky, you might even witness an archaeologist painstakingly brushing off a centuries-old figurine.

REGION OF CHOICE

Xinjiang (p198) is so remote and so ethnically distinct from the rest of China, it's like another country altogether. In fact, Xinjiang was once known as Eastern Turkestan, testimony to its Central Asian roots. Its boundless deserts and towering mountain ranges make for serious adventure, and fans of Uighur culture can gorge on spicy mutton and wander through Kashgar's market to their heart's content. Xinjiang is enormous, and travel is slow. So pack your sturdiest boots, and get ready for the long haul. It'll be worth it

– Rebecca Chau

Volunteering opportunities abound. The Sea Turtle Protection Society of Greece (www.archelon.gr), and the Hellenic Society for the Study & Protection of the Monk Seal involve volunteers in monitoring programmes on the Ionian Islands and the Peloponnese. The Hellenic Wildlife Rehabilitation Centre (www.ekpazp.gr) on the island of Aegina takes in about 4000 animals and birds from all over Greece and volunteers are needed, particularly in the winter months.

To get under the skin of Greece is both a traditional yet personal journey and most Greek locals (save that grumpy kiosk owner) will invite your presence to the table, into the dance and into the Greek spirit. Please, when you've finished playing, give Greece back her marbles.

GREECE

BEYOND THE STEREOTYPE

All Pausanias did was to pen some travel diaries about Greece in the 2nd century AD and then souls the world over wanted to set off to see what Pausanias saw. Almost 2000 years later, nothing's changed. For centuries people have been inspired by the sacred and proud Parthenon, the iridescent Aegean, glamorous Santorini sunsets, warm *filoxenia* (hospitality) and souvlaki. Visitors also discover that the country's true grit lies in the determined, artistic and fiercely patriotic Greeks; they have a zest for life, love and country unrivalled across East or West.

Of course, there's a whole lot more to Greece than simply art, culture, food and wine. Playing host to some major international events hasn't hurt the old girl's image either. It's not every day you get to welcome the Olympics home, or fire up the national belly with a UEFA soccer cup triumph. And the Eurovision Song Contest? Just another excuse to wear white, really. Hey, Greece is hot right now, Athens rocks and even her spiffy new metro works.

A DEEPER LOOK

Stop treading the same old worn-out goat tracks and take your cue from the Greeks themselves: get out of Athens in the summer and head to the hills, the villages or the quiet, seaside hamlets. Give yourself more time to devour regional specialities, and sample the great, sacred fruits, the olive and the grape.

HOT FOR 2007

Greece spent the first half of the noughties in a mad and expensive flurry of hosting international parties and pop acts, and the glory must have gone to her head like a bad wine. Save for the odd rock festival and summer theatre programme, it seems Greece is content to sit beside the international stage in 2007, licking her multibillion-euro wounds and nursing one mother of a hangover.

SIGHTS UNSEEN

The glitz and glam of the popular Cycladic island hop between Mykonos and Santorini is alluring and seductive, but it can also mean a shit-fight for the best beach spot. Grab some sanity

Stop treading the same old worn-out goat tracks…get out of Athens in the summer and head to the hills, the villages or the quiet, seaside hamlets.

space by ferrying your way over to the little-visited island of Amorgos, a peaceful detour to a dragon's back of dramatic, rugged mountains that lie wriggling their way through the vibrant blue. Here visitors can spot lovely old windmills, explore dazzling white monasteries that cling precariously to cliff faces, and simply escape the party gloss-pods (though Mykonos and Santorini are only a ferry-hop away should you get lonely).

Those in need of a distinctive urban character, cultural stimulation and intelligent nightlife that rivals New York should zip up north to Thessaloniki, Greece's second-largest city and one that's too often missing from the itinerary. It's worth exploring this city's vibrant culture, magnificent regional cuisine and quirky pulse.

REGION OF CHOICE

Remote enough in ancient times to remain untouched by the battles of Spartan warriors and Dorian upstarts, the prefecture of Arcadia is a fine Peloponnesian hideout. It's dotted by the legacies of the many civilisations that have come and gone: Mycenaean palaces, classical Greek temples, crumbling Byzantine cities, Frankish and Venetian fortresses and ornate Turkish fountains. Peeking into its peaks, you'll discover a tangle of medieval mountain villages, remote monasteries, precipitous ravines woven into valleys of dense vegetation and plateaus with vistas of tiny hamlets. So, while others are roasting on the coast, hire some wheels and start curling your way through gorges along dramatic hairpin bends. Arcadia is also a mecca for hikers, snow skiiers, whitewater rafters, mountain bikers, canyonists and those other adventure fiends, twirlers of *komboloi* (worry beads).

– *Gina Tsarouhas*

EXPLORE MOUNTAIN VILLAGES AND MONASTERIES ON YOUR OWN GREEK ODYSSEY.

'treasure' when its least expected. It may take the form of spending an afternoon discussing samsara (the cycle of life, death and rebirth), over a pot of masala chai (spiced tea), with a *pujari* (priest) whom you initially approached for directions after getting lost in a city bazaar, or, spontaneously ditching travel plans with friends to join a short-staffed rural volunteer group you heard about while queuing for bus tickets in Mumbai. Ultimately, it's all about being open to the unknown: this is the India that nothing can quite prepare you for, because its very essence lies in its mystery.

Another way of diverting from the tourist track is to enrol in a course. Whether its hatha yoga, classical dance, Vedic chanting or miniature painting, a course

INDIA

BEYOND THE STEREOTYPE

With its utterly astonishing diversity – from crumbling historic monuments to state-of-the-art shopping malls, snow-laden mountains to sun-washed beaches, pin-drop-quiet places of worship to music-thumping nightclubs – it's hardly surprising that India has been dubbed the most multidimensional country on earth. With its billion-plus population, the subcontinent has a rich melange of ethnic groups, which translates into a head-spinning cultural concoction of experiences for the visitor. There's a glorious mix of architecture, from the iconic Taj Mahal to ancient ruins well off the tourist trail, oodles of fantastical festivals and time-honoured traditions, and a positively seductive smorgasbord of regional recipes, from delicate south Indian *idlis* (spongy, white cakes that are great for breakfast) to robust north Indian curries. Yes, if there's any country in the world that really does justice to the widely flogged 'Land of Contrasts' cliché, it's India.

A DEEPER LOOK

India has the ability to inspire, frustrate, charm and bamboozle all at once, and although its wild unpredictability is often dismissed as a glaring drawback, it can actually lead to the defining moment of your journey. Those travellers who are willing to embrace – rather than lock horns – with the uncertainty that is India, are most likely to fortuitously discover

will not only give you inimitable cultural insights, it'll also hook you up with locals who can show you the India that exists beyond glossy tourist brochures.

HOT FOR 2007

India is festival crazy; no matter what the season, you can always catch a festival or three. Apart from the widely known Diwali and Pushkar Camel Fair, both taking placed in October and November, there's also a mind-boggling array of less flaunted yet uniquely scintillating regional offerings taking place in 2007. Among them are Rajasthan's Nagaur Cattle Fair in January and February, Madhya Pradesh's Festival of Dance in February and March, the Nehru Trophy Snake Boat Race in Kerala in August, Bihar's Sonepur Mela in

HEAD TO THE PUSHKAR CAMEL FAIR FOR TIMELESS RITUALS AND DESERT TALES – AND MAYBE A CAMEL AS WELL.

Ultimately, it's all about being open to the unknown: this is the India that nothing can quite prepare you for, because its very essence lies in its mystery.

November and December and the Festival of Carnatic Music & Dance held in Tamil Nadu in December and January – just to name a few. Dates vary annually; contact regional tourist offices to check festival calendars.

SIGHTS UNSEEN

Almost all travellers to Rajasthan flock to the much-photographed Jaisalmer Fort, however, few even know that Rajasthan is home to one of India's most legendary forts – that of Chittorgarh. This sprawling hilltop complex abounds with jaw-dropping tales of ferocious battles and fairytale romanticism. Indeed the fort at Chittorgarh epitomises the Rajput's unrivalled code of chivalry. It was here in 1535 that 32,000 Rajput warriors donned the saffron martyrs' robes to face imminent death in battle, while 13,000 Rajput women are said to have committed jauhar (ritual mass suicide on a huge funeral pyre) to avoid being dishonoured by their captors.

REGION OF CHOICE

Desperate to jump off the tourist treadmill? Then head straight for the rugged east Indian state of Orissa. Not only does it have a captivating tribal culture – Adivasis (Orissan tribal groups) are 25% of the population – it also hosts one of India's most spectacular events, Puri's Rath Yatra festival, when enormous chariots are hauled through the streets. Other Orissan gems include the striking Unesco World Heritage–listed Sun Temple at Konark, as well as a jumble of fine beaches and wildlife sanctuaries; don't miss the Similipal National Park, home to a bevy of beasts including big jungle cats.

– *Sarina Singh*

food when Florentines are drinking, which may explain why they never seem as tipsy as the travellers here. Try the spread of *aperitivi* (appetizers) at Il Rifrullo, a great little bar on a quiet corner of San Niccoló. This place, which attracts a chirpy, suave crowd, is a wonderful spot to mingle with the locals.

✪ KAERTNER BAR, AUSTRIA

Former capital of the Hapsburg empire, Vienna has some very well-appointed drinking holes. For a really intimate taste of the city, try to get a seat at Kaertner Bar. Lavishly designed by Adolf Loos in 1907, you'd be hard pressed to fit 20 people in here. For the eight who are standing, it's a great recipe for meeting locals. Start with a glass of Austrian wine or some cocktails and move on to the schnappy Viennese schnapps or fruit liqueurs.

✪ KARAOKE BARS, PHILIPPINES

The Philippines is chock-full of naturally talented musicians. Perhaps that's why many Filipinos head for karaoke bars on their nights off. Kakaoke is taken seriously: no matter how bad the singer, they'll still get respect. This is just a warm-up, however, as most towns have live music bars with local talent belting out flawless cover versions of classic rock and

#1. BEST BARS WITH LOCAL ✪ FLAVOUR

✪ FISHAWI'S COFFEE-HOUSE, EGYPT

Cairo has thousands of *ahwas* (coffeehouses) where you can while away the hours over a glass of *shai* (tea), a *sheesha* (water pipe) and a few games of *towla* (backgammon). Smoking *sheeshas* used to be strictly for men, but now it's not at all unusual to see women smoking, even at the regular *ahwas*. Fishawi's Coffeehouse (in an alley off Midan Hussein, in the Khan al-Khalili market area) is one of the oldest and the most famous.

Despite being swamped by foreign tourists and equally wide-eyed out-of-town Egyptians, it is a regular *ahwa*, serving stallholders and shoppers alike. It's especially alluring in the early hours of the morning.

✪ IL RIFRULLO, ITALY

You'll find the best dark local haunts in Florence's Oltrarno and Santa Croce, where happy hours can stretch for half the night. Cheap drinks are often accompanied by nibbles on the counter; *enoteche* (wine bars) like to serve

✪ RAFFLES BAR, SINGAPORE **1**

Famous for a drink that tastes like cough medicine and is more expensive than a flu shot, Raffles Bar is still worth a visit for the sense of times gone by. Despite Raffles' colonial connotations, Singaporeans do come here, bringing clients or visitors. Patrons nestle into a dark-boothed interior, or lounge on the wide white balconies littered with the shells of small salty peanuts. The staff are distressingly demure; fortunately the fans are now automated. The Top 40 music mocks the elegance, but after a few slings you'll be aiming for the central circular stairwell: go on, make an entrance!

✪ COOGEE BAY HOTEL, AUSTRALIA **2**

An hour's stumble from Bondi and the Beautiful People of Sydney, and across the road from the lazy wide expanse of Coogee Beach itself, the Coogee Bay Hotel is the place where locals come. They'll be watching the game – usually rugby – and downing close-to-Antarctic beers. You'll find blokes in the front (sports) bar and backpackers dancing at sassy, brassy Selina's nightclub out the back. In between is a beer garden, a bottle shop and a view of low-lying Wedding Cake Island. The cocktail lounge caters to the city slickers, and open-mic night usually produces an idol or two; beware parochial hits by Australian bands that split long ago.

✪ BON'S, JAPAN **3**

Welcome to Tokyo's Golden Gai night zone. Once here you'll feel like you've left the futuristic city behind: the Shinjuku skyscrapers tower several blocks back and you find yourself wandering among other traditionally low-lying *nomiya* (drinking establishments). Bon's, next to the police box near the Hanazono steps, is one of the only bars here that welcomes foreigners as well as locals. Cosy and old-school, it's a place to kick back and savour a round. Remember to keep the glasses of your friends full, but people will think you have a drinking problem if you fill your own. *Kampai!*

recent hits. Three commonly heard renditions are *I Will Always Love You* (Whitney Houston), *Dancing Queen* (ABBA) and *Wind Beneath My Wings* (Bette Midler).

✪ BARASTI, UNITED ARAB EMIRATES

Pubs and bars in Dubai are open until the early hours of the morning. You'll find beers from all corners of the earth here and the wildest cocktails conceivable. You'll also get to listen to an extraordinary mix of music on any one night, from *bhangra* (lively northern Indian music) and Bengali to Arab-Latin fusion and Persian pop. Barasti at Le Meridien hotel is the locals' top drinking spot for laid-back sundowners on a hot afternoon. It's the kind of place that you don't have to dress up for, and can head to straight after a day at the beach.

✪ RISE, USA

Yes, we heard you the first time (from across the room) – you're in the mood for a martini. A snazzy beverage can be found in many places in New York: sleek lounges, cosy pubs and straight-up alcoholic dives. New Yorkers don't hold back, and the jury says downtown's best bet is Rise at the Ritz Carlton. Even US$13 martinis won't make you think twice about hanging here, where the high-up lounge affords views of the sunset over the Hudson River.

✪ PRATER, GERMANY

As you'd expect from the capital of beer-obsessed Germany, Berlin elevates drinking culture to a fine art, offering everything from spit 'n' sawdust Kneipen (pubs) to shiny-smart cocktail lounges. Prater, on Eberswalder Strasse, is Berlin's oldest beer garden and also one of the prettiest, and is a great place for quaffing away beneath the chestnut trees. The complex includes a small stage operated by the Volksbühne (people's theatre), a cocktail bar, an old-fashioned restaurant and the popular Bastard club.

✪ MOUNTAIN BIKING IN MOAB, USA

Moab is the mother of all mountain-biking destinations, its fame riding on the slickrock that makes mountain biking in this Utah town so unique. Top of the pops in Moab is the Slickrock Bike Trail, arguably the most famous mountain-biking route in the world. This 20km loop crosses sandstone ridges above the town, a roller-coaster route of supersteep climbs and plunging descents. If you're nervous about whether you're slick enough for the Slickrock Bike Trail, you can always pluck up courage on the 3km practice loop.

1

LOOKING FOR THRILLS AND SPILLS? PUT MOAB ON THE ITINERARY...

✪ TREKKING AT TORRES DEL PAINE, CHILE

Like a fistful of broken fingers, the Torres del Paine rise more than 2000m from the Patagonian steppe. For trekkers these towers of pain (not a translation!) are some of the most instantly recognisable features on the planet. The classic walk here is the so-called 'W' trek. Beginning at Laguna Amarga, the W climbs to the spectacular Torres del Paine Lookout, immediately below the towers, and continues via Los Cuernos and Lago Pehoé to Lago Grey, famed for its flotillas of icebergs, some as big as houses.

2

FIND YOURSELF AND NO-ONE ELSE TREKKING THE 'W' IN CHILE.

✪ HIKING THE LARAPINTA TRAIL, AUSTRALIA

For 223km of desert delights, set aside a fortnight to walk the Larapinta Trail through central Australia's West MacDonnell Ranges, one of the oldest mountain chains in the world. Stretching between Alice Springs and Mt Sonder, the Larapinta winds through oasis-like gorges, over the ranges' sharp quartzite ridge tops and across desert plains. Regular camp sites and water tanks mute the desert's ferocity but not its beauty – this is the Red Centre at its finest. Food drops can also be arranged to ease the load on your back.

3

#2. BEST ADVENTURE
TRAVEL IDEAS

☆ SKI-TOURING THE HAUTE ROUTE, FRANCE & SWITZERLAND

Strap on the skins for one of the world's great ski experiences as you tour between the famed Alpine resorts of Chamonix and Zermatt. Most skiers take around a week to complete the 140km, hut-to-hut route, crossing 20 glaciers and savouring views of many of the Alps' highest and finest peaks. Expect more than a leisurely jaunt: the terrain is challenging, and climbs along the route total more than 10,000m. If you prefer feet to skis, you can always wait for summer and hike the Walkers' Haute Route.

☆ CYCLING THE ICEFIELDS PARKWAY, CANADA

Stretching 230km between Jasper and Lake Louise and following a lake-lined valley between two chains of the Rocky Mountains, the Icefields Parkway is considered one of the world's most scenic roads. Cyclists also know it as one of the great cycling tours. The impatient can ride it in two days, but well-spaced camping grounds and hostels mean it can also be lingered over for four or five days. Expect mountains, lakes and a menagerie of mammals – goats, bighorn sheep, elk, moose and perhaps even black and grizzly bears.

☆ KAYAKING ON GLACIER BAY, USA

The name alone ought be enough to tempt any sea kayaker, but the reality goes beyond even the moniker. In Alaska's Glacier Bay, 10 glaciers flow down from the mountains, filling the sea with an assortment of icebergs. The tour boat MV *Spirit of Adventure* can drop kayakers at various points in the bay, so you can pretty much paddle where you please. The truly hardy eschew the boat and paddle from Bartlett Cove to the glaciers of Muir Inlet (allow about two weeks). The blockbuster 'bergs are in the West Arm, though camping here is limited.

☆ WALKING IN KRUGER NATIONAL PARK, SOUTH AFRICA

What better way to mingle with a hungry horde of lions, cheetahs, rhinos, elephants and giraffes in South Africa's most famous park than on foot? Kruger has seven wilderness walking trails, along which you can take guided overnight walks with armed guides. Of the trails, the Napi Trail is noted as the best for spotting the Big

Five (the black rhino, Cape buffalo, elephant, leopard and lion). Most of the walks last for two days and three nights, covering around 20km each day at a leisurely pace…unless, of course, you notice a lion behind you.

☆ SWIMMING WITH KILLER WHALES, NORWAY

Think of them as orcas and not killer whales, and you might find it easier to roll overboard and into Norway's Tysfjord, around 250km north of the Arctic Circle. For three months each year, orcas settle into this fjord, chasing a feed of herring. Hard behind them are the whale-watching boats and the few hardy snorkellers prepared to brave both the Arctic waters and their visiting killer whales. For something marginally warmer, you may prefer to hire a kayak for a paddle among the cetaceans.

☆ ROCK CLIMBING IN KRABI, THAILAND

Fancy a tropical beach that's more about cams than tans, and where the closest thing to a thong is your harness? Then you should come to Krabi. This city on Thailand's Andaman coast is blessed with spectacular karst formations, even in the middle of Krabi River, making it one of the world's great climbing destinations. If you're serious about scaling a cliff, you'll want to head for

Railay, west of the city. This peninsula's steep, pocketed limestone cliffs offer a liquorice all-sorts of climbing features, including good overhangs and the occasional hanging stalactite.

☆ BUNGY JUMPING AT VERZASCA DAM, SWITZERLAND

They call it the GoldenEye jump, as it was on this Ticino dam that Pierce Brosnan, aka James Bond, fell so far that in order to re-create the stunt you must submit yourself to the world's highest commercial bungy jump, a leap of 220m. Make the classic swan dive or leap backwards, then endure a 7.5-second fall that will border on eternity. Only later will you appreciate the fact that you've just relived the stunt once voted the best in movie history. Jumps are conducted from Easter to October.

✪ HOT DOG IN NEW YORK CITY, USA   ①

So what if Nu Yawk has one of the greatest varieties of dining options of any city in the world? Everyone knows that the only truly meaningful foodie ritual here is to head to a busy inner-city intersection, find a shabby metal cart topped by colourful umbrellas, and order a dog with ketchup, mustard, onions and either sauerkraut, relish or chili sauce. To make the consumption of this gourmet treat a bit more challenging, head to Nathan's on Coney Island on 4 July and enter the famous hot-dog eating contest; the record is 53.5 dogs in 12 minutes.

✪ FEIJOADA IN RIO DE JANEIRO, BRAZIL   ②

Taste buds stage their own Carnaval in honour of Brazil's national lunch, *feijoada*, a dark and spicy stew built upon a foundation of black beans and pork. Note that the *feijoada* prepared for mass consumption in Rio's restaurants usually just contains pared down pieces of pig flesh, but it may also contain less familiar porcine treats such as ears, tongues and those cute curly tails. Also note that this hearty recipe is a challenge for any stomach to digest, so plan on hitting a couch rather than the waters off Ipanema after eating it.

✪ GUMBO IN NEW ORLEANS, USA   ③

Scooping out a steaming pot of gumbo is as central to New Orleans life as listening to jazz, zydeco or swamp blues, or chomping on the sugary pastries called beignets. This Louisiana favourite is essentially a hearty broth of seafood or smoked meats, thickened with okra or a wheat-and-fat mixture called roux before being splashed over a mountain of rice. But New Orleans serves up countless variations of the basic gumbo recipe, from classic Creole to pungent Cajun. The Big Easy hasn't had it so easy in recent times, but at least it has one of the world's great comfort foods.

TASTE THE COLOUR AND FLAIR OF NEW YORK, ALL WRAPPED UP IN A BUN.

#3. BEST FOOD & PLACE
⭐ COMBINATIONS

✪ COUSCOUS IN CASABLANCA, MOROCCO

The minute you arrive in Casablanca, make straight for Blvd de la Corniche down on the waterfront, pick an appealing café or restaurant and order a cup of mint tea and a plate of Morocco's staple food, couscous. The couscous grain is made from semolina (ground durum wheat) and is ideally prepared by being repeatedly steamed in a special pot called a *couscoussier*. It's then topped with a spicy stew containing either vegetables or a mixture of veggies and meat such as chicken, lamb and fish. Eat it again, Sam.

✪ CURRY IN MUMBAI, INDIA

Curries are a Pan-Asian phenomenon, with these spicy meals cooked up almost everywhere between the Punjab and Japan. But the birthplace of the curry is India, and you haven't really tasted one until you've wandered into Mumbai (Bombay) in the state of Maharashtra and delighted your palate with one of the local concoctions. As Maharashtra is a coastal state, a Mumbai curry typically contains seafood and coconut blended with a masala (mixture of spices). Standard spices include turmeric, coriander, ginger and red chilli.

✪ DÖNER KEBAP IN ISTANBUL, TURKEY

A traditional döner kebap consists of a plate of grilled mutton on a bed of buttered rice, and many of Turkey's restaurants still serve it this way. Far more prominent nowadays, however, is its fast-food cousin, which takes the form of a pita bread sandwich containing marinated meat that has been sliced from a rotating spit and bundled together with salad and a yoghurt-based sauce. It's *de rigueur* in Istanbul to equip yourself with a weighty döner and then wander around Sultanahmet or along the Bosphorus while casually wiping sauce and stray strands of lettuce from your chin.

✪ NASI GORENG IN PENANG, MALAYSIA

Visitors to Malaysia inevitably find themselves ordering the ubiquitous, delightfully simple meal called nasi goreng. Literally meaning 'fried rice' and also enjoyed across Indonesia and Singapore, this dish is prepared by stir-frying rice with chicken or seafood, vegetables, eggs and a sweetish soy sauce. Nasi goreng is available practically anywhere in Malaysia that serves food but is best sampled within the wonderfully crowded hawker centres that dot the island of Penang. It's here that the diverse Malay, Chinese, Indian and Baba-Nonya cooking styles conspire to give an otherwise humble dish some special flavours.

✪ PASTA IN NAPLES, ITALY

Food historians still debate whether Marco Polo introduced pasta to Italy by importing it from China in the 13th century, or whether the Etruscans had already embraced it long beforehand. But it's generally agreed that by the 18th century, Naples had turned the mixing of flour and water into a bona fide industry and was the world's pasta capital. As an encore, Naples also arranged a blind date between pasta and squashed tomatoes, and romance blossomed. So the next time you're wandering the crumbling streets of Naples' historic centre, make a beeline for the nearest trattoria and tuck into some authentic *pasta napolitana*.

✪ STEAMED DUMPLINGS IN SHANGHAI, CHINA

Shanghai dumplings have to be tasted to be believed. The Chinese call them *xiǎolóngbaō*, and they are one of the items most fought over during dim-sum feasts. These delicious morsels seem like ordinary dough balls until you discover that they are filled with a hot broth flavoured with ground pork, crab meat or vegetables. This little surprise is achieved by filling the dumplings with a hardened gelatin that liquefies when the bun is steamed. To avoid scalding your gums with hot soup, do not crunch the dumpling between your teeth but instead nibble it until the liquid seeps out.

✪ TAPAS IN BARCELONA, SPAIN

Patatas bravas (potatoes in a spicy tomato sauce), *calamares fritos* (fried squid), *boquerones* (anchovies), *croquetas de jamón* (ham croquettes), *chorizo* (pork sausage), *pimientos asados* (roasted peppers), *albóndigas* (meatballs), *berenjenas gratinadas* (cheese-baked aubergine) – just some mouthwatering examples of the fabulous Spanish snacks known as tapas. The vivacious Catalonian capital of Barcelona excels in the creation and consumption of tapas, particularly along La Rambla late in the evening when residents and tourists alike slowly graze their way south from Plaça de Catalunya. Become a local by leaving the cutlery on the table and claiming the tapas with a toothpick or your fingers.

'MUST-HAVE' DISHES IN ASIA

✪ BLACK-PEPPER CRAB, SINGAPORE

Of all the tasty delights in Singapore, perhaps the most widely accepted and well-loved by globetrotters from all over the world is black-pepper crab – large crabs smothered with a mixture of butter, soy sauce and black pepper (duh!).

✪ PENANG HOKKIEN MEE, MALAYSIA

Tastier than its counterparts from neighbouring cities, this dish features fresh egg noodles soaked in prawn and chilli soup, and served with various meat condiments. Yum!

✪ ADOBO, THE PHILIPPINES

Mix lots of soy sauce, a dash of vinegar, garlic and bay leaves, add meat and voila! – you get the Philippines national dish, adobo. The meat of choice is usually pork or chicken; both are equally good.

✪ XIǍOLÓNGBAŌ, SHANGHAI

The Chinese name *xiǎolóngbaō* means 'small dragon buns'. Looks like a dumpling, tastes like a dumpling...but watch out for the boiling soup trapped inside when you bite in. Great as a snack or as a meal on its own.

#4. BEST VALUE ENTERTAINMENT AROUND ★ THE WORLD

✪ HOGMANAY, SCOTLAND

In Scotland debate still rages about which of its ancient traditions are worth preserving, but one custom that's survived just fine is the legendary night of hedonism, celebrated on New Year's Eve, known as Hogmanay. Although the origins of the name are uncertain, the occasion itself is said to date back to pagan times and is associated with pre-Christian celebrations to mark the winter solstice. Standing among the 100,000-strong crowd in the freezing cold before an iridescent Edinburgh Castle at the stroke of midnight is unforgettable, as is singing *Auld Lang Syne* and kissing your neighbours, which traditionally follows.

✪ RIO CARNAVAL, BRAZIL

Long regarded as the carnival capital of the world, Rio de Janeiro hosts a street spectacular that officially kicks off on the Saturday before Lent and continues until Shrove Tuesday, at the height of summer. The Samba Parade is the most publicised part of the festivities, which often last several weeks before, during and after the main Carnaval. The parade is actually a competition that takes place before 40 judges and 70,000 ticketed spectators. Tickets are expensive, but to see with your own eyes the lavish floats and unbelievably sexy Brazilians, dressed to beyond the nines and shak-ing their booty, is a once-in-a-lifetime experience.

✪ CHICAGO'S MILLENNIUM PARK (FEATURING 'THE BEAN'), USA

Since the opening of its 10-hectare park in 2004, Chicago has become famous for the quality of its public art as well as its blues. Already attracting millions of visitors, easily making it the city's most popular destination, Millennium Park has highlights that include the Jay Pritzker Pavilion (the USA's most sophisticated outdoor concert venue), an interactive fountain replete with surreal digital images of babies squirting water, and the insanely fascinating sculpture by Anish Kapoor entitled *Cloud Gate* although better known as 'The Bean'. This shiny 100-tonne 'kidney bean' made of highly polished stainless steel will mesmerise you with its reflections for hours.

✪ TATE MODERN, ENGLAND

Open as late as 10pm, the Tate Modern is the UK's biggest and most accessible gallery housing modern art (defined as artworks created since 1900). The inspired setting, inside the shell of a disused power station on the banks of the Thames, offers a fantastic sense of wide-open spaces making it feel more like a park than a gallery. Locals meet here as well as coming to check out the internationally famous collection, which includes works by Salvador Dalí, Tracey Emin and Henri Rousseau. Take the main entrance into the Turbine Hall to be amazed by the latest enormous artwork occupying this portal to postmodernity.

✪ SOLAR & LUNAR ECLIPSES

For millennia, solar and lunar eclipses have fascinated those who witness them; Homer wrote about a total eclipse in the ancient Greek epic *The Odyssey*. Eclipses are some of Nature's most awe-inspiring spectacles, and one helluva good excuse for a party. In the next few years, there will be numerous festivals taking place at various locations where eclipses can be seen clearly (there are four eclipses occurring in 2007, and a trio to follow from 2008 to 2010). Festival organiser IndigoKids has a simple ethos behind its open-air parties: 'Witness one of the most awesome sights displayed by nature and be immersed in its universal cosmic energy cycle.'

✪ THE BOAT RACE, ENGLAND

In 2004 the world's most famous inter-university rowing race, between ancient rivals Oxford and Cambridge, celebrated 150 years of getting people to spend their afternoons lining the Thames come rain, hail or shine. Crowds gather just to catch a fleeting glimpse of two teams of heavyweight eights straining along the 6.8km course that stretches across London from Putney to Mortlake. The spring race attracts around 250,000 spectators supporting either the light blues (Cambridge) or dark blues (Oxford), so-called because on dry land team members wear blue jackets. Upon sighting the boats, you are expected to start cheering maniacally and keep it up until they disappear again.

✪ EID AL-FITR, EGYPT

Celebrated on the first day of Shawwal, the 10th month of the lunar calendar, this festival marks the end of Ramadan (a month-long fast observed by Muslims). Not surprisingly food is high on peoples' agenda, with home-baked *kakh* (cookies filled with nuts and covered with powdered sugar) especially popular. Eid al-Fitr, which is a three-day holiday throughout Egypt, is a real family affair; you'll spot lots of picnics along the Nile, as well as groups of kids gathered around storytellers, puppeteers and magicians. Shopaholics should note that the commercial districts are empty at this time of year so it's a good time for bargain hunting.

WITNESS HONG KONG'S COLOURFUL NEW YEAR'S CELEBRATIONS AND RELEASE YOUR INNER DRAGON.

✪ CHINESE NEW YEAR, HONG KONG

1

When the world's most populace nation ushers in the Lunar New Year it's time for celebrations on an unprecedented scale. For the 10-day lunar period in late January or early February, Hong Kong welcomes 600,000 extra visitors looking to be immersed in the hectic carnival atmosphere. Fiery dragon dancers lead the legendary New Year parade, joined by endless floats, sizzling street performers and musicians. A genuine warmth pervades the city as everyone passes on their goodwill to others. A lavish pyrotechnic display over Victoria Harbour ends the official festivities.

LOVE IS IN THE AIR – WITH A BIT OF INFLATABLE ACTION, PARADISE IS NEVER FAR AWAY.

✪ LOVE PARADE, GERMANY

2

Berlin's Love Parade is the loved-up techno street-carnival manifestation of the Eurovision Song Contest. It's wild, tacky, flamboyant and sizzling with raw energy, as over a million whistle-blowing hardcore ravers, party people, freaks and queens dance the length of Unter den Linden. They follow up to 50 massive floats bedecked with models and DJs pumping out trance, dance, techno and house (gabba is banned), en route to the Tiergarten via the Brandenburg Gate. Funding issues meant the event was cancelled in 2004 and 2005, but it's still Europe's premier mash-up, as ecstatic revellers transform the entire city into one heaving nightclub.

CLOSE TO A THOUSAND YEARS OF HISTORY IS PLAYED OUT DURING IL PALIO – THE FIRST RACE OCCURRED IN THE 11TH CENTURY.

✪ IL PALIO, ITALY

3

Siena's Piazza del Campo is the quintessential medieval town square, particularly when it's just been converted into a horse track for the spectacular Il Palio. Twice every summer, thousands of spectators amass at the centre of the square to view the race for the *palio* (a secretly made banner), a tradition that dates back to the Middle Ages. This gorgeous ancient city is divided into 17 *contrade* (districts), and each summer 10 are selected to compete in Il Palio; although the race lasts less than two minutes, winning secures the triumphant *contrada* bragging rights for the rest of the year. This is Italian passion at its wildest.

⭐ ARCHAEOLOGIST

Archaeology is just as thrilling as Indiana Jones portrayed it, right? You travel to exotic places, dig up treasures such as the Ark of the Covenant, and end your days by beating up a few baddies, right? More likely you'll spend your time in the field painstakingly brushing off and chronicling shards and relics from prehistory. If you're lucky it might be a dinosaur bone you're pondering; more likely it will be the household detritus of your ancestors.

#5. PAID TO ⭐ TRAVEL

⭐ PILOT/AIRLINE CREW

At a glance it's a life of glamorous jet-setting, tempered by the knowledge that your working hours will be spent inside a tin can. You can sit at the pointy end of the plane and enjoy the views as you fly the thing, or you can serve food and nurse babies in the back. The travel rewards are at the end, when you wheel your suitcase out into the streets of a different city at the completion of each shift. Now you just have to remember which city it is.

⭐ TOUR GUIDE

Grab an umbrella, hold it unopened above your head and walk around the streets for a while. If a bunch of purple-haired grannies follow along behind, you're probably a natural-born tour guide. While much tour guiding involves figurative hand- (and umbrella-) holding, you will also be getting paid to see the attractions the rest of the travelling world forks out to see. All the while you'll become an expert on everything from the number of windows in the Petronas Towers to the location of the nearest toilets.

✪ TRAVEL WRITER

This is the job that you've dreamed about ever since your family and friends told you that your emails and postcards were so good you should be published. In essence, travel writing is simple and sensational: travel the world, doing all the things you love, and get paid for it. Trouble is, for every hour you'll spend looking at something, you'll probably spend two hours in front of a computer writing about it. And everybody you know will wonder when you're going to get a real job.

✪ FOREIGN CORRESPONDENT

Travel writing with a purpose, if you like. Instead of writing about what you see and do in a foreign country, you'll be able to write about what other, more interesting people see and do in a foreign country. Foreign-correspondent jobs are the cream of journalism posts, and you'll have to do plenty of foot soldiering – court reporting, ambulance chasing, police rounds – before you land that plum job in the New York bureau.

✪ YACHT CREW

The rolling romance of the open seas might be reserved for the wonderfully wealthy, but you can always tag along by becoming a deck hand – Gilligan to somebody else's Skipper. Crewing duties range from cooking to mending sails, from staffing the radio to unblocking the toilet. Places to seek crewing work include Antibes (France) for the Mediterranean; San Diego (USA) for the Pacific; or Miami (USA), the US Virgin Islands and Guadeloupe for the Caribbean.

✪ FILM LOCATION SCOUT

Loved the scenery in *Lord of the Rings* or *Brokeback Mountain*? Then how about the prospect of being paid to unearth such treasures for upcoming blockbusters? It won't all be magnificent mountainscapes and dramatic deserts; you might have to find a kitchen or toilet that's just-so for a particular scene. You might knock on more doors than a Mormon, or you might drive free and open-topped through the countryside for days on end. And you can always check out your handiwork later at the cinema.

✪ ROADIE FOR A ROCK BAND

They're not called roadies for nothing. Quite simply, your job will be to go on the road with a band and do all the grunt work. You'll travel to a different city every night, there'll be more scaffolding to erect and disassemble, and the same old guitars to place on the same old stands, sometimes for months on end. For many it's consolation for the rock stardom that never came their own way. And at least there's always a tour T-shirt thrown in.

✪ VOLUNTEER FOR AN NGO

Give to the world instead of taking from it by volunteering for disaster relief or general fieldwork. There is a myriad of NGOs across the world, and fieldwork is as variable as the organisations that run them, though primarily you'll be working towards the betterment of communities or people's lives. This might involve building schools, providing safe water supplies or improving agricultural practices. It's anything but sensational work, but it may ultimately be more rewarding than any of the perceived glamour jobs.

✪ TEACHER OF ENGLISH AS A FOREIGN LANGUAGE

With English now the lingua franca of, well, just about everywhere, there are growing opportunities to convert your travels into an occupation by Teaching English as a Foreign Language (TEFL). The obvious prerequisite is a full grasp of the English language; teaching skills can be acquired through a raft of TEFL courses. One TEFL college claims the job is 'all about giving something back, and doing a job that is enriching, uplifting and culturally interesting', which is another way of saying it pays bugger all.

✪ TOKYO DURING HANAMI ①

The Japanese delight in the brief *hanami* (blossom-viewing) season from February to April. The fruity sequence goes from plum in February, to peach in March, and then cherry in late March or early April. There are two spots in Tokyo known for blossom adulation: Ueno Park, and Yoyogi Park, former barracks turned public park. Yoyogi is the most famous vantage point and it gets frantically busy. A more serene post is Shinjuku-gyōen, one of the city's largest green spaces (58 hectares).

#6. BEST PLACE & SEASON
✪ COMBINATIONS

✪ LONDON IN MAY WHEN EVERYONE HAS A PERSONALITY CHANGE

At the first ray of spring sunshine, London kicks off its drab pinstriped image and jumps into sequins and nonsensical T-shirts. On days when hot-blooded types would shrug and go indoors, the number of Londoners with faces turned to the sun is endearing. City folk pull up a smidgeon of lawn in a tiny park at lunchtime, or sit outside under newly flowering window boxes at the pub. Jubilant music booms from open windows, and the plane trees boast their green. You may even get an accidental smile from one in a million on the tube.

✪ ANCHORAGE IN SALMON SEASON

In Anchorage, the office workers go salmon fishing during their lunch hour. In early June the king salmon begin spawning in Ship Creek. But the wildest salmon here are found spawning along downtown streets as part of the Wild Salmon on Parade, an annual event in which local artists turn fibreglass fish into anything but fish.

The art competition has resulted in an Elvis Presley salmon; a salmon turned into a floatplane; 'Uncle Salmon' painted in red-white-and-blue stripes; and 'Fish & Chips', a poker-playing halibut. The 30 or so colourful fish appear on the streets and stick around until September.

✪ GOA OUT OF PEAK SEASON

It's said that the best time to visit the Indian state of Goa weather-wise is during the cooler months, from November to March. But many Goans feel that the monsoon, between June and the end of September, is when the state is at its best. Parties and celebrations are held to welcome the rain, and the countryside turns lush and green almost overnight. The plus side to visiting at this time is that you'll have the place to yourself at very little cost. If you arrive in October, right at the start of the tourist season, you'll still find the beaches pleasantly empty.

✪ DUBLIN AT CHRISTMAS

December in Dublin is remarkably high-spirited. Check out the icy 'Christmas Dip at

CHERRY BLOSSOMS TURN JAPAN INTO A MARSHMALLOW WONDERLAND.

MARTIN MOOS | LONELY PLANET IMAGES

⭐ ROME IN SUMMER

2

From late June to August it's hot and humid in the Eternal City, sometimes unbearably so. But this is when Rome is most vibrant, with life spilling onto the streets and open-air festivals in abundance; a sultrier city you will not find. Gorgeous dresses, gelati, alfresco dining – ignore the bad smells and concentrate on the good ones. The spires of Christianity's capital create an ochre-and-orange skyline, piercing a usually blue sky (after all, Rome's home to the Pope). Make time to idle in sunny cafés, get lost in narrow cobbled streets and while away hours at local *trattorie* (eating houses).

⭐ REYKJAVÍK IN MIDNIGHT SUNSHINE

3

'Prepare for the unexpected' is a good rule of thumb: Icelanders joke that if you don't like the weather, just wait 10 minutes for it to change. Generally, in summer the climate is cool and the streets are washed in light 22 hours a day. The best months to visit Iceland are May, June and July, the driest and warmest months of the year. Peak season runs from early June to the end of August; outside these months, many galleries, museums and attractions in the city have reduced opening hours.

the Forty Foot', 11am on Christmas Day, at the famous swimming spot in Sandycove immortalised in James Joyce's *Ulysses*: a group of the very brave swims 20m to the rocks and back before Christmas lunch. Then drink a toast to the soundtrack of the Christmas masterpiece, The Pogues' 'Fairytale of New York'. Blow your dough and your post-Christmas crankiness at the hugely popular Leopardstown Races, from 26 to 30 December. Top it off with Dublin's traditional funfair, Funderland from 26 December to 9 January.

⭐ PRE-EASTER FESTIVAL SEASON IN BARCELONA

Celebrated in February or March, Barcelona's *car-nestoltes* (carnival festival) involves several days of fancy-dress parades and merrymaking, ending on the Tuesday 47 days before Easter Sunday. The Gran

Rua (Grand Parade) starts on or near Plaça d'Espanya and proceeds west along Carrer de la Creu Coberta. All sorts of marvellous floats and carriages participate to welcome the Carnival King. The festivities culminate in the Enterrament de la Sardina (Burial of the Fish), often on the hill of Montjuïc on the following Wednesday, to mark the beginning of Lent. Down in Sitges, a much wilder version of the festival takes place. Party-goers keep the bars and clubs heaving to all hours, for several days running.

⭐ CHAMPAGNE OUTSIDE GRAPE HARVEST

Known in Roman times as Campania (Land of Plains), Champagne is a largely agricultural region celebrated around the world for its sparkling wines. According to French law, only bubbly from the region – grown in designated areas, then aged and

bottled according to the strictest standards – can be labelled as champagne. The Route Touristique du Champagne (Champagne Route) weaves its way among neatly tended vines covering the slopes between small villages. All along the route, beautiful panoramas abound and small-scale *producteurs* (champagne producers) welcome travellers in search of bubbly; but many are closed around the *vendange* (grape harvest), in September and October.

⭐ NEW YORK IN JUNE

The song tipped you off: the first full summer month in New York brings a slew of parades, street festivals and outdoor concerts. SummerStage

in Central Park has an amazing line-up of pop, rock and world musicians, plus temperatures above 20°C. There are big-time discounts at top-notch eateries during Restaurant Week. Gay Pride month in June culminates in a major march down Fifth Ave on the last Sunday of the month, a five-hour spectacle of drag queens, gay police officers, leathermen, parents and representatives of just about every queer scene under the rainbow.

☻ MOUNTAIN GORILLAS, RWANDA & UGANDA

Few experiences compare to crouching within a whisper of the greatest of the great apes and holding your breath because there's nothing separating you from these amazing animals except for a rather tangled family tree. This is all thanks to the willingness of mountain gorillas in Rwanda's Parc National des Volcans and Uganda's Bwindi Impenetrable National Park to let you get close to them. You'll only spend an hour in the vicinity of the gorillas once you've tracked them in their native jungle, but those 60 minutes will endure for a lifetime.

1

GORILLAS NOT TO BE MISSED. GET A GLIMPSE OF THE GREAT APES OF RWANDA AND UGANDA BEFORE THEY DISAPPEAR.

☻ BHUTAN

The Kingdom of Bhutan, known to its inhabitants as Druk Yul (Land of the Thunder Dragon), is imagined by many outsiders to be a land frozen in a highly traditional past. This is not true – a thoughtful programme of modernisation began here 40 years ago. However, Bhutan's culture is underpinned by an ancient Buddhist mythology, emblemised by the ethereal *dzongs* (fort-monasteries) of the Bumthang region. Combined with Bhutan's extraordinary geography, it's this that brings visitors to a standstill while they're trekking between Himalayan peaks in the north, delving into deep central valleys, or roaming the rolling southern hills.

2

THE WORLD TURNS A DIFFERENT PACE IN THE NATIO CHORTEN OF THIMPHU, BHU WHERE PRAYER WHEELS SPIN DIZZYING SPEE

☻ DJENNÉ MOSQUE, MALI

The mosque in the island-bound Mali town of Djenné seduces travellers with the mud-brick hue of its fortresslike exterior and the large supporting cast of wooden beams that protrude through the walls into the brilliance of the African sun. So captivating is this earthen marvel, the world's largest mud-brick structure, that it makes little difference to the experience to learn that the current building only dates from 1907. It was modelled on the Grande Mosquée erected on the same site in 1280; the original building fell into ruin in the 19th century.

3

FOUR THOUSAND PAIRS OF HAN WORK FOR A MONTH EVERY YEAR MAINTAIN THE DJENNE MOSQUE, MA MONUMENT TO ISLAMIC DEVOT

#7. EXPERIENCES THAT MAKE
★ TIME STAND STILL

★ AMAZON RIVER, BRAZIL

A slow trip down the world's second-longest river means unbearable monotony to some, but glorious idleness and immersion in nature's timelessness to others. To decide for yourself, board one of the *gaiolas* (river boats) that navigate the Brazilian Amazon between the interior settlement of Manaus and the port of Belém. These boats get insanely crowded and their open-sided nature (hence the name, which means 'birdcage') guarantees exposure to fierce Amazonian rainstorms. But just climb into a hammock near the railing, consign the sounds of boat life to background noise, and lose yourself in the passing of the world's greatest rainforest.

★ ANTARCTICA

Travel to Antarctica is expensive – the average cost of a two-week cruise taking in the best of this continental ice-mass is around US$8000. Getting there by boat also involves a challenging sail across the Southern Ocean from bases like Hobart (Australia) and isolated Punta Arenas (Chile). But those who make the trip

are rewarded with close-up views of the stunning cliffs marking the extremities of ice shelves, mountainous icebergs, the wildlife of the island-crowded Antarctic Peninsula, and fierce sunsets that can last for hours. Notwithstanding the presence of other cruise-ship passengers, visitors also get to experience a glacial solitude that freezes the present.

★ SERENGETI NATIONAL PARK BY BALLOON, TANZANIA

Imagine being hoisted up into the sky at daybreak and sailing serenely over expansive savanna plains dotted with wildlife, warmed by the rising sun and with only the occasional sound of a burner to break the silence. Such is the experience you'll have in Tanzania's epic 1.5 million–hectare Serengeti National Park if you forego the standard on-the-ground safari and opt instead for a hot-air balloon odyssey over this African wildlife playground. The trip is at its most dramatic in May and early June when massive herds of wildebeest and zebras dodge predators during their annual migrations.

★ MONT ST-MICHEL, FRANCE

Mont St-Michel is a mesmerising mix of town, castle, island and abbey. The Benedictine abbey's striking Gothic architecture was completed in the 16th century and is surrounded by a village that is in turn surrounded by defensive ramparts and towers, all of it perched on a large granite islet in the English Channel that's connected by a causeway to Normandy's shoreline. Mont St-Michel is often rated as France's most visited attraction, hence its narrow streets get absolutely jammed with pilgrims and other visitors. Some prefer to gaze at it from a distance and meditate on the beauty of its silhouette against the surrounding bay.

★ SWIMMING WITH WHALES, TONGA

Between June and November, humpback whales congregate in Tonga to mate and breed. Observing the whales from the deck of a boat as they slowly frolic and occasionally slap their flukes on the water's surface is one thing. But strapping on a snorkel and paddling amongst these majestic cetaceans is something else entirely, particularly when a mother and calf are nearby. Swimming with whales is mostly undertaken around the Vava'u and Ha'apai island groups. The wellbeing of the whales is a very serious

issue in Tonga, so anyone thinking of reprising Pai's exploits in *Whale Rider* should think again.

★ PETRA, JORDAN

Petra is an ancient city that was sculpted out of sandstone cliffs in the southern deserts of Jordan to become the capital of the Nabataeans. This staggering feat of rock-carving is entered via the Siq, a narrow, high-walled gorge that leads directly to Petra's Treasury – the squeezed view of its elaborate façade from within the Siq has to be one of the world's most snapped photographs. Many visitors devote themselves to the hillside tombs along Petra's one 'street'. But for some quiet reflection and an awesome view, tackle the more than 800-step climb up to the monastery.

★ LHASA, TIBET

The name of the Tibetan capital means 'Holy City', a fitting description for a city lodged in the Himalayas at an altitude of about 3600m and the spiritual centre of Tibetan Buddhism. The thin air will take your breath away, but so will the incredible spectacle of the surrounding Himalayan peaks and the golden-roofed Jokhang Temple. And, unlike the exiled Dalai Lama, you can also enjoy the serenity of Potala Palace. Most beguiling, however, is the indomitable cheerfulness of the Tibetan people amid the impositions of Chinese administration.

✪ SOMALIA

Occupying the tip of the Horn of Africa, Somalia has been without an effective government since President Siad Barre was overthrown in 1991. Warlords have become the country's power brokers; the northwest of the country has broken away, declaring independence; and gunmen roam the streets of the capital, Mogadishu, a city in virtual ruins. Such are Mogadishu's dangers that elections in 2004 were held in Kenya because it was considered unsafe to hold them in the Somali capital.

1

TREAD CAREFULLY – THOUGH UN PEACEKEEPERS HAVE WITHDRAWN FROM SOMALIA, THE COUNTRY CONTINUES TO SUFFER UNDER RIVALLING WARLORDS.

✪ AFGHANISTAN

Another haunt of the hippie trail fallen on hard times. Invaded by Soviet Russia in 1979, landlocked Afghanistan has lurched from conflict to conflict: civil war; the US invasion after the 9/11 attacks; and ongoing struggles between the now-rebel Taliban, international troops, the Afghan government and resurgent warlords. Couple this with the country's re-emergence as the world's largest opium provider, and it's difficult to see Afghanistan finding its way back onto any traveller's beaten track.

2

THE TALIBAN HAS LIFTED I RULING ON WEARING THE VEIL, BI MANY WOMEN IN AFGHANISTAN CONSERVATIVE ISLAMIC SOCIE REMAIN SHROUDE

✪ SIERRA LEONE

While sun-seeking visitors descend on Gambia, just to the north, few of them will consider extending their happy holiday to take in Sierra Leone. Though the civil war in the West African nation ended in 2002, the images of its atrocities linger. Fifty thousand people were killed and rebels were notorious for hacking off the hands and feet of supposed enemies. Elections in 2002 and 2004 have restored much order to the country and travel warnings have even been lifted, but perception is usually stronger than reality.

3

HAPPINESS WITH A WARM GUN – A REBEL SOLDIER IN THE STREETS OF FREETOWN.

#8. TOUGH TRAVEL & ⭐ RISKY VISITS

⚙ IRAQ

It's difficult to believe now that Iraq's capital, Baghdad, was once a favourite stop along the so-called hippie trail, the famed overland route between Europe and Asia in the 1960s and '70s. Here was the legendary Babylon, the mythical Hanging Gardens, gold-tipped mosques and the Biblical familiarity of the Tigris and Euphrates Rivers. Today, Saddam Hussein is gone from Iraq but so are the travellers, and with an ongoing insurgency and almost daily bombings, they're not about to hurry back.

⚙ DEMOCRATIC REPUBLIC OF THE CONGO

Joseph Conrad's *Heart of Darkness* has become no lighter. Five years of war and millions of deaths have turned one of Africa's largest countries into a no-go zone. Disease and starvation are rampant in the Democratic Republic of the Congo (DR Congo; formerly Zaïre) as government forces backed by Namibia, Zimbabwe and Angola battle rebels backed by Uganda and Rwanda, turning this into a fight that has been termed 'Africa's world war'. Despite being far from the news, DR Congo has the UN's largest peacekeeping mission, with around 17,000 troops stationed here.

⚙ CÔTE D'IVOIRE

Long a West African beacon for stability, Côte d'Ivoire imploded after a 1999 coup. Thousands were killed after a troop mutiny in 2002 escalated into civil war. Fighting has now ceased, but weapons are still common on the streets of the administrative centre, Abidjan. Car-jackings are rife and armed hold-ups, even in restaurants, are common. Elections planned for October 2005 were postponed, and there were sporadic outbreaks of violence in the early months of 2006. It reads like anything but a travel brochure.

⚙ PALESTINIAN TERRITORIES

Since the creation of Israel in 1948, some of the holies ided into two parcels of land – the West Bank and the Gaza Strip – housing 3.6 million Palestinians. Entry for visitors into the Gaza Strip is not difficult but still few venture behind the razor wire that encloses it. A halting peace process offers occasional hope, but reciprocal violence and political disputes over Jewish settlements in the territories and the possession of Jerusalem are constant stumbling blocks.

⚙ SUDAN

Africa's largest country may also now be its biggest headache, as Sudan tries to emerge from the continent's longest-running civil war. Although a fragile peace agreement between the government and the rebels was signed in January 2005, there remains a separate conflict in Darfur, in the west of the country, which the USA has labelled as genocide and the UN has called the world's worst humanitarian crisis. Far from Darfur, the capital of Khartoum has a relatively low crime rate but, in the face of such bad press, that's hardly likely to win it a rush of tourists.

⚙ NORTH KOREA

Still happily shivering in the drafts of the Cold War, North Korea is a land unto itself. In 2004, mobile phones were banned in the country (although Chinese communications towers along the border are helping many people overcome the prohibition), and only a handful of flights arrive in the capital, Pyongyang, each week. If you're a US or South Korean citizen you can definitely rule out visiting communism's greatest stalwart – one third of the so-called 'axis of evil' – as visas will not be issued to you. (One exception to this rule are visas granted for the Mass Games in Pyongyang in 2007.)

⚙ RWANDA

In 1994, 800,000 people were killed in an act of genocide in Rwanda. All but ignored by the world at the time, it has subsequently become a cause célèbre, the brutality of the blood-letting attested to by books such as Philip Gourevitch's *We Wish to Inform You That Tomorrow We Will Be Killed with Our Families* and Gil Courtemanche's *A Sunday at the Pool in Kigali,* and the movie *Hotel Rwanda.* The country has come a long way since, but the flip side of this global hindsight is that beautiful but brutalised Rwanda still wears its international scars like welts.

✪ WOLLMAN RINK, USA

1

Embedded in Central Park is one of the few places in Manhattan where you can escape the swoosh of passing yellow cabs and the jostle of playing sidewalk pinball with fellow pedestrians. Wollman Rink opened to ice-skaters in 1950 and remains a cool refuge from New York's urban chaos. Skaters glide, speed and tumble across the ice, surrounded by Midtown's spectacular skyscrapers. It's magical, particularly when rink and enfolding city are lit up at night. Unfortunately, what was once a cheap Big Apple experience has become a capitalist wet dream thanks to one toupee-wearing entrepreneur.

✪ JONGMYO, SOUTH KOREA

2

a Bluelist suggestion from Sim Jui Liang

Jongmyo (also called Chongmyo) was built in 1395 and is the oldest Confucian shrine in South Korea. It was erected by members of the Joseon (Choson) dynasty to house tablets inscribed with their royal teachings and is suffused with a meditative air. Just about the only time this Seoul shrine gets really busy is when Joseon descendants gather here each May dressed in traditional garb to perform Jongmyo Daeje, an elaborate ceremony that pays respect to their ancestors. Jongmyo was designated a Unesco World Heritage site in 1995.

✪ KOWLOON PARK, HONG KONG

3

It's not only credit cards that exhaust themselves in the retail vortex of Tsim Sha Tsui on the Kowloon side of Hong Kong's Victoria Harbour. Their owners also find their energy sapped after zig-zagging between shops along the Golden Mile and squeezing through the district's trademark crowds. If this happens to you, head immediately for the commerce-free oasis of Kowloon Park. The park has plenty of relaxing greenery to wander through and its Sculpture Walk, lined with interesting marble and bronze creations, will give your eyes a chance to recover from window-shopping syndrome.

✪ BROMPTON CEMETERY, ENGLAND

a Bluelist suggestion from Comet_Ed

London's Brompton Cemetery was created in 1840 to accommodate an explosion (metaphorically speaking) in the number of existential retirees over the preceding half-century. Nowadays the cemetery's 16.5 hectares of tranquillity and its ranks of wonderful Gothic monuments are enjoyed as much by peace-seeking visitors as by its permanent residents. Animals enjoy the grounds here too and you'll spot the odd fox roaming around without fear of being pursued by silly peoplein white jodhpurs. If you suddenly get a flashback involving leather and pasta, don't panic – it's probably because the central chapel is modelled on St Peter's Basilica in Rome.

✪ CHARITY BIRDS HOSPITAL, INDIA

Old Delhi's main thoroughfare, Chandni Chowk, is the backbone of the city's busiest marketplace, where silver jewellery, spices and perfumes are snapped up by voracious crowds. In the midst of this overwhelming bustle, opposite the Red Fort, is the Digambara Jain Temple, and inside this temple is a donation-funded bird sanctuary. True

#9. THE MIDDLE OF

★ SOMEWHERE

FIND A PLACE THAT TAKES YOU AWAY FROM IT ALL

to its name, the Charity Birds Hospital offers free treatment to injured or diseased birdlife. The most common patients are partridges that have been wounded by hunters or pigeons that have flown into ceiling fans, but doctors also try to heal parrots, doves and the odd rabbit.

★ CHIJMES, SINGAPORE

Because the Chijmes complex in the heart of Singapore's Colonial District is bursting with shops, restaurants and bars, you may imagine that it's identical to every other crowded, soulless retail mall in this city of commerce. But Chijmes is actually a restored, century-old convent school with some wonderful Gothic and neoclassical architecture separated by quiet courtyards, none more serene than the central space that contains a beautiful little Anglo-French Gothic chapel. The name stands for Convent of the Holy Infant Jesus, with the final 'mes' added to make the moniker sound appealingly like 'chimes' (pun intended).

★ PALATINE HILL, ITALY

a Bluelist suggestion from hansolo
What better place to take a break from Rome's abominable traffic and all those well-dressed Italians than on Palatine Hill, one of the seven mounds that prevent the city from being flat, and the place where legend says Rome was founded in 753 BC. The hill is littered with the ruins of emperors' palaces that once belonged to humanitarians such as Caligula, and it's an enigmatic place for contemplating the rise and fall of civilisations. You're also relatively safe from handbag snatchers and pickpockets up here, though there have been reports of a she-wolf in the area.

★ PARC MONCEAU, FRANCE

a Bluelist suggestion from moineau
Stroll with the ghosts of longtime patrons Claude Monet, Marcel Proust and Hector Berlioz in this wonderful Parisian park. The tree-filled grounds were sculpted in the late 18th century by the Duke of Chartres for his own aristocratic enjoyment, a fact not lost on those who introduced him to the guillotine during the French Revolution. The Duke was fond of all things English, which is why Monceau eschews French formality in favour of meandering paths and the haphazard placement of statuary, though the presence of scaled-down Roman ruins, an Egyptian pyramid and a Chinese fort is harder to explain.

★ PETŘÍN HILL, CZECH REPUBLIC

To get some relief from the tourist bottlenecks in the labyrinthine laneways of Prague's Old Town, cross Charles Bridge into Mala Strana and let the funicular railway haul you to the top of lovely Petřín Hill. The hill's leafy trails are ideal for an aimless wander.

Alternatively, stroll over to the southern side of the hill and try to find the eerie, derelict Church of St Michael within the tangle of Kinský Gardens. When you're ready to reconnect with civilisation, climb Petřín Tower, a 5:1 scale model of a certain Paris landmark, and take in the stupendous view.

★ SANTICHAIPRAKAN PARK, THAILAND

a Bluelist suggestion from Sim Jui Liang
The 1.2 hectares of Santichaiprakan Park laze beside Bangkok's sluggish Chao Phraya river. During the day it's often full of backpackers who have escaped Khao San Rd to sprawl under its many trees clutching old paperbacks, but at dusk the travellers make way for large groups of exercising Thais. The park is arrayed around the eye-catching whitewash of the restored Phra Sumen Fort, which dates back to 1783. In November, Santichaiprakan hosts the popular Thai festival Loy Krathong or 'Festival of Light', famous for its tradition of setting candles adrift on the river in banana-leaf boats.

LEH, INDIA

From the town of Leh in the northern Indian region of Ladakh you can depart for a two-day trip (only from mid-July to mid-September) across the 'roof of the world', a lovely global precursor for the roof over your heads. Get married at the end of day one and test your bond on day two. This strenuous pass will take your breath away at 5600m. Make each other proud by crossing the perilous swing bridges between canyons. Buddhist monasteries dot the serene landscape: pay a visit for first-hand instruction in kindness and tolerance.

TUSCANY, ITALY

Why not make the wedding just as memorable for your friends as it will be for you? Schedule the event as follows: hire the main villa for you and your mates, and a series of connected cottages nearby for both sets of family. Get everyone to arrive the night before and meet up in the irresistibly convivial atmosphere of the local pizzeria – ideally it'll be in a hilltop town, accessible only by foot. The next day, after a lazy, sunny morning getting ready, be married in the little fresco-painted chapel on the property. The evening reception is on the lawns, surrounded by fireflies and caterers with gallon jars of homemade red plonk.

WESTERN CAPE, SOUTH AFRICA

Here's one way to rock the boat. Say your vows (and your prayers?) in a shark cage off Gansbaai, 175km southeast of Cape Town. For those who dated at scary movies, this is just a natural progression. Admittedly your celebrant will have to be capable of some depth and your parents might be practising speeches long before the event. But if the cage is as strong as your love, you'll be fine. Great white sharks are now on the IUCN Red List of Threatened Species – although critics maintain that humans are more endangered since shark-cage diving started, as the pelagic predators are encouraged to associate bait with us.

ANTARCTICA

For those who have decided to ignore the cold feet and dedicate themselves to the mating season, what better place than Antarctica? Join your life partner on the good ship *Aurora,* on your deliciously slow way down to the largest continent on earth (you could propose here too, as it's the ultimate icebreaker). Ecotourism honeymoon expeditions can include polar adventure activities such as sea kayaking, scuba diving and camping. There's the potential for interaction with whales. Take a tip from the emperor penguins: the best answer to the weather is to go into the most natural of huddles. Life will seem cosy after this trip.

NICOBAR ISLANDS

It's a rare thing when two 'morning people' find each other. What better way to demonstrate your purposeful compatibility than to marry at dawn? Somewhere along a line in the Indian Ocean, the sun creeps first onto hundreds of tiny islands, islets and rocks. Sparrows fart first here, in the idyllic Nicobar Islands, a union territory of India, located in the Indian Ocean. Isolation has preserved lush forest cover and flourishing fauna, and there are people of many faiths: Hindus, Muslims, Christians, Sikhs. Should make designing a wedding ceremony all the more interesting.

#10. BEST PLACES ⭐ TO WED

& BEST DESTINATIONS AFTER A BREAK UP

✪ HUSTADVIKA, NORWAY

Chaotic and tumultuous, salt-stained, yet free – this stretch of ocean in a storm is a perfect metaphor for your dark heart. Stare out at the fantastically wild waves and contemplate how you got dumped. Or muse over the notorious history of this coast: ships have been sinking here since the Middle Ages. Then jump into an appropriately Scandinavian car and head down the Atlantic Road towards the western fjords and the fishing village of Kristiansund. Along this winding stretch you'll cross no fewer than 12 bridges over less troubled water.

✪ BUENOS AIRES, ARGENTINA

The World Tango Festival, held in venues all over a summery Buenos Aires, is a perfect opportunity to find a new partner who'll hold you like you want to be held. Workshops are run by the Great Masters of Tango, *milongueros.* Held in the best dance halls and sports clubs and culminating in the grandest ballroom in the city, the Palais Rouge, the workshops are accompanied by six 'orchestras'. In broader terms, this dance is also a physical interview for that greater tenet of coupledom: commitment. Can he take the lead and is she capable of following? Has he got big feet? Will he drop her? Test it out.

✪ MANCHESTER, ENGLAND

Make an instant chemical friend every night in one of Manchester's myriad dance clubs. You may not even have to talk, but you'll immediately know you've found one of your kind at Poptastic or the Northern Monkey Music Club.

Intellectuals can be found at the Best Indie Night in the World…Ever!, while simpler types bust a move at Giggle & Funk. But don't expect these clubs to stay the same. Tomorrow's a new day – possibly even a Happy Monday.

✪ ELORA, CANADA

Just over an hour out of Toronto, this rustic sandstone mill town preserves the pious ways of the old world, when couples huddled together through fierce Canadian blizzards (despite their sometimes icy relationships). The local Mennonite community will teach you how to cook and sew. You'll learn to survive without TV, takeaway, Gameboy, shoe therapy, haircuts or counsellors (no powerlines = time to talk to people around you). Best of all, now you can eat what you like: try locally produced maple syrup with every meal or organically grown veggies, the choice is yours. Go on a date with a new prospect in a horse-drawn buggy.

✪ AITUTAKI, COOK ISLANDS

Your return to the blue lagoon of Aitutaki, just an hour's flight north into the South Pacific Ocean from the Cook Islands' main island of Rarotonga, is long overdue. Nominated as the world's most beautiful island by Lonely Planet's founder, Tony Wheeler, it's better looking than your ex too. The truly buff inhabitants have won the Cooks' 'best young island dancers' award the last three years running. They perform every night at alternating beachside restaurants, so learn how to shake it and get on with attracting your next partner. Alternatively, hire a moped for a circuit of the island and feel the breeze in your free-flowing, newly single hair.

#11. GREAT LITERARY
✪ ITINERARIES

✪ KELLY COUNTRY, AUSTRALIA

Fancy yourself an outlaw? Ride into the heritage town of Beechworth and pull up at the pub, following the trail of bushrangers, as in Peter Carey's *True History of the Kelly Gang*, winner of the Man Booker Prize in 2001. These parts of the Victorian Alps are still known as 'Kelly country': it's not hard to imagine armoured showdowns in the bush near Glenrowan. Head southwest for the big smoke of Melbourne, where Carey did plenty of time in the city's archives. Ned's rough, sardonic voice in the novel is derived from the genuine 'Jerildirie letter', recorded before the bushranger was hanged at Old Melbourne Gaol in 1880; you can still see his waxen death mask here.

✪ FLEET STREET, ENGLAND

You'd be hard pressed to nominate a more literary itinerary than the Street of Shame (Fleet Street), London. Here you can still see the spookily pale Victorian Gothic–era Royal Courts of Justice, where Sherlock Holmes would have dusted his hands of villains. Here you can drink in the same 17th-century pub, Ye Olde Cheshire Cheese, where Samuel Johnson, Sir Arthur Conan Doyle and Charles Dickens put their warm ales away. (WB Yeats, George Bernard Shaw, GK Chesterton, William Makepeace Thackeray, EM Forster, Voltaire, Alexander Pope and Mark Twain also popped in). Mind your head.

✪ INDIA

Ruth Prawer Jhabvala wrote her novel *Heat & Dust* as a housewife in Delhi. The novel, which won the Booker prize in 1975, captures India as successfully as any reel of film, depicting the country under British rule in the 1920s, and again in the independent 1980s. Switching between these eras, it explores what happens when a bored young Englishwoman, Olivia, begins going to Khatm to spend time with the intensely charismatic Nawab (Prince) and they engage in an affair. Years on, her great niece is part of a backpacker wave, drawn to the idea of the exotic, wishing to uncover the past and to make a new future for herself through travel.

✪ ST PETERSBURG, RUSSIA

Is Leo Tolstoy's *Anna Karenina* the best novel ever written? Certainly it's one of the most famous works of the 19th century, set for the most part in the upper echelons of St Petersburg society. Start your itinerary here, in the city that, for more than 200 years, served as Tsar Peter's 'window to Europe' and the capital of the Russian Empire (until the Russian Revolution of 1917). Today, St Petersburg is Russia's second-largest city and Europe's fourth largest. To end proceedings, head to Moscow. Vronsky and Anna lay eyes on each other for the first time at the main railway station; Anna also ends her thoughtful but short life here.

✪ ROUEN, FRANCE

Madame Bovary takes place in provincial northern France, near the town of Rouen in Normandy. The protagonist, farm girl Emma Rouault, is filled with a desire for opulence and romance – the result of reading popular novels (as opposed to guidebooks) – and she embarks on a series of affairs. The scenery changes from the village of Tostes (now Tôtes) into the equally dull village of Yonville, based on the town of Ry. Then there's a fateful night at the opera house in Rouen. Flaubert himself is buried Rouen.

✪ YORKSHIRE, ENGLAND

Wend your way across the bleak moors to visit the Brontë Society and Parsonage Museum in the hilltop town of Haworth. The family house preserves rooms as they would have appeared in the writers' day. See the small table Charlotte and Emily circled as they read *Jane Eyre* to each other (while wearing extremely tiny shoes). Sadly, all four highly creative siblings died before age 40. Charlotte, prevented from finding love until her late thirties by their exacting father, only knew brief romantic happiness. You may well go away subdued, an appropriate mood in which to approach the (all the more remarkable) bruising passions of *Wuthering Heights*.

✪ DEMOCRATIC REPUBLIC OF THE CONGO

Conrad's *Heart of Darkness*, set in the late 1800s in what was then Belgium's Congo Free State (now the Democratic Republic of Congo; DR Congo), leads you simultaneously, more deeply and irretrievably into the jungle of the mind. Investigating the same part of the world 60 years on, Barbara Kingsolver's *Poisonwood Bible* reflects on the Congo from a postcolonial, female point of view. Both novels capture atmosphere as tangibly as leaves within their pages. Ditch the itinerary! Sometimes it's the view across the river, the colour of flora, scales, dirt, skin, or the voices around you that stay with you.

⭐ FLORENCE, ITALY ①

Isn't it trying when you book a Florentine *pensione* in advance but when you arrive, there's no view of the River Arno from your window? Like Lucy Honeychurch in EM Forster's *A Room with a View*, wander the Medici city in your Sunday best. Tour the Piazza di Santa Croce, the statue of David and the Duomo, as you too consider Truth, Beauty and Love. Beware the peasants, under whose guidance you're liable to be kissed in a waist-high Tuscan wheat field. But at the very least, never venture forth without your mackintosh squares – at any time you may have to sit on damp ground.

LEAVE COUSIN CHARLOTTE AND MISS LAVISH BEHIND AND HAVE YOUR OWN FLORENTINE ADVENTURE.

⭐ LOS ANGELES, USA ②

A most celebrated low-life writer, Charles Bukowski worked at a post office, the Terminal Annex building in downtown LA, until he was 50. For a degenerate, he was prolific: from 1979 to 2001 there were only a few years when he didn't publish. When not at his typewriter he was regularly to be found at Sunset Strip bars. His novels and poetry all draw on real life scenes downtown, in East Hollywood and on Hollywood Boulevard. He lived his last years to the south, in the port town of San Pedro; see his grave, which reads 'Don't try', at Green Hills Memorial Park.

THE GOOD, THE BAD AND THE UGLY – EXPLORE SOME DARK INSPIRATION IN HOLLYWOOD.

DON'T JUST READ ABOUT IT – RELIVE THE HIGHS AND LOWS OF MOSCHUS' MIDDLE EAST JOURNEY.

⭐ MIDDLE EAST ③

From the Holy Mountain by William Dalrymple traces the route of a pilgrim monk on a journey through the ancient Christian Middle East. It begins on Macedonia's Mt Athos, examining the oldest surviving manuscript of *The Spiritual Meadow*. From there, the itinerary next stops at Istanbul; goes on to eastern Turkey and Tur Abdin; then Syria, Lebanon, Israel, and finally Egypt. Dalrymple endeavoured to stay in the same monasteries as Palestinian monk Moschus had many centuries before. The modern journey is full of encounters in the Muslim realm, as the author is challenged on his journalist's visa.

★ ANGKOR, CAMBODIA

*a Bluelist suggestion from
jemima_price*

Tourists crawl over Angkor like ants over a picnic blanket. But it's worth joining them to register your first glimpse of this shrine-city's awesome main temple, Angkor Wat, with its lotus-shaped towers and extraordinary bas-reliefs. Angkor was sculpted from sandstone between the 9th and 13th centuries to satisfy the egos of a succession of Khmer *devaraja* (god-kings), providing the ancient empire with the grandest capital imaginable. The site contains hundreds of temples besides Angkor Wat, deemed the world's biggest religious structure, and is still being reclaimed from the jungle that overgrew it when it was abandoned in the 15th century.

★ EIFFEL TOWER, FRANCE

Men love to build towers (perhaps it's something about the shape) and Gustave Eiffel was no exception. Commissioned to build an eye-catching entryway for Paris' upcoming Exposition Universelle, he finally unveiled his 300m-high iron icon in 1889. The structure was only meant to stand for 20 years but won global admiration for its beautiful architectural form and has stood its ground, despite attempts to demolish it by aliens *(Mars Attacks)* and Thunderbird puppets *(Team America: World Police)*. Put it on your 'must visit' list – after all, six million people a year can't be wrong.

#12. TOURIST TRAPS WORTH ★ THE CROWDS

★ FLORENCE, ITALY

The capital of *bella* Tuscany can test the endurance of the most hardened traveller. Its piazzas are filled with the whir of digital cameras, the leather and jewellery shops hem you in, and money belts can disappear faster than kisses. But Florence is also Italy's Renaissance jewel and few cities can match its classic beauty. Swoon over Michelangelo's *David* in the Academy of Design Gallery, the gorgeous headpiece of the Brunelleschi-built Duomo, and the stunning sculptural landscape of the Boboli Gardens, or just sit in a café and swoon over handsome passers-by.

★ GRAND CANYON, USA

Arizona's desolate backcountry is one of the last places where you'd expect to get stuck in traffic, but this is typically what confronts visitors to the Grand Canyon. Once your vehicle is stowed away, however, you can check out one impressive hole in the ground, a 446km-long channel dug out of the surrounding rock by the Colorado River. The canyon measures 29km at its widest point and 1500m at its deepest. Stare into its magnificent depths from up on the South Rim or hike to the canyon floor and back; lazy types impose themselves upon a mule.

★ PYRAMIDS, EGYPT

Judging by the scale of many of the pyramids anchored in the desert around Cairo, the word 'modesty' wasn't in the vocabulary of ancient Egypt's pharaohs. This is particularly true of Khufu, who around 2560 BC commissioned the Great Pyramid that dwarfs two similar structures at Giza. Khufu's gigantic burial monument is the only surviving member of the

✪ ULURU, AUSTRALIA

a Bluelist suggestion from jemima_price

Massive, monolithic Uluru is embedded in the remote Australian outback and draws hundreds of visitors at dawn and dusk to watch the rock's colours magically change with the rising and setting of the sun. Some people choose to scale this sandstone giant even though the rock's custodians, the Anangu people, ask visitors to keep their feet on the ground out of respect for Aboriginal spiritual beliefs. A more respectful way of exploring enigmatic Uluru is to circumnavigate it via the Base Walk, a 9.5km trail that often allows you a little solitude.

1

✪ PRAGUE'S OLD TOWN, CZECH REPUBLIC

Prague's Staré Město (Old Town) is wildly crowded day and night. Restaurants and bars around Old Town Square criminally overcharge visitors. Wandering the district's tight lanes on rainy days means constantly ducking to avoid being impaled on umbrella tips. And groups of drunken males stagger around at night ritually humiliating the groom in their midst. All of which is forgotten once you see Týn Church's delirious baroque trimmings, the Art Nouveau brilliance of Municipal House and the magnificent bulk of Prague Castle across the Vltava.

2

✪ MACHU PICCHU, PERU

The fabulous stonework of the ruined Inca city of Machu Picchu is nestled high up in the Peruvian Andes. It was built in the mid-15th century but abandoned only a century later, around the time some Spanish gentlemen arrived bearing malice and smallpox. Archaeologist Hiram Bingham rediscovered the site on behalf of the outside world in 1911 and Peru's tourism bureaucrats are still thanking him. The ruins and the Inca Trail connecting them with Cuzco were becoming buried under tourist numbers and waste until several years ago, when toilets were installed and visitors limited to a mere 500 per day.

3

---

original seven wonders of the world, and that should be enough to tempt you to see it silhouetted against a North African sky. By the by, 'pyramid' comes from a Greek word meaning 'wheat cake'; apparently the pharaohs liked pointy desserts.

★ TAJ MAHAL, INDIA

The Taj Mahal was completed at Agra in 1653 by Mughal emperor Shah Jahan to glorify the beauty of his favourite (but dead) wife. So is this minaret-ringed marvel with its domed mausoleum, white-marble calligraphy and bejewelled inner chambers a romantic dream come true, or is it a lavish folly to which the labours of 20,000 people over 22 years should not have been devoted? You be the judge. The story behind the Taj Mahal has already been dealt with on-screen by Bollywood director Akbar

Khan; it's only a matter of time before the Hugh Grant version appears.

★ VICTORIA FALLS, ZIMBABWE & ZAMBIA

Victoria Falls is an astonishing sight, the result of a 1.7km-wide stretch of the Zambezi River falling into a crack in a basalt plateau to be crunched in a narrow gorge. In 1855 explorer David Livingstone presumed to name Victoria Falls after his homeland monarch, but its local name is Mosi-oa-Tunya (Smoke That Thunders). Try to catch these 108m-high falls during the wet season. But regardless of when you go, plan your trip carefully, as the turbulence of this enormous cascade unfortunately reflects the current social climate of Zimbabwe and Zambia, the two countries providing access to it.

#13. MOST ECCENTRIC
⭐ PLACES TO STAY

❂ CUEVAS PEDRO ANTONIO DE ALARCÓN, SPAIN

If you're tired of self-development and want to indulge in a bit of regression, head for Guadix in the foothills of Spain's Sierra Nevada and play caveperson by staying in the town's cave hotel. Cuevas Pedro Antonio de Alarcón consists of 23 rooms occupying caves in the clay of a local hillside. These caves were apparently once occupied by prehistoric folk, and to exploit this connection the hotel has, according to its website, decorated them '…with a lot of details to look like the primitive ones'. This probably doesn't refer to the fully equipped kitchens, jacuzzis or wheelchair access.

❂ HOTEL 1929, SINGAPORE

Tracing the origin of Hotel 1929's name is easy – the elegant building is one of Singapore's trademark shophouses and dates from (you guessed it) 1929. Deciding what prompted the owner to centre the décor on a collection of designer chairs is much harder. Those who choose their accommodation based on snob value will overlook the fact that the rooms are less spacious than the average prison cell and will instead swoon over the see-through shower stalls, pyschedelic bedspreads and the artwork seating, not to mention the groovy young things twittering away in the downstairs restaurant.

❂ HOTEL DU PETIT MOULIN, FRANCE

a Bluelist suggestion from Sasha Arms

Quirky French fashion designer Christian Lacroix recently tired of dressing up models and so decided to dress up a hotel instead. The place in question is the four-star Hotel du Petit Moulin, which occupies a 17th-century Parisian building once devoted to a *boulangerie* (bakery). The building's warren of tight passageways now accommodates Lacroix's flamboyant (some might say half-baked) sense of style. Each of the hotel's 17 rooms is uniquely decorated: some are encrusted with exotic murals and fittings like the set of a new cabaret, while others are more restrained in style but just as playful.

❂ HYDROPOLIS, UNITED ARAB EMIRATES

a Bluelist suggestion from Sasha Arms

The emirate of Dubai in the United Arab Emirates loves extravagant accommodation. It already has the world's tallest hotel, the 320m-high Burj Al Arab, and is building the globe's biggest artificial islands for its Palm Islands resort. Soon Dubai will also have Hydropolis, the world's first underwater hotel. This bizarre US$560 million undertaking will be located 20m below the surface of the Persian Gulf, and its 220 suites will be accessed from land by a plexiglass railway. Hydropolis isn't slated to open until the end of 2007; in the meantime, Atlantis is still taking bookings.

❂ KADIR'S TREE HOUSE HOTEL, TURKEY

Among the pine and bay trees that crowd the valley of Olympos in southern Turkey, you'll find a grown-up version of the childhood living-in-a-tree-house fantasy. Kadir's specialises in tree-top living, with a number of its cabins perched atop large trunks. Some of the cabins have an alarmingly realistic rustic look, a kind of tumbledown style that may make some nervous that high above the ground. But by all reports, these lodgings are as safe as houses. The biggest thing to cope with here is the lack of intimacy, as around 300 sleepers can be accommodated in Kadir's tree houses and ground-level cabins.

❂ LIBRARY HOTEL, USA

Talk about niche markets. Surely only a committed bibliophile could possibly care that each floor of this hotel on Madison Ave, New York, pays homage to one of the main classifications of the Dewey Decimal System, which is used around the world to categorise library stock. Each room is decorated according to a sub-genre of the theme of its floor, which means that the the 8th floor (Literature) has rooms devoted to the enjoyment of poetry and erotic literature. No prizes for guessing that the quietest floor in the hotel is the 10th (Computer Science).

❂ ST BRIAVEL'S CASTLE, ENGLAND

What could be more empowering for an all-conquering backpacker than to call a moated Norman castle home for a night or two? This is what's on offer at St Briavel's Castle, a 13th-century fortress in the leafy rural environs of Gloucestershire. Originally a hunting lodge for King John, the castle was invaded by the Youth Hostel Association in the mid-20th century and its Great Hall renovated to suit the demands of frugal travellers. Medieval-style banquets are held here each week, just in case the history of the place isn't obvious from the surrounding stonework.

CHILLY CONDITIONS ARE THE PERFECT REASON TO FIND SOMEONE TO SNUGGLE UP TO.

✪ MAMMUT SNOW HOTEL, FINLAND ①

By January each year, a castle has been magically sculpted from the snow and ice blanketing the Lapland community of Kemi in Finland's Arctic north. Within the Snow Castle is the Mammut Snow Hotel, a giant igloo of a place where guests snuggle down in rooms where the temperature is maintained at a comfy -5°C. After emerging from their sleeping bags, guests can go and eat in the Snow Restaurant, with its ice-block tables and seats swaddled in reindeer fur. If they're feeling particularly committed to the experience, they can also go and get married in the ecumenical Snow Chapel.

SWAP THE STARS ON THE HOTEL FRONT DOOR FOR STARS OVERHEAD IN THE JORDANIAN DESERT.

✪ BEDOUIN TENT, JORDAN ②

Lawrence of Arabia wannabes should make their way to the awesome desert valley of Wadi Rum in the south of Jordan to sleep under the stars in a Bedouin tent. The landscape here could hardly be more spectacular, particularly when the sun sets behind the sandstone monoliths that rear up out of the sand. However, your taste of desert-dweller life is likely to be less authentic, as most of the accessible Bedouin encampments are tailored towards tourists. Still, lying down amid ornate rugs and cushions within a goat-hair tent after digesting a meaty feast makes it all worthwhile.

SAIL FOR A SEA OF ~URY – NO LIFE JACKET ~UIRED.

✪ IMPERIAL BOAT HOUSE HOTEL, THAILAND ③

If you like the idea of sleeping on boats but are prone to seasickness, then the Imperial Boat House Hotel on the Thai island of Ko Samui is the answer to your prayers. The idea behind the hotel was to buy several dozen old rice barges, haul them onto dry land and convert them into luxury villas. Each of the landlocked vessels gleams with polished teak and is fitted out with all the luxuries that a life nearly-at-sea demands. Guests who pine for some salty water to round out the experience can walk into the ocean off nearby Choeng Mon Beach.

⊛ BOLLYWOOD POSTERS, INDIA

Not only is India's film industry the world's oldest and largest, it's also responsible for some of the most bizarre, and charmingly kitsch moments ever captured on celluloid. Naturally, the posters promoting Bollywood films tend to reflect the grandiose weirdness of the industry's conventions. Up until a few years ago posters were hand-painted in every city by local artists with varying degrees of artistic integrity, which sometimes resulted in the movie's stars being unrecognisable. With the introduction of digital artwork these hand-painted posters have been reappraised as works of art, appearing in exhibitions from London to Milan.

1

HUNT DOWN A POST FROM YOUR FAVOUR MELODRAMATIC MARSA IN MUMB

AN AAMIR KH

⊛ BIG THINGS, AUSTRALIA

Given the country covers approximately 7.7 million sq km, it seems appropriate that when you head down under size matters, especially when it comes to public sculptures of fruit, animals and historical icons. Australia's love affair with bigness began in 1964 when American John Landi erected an 11m-long, 5m-high concrete banana along the Pacific Highway at Coffs Harbour, New South Wales, to promote roadside fruit sales. Since then more than 140 Big Things have popped up across the country, including sculptures of a cow, a bee, a peanut, a pineapple and Australia's legendary outlaw Ned Kelly.

2

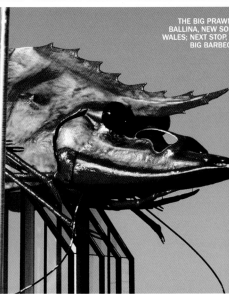

THE BIG PRAWN BALLINA, NEW SOU WALES; NEXT STOP, T BIG BARBEC

⊛ LIBERACE MUSEUM, USA

It's no coincidence that the museum dedicated to one of America's most flamboyant entertainers is found in Las Vegas, the world's most outrageously excessive city. Classically trained pianist Wladziu Valentino 'Lee' Liberace's career spanned four decades, peaking in 1960 with a star on the Hollywood Walk of Fame. His notable charisma, garish costumes and camp performances won Liberace admiration worldwide. The museum, exhibiting Liberace memorabilia, family photographs, stage costumes and a collection of the great man's pianos, opened in 1979 and is the third most popular attraction in Nevada state.

3

GLAM UP AND TINKLE THE IVORIES WHEN YOU WORSHIP AT THE LIBERACE SHRINE.

#14. THE KITCHEST OF
⭐ THE KITCH

⭐ COOLIDGE ARTWORK, USA

We've all engaged in anthropomorphism (the act of projecting human behaviour onto animals) at some stage, but few to the extent of American painter CM Coolidge, whose pictures of gambling dogs are among the world's most recognisable artworks. After unremarkable stints as a druggist, sign writer and publisher in Antwerp in New York state, Coolidge took a trip to Europe and began painting dogs whose actions mirrored those of middle-class humans. In the 1920s, Coolidge, having returned to Rochester, New York, painted his series of dogs playing poker that would make him world famous. He died in his 90s the following decade.

⭐ NEIGHBOURS TOUR, AUSTRALIA

Shot in Melbourne's drab outer suburbs, *Neighbours* is one of Australia's most visible and highly praised exports. For more than 20 years the TV soap, screened in 57 countries worldwide, has been launching inter-national careers for Aussie stars such as Jason Dono-van, Natalie Imbruglia, Holly Valance, and, of course, Kylie Minogue. Now discerning visitors can take their own trip through Erinsburgh High and have their picture taken with Neighbours demigods like Harold Bishop (Ian Smith), Dr Karl (Alan Fletcher), Jarrod 'Toadfish' Rebecchi (Ryan Moloney) and the delectable older woman Susan Kinski, nee Smith (Jackie Woodburne). Everybody's good friends down under, mate.

⭐ RUSSIAN KITSCH RESTAURANT, RUSSIA

Exquisite faux luxuriance exudes from every comical inch of Russia's priceless epicurean nod to the kitsch and famous. Green marble, polished gilded bronzes, garlands of flowers, hand-painted ceiling murals, divine sofas and a gallery adorned with naked busts – if you could dream it up after a night at an opium den, chances are the Russian Kitsch Restaurant has it in spades. Despite its tasteless opulence, the vibe is totally relaxed and the only thing that's stiff is the vodka. The menu reflects the décor's absurdity with mismatched food, such as herring pickled in pistachio, adding to the fun flavour.

⭐ BUTLIN'S HOLIDAY CAMP, ENGLAND

The first Butlin's Holiday Camp was established in 1936 by William 'Billy' Butlin at the seaside town of Skegness, in the cold north of England. The idea was to create a holiday venue for working-class Brits that offered a range of activities so they wouldn't get bored. To encourage customers to mix and have fun, Butlin employed a staff of 'Red Coats' (so called because of their uniforms) whose job it was to explain the facilities and get the party started. The Red Coats' boundless enthusiasm has been parodied by comedians ever since, especially in the hit TV comedy *Hi-de-Hi!*

⭐ LEOPARD LOUNGE, USA

While the world's superpower certainly boasts more than one Leopard Lounge, it's the one in Chicago that's got us purring. As you would expect, every seat and chair in this too-cool-for-cats bar is adorned with delightfully decadent leopard-print motifs. There's a definite swinger-style vibe with crooning tunes by the likes of Sinatra promoting a sultry, intoxicating theme. This is further implied by the unrestrained use of red for just about everything that isn't covered in leopard print, such as the walls, lighting and bar staff. Dress up and slink around but, no matter how tempting it may be, leave the leopard-print leotard at home.

⭐ PASSPORT STAMP, LIECHTENSTEIN

Sandwiched between Austria and Switzerland, the tiny principality of Liechtenstein nestles among the Alps busily minding its own business. In a country where the major export is high quality hand-drills it may not be too surprising that its major tourist attraction, apart from the picture-postcard scenery, is a souvenir passport stamp. In the capital, Vaduz, you must pay staff at the tourist office a small fee before they will lovingly caress your passport with their tasteful stamp. Then it's off to the hills to find and make friends with the Prince of Liechtenstein, reputed to be the world's fifth wealthiest head of state.

⭐ LEDERHOSEN, GERMANY

To many outside the German-speaking nations, the idea that lederhosen (leather trousers) are a symbol of masculine virility is greeted with considerable scepticism. These smartly embroidered three-quarter trousers, usually fashioned from the hide of an elk, goat, calf or pig, were first donned during the 18th century, being the favoured attire of butch Bavarian mountain men with an additional penchant for leather suspenders, or braces, to hold them up. Old photographs reveal that lederhosen could indeed look rather fetching but this was largely due to the athleticism of the models. Nowadays lederhosen retailers sell calf implants to make customers' legs seem manlier.

#15. MOST DESERTED
⭐ISLANDS

⭐ ELEPHANT ISLAND, SOUTH SHETLAND ISLANDS

You'll probably want to spend less time on this Antarctic island than did the crew of Ernest Shackleton's *Endurance* expedition in 1915 – 135 days – but you will enjoy the dramatic landscape, the ice-covered land mass and, reportedly, good surfing (if you've brought your board and a survival suit). Shaped vaguely like an elephant's head, hence the name, this cliff-ringed island now sports a bust in honour of the rescue of Shackleton's crew, as well as populations of chinstrap, gentoo and macaroni penguins. The heavy surf and crowds of fur seals and penguins can make landings difficult.

⭐ PRINCESS ROYAL ISLAND, CANADA

Once inhabited by the Tsimshiam people, this remote island 500km north of Vancouver is now primarily home to one of nature's most beautiful creatures, the Kermode bear. Endemic to British Columbia the Kermode bear, or spirit bear, is a black bear that is, by a trick of nature, actually white. Princess Royal Island has the largest population of Kermode bears, and around 10% of the island's bears are white. Tours to the island operate out of Terrace and Prince Rupert. You can also paddle here from Swindle Island, 12km to the south.

⭐ ISLA FERNANDINA, ECUADOR

The Galápagos Islands are a volcanic archipelago of 15 islands, famed for their wildlife and their role in the formation of Charles Darwin's theory of evolution. Only four of the islands are inhabited; of the others, Isla Fernandina is among the most appealing to visitors. Rising 1500m from the Pacific Ocean, it is also the most volcanically active of the islands. Visitors land at Punta Espinosa, where hundreds of marine iguanas, the world's only sea-going lizards, bask in the equatorial sun. Expect also to see flightless cormorants, Galápagos penguins and sea lions.

⭐ ROCK ISLANDS, PALAU

Resembling marine mushrooms, the 200-plus rounded knobs of limestone that comprise the Rock Islands are sprinkled over a 32km stretch of the Pacific Ocean southwest of Koror. Famed among divers and kayakers, the translucent waters around the islands contain more than 1500 varieties of fish. To test your survival skills, follow the lead of the *Survivor: Palau* contestants by plunging into the waters of Jellyfish Lake – one of 80 marine lakes in the Rock Islands – to swim among millions of harmless jellyfish.

⭐ MOTUARA ISLAND, NEW ZEALAND

On 31 January 1770, James Cook raised the Union Jack on Motuara Island, at the head of Queen Charlotte Sound, and claimed British rule over New Zealand. Today, the tiny, predator-free island is like a kiwi's revenge, having been transformed into a bird sanctuary that's home to kiwis, South Island robins, little blue penguins and other native bird species. The fearsome-looking weta is also an island resident. Dock at the pier on the western side of the island and ascend the trail to a Cook monument and a view across the Sound and Cook Strait.

⭐ HALFMOON ISLAND, NORWAY

Bare, barren, bleak and inhabited by polar bears, Svalbard's Halfmoon Island is no pin-up deserted island but it is the likely site of one of history's great survival tales. Stranded on Svalbard – most likely on Halfmoon Island – in 1743, three Russian walrus hunters survived through six Arctic winters before being rescued. Their ingenuity stretched to a hunting bow made from driftwood and the tendon from a polar bear. Modern travellers can glimpse Halfmoon Island in more comfort, from the deck of the cruise liners that plough around the Svalbard archipelago each summer.

⭐ RAMSEY ISLAND, WALES

A Royal Society for the Protection of Birds reserve off the coast of St David's, Ramsey Island is a twitching paradise – up to 130 bird species can be found here each season. Rimmed by 120m-high cliffs, Ramsey is rich also in flowers and seals, and in autumn its beaches becomes a breeding ground for grey seals. Travel to the island is only possible between April and October, and visitor numbers are limited to 40 per day. Seabird numbers peak between April and July.

✪ BALL'S PYRAMID, AUSTRALIA

One of the most shapely rocks in the sea, Ball's Pyramid rises 562m from the Pacific Ocean like a cockscomb. A remnant stack from a shield volcano, it has long been ogled by climbers, and was first scaled in 1965 by four members of the Sydney Rock Climbing Club. Climbing was banned in 1982, and it's more likely to be visited now as part of a diving or fishing trip out of nearby Lord Howe Island.

1

✪ SANTA CRUZ ISLAND, USA

Immediately off the coast of Los Angeles, Santa Cruz is California's largest island and was once home to around 2000 people. Today, it's jointly protected as a national park and nature conservancy and is visited by few people, though it has wonderful natural features. Here you'll find the Channel Islands' highest peaks, deep canyons, beaches and around 140 bird species. Most impressive are Santa Cruz' sea caves, which are among the world's deepest. Boats for Santa Cruz depart from Ventura, and there are two primitive camping grounds on the island.

2

✪ KRAKATAU, INDONESIA

Pinched between Java and Sumatra, Krakatau rendered itself all but uninhabitable in one mighty volcanic sneeze in 1883. On 27 August of that year, Krakatau erupted with the loudest bang ever recorded on earth – people in Alice Springs, Australia, recorded hearing explosions. Ash fell on ships as far as 6000km away, and more than 36,000 people were killed by the resulting tsunamis. Though Krakatau has been erupting almost continuously for the past few years, boats can sometimes land on the eastern side of Anak Krakatau (Child of Krakatau). Boats can be arranged from the Javanese beach resort of Carita.

3

✪ SURINAME

Resting atop South America's eastern shoulder, Suriname is a former Dutch colony turned ethnic melting pot, where indigenous cultures mingle with British, Dutch, Chinese, Indian and Indonesian influences. There is much to like here. The capital, Paramaribo, retains some fine Dutch colonial architecture, but the nature reserves are the country's true gems (though the infrastructure is less dazzling), with Raleighvallen Nature Reserve and Brownsberg Nature Reserve noted for their rich bird life. Bordered by the equally anonymous Guyana and French Guiana, this is the last frontier of South American travel.

1

IN SURINAME, CALM CELEBRATIONS MARK THE END OF RAMADAN.

✪ TOGO

About as wide as a cigarette paper, Togo bounces off the tongue and into the hearts of those who make the journey to this West African nation. The capital, Lomé, fronts the Atlantic Ocean in a line of beaches and palm trees, but from here the country heads inland through deep valleys and tall mountains that peter out into flat savanna. Togo can be all things to all people – you can be windsurfing on Lake Togo one hour and sifting through voodoo medicines such as monkey testicles and snake heads at Lomé's fetish market the next.

2

WITH AROUND 2.5 MILLION FOLLOWERS OF THE VOODOO RELIGION IN TOGO, YOU MAY WITNESS TRANCES AND SEE FETISH MARKETS AROUND THE COUNTRY.

✪ KUWAIT

Famous only for being invaded, tiny Kuwait is on few travel agendas, partly because its only land crossings are with Iraq and Saudi Arabia, making overland entry all but impossible. For those who think about flying in, there's not a whole lot here to justify the effort, unless you like gleaming Middle Eastern shopping malls and four-lane highways. Away from the spit-and-polish of Kuwait City you can ascend all 145m to the country's highest point on the Mutla Ridge, or check out Al-Ahmadi, the birthplace of Kuwait's oil industry. Go nuts.

3

FIND A DIFFERENT KIND OF BEATEN TRACK AT THE KUWAIT CAMEL RACING CLUB.

#16. UNDER ★ THE RADAR

LOW PROFILE DESTINATIONS NOT TO MISS

★ KYRGYZSTAN

Think of great mountain countries – Nepal, Peru, Canada – and Kyrgyzstan will inevitably get overlooked. It shouldn't. The former Soviet republic, closed to foreigners for much of the occupation, contains the highest and most dramatic mountains in Central Asia; its highest peak is almost 7500m above sea level. Trouble is, Kyrgyzstan has little else, being low on resources and tourist infrastructure. It's a good thing, then, that most visitors head straight for the relatively developed Lake Issyk-Kul, the second-highest lake in the world and a launching pad for the region's finest trekking.

★ SÃO TOMÉ & PRÍNCIPE

Fancy a slice of the Caribbean just off the coast of Africa? With their uncrowded calm, the two sleepy islands that make up Africa's smallest nation are the antithesis of all things African. Few people have heard of them, and even fewer visit, though news of their charms is leaking out. There are miles of deserted beaches, crystal-blue waters with excellent and uncharted diving, jagged rock formations and lush rainforests. There's also a laid-back café lifestyle with real coffee, delicious fresh fruit and seafood.

★ COMOROS

In the glory days of ocean travel, Comoros was a traditional stopover for ships rounding the Cape of Good Hope. Obscurity came with the construction of the Suez Canal, and today there are only 25,000 visitors each year. Neighbouring the Seychelles, and just a few freestyle strokes from Mauritius, Comoros should be a tropical idyll, but it's as fragmented as its islands, enduring 20 coup attempts since gaining independence from France in 1975. Skip across to Mayotte, a part of the archipelago but not of the country, and you can visit one of the world's largest lagoons.

★ NAURU

There was a time when the tiny, potato-shaped island of Nauru was among the richest nations on earth on a per capita basis, its people made wealthy by an abundance of phosphate deposits. Today, the phosphate is all but gone from the Pacific island, leaving the interior looking like a treeless moonscape of coral pinnacles. Most visitors who come do so unwillingly (asylum seekers deposited into a detention camp by the Australian government) and there's more talk about abandoning the island than bringing in tourists.

★ GUINEA-BISSAU

With some of the most unconditionally welcoming people in West Africa, Guinea-Bissau is like a rare find in a disorganised record store. On the mainland there are sleepy colonial towns, quiet beaches and sacred rainforests, while the country's single entrant into mainstream tourism is the Arquipélago dos Bijagós, a cluster of wild and remote islands with fantastic marine and animal life. The laid-back, small-town feel of the capital, Bissau, sets it apart from the frenzy of most West African capitals, but if you're sightseeing you're mostly going to be looking at war damage.

★ NIUE

A speck of an island 600km from its nearest neighbour, Niue sees so few visitors there are just two flights in every week (one each from Auckland and Apia). This is not your classic Pacific beach paradise as there are few beaches here; but there's some fantastic cave exploration through the Vaikona and Togo Chasms, and as the island has no rivers running into the sea, visibility for divers is exceptional. The name of the Toilet Bowl, a dive site off the west coast, is no reflection on the quality of Niue dives.

★ BELARUS

As other former Soviet states fill with visitors, Belarus only looks on, despite being the straightest line between Moscow and the rest of Europe. The last dictatorship in Europe to fall, Belarus is the place to come if you want to reminisce about all things Soviet – the capital, Minsk, was all but destroyed in WWII and rebuilt to a Stalinist blueprint. For natural grandeur, there's the Belavezhskaja National Park, straddling the Polish border. This is Europe's largest primeval forest, a Unesco World Heritage site and a home to European bison, the continent's largest mammal.

KYRGYZSTAN MAY NOT HAVE MANY TRAVELLER FACILITIES, BUT IT'S GOT PLENTY OF CULTURAL AND NATURAL BEAUTY.

ANTHONY PLUMMER | LONELY PLANET IMAGES

EAT ODORI EBI
a Bluelist suggestion from Svjetlana Mlinarevic

If your restaurant dinner moved when it was served to you, you'd probably scream and health inspectors would close the place down. However, aficionados of the Japanese dish called *odori ebi* actually look forward to the movements of their meal. *Odori ebi* translates as 'dancing prawns', which is an attempt to avoid saying that the creatures are still alive when you munch them. The prawns are soaked in sake to sedate them, but the drunk crustaceans are nonetheless still capable of greeting you with a wiggle of the antenna and a twitch of the leg when they reach your table.

WATCH NIRAMEKKO OBISHA, ICHIKAWA
a Bluelist suggestion from Keridwen Cornelius

The Niramekko Obisha festival takes place each January at the Kamagata Shrine in Ichikawa, Chiba Prefecture, and is an example of how it sometimes pays to be a loser. During this centuries-old event, two people try to outstare each other without smiling or laughing while a raucous crowd attempts to crack the contestants up. The loser is 'punished' by draining a large bowl of sake. Some believe that this highly entertaining ritual was devised to help priests predict the success or failure of the upcoming harvest; others believe the priests were just looking for an excuse to guzzle rice wine.

CATCH THE LAST TRAIN HOME
a Bluelist suggestion from kimba111

The Japanese white-collar term 'salaryman' was once a job description in itself and implied a strong work ethic, impeccable appearance and loyalty to a single company, often for life. But the salarymen's 'live to work' mantra has taken its emotional and physical toll, particularly during Japan's recent economic depression, and some now end their long working days by drinking until they literally pass out. Catch the last train home from an inner-city station and you may see a few business suits sprawling unconscious in the shadows of the platform, briefcases clutched to their chests.

CONFRONT HARAJUKU FASHION, TOKYO

Barbarella-style vamps in foot-high boots, satin glam-rock ensembles, sci-fi schoolgirls, rockabilly quiffs, *Alice in Wonderland* pinafores, Goths and Pierrots, *anime* heroines – just some of the things you might see when Japanese girls strut their sartorial imaginations every Sunday around Tokyo's Harajuku train station. The street performers are thinner on the ground than they were a few years ago and a peek into one of the area's trendy boutiques reveals

#17. SPIN OUT ★ IN JAPAN

...THEN GET SOME BALANCE

GO TO THE GHIBLI MUSEUM, TOKYO
a Bluelist suggestion from Sheila Scarborough

Anyone with a soft spot for flying fortresses, spirit-world bathhouses and reclusive wizards will love the Ghibli Museum in the Tokyo suburb of Mitaka. It showcases the surreal *anime* output of Studio Ghibli, which is headed by director Miyazaki Hayao and is responsible for popular flicks like *Spirited Away* and *Howl's Moving Castle*. Wander through galleries of vivid artwork, watch short films specially produced for the museum, and head up to the rooftop to give a giant Laputan robot a hug. As an extra reward for your devotion to animation, you'll find several film frames embedded in your admission ticket.

HANG OUT AT HIMEJI-JŌ, HIMEJI
a Bluelist suggestion from NewMexican

Himeji-jō (Himeji Castle) is one of Japan's best pre-served medieval buildings. Dominated by an enormous central tower, the castle is raised up on a small hill within the city of Himeji and is nicknamed the 'White Egret' because of an outer coating of white plaster that flashes back the sunlight. Himeji's good looks belie its age (the original fortifications date from the mid-14th century) thanks to scrupulous maintenance and the fact that the structure has never been involved in a battle. Perhaps the castle's most extraordinary character-istic, however, is that it is made entirely out of wood; put out your cigarette before you visit.

HAVE A BILL MURRAY MOMENT IN THE NEW YORK BAR, TOKYO

In the film *Lost in Translation*, Bill Murray's character Bob first meets Scarlett Johansson's Charlotte in the New York Bar on the 52nd floor of the Park Hyatt Tokyo, where both characters are staying. To take the life-imitates-art path to deal with your own sense of being culturally overwhelmed in Tokyo,

just how contrived the scene has become. But it's even more entertaining than watching the comings and goings of identically dressed salarymen.

● BATHE AT A SENTŌ

a Bluelist suggestion from kimba111

A visit to a *sentō*, one of Japan's sex-separated public bathhouses, is not for the self-conscious. Leave any introversion at the front door along with your clothes and shoes, and join the unwashed masses as they first cleanse themselves thoroughly and then shuffle over to one of the relaxation baths. Bath temperatures range from tepid to sulfurically hot, with one version carrying an electrical current – the ultimate muscle relaxant, apparently. The primary idea behind the *sentō* is one of respectful communality. But women may dispute this when crinkly old men wander casually into their section to use the toilet.

JOHN ASHBURNE | LONELY PLANET IMAGES

you'd need to start by paying at least US$400 per night for a room here. Alternatively, just sit in the New York Bar and gaze down at Tokyo's cityscape through the floor-to-ceiling windows while listening to soothing jazz and nursing a drink (ideally a tumbler of Suntory whisky).

VISIT OKUNO-IN, MT KOYA

a Bluelist suggestion from Karly Straitton

South of Osaka lies Mt Koya, a spectacular Unesco World Heritage site that accommodates more than 100 temples and Japan's largest cemetery, Okuno-in. The centrepiece of Okuno-

in is the tomb of Kūkai, the wise monk who founded the Shingon school of Buddhism before he died in the 9th century. A pilgrimage to Kūkai's mausoleum, which is lit by hundreds of lanterns, involves walking through dense forest along a stone path lined with thousands of graves. The quantity of graves is eerie enough, but spookier still are the communal tombs maintained by corporations such as Toyota for their most devoted employees.

TAKE IN TŌDAI-JI, NARA

a Bluelist suggestion from Alphazack

Buddha statues don't get much grander than the one in the Tōdai-ji complex in the one-time Japanese capital of Nara. The bronze Daibutsu (Great Buddha) here is 15m high and weighs in at a hefty 500 tonnes. The building enclosing it is reputedly the largest wooden structure in the world, which sounds impressive enough until you learn that the current structure only dates from 1709 and that its predecessor was another 30% bigger. While you're here, wander into the Shōsō-in Treasure Repository to have a peek at treasures once gloated over by 8th-century Japanese emperors.

BLUELIST // ONLINE

THINGS THAT GET 'LOST' IN JAPAN

✪ SHOES

Japan has little crime, but the things that are stolen are petty. My friend's new shoes were stolen at a restaurant. As the last to leave, he was left with smelly sports shoes – the right size.

✪ UMBRELLAS

Outside stores, restaurants and offices are racks of umbrellas. Some people simply help themselves when it rains.

✪ BICYCLES

Around train stations or supermarkets you'll find rusty old bikes that have been dumped. Occasionally you'll see fathers and daughters checking through the racks for their missing ones.

✪ BURROUGHS IN TANGIERS, MOROCCO

1

After accidentally shooting his wife while playing William Tell, American beat writer William Burroughs wound up in Tangiers where there was cheap hashish and young boys aplenty. Drugs, alien Moorish culture and the city's labyrinthine streets fuelled his imagination. Holed up in a small room overlooking the Atlantic, he wrote incessantly, leaving the pages where they fell from his typewriter. In 1957, with Allen Ginsberg's help, the manuscript was put in order. Entitled *Naked Lunch,* it starkly depicts drug use, cannibalism and Burrough's decadent life in Tangiers.

✪ KAFKA IN PRAGUE, CZECH REPUBLIC

2

To really explore Franz Kafka's Prague, visit in winter when the light is most bleak and mysterious. Especially at night the city is dominated by its medieval castle, towering forebodingly over the baroque streets below. This was one of many landmarks described by surrealist literary and metaphysical icon Kafka, who spent his formative years lurking around the streets near the Old Town Square. Read *The Castle* or *Metamorphosis* to heighten awareness of the disorienting layout of Prague's back alleys, dimly lit passageways and bewildering living spaces. Very trippy.

✪ GHANDI IN NEW DELHI, INDIA

3

No relation to serene Mahatma Ghandi, although they were friends, Indira Ghandi often divided public opinion during her two tenures (1966–77 and 1980–84) as Indian prime minister. Controversial for authorising violent actions against Punjabi Sikhs and an administration marked by rampant nepotism (her son took over the leadership following her death), Ghandi nevertheless secured her place in history as the country's first female head of state and by achieving success in the war against Pakistan in 1971. A memorial in New Delhi commemorates the place where Sikh militants assassinated her in 1984.

⭐ GREAT PEOPLE

MANDELA ON ROBBEN ISLAND, SOUTH AFRICA

South of Robben Island, Table Mountain rises majestically above the city of Cape Town. It was here in 1652 that Europeans established their first settlement in South Africa, initially as traders, later as captors of the men detained on this island. The most prominent of the prisoners was Nobel Laureate and former South African prime minister, Nelson Mandela, who spent 27 years languishing in a cell measuring 5 sq metres. The 500-hectare island prison lies just 12km off the mainland across a notorious stretch of water frequented by great white sharks. Today, the site is a memorial and museum with guided tours offered by former inmates.

NORGAY IN THAME, NEPAL

The small, high mountain village of Thame might be off the beaten path taken by climbers on their way to Everest, but it is the former home and birthplace of the Sherpa who made the first summit possible. Unlike most of his fellow countrymen at the time, Tensing Norgay believed it was his destiny to be one of the first to ascend the world's highest peak. After breathlessly scaling Everest on 29 May 1953 along with New Zealand's Edmund Hillary, Norgay instantly became a global legend. Lofty Thame, meanwhile, continues to produce many of Nepal's most respected mountain men and women.

MOZART IN VIENNA, AUSTRIA

Had Emperor Joseph had any idea how popular his court composer, Wolfgang Amadeus Mozart, would become it is doubtful he would have had him buried in a commoner's grave, the location of which remains unknown. Born in Salzburg, near Vienna, Mozart was a prodigy, writing his first symphony aged eight. But it was in Vienna that he really let loose, composing pieces that would comprise a virtual honour roll of classical masterpieces. A maverick in an age of powdered wigs and courtly manners, Mozart's legacy still thrives in Vienna, where he flamboyantly lived and died aged 35 in poverty, despite his genius.

THE BEATLES IN LIVERPOOL, ENGLAND

All four members of the world's greatest rock band were born and raised in England's northwest city of Liverpool. It was also here the Fab Four got their first break, performing at underground jazz club, the Cavern. After initial resistance from the club's manager, The Beatles took to the stage on 7 August 1957. And the rest is history. The current manifestation of the Cavern occupies 50% of the original site, while other Beatlemania buildings, such as the childhood homes of John Lennon and Paul McCartney, are considered national treasures.

SESANA IN THE KALAHARI, BOTSWANA

Most visitors agree that surviving in the Kalahari would be impossible without taking in your own supplies of food and water. To Roy Sesana, a Gana Bushman, the desert provides everything needed not only to survive, but also to thrive. In order to escape persecution at the hands of white settlers and other African tribes the Gana people took refuge in the desert, where their pursuers were too afraid to follow. But since the Botswana government discovered mineral deposits, Gana land and livelihood are again under threat. In 2005, Sesana was awarded the Right Livelihood Award (known as the 'alternative Nobel prize') for 'resolute resistance against eviction from ancestral lands'.

FRANK IN AMSTERDAM, NETHERLANDS

On 6 July 1942, fearing immediate deportation to a Nazi work camp, Otto Frank moved his small family into the abandoned offices, later known as 'the annexe', that he had been preparing for them to go into hiding. His daughter, Anneliese Marie Frank, had just turned 13 and was given a diary for her birthday. Anne's vivid portrayal of the German military occupation, her personal aspirations for after the war and the assistance provided to the family by non-Jewish 'helpers' would posthumously make her famous. Anne Frank House commemorates the brave teenager who died at Bergen-Belsen concentration camp one month before it was liberated in 1945.

JOAN OF ARC IN DOMRÉMY, FRANCE

Joan of Arc (Jeanne d'Arc) was born in the village of Domrémy (now Domrémy-la-Pucelle) on 6 January 1412, an auspicious date celebrated as the Feast of the Epiphany. For a woman destined to become one of the most feared military commanders of her day, as a youth d'Arc was said to have been 'a quiet, serious girl who was dutiful in helping with the housework and unusual only in her extreme degree of piety'. Today scholars and pilgrims still flock to Domrémy to explore the forest where d'Arc experienced her visions of popular saints and to check out the d'Arc family home.

☆ POLAR LIGHTS ①

A space spectacular, the polar lights are a dazzling Arctic and Antarctic display, their colourful sheets of light transforming the endless winter nights into natural lava lamps. The polar lights – aka aurora borealis and aurora australis – form when solar particles, thrown out by explosions on the sun, are drawn by the earth's magnetic field towards the north and south poles, colliding with atmospheric gases to emit photons, or light particles. What results are brilliant sheets of green, red, white, purple or blue light.

☆ DON JUAN POND, ANTARCTICA ②

Antarctica's McMurdo Dry Valleys are remarkable enough: huge, desolate spaces covering 4800 sq km without snow or ice. Here, algae, bacteria and fungi, some of it thought to be 200,000 years old, have been found growing *inside* rocks. The Onyx River flows inland from the coast and there's a lake, Lake Vanda, that's 25°C at its bottom. There's also Don Juan Pond, which is only 10cm deep but the most saline body of water on the planet, 14 times saltier than the ocean. It is so salty, in fact, that this shallow pond never freezes, even at temperatures of -55°C.

#19. MOST AMAZING NATURAL
☆ PHENOMENA

☆ RACETRACK, USA ③

Who wouldn't expect a few oddities in a place like California's Death Valley? Prime among them is the mystery of the 'racing' stones in the valley's remote north. These large, flat stones, some weighing as much as 180kg, have 'raced' across the earth, leaving grooves in the dry, cracked lake bed behind them. Nobody has ever seen any of the rocks move, and science's best guess is they've been blown across at times when the lakebed is slippery with rain or frost.

✷ SEQUOIA TREES, USA

So you think Shaq is tall? Then head into the Sierra Nevada in California to meet the largest living organisms on the planet. Sequoias, or giant redwoods, can live for up to 3000 years, and can grow to around 100m; the tallest, the so-called Stratosphere Giant in Humboldt Redwoods State Park, has been measured at almost 113m. Sequoias grow only on the Sierra Nevada's western slope, and there are protected groves in Yosemite, Sequoia and Kings Canyon National Parks.

✷ KILAUEA, USA

Hawaii's Kilauea may be less headline-grabbing than some of its volcanic counterparts, but the world's most active volcano just keeps on spewing lava. An eruption began here in 1983, and continues today, flowing around 11km to the sea. On its way it has destroyed villages, engulfed the coastal highway and covered more than 100 sq km of the island. Daily it adds new land – more than 200 hectares to date – turning Hawaii's Big Island into Bigger Island.

✷ WILDEBEEST MIGRATION, TANZANIA & KENYA

The thundering of two million hooves through the Serengeti and Masai Mara is surely one of the most spectacular moments in the extravaganza that is the animal kingdom. This annual migration is a continuous cycle of movement: wildebeest give birth in the Serengeti during the wettest part of the year and head for the Mara in the dry season, an endless if relatively recent phenomenon prompted by the increasing numbers of wildebeest. The most spectacular moment of the migration is the crossing of the Grumeti River, where gigantic Nile crocodiles lie in wait for a wildebeest steak.

✷ BOOMING SAND DUNES

With a haunting moan almost like a didgeridoo, booming sands have spooked more than a few people; Marco Polo blamed evil spirits when he heard booming sands in the Gobi Desert. Booming sands have been heard at around 30 places around the world, the sound lasting up to 15 minutes and audible up to 10km away. Their cause isn't yet fully understood, though it's believed they result from a rare combination of factors: sand grains must be of a similar size, they must be smooth and polished and conditions must be dry. A wind-blown sand avalanche then supposedly creates the sound.

✷ RED LAND CRABS, AUSTRALIA

For most of the year you'll see little of the red land crabs of Australia's Christmas Island, living away in shady sites inside the forest that covers much of the island's plateau. Then, suddenly, at the beginning of the wet season, around October or November, more than 100 million enormous red crabs suddenly emerge, breaking out of the forest like escapees, climbing down cliff faces and – more dangerously – crossing roads. All this so the female crabs can release their eggs into the Indian Ocean at precisely the turn of the high tide during the moon's last quarter.

✷ LAMBERT GLACIER, ANTARCTICA

In a world of shrinking glaciers it's nice to know there's always Lambert Glacier. The world's longest glacier drains about 8% of the Antarctic ice sheet and is up to 400km long and 200km wide at the point where it reaches the Amery Ice Shelf. The shelf itself is a seaward extension of the Lambert, and is a source for one of the rarest and most beautiful sights in the natural world: bottle-green icebergs, resulting from the high content of organic material inside the ice.

✪ MT SINAI, EGYPT

Moses climbed it and carried back some stone tablets, but all you'll need is a sleeping bag and some warm clothing if you want to be here for the requisite dawn vigil atop the Sinai Peninsula's signature mountain. The climb commences at Unesco World Heritage–listed St Catherine's Monastery, from where you can follow the camel trail, or sweat out your sins on the Steps of Repentance. The 2285m summit, which offers stunning views of the surrounding bare, jagged mountains and plunging valleys, is reached after around two hours along the camel trail.

1

FIND DIVINE INSPIRATION IN THE COMMANDING VIEWS AT THE TOP OF MT SINAI.

✪ MATTERHORN, SWITZERLAND

For those who know that a crampon is more than a sporting injury, there are few more alluring peaks than the mighty Matterhorn. Shaped like a broken finger, the Matterhorn is a technical climb, and though its distinctive rock pyramid frightened the ice screws out of early alpine climbers, its Hörnli Ridge route – the approach used by most climbers – is today considered a straightforward mountaineering ascent. The standard climb begins at the top of the Schwarzsee cable car, with climbers spending a night at the Hörnli Hut before making a dawn approach to the summit.

2

FOR A REAL CHALLENGE, RE-ENACT A FEW OF YOUR FAVOURITE SCENES FROM THE SOUND OF MUSIC AS YOU SCALE THE MATTERHORN IN SWITZERLAND.

✪ MT FUJI, JAPAN

Welcome to the mountain sometimes said to be the most climbed in the world, and one that is certainly among the most recognisable. Rising 3776m behind Tokyo, Mt Fuji is the highest mountain in Japan. It has an official climbing season running during July and August, although you may want to come just outside this peak season to avoid crowds that are as large as the mountain itself. The climb up from the traditional starting points takes around 4½ hours; aim to reach the summit in time for dawn to witness sunrise and to beat the clouds to the top.

3

GET SNAP-HAPPY AT MT FUJI, THE MOST PHOTOGRAPHED MOUNTAIN IN THE WORLD.

#20. TOP MOUNTAINS TO CLIMB
✪WITHOUT A PORTER

✪ HALF DOME, USA

Looming over Yosemite Valley like a stony wave, Half Dome is one of the world's most stunning pieces of rock architecture, and a major lure for hikers. The trail begins at Happy Isles in the valley, climbing more than 1000m to the bare summit – steel cables lend some assurance on the final haul along the exposed northeast shoulder. There's a flat two-hectare expanse on top with glorious views across Yosemite, especially from the overhanging northwest point. The climb can be made in a mammoth day, or you can camp on the northeast shoulder.

✪ TABLE MOUNTAIN, SOUTH AFRICA

The flat-topped, 1086m-high mountain that gives Cape Town its visual splendour is also said to contain more than 300 walking paths. For most people, however, it's all about getting to the summit, and pronto. For this, the route through Platteklip Gorge is the most straightforward. The gentlest climb is along the Jeep Track, through the Back Table, though the gentle gradient also means that it's one of the longest approaches. The Platteklip Gorge route should take two to three hours; you can descend in about four minutes on the cable car if you wish.

✪ BEN NEVIS, SCOTLAND

Britain's highest mountain has an attraction that belies its numbers. Only 1344m above sea level, its paths are pounded by hordes of walkers and climbers. For most, the ascent means following the queues up the Mountain Track but mountain connoisseurs prefer the more difficult approach across the satellite peak of Carn Mór Dearg, a climb that involves picking along a thrilling rock ridge between the two summits. And if Ben Nevis whets your mountain appetite there are another 283 'Munros' – Scottish peaks above 914.4m – you might want to climb.

✪ JEBEL TOUBKAL, MOROCCO

North Africa's highest mountain (4167m) is surprisingly kind on climbers. From the trailhead at the village of Imlil, a two-hour drive from Marrakesh, it's a five-hour walk into Toubkal Refuge, at around 3200m, situated immediately below the western flank of this High Atlas giant. From here, trekkers usually scurry up and back and return to Imlil in a day. The climb's greatest challenge is in Toubkal's famously long scree slopes; be prepared for a walking experience like quicksand.

✪ MT ELBRUS, RUSSIA

Far from the glory-grabbing summits of the European Alps are the shy twin peaks of Mt Elbrus (5642m), Europe's highest mountain. Straddling the Russia–Georgia border and bulging above the Caucasus Ridge, Elbrus looks a daunting prospect. It's nearly 1000m higher than any peaks around it, and glaciers chew at its edges, yet it offers no real technical difficulties – there's even a chairlift to 3800m, where most climbs begin. A short distance above the chairlift is Camp 11; from here it's an eight-hour push to the summit.

✪ MT OLYMPUS, GREECE

Rub hiking boots with the gods as you ascend Greece's highest mountain, the legendary home of the Olympian gods. Mt Olympus still draws worshippers of a sort, as trekkers make the two-day climb to its highest peak, Mytikas (2918m). The most popular trail up the mountain begins at the tiny settlement of Prionia, 18km from Litohoro. From here it's a 2½-hour climb to Refuge A, with the summit of Mytikas about three hours further on.

✪ GUNUNG BROMO, INDONESIA

Emerging from the crater floor of Java's massive Tengger crater are three volcanic peaks. The smoking tip of Gunung Bromo (2392m) is the smallest of these but it's the one all who visit come to climb. The easiest and most popular route is from Cemoro Lawang, on the crater rim, accessed from the city of Probolinggo. The route crosses the crater's Sand Sea, and within an hour you'll be on the summit of Bromo, savouring views into the steaming crater. Like mountains the world over, the favoured time to reach the summit is for the sunrise.

✪ INDONESIA

A country also deserving of two entries on this list. *Buah keluak* translates as 'the fruit that nauseates'. In fact, it is not a fruit at all, nor a nut, as many of its champions think, but is the soft interior of a hard seed case about the size of a small egg. It's found

#21. DINING ON THE
 WILD SIDE

☞ BLUELIST ONLINE

MOST MEMORABLE FOOD EXPERIENCES

✪ DEEP-FRIED ANEMONES IN SEVILLE, SPAIN

You know those globs of jelly that cling to rocks and give you the creeps if you touch them? Well, in Seville they cover them in batter and fry them. They taste of salt water and have the colour and texture of that slimy shave gel in tins. Mmmm, nice.

✪ HIMALAYAN HOME-STYLE, TIBET

Tibetan cuisine at its best, although most surprising. Momos are the zenith of comfort eating. Shaped like fortune cookies and filled with hot, melted yak cheese. Delicious, just watch out for the chillies on the side – they cause blisters!

✪ GOURMET GAME SOUTH PACIFIC-STYLE, VANUATU

Short of the usual winged varieties of highly prized game, Vanuatu has come up with its own use for rich red wine sauce…fruit bat. The furry critters cook up pretty well, although the head can be a little disconcerting for the discerning diner…

✪ BUGGING OUT IN LONDON, ENGLAND

The Birdcage restaurant does a nice line in invertebrates to rival any third-world road stall. Start with a love-bug salad (caterpillars and crickets) and finish with a deep-fried chocolate scorpion. Looks scary, tastes like Kit Kat.

ESTHER GOLDSBY

within the fruit of the great *kepayang* tree. In its uncooked state, it's used in the Indonesian jungles to coat spears, arrows and blowgun darts for hunting, providing a clue to its deadliness. *Buah keluak* contains glucoside, which readily yields prussic acid; fortunately, soaking in water neutralises this.

✪ JAPAN

If you're unfazed by seafood that actively threatens to dispatch you into the next life, then you may be a candidate for a meal that is still kicking in this life. Sushi chefs have been known to slice the leg off an undeserving octopus, pop it on a plate with soy sauce and serve it up, wriggling and writhing. The sensation of suckers on your palate is only slightly more distressing than the knowledge that you are murdering something in your mouth.

✪ NORWAY

In the north, you can sample 'Arctic menus', which undertake to use local ingredients pulled from the icy waters. This includes seal, reindeer; and the ubiquitous cod, from which nothing's wasted. Locals eat cod cheek, roe,

liver and stomach. Cod tongue in particular is a delicacy; children extract the tongues and are paid by the piece. The roe is salted in enormous wine vats. And the livers? Steam-boiled in a cauldron, steamed in a vat, then pressed to provide the tasty oil that combats depression in the Arctic winter.

✪ CHINA

Given the mind-boggling array of regional specialties, it could take years to sample all Chinese cuisine has to offer. See if you can fool yourself with elaborate 'mock meat' dishes, some of which are quite fantastic – and more than a bit creepy – to look at. Typical dishes include fake fish, braised vegetarian 'shrimp' and vegetarian 'ham'. Ingredients (made from tofu, wheat gluten and vegetables) can be sculpted to look like spare ribs or fried chicken. Sometimes chefs even go to great lengths to create 'bones' from carrots and lotus roots.

✪ GREENLAND

In coastal areas of Greenland, dark rich whale meat is popular, though it's quite salty to the unaccustomed palate. The choice cuts are served as steaks and others often end up in a stew. Whale blubber *(mattak or muttak),* which is relatively tasteless and difficult to chew, is rich in vitamins and fats that the body uses to retain heat. Even a thin slice will take several hours of jaw work. It tastes less fishy and salty than seal.

✪ WEST AFRICA

Many people here have strong loyalty to their native *fufu*. It is made from pounded yam, which stiffens as you beat it with a giant wooden mortar and pestle. You'll hear this thumping sound every morning in rural West Africa as the food is prepared for the day. *Fufu* is then eaten in slimy balls without chewing, normally with a spicy peanut sauce. It is a strong identity issue, notably in Ghana.

✪ INDONESIA

A certain Indiana Jones movie has engrained the image of monkeys brains in the minds of many 1980s children. However, there have been protests due to the practice of some eating establishments in Indonesia. A table with a hole in it becomes a space for the top of the monkey's head, which has been removed with a sharp knife. Local rocket fuel, *arrack* (rice wine) is then mixed in. The long-tail macaque is most likely to suffer this fate.

CHOOSE YOUR CUT CAREFULLY – EATING PUFFERFISH CAN BE A LIFE-OR-DEATH EXPERIENCE.

⭐ JAPAN 1

The Japanese are so good they get two entries on this list. The first is the (in)famous *fugu* (pufferfish), so deadly that its ancient nickname translates as 'the pistol', from its potential to knock you off fast. The pufferfish's active ingredient is tetrodoxin, which is 13 times stronger than arsenic. Prepared by chefs who remove the poison, the delicacy makes rather bland eating and numbs your lips...or can be taken in a shot of *hirezake* (toasted *fugu* tail in hot sake), the traditional accompaniment to dinner. Only the wealthy can afford to flirt with death by fine dining: a dish of *fugu* will set you back ¥10,000.

AUSTRALIA – WHERE YOU CAN MEET A NATIONAL SYMBOL ON THE ROAD OR ON A PLATE.

⭐ AUSTRALIA 2

On the remote, striking plains of the southern Flinders Ranges in South Australia, you can eat the Australian emblem. (In case it has escaped your memory, that's a tasty combination of kangaroo and emu.) In the tiny town of Parachilna, a settlement of six people, the superb Prairie Hotel specialises in bush tucker. The menu features scrambled emu eggs for breakfast and tender roo fillets for dinner. An indigenous chef cooks up local ingredients, known to the Kaurna people for many thousands of years, presented with a terrific Mod Oz twist.

PUT YOUR INSECT REPELLENT ASIDE AND TRY A LOCAL SNACK.

⭐ MYANMAR (BURMA) 3

Locals here have been heard to say that 'anything that walks on the ground can be eaten'. Translation: it's a bug's life. At the night markets of Yangon (Rangoon), and all around the country, *thăye-za* (literally meaning mouth-watering snacks) come in the form of fried crickets, beetles and larvae. The crickets are sold threaded onto skewers and can be bought in a 10-pack for about K400, while the bamboo-inhabiting larvae are lightly grilled and served still wriggling. A tip when you're eating the beetles is to suck the stomach out, then chew the head apart.

✪ BALLOONING OVER LUXOR, EGYPT

Top off your explorations of the ancient Theban temple ruins in Luxor with a dawn hot-air balloon ride over the fabulous pharaonic cemetery on the other side of the Nile. These gentle flights waft over the Nile's West Bank, revealing spectacular mortuary temples such as Medinet Habu and Ramesseum, as well as the rocky cliffs and scree that encase dozens of royal tombs in the Valley of the Queens and the nearby Valley of the Kings. The ride also reveals the startling contrast between the greenery of the Nile Valley and the washed-out stoniness of the adjacent desert.

1

✪ FLOATING IN A GONDOLA AROUND VENICE, ITALY

Even though gondolas may be overpriced and disregarded by locals in favour of the *vaporetto* (waterbus), that doesn't change the fact that gliding around the submerged streets of Venice in one of these hand-crafted wooden vessels is still a wonderful journey to make. Let a gondolier punt you along the Grand Canal and through the city's labyrinth of smaller canals, allowing you and your thoughts to drift quietly through Venetian life. You can shatter this reverie by hiring an accordionist and a singer to serenade you from an accompanying gondola, but why on earth would you?

2

GAIN A NEW PERSPECTIVE ON HISTORY, DRIFTING OVER THE RUINS OF ANCIENT EGYPT AT DAWN.

✪ EXPERIENCING THE TRANS-SIBERIAN RAILWAY, RUSSIA

Siberia is not noted as one of the world's great holiday destinations, but its vast steppe does accommodate one of the planet's longest tourist attractions. The Trans-Siberian Railway runs a staggering 9288km from Moscow in Russia's west to Vladivostok on the Sea of Japan. This incredible trip introduces you to the Ural Mountains, the world's deepest lake (Lake Baikal) and the importance of vodka lunches. You could just ride the railway nonstop for seven days, but then you would only experience Siberia through a window; also, your personal hygiene would never recover.

3

MAKE TRACKS FROM MOSCOW TO VLADIVOSTOK ON THE TRANS-SIBERIAN, SEVEN DAYS OF RAILWAY ADVENTURE.

4WD-ING THE CANNING STOCK ROUTE, AUSTRALIA

The only way to truly appreciate the vast, barren beauty of Australia's outback is to drive through it. Hear rocks crunch beneath you, taste red dust as it's blown into your face and feel the heat that bakes this extreme environment into submission. Many tracks crisscross Australia's interior, but none are as challenging or as long as the 1700km Canning Stock Route. This trail (if you can call it that) crosses the Gibson and Great Sandy Deserts, exposing you to enormous sand hills and fences of spinifex. Tradition demands you prepare lunch by frying eggs on your 4WD's bonnet.

SAILING THE GREAT BARRIER REEF, AUSTRALIA

The vivacious coral gardens that make up the biggest reef system on the planet, the Great Barrier Reef, set the scene for the most magical sailing adventure you can imagine. Around 2000km of reef shadows Australia's east coast between the tip of Cape York Peninsula and the Queensland town of Bundaberg, harbouring more than 400 types of coral and 1500 species of fish. Set sail from practically any town along the coast and while away the weeks by cruising spectacular coral cays, snorkelling along technicolour drop-offs and watching dolphins at play.

RIDING ON BULLET TRAINS, JAPAN

a Bluelist suggestion from Leo Maza

Japan's excitable *shinkansen* (bullet trains) sweep passengers at speeds of more than 300km/h between major cities such as Tokyo, Osaka and Kyoto, and are an exhilarating experience

★ JOURNEYS

despite the smoothness of the ride. The Tokyo–Osaka line is a good one for novices to try, as they'll get a good view of Mt Fuji as the train hurtles past. *Shinkansen* are the bane of trainspotters because they're almost too quick to track and are frustratingly punctual. There's worse to come, however, as Japan develops maglev (magnetic levitation) trains that have already been tested at speeds approaching 580km/h.

DRIVING A TRANS AM DOWN ROUTE 66, USA

Tick off two iconic American experiences simultaneously by jumping into a classic Pontiac Trans Am and taking it for a long spin down Route 66. The car should preferably be a black Firebird model, the one driven with a complete disregard for road rules by Burt Reynolds in the 1977 flick *Smokey and the Bandit*. The road speaks for itself: a 4000km trans-American stretch of tarmac between Chicago and Los Angeles that was the mother of all interstate roads until the mid-1980s. Don't forget to install a CB radio in the car and brush up on trucker slang.

ISLAND-HOPPING BY FERRY, GREECE

A seafaring voyage taking in Hydra, Naxos, Skiathos and Rhodes sounds like a trip only Odysseus should attempt. But these are in fact the Aegean, Ionian and Mediterranean treasures discovered by visitors to the soporific Greek islands. Island-hopping

THERE'S NO BETTER WAY TO PICK OUT YOUR NEXT ISLAND PARADISE THAN BY SAILING AROUND IT.

in this region is a classic European adventure, undertaken on vessels ranging from scuffed, sluggish old ferries to newer, faster hydrofoils. Whatever your route, allow plenty of time to visit legendary sites like Knossos on Crete and to be regularly marooned on the nearest beach.

MOTORCYCLING IN THE TRACKS OF CHE GUEVARA, SOUTH AMERICA

You've worn the T-shirt, read the diaries and seen the film; now, take the ride. First, acquire a roadworthy 1939 Norton 500 motorcycle. Next, brush up on some Marxist revolutionary ideas – they'll come in handy later. Now spend a year riding from Buenos Aires in Argentina to Caracas in Venezuela via remote Patagonia, unfriendly Atacama Desert, Peru's Machu Picchu and

Colombia. This 12,000km journey will leave you saddle-sore but profoundly familiar with the diverse landscapes and cultures of South America.

RIDING THE NEW YORK CITY SUBWAY, USA

Every working day, some four million people from all walks of metropolitan life funnel down into New York City's arabesque subway system. This makes a ride on one of the myriad trains that rattle along the tracks between the subway's 400-plus stations as much of a cultural journey as a physical one. As you travel around and between the boroughs of Manhattan, Brooklyn, Queens and the Bronx on battered rolling stock, you'll share your personal space (and often your opinions) with a remarkable assortment of attitudes and ethnicities. You won't want to come up for air.

SERGIO PITAMITZ / APL / CORBIS

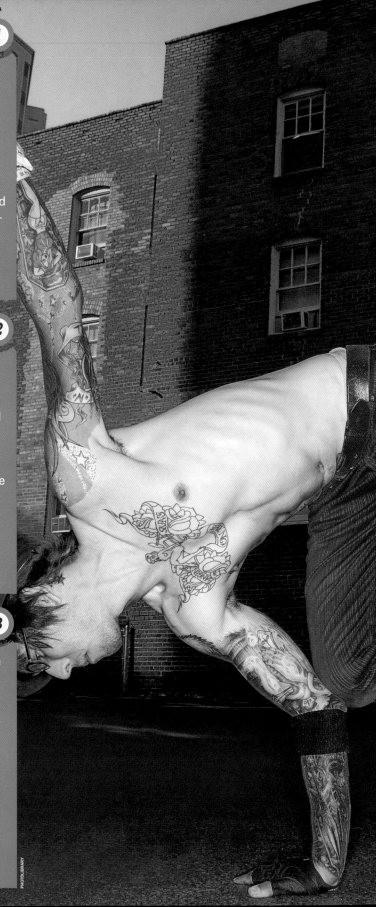

✪ HIP-HOP AND RAP & NEW YORK, USA   ①

Hip-hop and rap erupted in New York in the '70s, and the city still boasts the hottest underground rap scene to be found anywhere in the world. Small-scale venues like Demerara's and Club Pure host weekly 'battles', where rappers lyrically shred each other on stage and the baddest, most fluid rapper wins prizes and prestige in the eyes of his or her peers. The more time you spend in the original concrete jungle, the more hip-hop's raw energy will get under your skin, and you'll appreciate why this genre has become the most commercially successful musical phenomenon ever. Keep it real, yo.

✪ SALSA & HAVANA, CUBA   ②

In Cuba, salsa is a way of life. After the sun sets, the rhythm of the beat seeps through the city's dilapidated walls to get your hips swinging and your shoulders swaying. Most venues don't get started until close to midnight and with no licensing restrictions will stay open until the last customer dances into the night. Each of the city's 10 principal districts has its own unique flavour, but if you're looking for modern salsa in a trendy club check out the venues below Teatro National. For a bit of '50s retro, and dancers replete with extravagant headdresses, check out the legendary open-air Tropicana.

✪ PUNK & TOKYO, JAPAN   ③

The extent to which punk is becoming mainstream here is shown in the production of a set of Sex Pistols 'action figures' by a Japanese toy company to commemorate the 30th anniversary of the Never Mind the Bollocks, Here's the Sex Pistols album release. The punk scene in Tokyo has been around just as long and, as you'd expect, its proponents make up a highly visible minority in the metropolis. As is always the case in Tokyo you can expect the unexpected, with punks rocking out on street corners or outside Shinjuku station, sometimes accompanied by artists creating anarchic visions inspired by the music.

✪ OPERA & FLORENCE, ITALY

Italian intellectuals in the 16th century were well into ancient mythology and thought it would be cool to set the old Greek myths to music. A new art form was born. The world's first opera, Jacopo Peri's *Dafne*, was performed in Florence in 1598. The opulence and power of the music reflected the grandeur of a city at the height of its powers. The ruling Medici family was sufficiently taken with it to allow Peri's next work, *Eurydice*, to be performed as part of Maria di Medici and Henry IV's wedding celebrations in 1600. Relive the effusive wonderment of opera's infant years by attending performances at Florence's grand auditorium, the Teatro Comunale.

✪ COUNTRY & NASHVILLE, USA

It's a curious fact that all visitors to the spiritual and commercial home of country music are compelled to adopt a 'southern drawl' for the duration of their stay. Perhaps this is because your senses are flooded with images of country legends, from Dolly Parton to Garth Brooks, the second you step off the plane. Or maybe it's because you're simply overwhelmed by the rustic love emanating from Saturday night's Grand Ole Opry radio show, where every country singer dreams of cutting loose, and the 3716-sq-metre exhibition at the Country Music Hall of Fame. Ya'll find the place unique, family friendly and in love with country now, y'hear?

✪ JAZZ & NEW ORLEANS, USA

Wander around New Orleans' famous French Quarter, where the spirits of jazz greats such as Freddie Keppard and Louis

#23. BEST MUSIC & PLACE
✪ COMBINATIONS

Armstrong can be found within a myriad of fabulous clubs and bars, and you'll be hard pressed to notice the effects wreaked by Hurricane Katrina. The city's long association with jazz, which dates back to the 18th century, has been a buoy that locals have clung to in their efforts to revive their beloved city. The annual Jazz & Heritage Festival attracts legions of music-lovers who also come to savour the rich architectural heritage, sumptuous cuisine and genuinely warm welcome of this uniquely cosmopolitan place.

✪ BLUES & CHICAGO, USA

Forty years ago you could duck into any downtown Chicago bar or club and expect to hear one or several legendary musicians such as Buddy Guy, BB King or John Lee Hooker singing the blues. Today, little has changed, except some of the old guard have passed on and the baton has been taken up by a new breed, such as Blues in the Schools students Honey Boy Edwards, Henry Townsend and Homesick James. The annual month-long Blues Festival provides for a summer of scintillating sounds, but it's in the darkened clubs where

the tradition, a legacy of southern African Americans, is kept alive.

✪ DRUM AND BASS & LONDON, ENGLAND

If names like Mampi Swift, Andy C, IC3, GQ and Skibadee ('When I say "Skibadee", you say "bo!"') get your pulse racing at 180 beats per minute – the speed at which your average drum and bass or jungle track gets played – then head to the undisputed junglist capital of the universe. In London, you can go mental in your pick of small venues and superclubs serving up the best urban audio assaults nightly. Here, at laser-rich spots such as Fabric and the End, you can see the likes of Roni Size, Goldie and the above mentioned without having to pay through the nose for the privilege. Wicked!

✪ SYMPHONY & PRAGUE, CZECH REPUBLIC

The month of May means music in this pristine medieval citadel. Whether it's the world-renowned Prague Symphony Orchestra kicking off its annual concert season with a performance in the Old Town Square (Starom stské nám stí), or the Prague Academy of Music raising

the roof of the city's biggest concert hall, the Smetana (located inside the fabulous Municipal House), classical music-lovers and romantics will be captivated. If you don't know Brahms from Beethoven, then Prague is the perfect setting to sample a taste of high culture. The key to unlocking the city's great mysteries, concealed in its architecture, is to have an orchestra's strings reverberating within its buildings.

✪ POP & LIVERPOOL, ENGLAND

Since spawning the Fab Four, Liverpool has been at the forefront of global pop-music culture. It's interesting to ponder such metaphysical mind-benders as, 'If it hadn't been for John Lennon, would Justin Timberlake exist?' as you immerse yourself in the European Capital of Culture for 2008. You can still visit many venues associated with Liverpool's prominent bands (The Farm, Frankie Goes to Hollywood, Gerry and the Pacemakers), including the Cavern, where The Beatles got their first break. Ask the famously friendly locals for directions and they might even regale you with a humorous personal recollection about the artists before they became stars.

✪ CONCORDIA, PAKISTAN

To reach Concordia, the junction of the Baltoro, Godwin-Austen and Vigne Glaciers in Baltistan, northern Pakistan, you must walk for about 10 days, eventually arriving at the foot of K2, the world's second-highest mountain. Easy ways in do not exist, and there are few places on earth where you can be buried so deep within a mountainscape. Described by the photographer Galen Rowell as the 'throne room of the mountain gods', Concordia is as starkly beautiful as it is remote. Its name was given by European explorers, who thought it looked like a spot in the European Alps.

1

TO REACH CONCORDIA, YOU'LL TREK BENEATH SEVEN OF THE WORLD'S 25 HIGHEST PEAKS.

✪ EMPTY QUARTER, SAUDI ARABIA

Whether you call it the Empty Quarter (Rub al-Khali) or the Abode of Silence, the largest area of sand on earth is, well, rather empty. Covering an area of the Arabian Peninsula that's larger than France, Belgium and the Netherlands combined, it also has sand dunes as high as the Eiffel Tower, rising to more than 300m in height and stretching for hundreds of kilometres. And while the Eiffel Tower remains firmly rooted in Parisian soil, these dunes can move up to 30m a year, pushed along by strong winds.

2

FOR A DEFINING EXPERIENCE OF ISOLATION, HEAD TO THE EMPTY QUARTER.

✪ CAPE YORK, AUSTRALIA

Australia is renowned as a place of nowheres but even to Aussies, Cape York presents a remote and forbidding frontier. The northernmost tip in the country is reached along corrugated 4WD tracks that will rattle the teeth loose from your jaw. You'll find the cape approximately 1000km from Cairns, which means days and days of driving, including crossing creeks inhabited by estuarine crocodiles. For your reward, you'll find a rocky headland and, well, not much else. Now the only thing left to do is to turn around and clatter your way back.

3

750KM OF PENINSULA MEANS IT'S A LONG WAY TO ANYWHERE FROM CAPE YORK.

#24. BEST MIDDLE OF
⭐ NOWHERE PLACES

⊛ QUITTINIRPAAQ NATIONAL PARK, CANADA

Canada's second-largest national park is probably also its least visited. Straddling the 80th parallel on Ellesmere Island, it reaches to North America's northernmost point (Cape Columbia) and, for visitors, deep into their pockets – a charter flight in from the town of Resolute will set you back an immodest C$32,000. The park has no facilities, roads or even trees. What it does have are bears and bares: polar bears and beautiful, bare mountains. While here you may as well pay a visit to Grise Fiord, Canada's most northerly town, with a population of fewer than 50 people.

⊛ NORTH POLE

The earth's northernmost point is a place so far off the human radar that somebody turned it into the mythical home of Santa Claus – after all, who'd come here to prove the story wrong. Unlike the South Pole, there is no land at the North Pole. The few adventurers who come here do so by literally walking on water across the frozen Arctic Ocean. The ice cover fluctuates between nine million sq km in summer and 16 million sq km in winter, and is rarely more than 5m in depth; a disturbing thought when compared to the 3000m-thick Antarctic ice shield.

⊛ ROBINSON CRUSOE ISLAND, CHILE

Name the loneliest person in literary history and Robinson Crusoe vies only with Yann Martel's Pi (and perhaps the Elephant Man). As lonely as the man is the island that bears his name, 670km off the South American coast. It was here, in 1704, that Alexander Selkirk asked to be put ashore after a dispute with his ship's captain. He lived here alone for four years, inspiring Daniel Defoe to create Robinson Crusoe. Today, around 500 people live on the Pacific island named for its very solitude. Few others come here; visitor numbers rarely top 100 in a year.

⊛ NEVADO MISMI, PERU

The Amazon is the world's most voluminous river but it wasn't until a few years ago that anybody could truly pinpoint its headwaters. In 2001 a GPS-laden *National Geographic* survey team climbed high into the Andes of southern Peru, about 700km from Lima and 3000km from the Amazon's mouth. Here, on a rock wall on the 5597m-high mountain, Nevado Mismi, they identified a dribble of water as the river's origin. If you're intrepid enough to want to visit Nevado Mismi, begin in Arequipa and head for the village of Tuti; the walk in is not difficult.

⊛ OLKHON ISLAND, RUSSIA

Travel on the Trans-Siberian Railway as it skirts Lake Baikal, the world's deepest freshwater lake, and you appreciate the place's remoteness – about 3½ days by train from Moscow, and three days from Beijing. Containing around 20% of the world's fresh water, the lake also contains Olkhon Island near its midpoint. Around 72km long, Olkhon is Baikal's largest island, and by some climatic quirk it's said to get more sunny days than the Black Sea coast, even as the rest of the lake and its surrounds mope beneath heavy cloud.

⊛ KAMCHATKA PENINSULA, RUSSIA

Want a sense of just how big Russia really is? Then picture this: Kamchatka Peninsula, drooping off its east coast, is closer to Los Angeles than Moscow. Among Russia's least visited areas, the 1200km-long peninsula is also perhaps its most spectacular, a hyperactive geothermal land containing more than 200 volcanoes. The surrounding lava fields were used as testing grounds for Russia's lunar vehicles. Once, it was a six-month journey to get here; today you can fly from Moscow, though it's still an 11-hour flight, surely the longest domestic flight on the planet.

⊛ SCOTTY'S CASTLE, USA

In the 1920s Chicago millionaire Albert Johnson was sold the ultimate snake oil – the idea that there was gold in California's Death Valley. In the dry, scorching conditions the ailing Johnson found something more precious: improved health. So, he built a castle in the desert valley with the second-highest temperature on record. Today, the Spanish-style ranch 70km from the nearest Death Valley settlements looks like a folly, although it's rather snug behind its sheepskin curtains and with its 1000-pipe theatre organ.

#25. TINY COUNTRIES PACKING
⭐ A BIG PUNCH

SAN MARINO, 61 SQ KM

Because of San Marino's high altitude, the view when walking around this enclave of central Italy is a bit like looking out of an aeroplane window onto endless clouds and the spectacular snowcapped Apennines. Founded in AD 301 by a stonemason named Marino, the rugged city-state claims to be the world's oldest republic. Steeped in medieval history, a visit here is not complete without trekking up to the three imposing tower-fortresses perched along the cliff tops, the oldest of which, the Rocca Guaita, dates back to the 10th century. Also check out the infamous torture museum, which uses diagrams to explain how the gruesome instruments were used.

LIECHTENSTEIN, 160 SQ KM

Despite being the butt of jokes told across its borders in Switzerland and Austria, Europe's fourth largest principality has much to offer the open-minded traveller. Within its 160 sq km are awesome ski-fields, centred on the enchanting hamlet of Malbun, that have produced 11 Olympic alpine-skiing medals for the tiny country. Cyclists of all levels can burn along more than 90km of trails in the Rhine Valley and around the Eschnerberg mountain. And connoisseurs of urban culture can take the innovative new 'Visiting Vaduz with Goethe' audio trail to discover the capital through art, architecture, culture, history, gastronomy and wine.

MARSHALL ISLANDS, 181 SQ KM

Mums and feminists get an especially warm welcome when they visit this remote chain of around 60 coral atolls and islands in the Pacific. The republican population of just over 52,000 has retained the matrilineal traditions of original Marshallese culture, and at a young age children are taught politeness and respect for women and elders. The region is celebrated for its juicy coconuts, and as a world-class haven for divers, the crystal waters concealing WWII wrecks and endless reefs. Wotje Atoll is generally regarded as the most beautiful atoll in the world, with a lagoon filled with giant clams harvested by the islanders.

SAINT KITTS & NEVIS, 261 SQ KM

Comparisons are often made between the dual Caribbean island nation of St Kitts & Nevis and the lush, tropical paradises of the South Pacific. St Kitts, the larger of the two islands, is dominated by a central mountain range, with a dense covering of rainforest, above which rises the cloud-fringed peak of Mt Liamuiga, a dormant volcano. Natural preservation is a key government aim, with laws forbidding any construction above the height of the tallest palms. The beaches are pristine, as are the surrounding waters savoured by aquanauts from around the world. The country's colonial past has also been preserved and makes for a revelatory visit.

MALDIVES, 298 SQ KM

As with most remote islands, some of the best adventures in the Maldives are to be had in the ocean. Particularly renowned are sunset cruises offered on most of the 200 inhabited islands (out of a total of 2000). Expect to find yourself clicking with joy as scores of dolphins put on an effortless natural display that you won't find at any marine park. Another popular excursion is night fishing, where even the lamest landlubber can expect to reel in a snapper. During the day it's a toss up between sunbathing or donning a snorkel and chasing angelic reef fish through corridors of coral. Marvellous.

TUVALU, 26 SQ KM

The nine low-lying atolls and islands of Tuvalu comprise one of the most isolated independent nations on earth, huddled together in an idyllic and unspoiled corner of the Pacific. Due to the high costs associated with getting there, Tuvalu is still rarely visited. The country's total land area of just 26 sq km is formed by a curving chain stretching 676km in length; it's the gateway to tranquil reef diving, uninhabited beaches and paradisiacal weather (except during hurricane season). In this idyllic setting, dancing and singing is still the number-one entertainment, with lively *fale kaupule* shows put on each night.

NAURU, 21 SQ KM

The main purpose of a trip to the world's smallest republic is education. Named Pleasant Island by its first European visitors in recognition of its lush vegetation and friendly locals, Nauru has since become a striking example of resource mismanagement. In just 50 years, a consortium of British and Australian mining companies has destroyed 80% of the island's 21-sq-km land mass, an area known as 'topside.' Standing in the middle of this wasteland, mined for its valuable phosphates, is a shocking lesson of how greed can decimate ecosystems. It is not something you are likely to forget in a hurry.

OW TRAVEL'S NOT THE ORDER OF THE
Y IN MONACO – PACK YOUR BAGS FOR A
LD RIDE THROUGH THE HIGH-LIFE.

✪ MONACO, 1.95 SQ. KM ①

If you want posh then you've come to the right principality. Monaco was established in 1297 when François Grimaldi seized the fortress that still dominates the area from a rival Italian faction. The 195-hectare independent state, which lies on an exceptionally picturesque, narrow coastal strip, has long been a tax refuge for the spectacularly rich and famous. Actress Grace Kelly, who married Monaco's Prince Rainier, is buried in the cathedral in the heart of the wonderfully preserved Monaco-Ville old town. Exploration on foot is facilitated by public lifts and escalators to help overcome steep hills. Dress smart if you don't want to stand out.

YOU WON'T KNOW WHICH WAY TO LOOK WITH ALL THE COLOUR AND ACTIVITY IN THE STREETS OF GRENADA.

✪ GRENADA, 344 SQ. KM ②

This oval landmass, known as the Spice Isle because it produces vast quantities of mace and nutmeg, contains some of the Caribbean's most spectacular natural vistas. From a narrow coastal plain, volcanic cliffs rise majestically through luscious rainforest to form Grenada's mountainous backbone, now under the protection of the Grand Etang National Park. Grand Etang itself is a water-filled crater that, legend has it, is bottomless; few have the nerve to swim in the eerily tranquil waters. Spectacular interior hiking trails lead to wonders such as Concord Falls, while beachcombers should head for the Levera National Park.

TAKE A TRIP BACK IN TIME TO THE 5000-YEAR-OLD RUINS OF HAGAR QIM TEMPLE.

✪ MALTA, 316 SQ. KM ③

You'll never say there's nothing to do in Malta. For its size, the tiny rock and limestone island puts on an inordinate number of festivals throughout the year, but particularly in summer. There's the Mediterranean Food Festival, the Malta Fireworks Festival, as well as a Jazz Festival and, most fabulous of all, a two-day event put on especially so that attendees can help select the country's entry into the Eurovision Song Contest. When you've had enough human interaction, head to a nearby uninhabited island to unwind, or wander into the interior to check out the megalithic ruins of the island's conquered indigenous inhabitants.

⭐ PRINCIPALITY OF SEALAND

A crumbling anti-aircraft tower in the North Sea, Sealand has become the world's most intriguing, secretive and disaster-prone micronation, 10km off the coast of Britain near Felixstowe. Paddy Roy Bates and Ronan O'Rahilly, both pirate radio-station operators, landed here in 1966. Bates seized the tower and settled there with his family. Ordered to surrender by the Royal Marines, Bates later won a court ruling that Sealand was beyond British territorial control. He went on to develop Sealand's own stamps, currency and national anthem. The micronation suffered UK£500,000 of fire damage in mid-2006; the Bates family has vowed to rebuild.

1

ATTEMPTS AT ECONOMIC STABILITY IN SEALAND HAVE INCLUDED HOSTING A CONTROVERSIAL WEBSITE, AND ESTABLISHING THE 'ROYAL BANK OF SEALAND' IN GENEVA.

⭐ COPEMAN EMPIRE

King Nicholas rules. His empire is a caravan in Sheringham, England; as one of the rare examples of a mobile micronation, it can be distinguished by the 'Monarch on Board' sticker in the rear window. King Nicholas recently published a book regaling the world with his royal adventures. Is it a joke? A fantasy? An exercise in ego massage? An especial example of whimsical British humour? A particularly clever way for a young jobless guy to make a name for himself? The king has initiated a number of ventures including the sale of peerages on the Internet. Stay tuned for the range of sweet-potato crisps.

2

HE'S GOT THE WHOLE WORLD IN HIS CARAVAN. KING NICHOLAS, RULER OF THE COPEMAN EMPIRE AND 'ENGLAND'S OTHER MONARCH', FOUNDED HIS MICRONATION AS A BET IN 2004.

⭐ KINGDOM OF ELLEORE

The Kingdom of Elleore, the oldest modern-day micronation, was founded in 1944 by Danish schoolteachers (the 'Immortals') on an uninhabited island. On delving into the island's history, the founders discovered an ancient lineage dating back to 944 and the settlement of a depleted band of Irish monks. In 1963 Elleore purchased the ship *Løvejagten* and inaugurated Elleorian Week. In 1975 the government purchased a 45-sq-metre tent and anointed it the City Hall of Maglelille. Ways to become a citizen include recommendation by two Elleorians; or being 12 years old and a pupil at Kildegaard School.

3

★MICRONATIONS
EXPERIENCE A SELF-PROCLAIMED, UNRECOGNISED COUNTRY

★ HUTT RIVER PROVINCE PRINCIPALITY

Regarded by some as the world's most established (and lucrative) micronation, the Hutt River Province Principality is something of a template for modern micronationalism. The Principality is in Yallabathara, Western Australia, 595km north of Perth. It all started in 1969 with a shift in Australia's agriculture policy. Feeling restricted, farmer Leonard Casley believed there was only one option open to him: secession. The following five years saw the emergence of the Hutt River Province's national structures and symbols, including the issuing of coins, banknotes and stamps. Tourism is important to the Hutt River economy: you can stay overnight in camping and caravan facilities.

★ REPUBLIC OF MOLOSSIA

This is surely the most delightful micronation on earth. While it describes itself as a 'developing country', this republic, surrounded on all sides by Nevada, USA, has a beautiful insight into the ridiculousness of the modern world. Founded in 1977 by one James Spielman (King James I), it was formed under the auspices of Article 1 of the UN's International Covenant on Civil and Political Rights, which recognises that all people have the right to self-determination. In 2000 (the year XXIII in Molossia)

the government inaugurated the first Intermicronational Olympic Games. His Excellency won a gold medal in the discus (with a Frisbee).

★ WHANGAMOMONA

This sleepy little New Zealand town is well on the way to being a country, as it has two rugby teams and the all-important beer. Set in the North Island's hilly interior, on the Forgotten World Hwy, it's the kind of spot where you could film a Kiwi version of *Northern Exposure*. The biggest day of the year is Republic Day when the townsfolk set up stalls along the main street aimed at fleecing city folk. The main event is the election of the president, where citizens cast their votes into a toilet.

★ CHRISTIANIA

Every country has its limits; in Christiania it's 'no hard drugs'. As recently as 2004, you could buy hash on the aptly named Pusher St in this bohemian enclave that broke off from Denmark to name itself a 'free town' in 1971. A group of squatters founded the micronation by breaking into the disused army barracks in Copenhagen. Christianites sought to make their town

car-free by barricading streets using rocks. These days, the fenced-in compound occupies prime riverside real estate in the merchant district. A backpacker haunt and magnet for young Danes, it's under increasing pressure from the government to pay taxes: an idea booed by its 1000 freethinkers.

★ LADONIA

Located on the southern tip of the Scandinavian peninsula at Kullaberg, this micronation is not a haven for lads but an artspace. Founded by a sculptor and constantly at war with neighbouring Sweden for its installations, Ladonia is the micronation for the rebellious artist in everyone. It was created in 1996 in order to protect Lars Vilks' works. Much like its two founding sculptures, *Arx* and *Nimis*, Ladonia has stood the test of local councils and bad weather. It has taken its love of aesthetics to the Swedish government and beyond. Cyber citizens outweigh residents.

★ AKHZIVLAND

When it came to the historical village of Akhziv, President Eli Avivi proved the micronational adage that if you look hard enough, you're bound to find a piece of 'turf' nobody wants. Surrounded by the state of Israel, the peaceful anomaly of Akhzivland became a beacon of hope for disaffected Israelis, and in the 1970s it embraced the

peace-and-love movement and hosted communal festivities and happenings. Today it's beloved of counterculture freaks and footloose backpackers. But it's also attracting a very different demographic: newly married couples. For Akhzivland has perhaps the most romantic setting of all micronations, surrounded by mountains, overlooking a beautiful beach.

★ REPUBLIC OF KUGELMUGEL

Kugelmugel is more than a micronation: it's simultaneously a house and a work of art. It's also a classic illustration of that age-old struggle, One Man against the System. Despite all attempts to squash it, exiled President Edwin Lipburger stands tall as Kugelmugel's founder, its head of state, its defence force and its sole citizen. Now 77, President Lipburger lives in Austrian exile, watching as his radical experiment in spherical housing is reappraised and hailed as a masterpiece of micronationalism (and postmodern architecture). Best of all, Kugelmugel is round, and as President Lipburger has said all along, 'round is free'.

For more on home-made nations see Lonely Planet's Micronations.

✪ MOTORHOME ①

If your main concern when you're on the road is having the freedom to go wherever, whenever, whatever the weather, then consider hiring a motorhome for your next adventure. You can rent these fully self-contained bad boys from many capital cities worldwide. Choose your level of opulence by selecting from an astonishing array of extras such as satellite navigation systems, central heating, air con, bathrooms with showers and toilets, fridges and freezers, microwave, TV, video, DVD, stereo, radio, generators, awnings, automatic transmission and power steering. If a truck can get there, so can you in a motorhome.

✪ DIGITAL CAMERA ②

Digital cameras are gold. You can review your snaps instantly and delete the ones where you look ugly. Extra memory cards mean you can keep virtually limitless numbers of images in which you look good. With digital you don't have to wait to get your snaps developed, but you have the option of getting them printed should you so choose. Most digital cameras also have a recording facility so you can literally capture poetry, or your friends, in motion. But perhaps the best thing is that you can send images via email to instantly share your experiences with friends and family wherever they may be.

✪ MP3 PLAYER/IPOD ③

Life is a journey but every now and then it can get a little tedious, like when your plane gets delayed or you're stuck on a never-ending bus ride. MP3 players are perfect for whiling away otherwise dull hours by listening to your fave tunes or random podcasts, flicking through photos, or even watching a movie on the miniscreen. The first workable MP3 player was created in 1997 by Tomislav Uzelac when he was still a student at Croatia's University of Zagreb. In recent years it has been estimated that MP3 sales have rocketed with well over a hundred million sold each year.

★ SWISS MEMORY USB

Geeks and tech-savvy citizens everywhere have been getting very excited about this one. Described as 'the perfect marriage of technology, practicality, materials and quality design', this exceptional unit has everything you need to survive in both rural and urban settings. In addition to the standard Swiss Army Knife features (knife, scissors, screwdriver, key ring) that have made the brand famous, this postmodern must-have also has its own USB flash drive, LED light and ballpoint pen. You can choose how much memory you want (from 256MB up to 1GB), and the deluxe version comes with built-in FM radio and voice recorder.

★ LEATHERMAN CORE MULTITOOL

Hard-core travellers demand hard-core accessories to ensure their adventurous lifestyle is hassle free, leaving them more time for more hard-core adventures. So for anyone planning a trek into the backcountry, this multitasking wonder is just the ticket. Featuring locking knife blades, three wire cutters, pliers and hollow-ground screwdrivers in standard sizes, with rounded handles to help every Action Man or Wonder Woman get a firm grip when putting it to use, the stainless steel Core will fix, open, mend and repair just about anything. If the A-Team had used one of these, they'd have been able to build a tank out of sand.

★ EMERGENCY MOBILE-PHONE CHARGER

You've been stranded out in the middle of nowhere with your erstwhile travelling buddy for weeks, stumbling around looking for signs of civilisation. At last your mobile has coverage and, believing salvation is at hand, you call for assistance. Then the battery goes flat. It's at times like these you'll be feeling ever so smug and superior for remembering to pack an emergency charger. Some chargers are model-specific, while others suit a range of phones. They use standard AAA batteries and typically give you around 40 to 60 minutes of talk time and four to six hours of standby time. Sorted.

★ UNIVERSAL PLUG ADAPTOR

Plugs and sockets are the bane of international travellers' lives. There are at least nine different types of plugs in use around the world. Europe uses two prongs, the USA has three, the UK also has three but they're different to the US ones, and so on. The International Electrotechnical Commission actually wrote a world standard back in the 1980s but governments are reluctant to give up their own standards. Luckily, universal plug adaptors can save the day. Ingenious as a Rubik's Cube, in one tiny box they fit all the prongs needed to produce a plug you can use wherever you wake up.

★ HEADLAMP

When you're travelling around with your world in your backpack you're always on the lookout for good things that come in tiny packages. That's why we really love the ultralight travel headlamp designed by the caving gurus over at Petzl Zipka. Weighing only 57g with batteries included, this mini-illuminato fits into the smallest of pockets ensuring it's always close at hand during a blackout or on those long, dark nights when you're stuck by yourself at the back of a plane, train or automobile. Anyone wishing to see the light should invest in one of these, a genuine travel essential.

★ QUICK-DRY TOWEL

Sometimes the best ideas are also the most simple. Anyone who's had to drag around a wet heavy towel in their backpack, unable to prevent it festering in its own dampness, or worse still, spreading mildew onto your spare set of clothes as you travel between places, will understand the straightforward brilliance of a lightweight towel that can dry super-fast – up to eight times quicker than a beach towel. Made from a combination of synthetic microfibres, the best brands also come with their own carry bag and are treated to prevent the build-up of bacteria, fungi and stench.

★ GPS WATCH

For those who like exploring well off the beaten track, and others who just want to be James Bond, the Suunto X9 Global Positioning System (GPS) watch uses 27 satellites to calculate its wearer's exact location, give or take a few metres, almost anywhere on the planet. Very handy if you get lost looking for the South Pole or charging through an Ecuadorian rainforest. What's more, it features a barometer, altimeter and compass, and will measure your travelling speed, guide you to your destination and store coordinates so you can retrace your steps. Amazingly, it also tells the time.

#27. BEST TRAVEL ★ GADGETS

⊗ MUSEO GUGGENHEIM, SPAIN

Some critics might argue that Frank Gehry's Museo Guggenheim in the northern Spanish city of Bilbao, opened in 1997, looks as though it's been taken to by a can-opener, but this is one of the most influential and striking buildings in modern architecture. With its ribbonlike sheets of titanium and its collection of interconnecting blocks, the museum gives a nod to Bilbao's industrialism but also to the saucerlike curves of Frank Lloyd Wright's Solomon R Guggenheim Museum in New York. Oh yeah...nearly forgot. There's art inside, too.

1

⊗ POTALA PALACE, TIBET

Perched high above the holy city of Lhasa is the former seat of the Tibetan government and the winter residence of the Dalai Lama. More notable now for its imposing presence than its residents, this huge construction is 13 storeys high, contains thousands of rooms, and is styled like a traditional Buddhist *gompa* (temple), if significantly more elaborate. More than 7000 workers were said to have been involved in its construction during the 7th century AD. The palace is now a state museum of China, and has been given a place on the Unesco World Heritage list.

2

LOSE YOUR WAY IN THE LABYRINTH OF BUILDINGS AT THE KING-SIZED POTALA PALACE.

⊗ BIBLIOTHECA ALEXANDRINA, EGYPT

Between the ancient pyramids and the Bibliotheca Alexandrina, Egypt now has the best of old and new. Like a giant discus landed at an angle or an enormous light switch, Alexandria's oceanfront library is arguably the first great design of the new millennium. Completed in 2002, it's inspired by the original Alexandrina library, founded in the 3rd century BC and acclaimed as the greatest of all classical institutions. The building's sloped design represents a second sun rising beside the Mediterranean. The vast rotunda space can hold eight million books.

3

WHAT GOES AROUND, COMES AROUND – THE BIBLIOTHECA ALEXANDRINA TAKES AFTER ITS 2300-YEAR-OLD PREDECESSOR.

★ BUILDINGS

★ SAGRADA FAMÍLIA, SPAIN

Surely the most extraordinary church on the planet, from the mind of one of history's most eccentric designers: Antoni Gaudí. With its tapering towers like the straightened arms of an octopus, construction of Sagrada Família began in 1882, though Gaudí's vision was so complex that the church is still unfinished. It will ultimately feature three façades and 18 towers, the tallest of them (170m) representing Jesus Christ. Plans are to have the Barcelona icon completed in 2026, the 100th anniversary of Gaudí's death, although it will almost be a shame now to see it finished.

★ TAJ MAHAL, INDIA

Is this the world's most famous building? And its most romantic (ignoring the sprawling, industrial city around it, and the hordes of rickshaw-wallahs and touts)? Described by Indian poet Rabindranath Tagore as 'a teardrop on the face of eternity', the Taj Mahal in Agra was built by Emperor Shah Jahan as a memorial for his second wife, Mumtaz Mahal, who died giving birth to their 14th child in 1631. It's an extravagant, white-marble monument to love, which may explain all the young, starry-eyed couples wandering around it.

★ EMAM MOSQUE, IRAN

Headlining beside one of the world's largest squares, Esfahan's Emam Mosque is a tiled wonder. Completely covered, inside and out, with pale blue and yellow ceramic tiles (which are an Esfahan trademark), it's a stunning 17th-century mosque, with its tiles seeming to change colour depending on the light conditions. The main dome is 54m high and intricately patterned in a stylised floral mosaic, while the magnificent 30m-high portal is a supreme example of architectural styles from the Safavid period (1502–1772). The mosque sits askew to the square, at about 45 degrees, so that it faces Mecca.

★ WINTER PALACE, RUSSIA

Best known as the outer casing for the remarkable State Hermitage Museum, this pistachio-coloured gem on the banks of the Neva River in St Petersburg was designed by Francesco Bartolomeo Rastrelli as the winter residence of the Russian tsars. Filling an entire block, it bears all the whimsy and ornamentation of the baroque period, and statues line its roof edges like divers about to plunge into the Neva. Little wonder it should be the showpiece of a city built specifically to highlight that Russia could match the architectural beauty of Europe.

★ CRAC DES CHEVALIERS, SYRIA

Described by TE Lawrence as the 'finest castle in the world', this hilltop Crusader fortress might be 800 years old but, like a good botox treatment, stands tight and taut against the ravages of time. It's the classic blueprint of a medieval castle, its thick outer walls separated from the inner structure by a moat dug out of the rock. Inside, it's a minitown, complete with a chapel, baths, a great hall and a Gothic loggia. The most visible sign of ageing is the vegetation that grows from its walls; nothing a good shave wouldn't fix.

★ MUSEU OSCAR NIEMEYER, BRAZIL

Designed by Oscar Niemeyer, the celebrated architect behind the creation of the Brazilian capital, Brasília, the Museu Oscar Niemeyer in Curitiba will test your view of aesthetics. Like all great buildings – and probably more so – the art museum's appearance has an element of love-it-or-hate-it, with its main gallery shaped like a reflective glass eye, balancing atop a yellow support, and approached on curving ramps above a pool of water. Once inside the building commonly called the 'Eye Museum', you'll see that every aspect of the museum's design seems to marry beauty with whimsy.

★ HAGIA SOPHIA, TURKEY

Hagia Sophia is the great architectural landmark at the heart of Istanbul, with its four minarets poised like moon-bound rockets. Constructed in the 6th century AD as an Orthodox church, it later became a mosque and, since 1935, a museum. The enormous structure was built in just five years, and its musk walls are topped by an imposing dome, 31m wide and 56m high. The dome's base is ringed by windows, so that from within the structure, the dome seems almost to hover ethereally above the building.

#29. BEST VALUE
⭐ DESTINATIONS

⚙ LITHUANIA
Rebellious and quirky, Lithuania is Europe's best-kept secret, an all-rounder when it comes to value. Shoved successively between Russian pillar and Nazi post, this tenacious little country stunned the world when it played David and Goliath with the might of the Soviet Union – and won its independence just over a decade ago. There's been plenty to enjoy since. The nation that vanished from the maps of Europe is back with a vengeance: it's part of the EU and is a fully fledged partner of NATO. It is *the* place to buy 'Baltic gold' (amber) or to explore 15th-century castles.

⚙ HUNGARY
In a world ever more obsessed with the drops squeezed from a grape, Budapest represents value when it comes to history and the knowledge that goes with it. Wine has been produced in Hungary for thousands of years, and it remains very important both economically and socially. You'll find it available by the glass or bottle everywhere in the capital – at very basic wine bars, food stalls, restaurants, supermarkets and 24-hour grocery stores – usually at good prices. If you're seriously into wine, visit the speciality wine shops on both sides of the Danube.

⚙ THAILAND
The land of smiles is still a generous destination. Value is most famously demonstrated in the nation's cuisine, which stands at the crossroads of numerous ancient culinary traditions (those of India, China and Asian Oceania). You'll quickly discover that eating is one of life's great pleasures here. The average Thai takes time out to eat, not three times per day, but four or five. Fortunately, most travellers are also lucky enough to be able to afford to do the same, whatever their budget.

⚙ LATVIA
A country in transition, hellbent on shedding its stalwart old-Soviet image, the Latvia of today is vibrant. Still relatively undiscovered by Europe's tourism masses, this Baltic star is poised to arrive on the continent's A-list. Many arrive expecting little and leave overwhelmed, certain they've uncovered long-buried treasure. Its capital Rīga has come an awfully long way in 10 years. Instead of making do with the best of a dodgy lot, for visitors these days there's a genuine choice of restaurants and places to stay, representing value, attention to detail and finesse.

⚙ LAOS
Opening its doors to tourism in the early 1990s, Laos has since changed rapidly, but not so fast that you've missed out. It retains its laid-back pace, and you're forced to relax because travel…is…slow. As with neighbouring Cambodia, the infrastructure is not yet there in the northern provinces; you'll be catching a boat, or winding over crazily rough roads on buses. In the towns and cities you can hire a scooter for less than US$8 a day. Ironically, most travellers here stick to a very well-trodden path, but if you can do without the niceties, you'll discover the potential of less-travelled terrain.

⚙ MALAYSIA
Want a five-star experience without the hip-pocket haemorrhaging? Then hit the hotel scene in Malaysia. The fast-paced, cosmopolitan capital city of Kuala Lumpur supports a fiercely competitive accommodation scene, where rack rates at luxury stalwarts are regularly slashed by more than 50%. If you get bored of living large in the big city, try breaking the bank in a laid-back beach chalet on Kecil, the bargain-friendly Perhentian Island. We tip that you'll struggle to spend more than US$20 a day lazing on white sands or snorkelling through crystal-clear waters. With your leftover cash, hop on a bus and make your way south to historic Melaka, to sample cheap and cheerful Nonya cuisine while soaking up the port city's multicultural heritage.

⚙ CZECH REPUBLIC
The focus has shifted from Prague, gaspingly overrun, to other towns in the republic. Travellers increasingly head straight for Kutná Hora and pretty medieval Český Krumlov, just an hour away. Křivoklát, which can be reached via train through the Berounka valley, has the same charms on offer as the capital – cheap beer, hearty food, red roofs – but fewer football teams running around with their postgame paunches on show. The region around the town is a Unesco 'biosphere preservation' area flanked by Bohemian forests.

⊛ INDONESIA

Despite its struggles with natural disasters and poverty, the Indonesian archipelago is as rich in natural beauty and culture as ever. Rippling across the equator for nearly 5000km, it embraces more than 18,000 islands, each with its own character. If you value variety, you can't go wrong. Bali's resorts and restaurants pamper, while threadbare backpackers are welcomed in Kalimantan. Yet the natural world remains its real treasure. The jungles of Sumatra and Papua are zoological wonders. For an experience to make you value your life, visit the last dinosaurs, the dragons of Komodo Island in Nusa Tenggara.

A TRIP TO INDONESIA EFFORTLESSLY MIXES THE SACRED WITH THE NATURAL.

⊛ CROATIA

2

When people think of Croatia, it's most often the old towns that they picture. The sober stone buildings lined up, the floridly sculpted public buildings and, above all, the magnificent walls circling the cities are point-and-shoot perfect. But even though it's full of architectural gems and drenched in history, Croatia is far from being a museum. People live here, raising their kids and growing old in the baroque houses. They shop in local grocery stores and chat with their neighbours in the local café. This is the real Croatia and this is its real value.

TURN OFF THE TOURIST TRAIL AND EXPERIENCE DAILY LIFE IN CROATIA.

⊛ UNITED ARAB EMIRATES

While modernisation speeds forward, Emiratis have something of value to show the world: they are proudly clinging to their traditions. The Emirates' history is in its songs and dance (there's nothing like coming across a traditional performance of the popular *liwa* dance), and its culture can be found in its Bedouin heritage and Islamic religion. Instead of discarding their national dress (like the Egyptians or Persians did when they swapped their *hijab* headwear for miniskirts and knee-high boots), Emirati women are calling attention to it by embellishing their *abayas* (overgarments) with gems and sequins. You gotta value a culture that values its own.

PITCH YOUR TENT BY THE HAJIR MOUNTAINS, FAR FROM THE BRIGHT LIGHTS AND BIG HOTELS OF DUBAI.

✪ BIRQASH CAMEL MARKET, EGYPT

PURCHASE YOUR VERY OWN SHIP OF THE DESERT AT THE BIRQASH CAMEL MARKET.

Friday is the day that traders get down to business at Birqash camel market, Egypt's biggest retail outlet for ships of the desert. Hundreds of camels that have been brought in from Sudan are paraded in front of prospective buyers and the frenzy that surrounds the buying and selling of these beasts makes for a fascinating spectacle. However, animal-lovers may want to think twice before coming out here from nearby Cairo, as the animals are often subjected to treatment and conditions that will not make you proud to be a member of the human race.

1

✪ CHICHICASTENANGO, GUATEMALA

GUATEMALA'S MARKETS OFFER A WHOLE LOT MORE THAN YOUR LOCAL SUPERMARKET.

a Bluelist suggestion from alaskanjade

The market beside the church of Santo Tomás in the Guatemalan town of Chichicastenango is one of the most colourful on the planet. Mayan people set up their stalls here every Thursday and Sunday, and go about selling craftwork, medicinal plants, incense and snacks in an atmosphere of good-natured chaos. The highlight of the market, however, is the vibrant presence of the woven traditional Mayan costumes known as *traje indígena*. The streets are filled with these indigenous works of art, collages of brilliantly coloured textiles that light up their wearers.

2

✪ ALEPPO'S SOUK, SYRIA

The labyrinthine souk in Aleppo is supposedly the longest in the Middle East, with an estimated 10km of covered passageways. Browse the souk's containers of meat and vegetables, mounds of spices and nuts, racks of clothing such as embroidered *jalabiyya* (caftans), handworked gold and silver, and piles of carpets and kilims, all while dodging shoppers, donkeys and small vans weighed down with goods. Every once in a while, you might find yourself suddenly sharing tea with a loquacious, convivial stall owner, with no memory of having agreed to do this.

3

HOURS OR EVEN DAYS BE SWALLOWED UP YOU STROLL UNDER VAULTED STONE CEILING ALEPPO'S MAIN SO

BIRMINGHAM BIZARRE BAZAAR, ENGLAND

On the third Sunday of every month, fetish suppliers gather over two floors of Birmingham's Nightingale Club to help make adult fantasies come true. Also known as BBB, this friendly, open-minded event attracts men and women, gays and straights, the experienced and first-timers. There are stalls dedicated to adult baby clothes, steel bondage gear, dungeon furniture, all manner of leather and rubber garments, erotic art and photography, electrical toys and pretty much anything else your body may desire. There are also useful demos of bondage and discipline, domination and submission, and sadism and masochism rituals.

MARCHÉ DE FER, HAITI

Some of the cramped walkways of the lively, sweaty Marché de Fer (Iron Market) located in the rundown downtown of Port-au-Prince overflow with scrap metal such as disassembled automobile parts. But iron is only one of the commodities that adventurous market-lovers will find in the maze of stalls here. After some of the fierce haggling that is traditional in Haitian marketplaces, money is also exchanged here for paintings, tinned food, voodoo fetishes and much more. The market is confined by an elaborate and colourful 19th-century metal structure that rates as an attraction in itself.

MARCHÉ DES FÉTICHEURS, TOGO

a Bluelist suggestion from GungaJim

Hoping to convince the man/woman/other of your dreams to feel the same way about you? Looking for a way to protect yourself against bad luck? Want to cure impotence? Then come on down to Lome's Marché des Féticheurs (Fetish Market), where the bewitched skulls, skin and teeth of various unfortunate animals are on offer to improve your lot in life. You can also purchase lucky charm stones, talismanic dolls and blessed medicines, or organise a consultation with a spiritually qualified fetish doctor or priest. This is one place where you definitely don't want to get on the locals' bad side.

MERCADO DE BRUJAS, BOLIVIA

The Mercado de Hechicería (aka Mercado de Brujas, the Witches' Market) in the cobbled centre of La Paz is famous for its range of potions and charms, guaranteed to improve things such as your sex life or your financial situation. The 'witches' who conduct business within this outdoor market's crowded aisles are almost exclusively Aymará, an ethnic group hailing from the Andes who still practise their indigenous religion under a thin veneer of Catholicism. The item most visitors find hardest to forget is llama foetus, which is meant to bring you domestic bliss if you inter it under your house.

#30. EXTRAORDINARY
★ MARKETS

PERFUME MARKETS, OMAN

a Bluelist suggestion from Izzi Robinson

Oman is recognised as a world leader when it comes to producing frankincense, the aromatic resin that is a key ingredient in fine perfumes. It's also where one of the world's most expensive smells, Amouage, is cobbled together. So it should come as no surprise to learn that the country's souks are a haven for stunning scents. The best places in Oman to go shopping for head-spinning *bokhur* (incense) and fragrant oils include the fabled Muttrah Souk in the capital Muscat, and the Al Haffa Souk in the southern Omani town of Salalah.

MINERS' MARKET, BOLIVIA

a Bluelist suggestion from alaskanjade

The Bolivian settlement of Potosí is famous for being the world's highest city, at an altitude of 3970m. It was once also famous for the wealth generated by its rich silver mines, but the deposits thinned out long ago. Despite this, local miners still risk their health by digging deep for new veins of ore, and it's this that makes a visit to Potosí's miners' market so poignant. The market seems to exist almost solely so tourists can buy dynamite, water, alcohol and chewable coca leaves to gift to the struggling miners during tours.

NILKHET BOOK MARKET, BANGLADESH

The Nilkhet district in Bangladesh's sprawling capital city of Dhaka is where hundreds of word-lovers congregate daily to browse preloved books and magazines stacked in tin-shed stalls. Many of the books here are in Bengali but English-language tomes are also prominent; you can find almost anything from Mills & Boon to Martin Amis. Bordered on one side by Dhaka University, the market does a roaring trade in academic texts, many of them illegally copied. This doesn't seem to bother the droves of wall-eyed students ticking off their reading lists amid the chugging of ancient photocopiers.

✍ BLUELIST // ONLINE

BEST BAZAARS

MOSTAR'S MARKETS, BOSNIA & HERCEGOVINA
Mostar has cobblestone alleyways with vendors selling old Yugoslavian one-million dinar banknotes, intricately decorated tea sets, and engraved bullet cartridges supposedly used in the 1992–1995 conflict between the Croats and the Muslims.

CREEKSIDE SOUKS, UNITED ARAB EMIRATES
Dubai's creekside souks offer aromatic spices and herbs, a plethora of gold jewellery glittering from afar, silks, electronics, and 'designer' hand bags, wallets and watches, located in tiny windowless rooms in back-street apartments.

PHNOM PENH'S RUSSIAN MARKET, CAMBODIA
Phnom Penh's Russian Market could engross you for days with its hidden treasures. Everything from DVDs, software and music, to replica temple statues to jewellery and silks will assure no-one will ever leave it empty-handed.

#31. THE BEST IN
⭐ SLOW TRAVEL

✪ CAMPERVAN AROUND AUSTRALIA

One of the most leisurely yet fulfilling adventures you can have is to climb aboard a fully equipped campervan and tootle around the enormous girth of the Australian continent. If you were to hug the coastline as much as possible on your circumnavigation, you would end up tallying more than 14,000km driving beside fantastic beaches, into remote rainforests and through almost all the major cities, setting up your bed and cooking your meals wherever you park. However, the trip simply wouldn't be complete without also taking a few detours into Australia's intimidating outback.

✪ CRUISE THE FJORDS, CHILE

The southern coastline of Chile is embellished with a plethora of grand fjords that swallow up travellers and time alike. These glacially eroded inlets provide a deep passage for cruise vessels skirting Patagonia and Tierra del Fuego, granting the curious sightseers on board some memorable close-ups of steep-sided cliffs, encroaching glaciers and pristine channels. Popular cruise departure points in southern Chile include Puerto Montt and Punta Arenas, while highlights include the huge fjord in Parque Nacional Laguna San Rafael and the magnificent Unesco Biosphere Reserve of Parque Nacional Torres del Paine.

✪ CYCLE AROUND AMSTERDAM, NETHERLANDS

The narrow, canal-threaded and, in some cases, vehicle-free streets of central Amsterdam are ideal for bicycles, a fact that locals cottoned on to long ago. Bike lanes shadow all the main streets and are usually brimming with Amsterdammers pedalling aimlessly around in the fresh air. So don't hesitate to join them by taking a relaxed cycle from Vondelpark past all of your favourite museums to your favourite brown café. Unfortunately, the immense popularity of this two-wheeled contraption in the Dutch capital also makes it an ideal place for thieves, who make off with tens of thousands of bikes each year.

✪ BUS ALONG THE KARAKORAM HIGHWAY, CHINA TO PAKISTAN

The fabulous slow road from Kashgar in China to Rawalpindi in Pakistan is known as the Karakoram Highway, or KKH. One reason this 1300km route is slow is because it traverses some colossal mountain ranges, making it the highest sealed road in the world – local buses are often reduced to crawling up steep inclines. Another reason is that the vehicles travelling this route are often hampered by rockslides and mechanical breakdowns. Tackling this branch of the legendary Silk Road means exposure to some incredible high-altitude scenery and a beguiling diversity of cultures.

✪ MOPED ALONG THE RIVIERA, FRANCE

The Riviera is a gorgeous section of the Côte d'Azur coastline stretching from the town of Toulon in the southwest of France almost all the way to the Italian border. For a luxurious taste of slow travel, jet into the principality of Monaco, hire yourself a top-of-the-line moped (think scooter), rev up that powerful 50cc engine, and then meander your way along the coast through glamour-conscious places such as Cannes and Nice, noting how many beautiful people you pass along the way. After you've had enough of bodies beautiful, motor west away from the Riviera towards Marseilles' rough charm and Nîmes' Roman amphitheatre.

✪ TRAMP THE MILFORD TRACK, NEW ZEALAND

The 53.5km Milford Track on New Zealand's mountainous South Island is regarded as one of the finest walking trails in the world. It's a four-day adventure that leads from Lake Te Anau up through rainforest to Mackinnon Pass, where you can make a side-trip to the country's highest waterfall (Sutherland Falls), and then follows a wilderness river north to the edge of the spectacular fjord called Milford Sound. The number of daily walkers allowed on this magnificent trail is limited from November to April, so book well ahead if you're visiting the Land of the Rings at this time.

✪ WINE CRUISE DOWN THE CANAL DE BOURGOGNE, FRANCE

a Bluelist suggestion from Marlon Kobacker

The premier French wine-making region of Burgundy is bisected by the 242km Canal de Bourgogne, along with a large number of locks that raise or lower vessels as required. This attractive, slow-flowing watercourse is trafficked by numerous well-stocked barges that will let you stow away on board and indulge in the best wines and produce the region has to offer. Cruise options range from relatively short wine-and-cheese tastings to seven-day crewed and fully catered excursions where you get to make strategic side-trips to some of the region's fabled wineries.

★ DOG SLED IN BRITISH COLUMBIA, CANADA

1

What could be more relaxing than having a half-dozen Siberian huskies pull you on a sled along back-country trails through a soft blanket of snow? Nothing, according to the numerous outfits that organise dog sledding excursions in the wilds of British Columbia, although the huskies in question may disagree. Not only do you avoid the whine of a snowmobile or the effort required to point those pesky skis in the right direction, but you also get to learn interesting aspects of this peaceful activity, such as how to mush a team of hard-working canines.

EACH DOG HAS ITS OWN POSITION IN THE TEAM – BUT YOUR POSITION IS A LITTLE MORE COMFORTABLE.

★ SLOW BOAT DOWN THE MEKONG, LAOS

2

a Bluelist suggestion from Louise182

The Mekong doglegs through Laos on its way south into Cambodia and Vietnam. You can catch basic river ferries at a number of places along its twisting length and drift casually down this mighty watercourse. A favourite stretch for locals and travellers is the superbusy section between the trading town of Huay Xai and the French colonial grandeur of Luang Prabang. You could cut the time spent on the river from two days to as little as six hours by catching one of the *héua wái* (speedboats), but the point of this trip is to slow down, not speed up.

MEANDER DOWN THE MEKONG, SOUTHEAST ASIA'S LONGEST RIVER, AND WATCH LIFE IN SLOW-MOTION.

★ CAMEL INTO THE SAHARA, MOROCCO

3

Camel jockeys head to the small village of Merzouga in central Morocco for an opportunity to ride one of the ill-tempered beasts of burden into a part of the Sahara that's drifted over from Algeria. The excursion involves a sure-footed plod across the Erg Chebbi – *erg* is an Arabic term for one of the massive sand dunes that the Sahara specialises in. Camel rides are normally arranged around dawn and dusk so that you can appreciate the changing colours of this immense sandscape. But you can also take longer treks that include camping in the desert.

TIMELESS SAND DUNES SURROUND YOU DURING A CHILLED-OUT CAMEL RIDE THROUGH THE SAHARA.

✶ STONEHENGE, ENGLAND

It's easy to see why
Stonehenge is on the must-
see list of anyone interested
in paranormal shenanigans.
It's old (built between
3000 and 1600 BC), it's
mysterious (no-one is really
sure what it was used for,
although an astrological
clock is currently the
most widely accepted
explanation), and it was
probably constructed by
druids, those tripped-out,
unkempt, hippy-forerunners
epitomised by Merlin the
Magician and Gandalf
in *Lord of the Rings*.
Since 1985, after police
forcibly removed revellers
occupying the 'Henge',
access to the stones has
been restricted, but you
can still feel the energy
surrounding the place.
Far out, man.

denied it's covering up any
first contact with aliens.
Truth-seekers be warned
that the military has set up
sophisticated surveillance
and regular patrols to deter
would-be intruders.

✶ HANGING ROCK, AUSTRALIA

It's quite hard to be
spooked by an oversized
volcanic rock just outside
of Melbourne, particularly
when the summit promises
close-ups of koalas and
panoramas of the wine
and spa region. Unless,
of course, a plot about
a picnic, schoolgirl
disappearances and
insoluble tragedy starts
to thicken. The cult
phenomena surrounding
Hanging Rock began
with Joan Lindsay's 1967
novel and Peter Weir's
subsequent film, and
an eerie sentiment has
shrouded the rock ever
since. Although touted
as fiction, readers and
viewers assume that the
story is true. Were the girls
kidnapped and tortured

#32. PARANORMAL
★ TRAVEL

✶ AREA 51, USA

The UFO conspiracy
surrounding the US military
facility known as Groom
Lake, or 'Area 51', exploded
onto the public arena in
1989 following revelations
by physicist Bob Lazar,
broadcast on a Las Vegas TV
network, that he'd worked
with alien spacecraft while
employed nearby. Since the
1950s Area 51, which lies
145km north of Las Vegas,
has been the testing ground
for 'black budget' aircraft,
including the B-2 Spirit
stealth bomber, but the
military has strenuously

in the dark hollows of
the rock? Did they vanish
into a time warp? Or were
they, as one Hanging Rock
enthusiast suggested,
flattened by an avalanche
of oversized meteorites?
Take your cucumber
sandwiches, hiking shoes
and a video camera
perhaps, but do leave
grandma at home.

✶ XALAPA, MEXICO

On 24 June 2005 the
city of Xalapa sent out
a beacon to ufologists
everywhere following an
extraordinary mass UFO

sighting in broad daylight.
Hundreds, including
Xalapa's governor,
Fidel Herrera Beltran,
dozens of police officers
and newspaper and TV
reporters, witnessed
the event, which caused
considerable commotion.
At least 14 UFOs were
spotted, interrupting
the governor's speech.
The aerial display was
captured on film as the
crowd screamed excitedly.
Nestled in the hills 1200m
above the Gulf of Mexico,
this heavenly university
town is one of the most

picturesque and cultured
destinations to explore
while on the lookout for
extraterrestrials.

✶ CITY CEMETERY, HAITI

Wildly embellished
'histories' of Haiti written
by 18th-century European
explorers immodestly
played up the indigenous
peoples' occult practices.
That said, this is one place
you wouldn't want to visit
on the night of a full moon.
Haitian voodoo contains
legends about child-eating
loup-garous (werewolves)

and innumerable ghosts, ghouls, zombies and *bakas* (people who are poisoned and agree to return from the dead). Nowadays the cemetery is frequented by hundreds of homeless street kids who allegedly break into the tombs to find goods they can sell. Come evening, they fear the police who come to round them up even more than they fear the *loup-garous*.

★ BERMUDA TRIANGLE

It's the stuff of a boy's-own adventure, with disappearing warships and aircraft quietly fading from radar screens. It may be a freak natural phenomenon, it may be a rip in the fabric of space-time. Maybe it's alien intervention. Accounts of missing ships attributed to the triangle date back to the 18th century, and still they flood in. Myth or not, there's something disconcerting about this pocket of the ocean. The triangle's three points are found in Bermuda, Miami and Puerto Rico, forming a polygon of more than one million sq km in area. Possessed by an *X-files*-like desire for investigation? Begin your own encounter in Miami, hire a boat and head out into the great unknown. What could possibly happen?

★ OLD CHANGI HOSPITAL, SINGAPORE

Enter the most haunted place in Asia's ghostliest city. At full moon locals come here seeking cheap thrills provided by its legion of poltergeists, screaming apparitions and generally macabre setting. Built in the 1930s the hospital is like a dilapidated version of the hotel in *The Shining*. During the Japanese occupation it housed POWs, some of whom were brutally tortured. Ghostbusters worth their salt should plan a trip here immediately, as the council may rejuvenate the building. But go with a friend, as individuals have been known to disappear.

✪ GREAT PYRAMIDS, EGYPT

It's one thing to sleep in a haunted house but another matter entirely to voluntarily stay locked up in the confines of the King's Chamber inside the world's most famous ancient landmark. Napoleon Bonaparte was the first European to do so in 1798. When he emerged the following day he was apparently 'visibly shaken' and refused to discuss the experience, even on his deathbed 23 years later. In 1904 Aleister Crowley, the infamous British occultist, repeated the feat, opting to read an incantation while sealed inside. To protect the innocent, visiting hours no longer permit nighttime vigils.

✪ CROP CIRCLES, ENGLAND

For at least 1200 years, weird patterns have been cropping up in agricultural fields and freaking out the locals. But over the past 15 years the area around Stonehenge in southwest England has been literally bombarded with geometric patterns, mind-bending for their size (some almost 1km long), mathematical precision (patterns based on fractal geometry) and consistency, season after season. Every year, 150 formations appear across the UK. Believers claim that electromagnetic anomalies surrounding the circles make you feel strange and can interfere with watch mechanisms.

✪ JOKHANG TEMPLE, TIBET

For more than 1300 years, this imposing grand temple has dominated Lhasa, one of the world's highest cities (3650m) and the spiritual capital of Tibet. From around AD 639 to 647, King Songtsen Gampo began construction over the site of a dark pool, after one of his wives contended the pool symbolised a witch's heart, and that by constructing a temple over it they could ward off its evil spirits. Pilgrims still trek here across the high mountain passes, prostrating themselves frequently as they approach. Although it can get crowded, there's always a supernatural aura of holiness surrounding the ancient complex.

#33.
★ BEST WAYS TO GIVE BACK

✿ ECOFRIENDLY TRAVEL, THAILAND

Each year this most popular of countries receives more than 15 million international tourists, and the southern region sees most of them. Some of the resultant problems here include waste dumping and water shortages. But there are ways you can give back. Try to deposit nonbiodegradable rubbish on the mainland rather than on the islands; on Ko Samui alone visitors and inhabitants produce more than 50 tonnes of rubbish a day, much of it plastic. Request glass water bottles. If you don't need a bag with your purchase, say so. Support genuine ecotourism outfits (Lonely Planet lists them where possible). Have speedy little showers.

✿ CAPITALISM FOR A CAUSE

Get behind brands or companies that are making an effort to demonstrate how they give back. Log on to a fair-trade website, or visit www.nosweatapparel .com, where you can buy your holiday flip flops designed by orphan survivors of the tsunami in Aceh. There are heaps of great things to buy on this site and they are all produced by workers paid a fair wage for their efforts. Take a fair-trade soccer ball (http://yfocus.ncf .ca/fairtrade/) as a present for local kids on your next trip away.

✿ OXFAM TRAILWALKER, HONG KONG, AUSTRALIA & NEW ZEALAND

Established in Hong Kong 30 years ago and based on a Ghurkha training exer-

cise, this event has spread to Britain, Australia and New Zealand. It adds the element of nature to getting fit, so that you can get some fresh air while giving back. Five hundred teams of all combinations and abilities enter each year, from the Ghurkas (who run the course in staggeringly quick times) to teams of workmates, who have stopped off for a full pub meal including red wine, and a nap. Teams must finish the 100km team event in the prescribed 48 hours. Proceeds go to Oxfam projects, which revolve around communities in 26 countries.

✿ DIY CHARITY

You don't actually need an organisation to tell you what to care about. It can be as simple and compelling as this: while on your trip, you see something or someone you want to help. This might

be a child with polio or a village without running water or a school that needs more resources. You collect the contacts you need while you're there. Then you go home, set up your own minicharity to help them directly and raise the money yourself. In nominating your own way of giving back, you get 100% of the satisfaction, and develop a special link with the place.

✿ INDIGENOUS-RUN OPERATIONS, AUSTRALIA

On a trip to Australia, if you'd like a taste of indigenous culture, go out of your way to seek out Aboriginal-controlled projects. Visit www .ananguwaai.com.au for good assessments on local tour providers. Go on a trip to Barmah-Millewa along the Murray River and enjoy the beautiful river red gum forests in the knowledge

✪ CHARITY MARATHONS IN BIG CITIES

Charity endurance events have become all the rage, a way for time-poor urban dwellers to give back while getting fit. The world's five top international marathons – the London, New York City, Chicago, Boston and Berlin Marathons – are all linked on the one site. Each year an official charity is selected to benefit from funds raised. Marathons make a genuinely fab excuse for you to train in your lunch hour. What's more, these events also give a sense of community and common endeavour to all those big-city isolates.

1

✪ COMMUNITY ART, INDIA

Not all giving back is about medical care, military security or logistical expertise. You could use your artistic skills to brighten the environment and educate simultaneously. After the Asian tsunami, Oxfam volunteers painted murals on their disaster-relief water tanks in coastal communities. The incidence of assault was increasing after the devastation of local homes and fishing fleets, which placed huge strain on already struggling families. The bright installations were designed to counter violence against women and children and featured simple messages in local languages.

2

that you are supporting local indigenous work to protect the forests from unsustainable forestry. Go to www.melbourne.foe.org.au/barmah to find contact details for the next trip.

✪ POST-EARTHQUAKE ASSISTANCE, PAKISTAN

You don't need to be part of Médecins Sans Frontières to roll up your sleeves and help after an earthquake. A group of volunteers from Melbourne travelled of their own accord to areas affected by natural disaster. The friends volunteered for a newly registered NGO called Australian Aid International, pooling their skills. They then spent their annual leave helping out in all kinds of ways. One member compiled reports on the extent of the damage. Another assisted in local villages and organised transport to evacuate people in need of serious

medical help. A primary focus for all was to build 'shelters' from their own design.

✪ SUPPORTING A COMMUNITY, VENEZUELA

Sometimes it doesn't take much more than a little positive action to have an impact on a community. Go to Venezuela to volunteer with Fundación Aldeas de Paz in the small southern town of Santa Elena de Uarién. The nature of this volunteering project means that tasks change regularly. You could help out in the daycare centre for kids with special needs and supervise excursions, or paint mandalas on the walls of the local psychiatric clinic, used as a unique form of therapy for troubled youngsters.

✪ AIDS AWARENESS, TANZANIA

Raise AIDS awareness by signing up with Student Partnership Worldwide (SPW), an international organisation supporting volunteers who've just finished high school. Volunteers raise their own funds before heading off (easier to do while still in your home town). They then live and work in an African community, organising events like plays and discos. These activities engage the locals and get the message across to young people – a message all the more powerful when it's coming from someone their own age.

3

#34. EXPERIENTIAL TRAVEL

PUT SOME CULTURALLY SPECIFIC LEARNING INTO YOUR NEXT HOLIDAY

⊛ ARCHAEOLOGICAL RESEARCH TRIPS AT CROW CANYON, USA

Crow Canyon Archaeological Center offers up to 11 trips annually for those willing to get their hands dirty as they dabble in amateur archaeology. Visitors' accommodation is in one of ten 'hogans', circular log cabins built in the traditional Navajo style, at the Center's 28-hectare campus; the campus is part of a site occupied by Ancestral Puebloans of Mesa Verde more than 1000 years ago. The trips, lasting seven to 10 days, allow visitors to explore the land in relation to what is known about the region's indigenous occupants, through studying the interaction of light, landscape and architecture, or participating in a dig.

⊛ BUSH SURVIVAL SKILLS IN ESINGENI, KENYA

If you can last a one-week survival course in Kenya's pristine wilderness, then chances are you'll emerge feeling more human than you've ever felt before. Qualified field experts lead small-group tours from the Esingeni Bush Camp, based on a private game reserve. Participants learn how to construct a shelter, make a fire, locate and prepare food, and extract water from plants. You will also be taught how to navigate using the stars as you traverse the countryside, which is abuzz with unfamiliar sights, sounds, smells and animals. Anyone who has imagined what life was like before the agrarian revolution can find out here.

⊛ YOGA IN RISHIKESH, INDIA

A trip to the birthplace of yoga is an obvious choice if you're looking for a mystical experience inside and out. Not only does yoga promote relaxation through meditation; research conducted by the University of Texas has revealed it can help alleviate the negative side effects of cancer treatment. At Rishikesh, in the serene foothills of the Himalayas, special retreats invite novices to practice stretching, breathing and contemplation alongside qualified yogi masters. Depending where you stay you might also be encouraged to help out in the organic garden and cook for the group, in between soul-enriching excursions into the mountains.

⊛ SPANISH IN PATAGONIA, ARGENTINA

The small town of Bariloche, surrounded by glacial lakes, forests and the valleys and mountains of the Andes, is so inspiring you'll probably learn more Spanish here in a month than you might elsewhere in a whole year. Sometimes called 'the Switzerland of South America', Bariloche is the base for most Patagonian language schools, so there's always a good mix of international students should you wish to slack off from speaking Spanish. There are plenty of optional excursions too, from nearby skiing at Cerro Catedral, South America's premier downhill resort, to a refreshing day trip through thick forest to the glorious Cántaros waterfall.

⊛ STOVE BUILDING IN CADMALCA, PERU

At the Cadmalca Community Lodge in Peru's remote northern highlands, a simple but potentially life-saving ecoproject allows travellers to do something challenging and useful, while becoming immersed in a culture they would otherwise find difficult to access. In return for being lodged and shown around by a local host family, visitors will source the construction materials for a cooking stove that's ideally suited to high altitude conditions – and then build it. The stoves have been shown to help reduce serious respiratory conditions associated with cooking over the open fires that are contained in the majority of mountain huts.

⊛ CALLIGRAPHY IN KYOTO, JAPAN

Anyone looking to make their mark using the traditional characters of Japanese calligraphy will find the course run by the Women's Association of Kyoto frustrating yet rewarding. Calligraphy written in Japanese is not easy, so you'll need to keep focused if you want to make your instructor proud. After receiving a lecture about the history of the Japanese literary art form, you will be shown and told how it's done. Then it's over to you, grasshopper, as you sketch your favourite Japanese character, such as the symbol for 'peace' or 'love', before adding your signature. One lesson is enough to ensure you pity Japanese school kids forever.

⊛ MOUNTAIN BIKING IN MARIN COUNTY, USA

Largely thanks to the pioneering efforts of bike designer Joe Breeze, Marin County and in particular Mt Tamalpais has become famous worldwide as the birthplace of mountain biking. Located just north of San Francisco across the Golden Gate Bridge, there's no more rugged or exciting arena to develop a passion for downhill riding. Throughout summer, countless tour operators, catering to kids, women, amateurs and pros, offer tuition and guided trail riding, including bike hire and transport to the start of hundreds of trails among more than 2550 hectares of redwood groves and oak woodlands. Trails range from the gently sloping and visually spectacular to the you-must-be-kidding-me steeply insane.

KICK IT KUNG-FU STYLE DURING YOUR TRAINING WITH THE SHAOLIN MONKS.

✪ KUNG FU AT SHAOLIN TEMPLE, CHINA

Every year foreigners can apply to attend classes at the Shaolin Temple, amid the beautiful Song Shan mountains in China's Henan province. Trainees at the 1500-year-old monastery, the birthplace of kung fu, embark on a steep learning curve led by extraordinarily disciplined 'warrior-monk' tutors. You won't notice who you're sharing a dorm with as the gruelling regime starts at 8.30am (Chinese students begin at 5am) and lasts until at least 7pm. For inspiration, watch the coaches prepare for daily tourist performances, in which they snap iron bars with their heads and break glass by throwing a pin at it.

SURF'S UP IN OAHU, HAWAII. LEARN TO TUBE RIDE, CUT BACK AND HANG TEN IN THE PLACE WHERE IT ALL BEGAN. GAUDY BOARD SHORTS OPTIONAL.

✪ SURFING IN HAWAII, USA

Learning to surf here is special. Polynesia was the birthplace of surfing – *he'e nalu* (wave sliding) was first observed here by Europeans in the 18th century – but Hawaii remains the focal point for the world's coolest lifestyle. Plenty of surf schools and instructors will patiently teach you how to read the ocean for swell, paddle into a wave and, critically, learn to stand and ride at beginner spots such as Waikiki Beach and Puena Point. Between sessions you can watch the pros shred heaving monsters at reef breaks such as Pipeline, Off the Wall and Sunset Beach.

NOT JUST ANOTHER SHRIMP ON THE BARBIE. LEARN TO COOK THE TRADITIONAL WAY IN VIETNAM OVER A CHARCOAL GRILL.

✪ COOKING IN HANOI, VIETNAM

On the banks of the Hoi An River, the Red Bridge Restaurant & Cooking School is one of many restaurants offering courses to meet the growing demand for tutorials in quality Vietnamese cuisine. Day and half-day cooking tours will match your culinary skills, from non-existent to cordon bleu. Starting with a trip to a local market, where you'll select ingredients and learn by observing street vendors, you then return to the restaurant for an expert demonstration before putting your new-found knowledge into practice. Expect to serve up rice-paper rolls and marinated beef, decorated with a pineapple boat.

● COCOS ISLAND, COSTA RICA

On Cocos Island, 600km off Costa Rica's Pacific coast, it's hammer time. Some of *Jurassic Park*'s most evocative scenes were filmed on this island, but it's under the sea that things are truly wild around Cocos Island. Here, hammerhead sharks shoal in enormous numbers, offering divers a jittery look at their fantastic features. The largest shoals are found around the submerged mountain at Alcyone, where you will also see white-tip reef sharks and possibly whale sharks. Divers will need to visit on live-aboard boats as nobody is allowed to stay on the island.

● GANSBAAI, SOUTH AFRICA

Move up the food chain, from hammerheads to great white sharks, as you climb inside a metal cage and come nose to snout with the ocean's most fearsome predator. Watch in awe, even as you wonder about the cage's strength, while the 6m-long great whites circle. Dive operators off this Western Cape town use bait to attract the sharks to the cage, virtually guaranteeing sightings (and controversy). You'll find operators based in Hermanus, though the boats leave from Gansbaai, 35km away.

● RAS MOHAMMED NATIONAL PARK, EGYPT

Covering the southern tip of the Sinai Peninsula, this national park is the final landfall before the underwater wonders of the Red Sea. The park itself contains 20 dive sites, many of them among the Red Sea's finest. Two submerged peaks, Yolanda Reef and Shark Reef, are the park's diving centrepieces, and both are rich in marine life. At Yolanda you can look forward to diving among the wreckage of the *Yolanda*, including its cargo of hundreds of toilet bowls (and a BMW). The vertical wall at Shark Reef is prized for its concentration of fish and, unsurprisingly, sharks.

● COCKLEBIDDY CAVE, AUSTRALIA

Australia's Nullarbor Plain may appear waterless, but beneath this enormous limestone block there's a series of caves, including Cocklebiddy Cave, a 6.7km-long, arrow-straight tunnel that's almost entirely flooded, making for one of the world's premier cave dives. It was here, in 1983, that French cavers racked up the world's longest cave dive by exploring to Cocklebiddy's end. The cave is situated 10km north of remote Cocklebiddy Roadhouse; divers must obtain permits from Western Australia's Conservation & Land Management (CALM) department.

● MANTA RAY VILLAGE, USA

No prizes for guessing the star attraction at this dive site off the Kona coast of Hawaii's Big Island, though half the fun is that dives here are conducted at night. Dive operators shine powerful lights into the water, which attracts plankton, which in turn attracts manta rays (which in turn attracts divers). Manta-ray sightings are unreliable – you might see up to 10 rays and their magnificent 'wings', or you might see none. Dives during the new moon seem to be the best bet for manta encounters.

● SAMARAI ISLAND, PAPUA NEW GUINEA

Get down and dirty in the world's muck-diving capital as you swim through Samarai's silty waters to appreciate the finer things of the sea. You won't encounter whale sharks, manta rays or moray eels on this island off Papua New Guinea's southeastern tip; Samarai is about the little critters, such as nudi-branches. Shallow waters make Samarai's tiny ocean goodies accessible even to novices, and you'll find exuberant corals and tropical fish as well as remnants of the island's turbulent history.

● RAINBOW WARRIOR, NEW ZEALAND

Bombed by French government saboteurs in Auckland harbour in July 1985, the Greenpeace boat *Rainbow Warrior* was later refloated and scuttled off beautiful Matauri Bay in New Zealand's Northland. Coated in colourful corals and populated by goatfish, moray eels and other fish, the *Rainbow Warrior* sits upright in 25m of water, wedged into the sandy ocean floor. Anemone, sponges and algae of all colours cling to the wreck; in its grave the *Rainbow Warrior* is far more rainbow than warrior.

#35. DIVE

★ THE WORLD

✪ GREAT BLUE HOLE, BELIZE

When seen from above, the Great Blue Hole looks like the pupil of an eye. Seen from within, this Unesco World Heritage–listed ocean sinkhole is a visual treat for divers. Ringed by fringing reef, and approximately 400m in diameter, the Great Blue Hole drops away to around 145m. About 40m down are the formations that lure divers from around the world: marine stalactites up to 15m in length. Marine life is noticeable only in its absence – you may not see a single fish – but when you're swimming among stalactites, who gives a Nemo?

1

✪ CHUUK LAGOON, MICRONESIA

Micronesia's Chuuk Lagoon is rich in colourful coral and tropical fish, but for divers these are almost peripheral to the main attraction. What draws divers to this 70km-wide lagoon are the wrecks – Chuuk may hold the greatest proliferation of shipwrecks in the world. Used as a Japanese naval base in WWII, dozens of ships were sunk, and many planes downed, during US attacks in 1944. Dives include the *Fujikawa Maru,* complete with intact fighter planes in its holds, and the *Shinkoku Maru,* decorated by nature in soft corals and sponges.

2

✪ PULAU SIPADAN, MALAYSIA

Slow things down to turtle pace as you take to the seas off the Malaysian island that invariably figures in all lists of the world's top dive sites, Pulau Sipadan. Green and hawksbill turtles abound; there's even a so-called turtle tomb, 22m underwater, containing the skeletal remains of vast numbers of turtles. For a marine adrenaline rush, try Barracuda Point, where the eponymous barracuda often gather in swirling, tornado-like formations. No diver will want to leave without witnessing the famous Drop Off, where, just a stroll from the shore, the ocean floor drops away 600m.

3

#36. CITIES
★ ON THE RISE

★ LUANG PRABANG, LAOS

Northern Laos' stunning city has been regulated in its development and as a result, has retained its character and sense of isolation. Its incredible French colonial architecture, delicate Buddhist wat and backdrop of emerald green mountains make it a travel photographer's dream. Placed on the Unesco World Heritage list in 1995, the once sleepy riverside city has become gentrified at a manageable pace. Restoration works and a tourism boom are assuring its ability to remain a postcard-perfect illustration of historic Indochina.

★ RĪGA, LATVIA

Growing up as the big boy of the Baltics, Rīga has always been a major metropolis with a proper big-city atmosphere hard to find elsewhere in the region. A pulsating place, its magnetism traps travellers long after their planned departure date. Once dubbed the 'Paris of the East,' it's building so fast that Unesco has warned Rīga it may withdraw its special protected status, due to the number of glittering glass hotels and business centres springing up faster than you can say 'bring me the tourist dollar on a platter, and make it snappy'.

★ VILNIUS, LITHUANIA

An incredibly small place (can this really be a capital city?), Lithuania's hub seduces visitors with astonishing old-town charm. Unesco has declared this, Europe's largest baroque old town, a World Heritage site. It's home to an eccentric artist community: where else could there be the world's only statue of psychedelic musician and composer Frank Zappa? Change has swept through with flair and panache. Using foreign cash and local vision, this stylish little city has big plans. But new business and infrastructure – even a skyscraper skyline – won't disguise its curious charm.

★ WELLINGTON, NEW ZEALAND

One of the world's cold-yet-cultural cities, New Zealand's capital is gaining in reputation as a place to be in the southern hemisphere. Why does this windy city foster an artistic culture? Maybe because it's somewhat isolated, sitting at the southern end of the North Island with a contemplative view over Cook Strait. Maybe, due for NZ's next big earthquake, it's busy living for the moment. Whatever the ingredients, youthful energy abounds – hip-hop dance-offs, plenty of live music and cafés, fashionable bars and bookshops. More beautiful than Seattle or Melbourne, the starry night is clearly young here.

★ BELFAST, NORTHERN IRELAND

A walk through the streets of Belfast late in the day seems to confirm the image of a place battened down and beleaguered by years of religious politics and violence. Yet Belfast recently celebrated the City Hall's 100th birthday with one of its biggest carnivals. It's possible to get a decent coffee, and the central mall these days seems like a smaller version of shopping districts elsewhere. Most symbolic of change is the latest wall mural, which depicts a unifying figure, the footballer George Best, rather than images of difference.

★ BELGRADE, SERBIA

It's not just the ridiculously cheap prices; this Serbian city has an infectious energy and a populace that's unfailingly friendly, mad about music and up for a big night out. A devastating combination of Nazi bombing and postwar central planning has given once-handsome Belgrade the architectural equivalent of a cauliflower ear and a crooked nose. Look beyond the carbuncular concrete, however, and you'll discover compelling reasons to stay. The sensationally located, unspoiled Kalemegdan Citadel is one. Spend more than a day here and you'll also realise why Belgrade is a burgeoning party destination.

★ PERTH, AUSTRALIA

Step off the plane in the most remote city of its size in the world and you'll feel the freedom: it's a big possible sky out here. The capital of Western Australia has got it good and it knows it. Due to resource-rich soils and a tenacious – and controversial – mining industry, the quality of life here is as obvious as a boat parked in front of a beach mansion. Liquid amber's just another local commodity: every week, year round, people queue to get into local beer gardens for the Sunday Sesh (session). No wonder there are still motions to secede.

✪ CHONGQING, CHINA ①

With an urban population of more than 12 million, Chongqing is a big city with even bigger plans, most of them related to the hype connected to the Three Gorges Dam. It already rates as the chief industrial city of southwestern China. Perched on the steep hills overlooking the confluence of the Yangtze and Jialing Rivers, it's one of China's more unusual cities, as dusty tenements and gleaming office towers cling to the side of the steep hills that make up most of the city centre. Something immediately noticeable is the absence of bicycles – all those hills would make for a coronary.

BEAT A PATH TO CHONGQING, A CHINESE CITY THAT'S ON THE UP-AND-UP.

✪ DUBAI, UNITED ARAB EMIRATES ②

Currently the fastest-growing city in the world, Dubai is a million things, depending on who you are and why you're here. For many of the more than five million visitors who fly into its sleek airport every year, it's a flashy, fun, often surreal yet uniquely Arabian city, with year-round sunshine, stunning five-star beach hotels, endless shopping, bubbling nightlife and world-class sports events. For Emiratis, it's a city that shows the rest of the world what an Arabic nation is capable of when given an opportunity to shine.

PACK YOUR SNOWSUIT FOR A TRIP TO THE MALL OF THE EMIRATES.

✪ TALLINN, ESTONIA ③

The 1990s saw Tallinn transformed into a contemporary mid-sized city, with a beautifully restored Old Town and a modern business district surrounding it. Today, a look around the centre indicates that the city is booming. It boasts 14th-century dwellings that have been given new life by its imaginative populace. The flair of the streets is decidedly fashion-forward, with boutiques bearing the imprint of rising Estonian designers, in contrast with centuries-old artisan traditions. The capital also boasts the largest wine cellars in the Baltics and plenty of medieval settings in which to imbibe.

DON'T EXPECT QUIET NIGHTS ON THE COUCH IN TALLINN.

⭐ FINLAND

Before Lordi blitzed the competition at Athens 2006, the Finns held one of the most dubious records in Eurovision history. In 45 years of competing, their highest placed finish was sixth, back in 1973. So, where other nations might have turned up their noses at entering a heavy-metal band, dressed as monsters, wearing latex Halloween masks and wielding flame-throwing guitars, Finland was happy to give them a go. The gamble paid dividends, as Lordi made the contest embrace a whole new realm of furiously freaky kitsch, while ensuring Finland will now be known for more than just the Moomins.

1

GRIMACES TURN TO GRI
AS LORDI EMBRACES
EUROVISION W

⭐ UNITED KINGDOM

Sandie Shaw, Cliff Richard, Lulu, Olivia Newton-John, Black Lace, Bucks Fizz, and Katrina and the Waves are just some of the greats whose careers were launched into orbit by the Eurovision Song Contest. In 50 years of competition, the UK has bent over backwards to host the event eight times, including once after a previous year's winners refused to host it themselves. In honour of the British tradition that 'it's the taking part that counts', the Brits have managed to finish second on 15 occasions, while self-deprecatingly blaming poor results on political voting or even, as commentator Terry Wogan once put it, 'post-Iraq backlash'.

2

TRAVEL TO FINLAND TO
DISCOVER LORDI'S INSPIRATION.

⭐ SWEDEN

Eurovision in Sweden means ABBA. After winning in 1974 with 'Waterloo', the foursome become the '70s most successful pop group, selling 300 million albums and being officially declared the country's biggest export since Volvo cars. Benny, Anni-Frid, Björn and Agnetha have arguably done more to promote the contest than any other Eurovision champions, but that's no excuse for Sweden's incessant attempts to recapture past glories by entering thinly disguised ABBA clones into subsequent contests. It's about as sensible as piling into dragon boats and invading England pretending to be Vikings. Stop it, ya?

3

EUROVISION

EXPERIENCE THE COUNTRIES THAT NEVER FAIL TO DELIVER AT THIS ANNUAL MUSIC COMPETITION

✪ UKRAINE

After debuting at Eurovision in 2003, Ukraine took top honours the following year. Raven-haired songstress Ruslana, now a member of parliament, whipped the judges into a lecherous frenzy by gyrating in a skimpy leather costume while belting out a Baltic pop number inspired by 'mystical elements' of the music of the Hutsul people (a mountain tribe with pagan traditions living in the Carpathian Mountains). When Ukraine hosted the contest's 50th anniversary edition, President Viktor Yushchenko assigned two cabinet ministers to organise the €10-million event, and assigned the country visa-free status for its duration.

✪ PORTUGAL

Everyone likes cheering for the underdog but in Portugal's case the dog's almost gone under. Even though the Portuguese have been 'competing' since 1964, the country is still awaiting its first victory. The last time it even made the top 10 was more than a decade ago. In fact, the only Eurovision honour Portugal has received is the award for Worst Dressed Contestant, declared by a fan website that picked out 2006 entrant Nonstop for its mismatched '80s-style *Pretty in Pink* attire. The awards are held in memory of Belgian contestant Barbara Dex, who caused the audience to crease up when she walked on stage in a homemade dress.

✪ NORWAY

And the record for the most number of last places goes to…Norway, for the 10 almost inconceivably terrible tunes it entered over five decades. But that's not all. The record of last places for an individual 'artist' is also Norway's, thanks to an outstanding solo effort by anti-diva Anne Karine Ström, who finished last not once but twice, with the monumentally forgettable 'The First Day of Love' (1974) and 'Mata Hari' (1976). However, the Norwegians did win in 1995, proving their Euro-know-how by entering an Irish-sounding song at a time when that country had just won three in a row.

✪ NETHERLANDS

If the Dutch selectors had a sense of humour, their next Eurovision entry would be a singer wearing a big nappy. In 2005 there was widespread media speculation that the Dutch were so incensed by their entrants ejection that they voted 'No' in a referendum about whether to join the European Union. And in the wake of Athens 2006, a leading Dutch newspaper ran the headline, 'Sick of the Eurovision Song Contest', suggesting that the country pull out of future contests because of vote-rigging by Eastern European countries. But having tasted success with 'Ding Dong' in 1975, we know they'll be back with bells on.

✪ GERMANY

A quick glance at the stats tells you everything you need to know about Germany's *rasende Leidenschaft* (raging passion) for Eurovision. It is the only country to have fielded entrants in every contest since the inaugural one in 1956, when it entered two songs. German singers have made the finals 50 times out of 51 attempts. The only year they didn't make it was in 1966 when the country's soccer players also lost the World Cup final. Being picked to represent Germany at Eurovision is still considered an honour, even though the only German victory in more than half a century of trying occurred in 1982.

✪ IRELAND

The mightiest of Europe's elite songsters. Not only has the country won the Eurovision Song Contest a savage seven times since 1965, but Ireland also posted the competition's only ever hat trick when it won three contests in a row during the mid-1990. Veteran crooner and former electrician, Johnny Logan, is the country's individual standout, winning as a performer in both 1980 and 1987. The emerald isle is so accustomed to success that the Minister for Arts, Sports & Tourism went so far as to issue a press release following Athens 2006 congratulating Irish entrant Brian Kennedy for winning, when in fact he came 10th.

✪ MALTA

If any one country can be accused of taking Eurovision too seriously it's Malta. The tiny island nation received a whopping 220 entries for the competition to select its entrant for Athens 2006. A two-day festival, televised nationally, is held each year so the public can choose the Malta Song for Europe. Whether or not to allow foreign composers to compete in this event is the subject of heated debate, and may have sparked a public slanging match between Malta Song board members, which ended in the chairperson filing a libel suit against his predecessor. Despite the passionate kerfuffle, Malta is yet to claim a victory.

#38. MOST OBSCURE
⭐ FESTIVALS

⚙ CAPE TOWN MINSTREL CARNIVAL, SOUTH AFRICA

One of the few great traditions to have emerged from the country's segregated past is this fascinating, high-tempo celebration of life, also known as the Coon Carnival. It was originally conceived as a way for black slaves and their descendants to make a mockery of their oppressors. In 1848 a troupe of white American minstrels performed here with their faces blackened by burnt cork. Dark-skinned locals caught on but instead whitened their faces in order to perform songs that, while seemingly full of joy and happiness, satirised the white rulers who remained oblivious to the performers' real motives. Today 13,000 minstrels continue their forebears' bittersweet tradition.

⚙ HINA MATSURI, JAPAN

On 3 March every year, doll enthusiasts know there is only one place to hang out. Since the Edo period (1600–1868), Japanese families have celebrated love for their daughters by presenting them with ornate dolls around the time when the first spring blossoms go into bloom. The special ceremonial dolls are beautifully ornate replicas of ancient emperors, empresses and their minions. Although the festival is traditionally a home-based event, the city of Katsuura in Chiba Prefecture holds a week-long 'Big Hina Matsuri' the week before, with as many as 12,000 dolls set up in lavish displays outside public buildings and in the streets.

⚙ NANAIMO WORLD CHAMPIONSHIP BATHTUB RACE, CANADA

For more than 40 years, apparently sane men and women have been building boats out of bathtubs and competing in this, the most prestigious event on the bathtub-racing calendar. Every July thousands of spectators converge at one of Canada's most picturesque bays to witness the spectacle of hundreds of hard-core 'tubbers' maniacally manoeuvring their motorised bathing devices along a looping 58km course that takes them down the Strait of Georgia. The fiercely competitive race is run by the Loyal Nanaimo Bathtub Society, which monitors entrants to ensure strict adherence to rules, such as tubs 'must have a minimum width of 20in [50cm]'.

⚙ HOMOWO FESTIVAL, GHANA

Travel through Ghana's Greater Accra Region along the magnificent Gold Coast in June, and you will notice things are unusually quiet. That's because local priests issue a month-long ban on all drumming in the lead up to the region's most joyous celebration. The Ga tribes have successfully managed to thrive here for centuries; the Homowo (Harvest) Festival commemorates the last famine faced by their ancestors, by marking a long period of abstinence followed by crazy celebrations. Such is participants' unbridled joy that at the apex of the festival any woman, whatever her status, must accept a hug from any man.

⚙ GREAT TEXAS MOSQUITO FESTIVAL, USA

The historic city of Clute, situated on the Gulf Coast, proudly claims to host the Lone Star State's daftest celebration, held every summer in honour of its peskiest residents, mosquitoes. Over three fun-filled days, locals and visitors slap on repellent and participate in such inane competitions as Mr and Ms Mosquito Legs and Willie Man-Chew's Goat Roping Competition. In the Mosquito Calling Contest, contenders must lure the blood-sucking insects using their own special sound, call or voice. Presiding over the proceedings is 'Willie Man-Chew', the world's largest mosquito, standing nearly 8m, replete with Stetson, cowboy boots and an enormous proboscis.

⚙ DENI UTE MUSTER, AUSTRALIA

There's nothing more quintessentially outback Australian than a trusty ute, the powerful open-backed workhorse utility automobile favoured down under for decades. And during the last weekend in September the otherwise sleepy town of Deniliquin, jewel of New South Wales' southern Riverina, pays tribute by declaring itself the Ute Capital of the World. For three days, thousands of ute-owning fanatics and admirers converge under the Southern Cross, chucking innumerable shrimps on the barbie and celebrating the Aussie way of life. There is also stiff competition for prizes awarded in categories such as Best Feral Ute, Best Chick's Ute and Ute That's Travelled Farthest. It's a veritable 'ute-opia'.

⚙ FESTIVAL IN THE DESERT, MALI

Billed as the world's most remote festival and modelled on traditional celebrations held by the Tuareg people – the desert's indigenous inhabitants – this unique event attracts musicians and performers from West Africa and beyond. The magical setting among steep sandy dunes is accessible only by camel or 4WD in a region where civil war once kept travellers at bay. The festival is now a symbol of local pride. It provides a public stage for Tuareg song, dance, poetry, camel racing, ritual sword fighting and cultural pursuits, as well as traditional and modern music performed by visiting artists.

COME ON BABY, LIGHT MY FIRE. THE GRASS IS ALWAYS GREENER AT THE ANNUAL FIVE-DAY CANNABIS CUP.

★ CANNABIS CUP, NETHERLANDS

Perhaps predictably, the history of the Cannabis Cup reads like the script of some tripped-out stoner movie. The first event was held in 1987 and attracted only a few judges who subsequently had to evade unwanted attention from the Authorities. Rita Marley, who inducted deceased husband Bob into the Counterculture Hall of Fame, attended the 10th Cup in 1997. The celebration is now in its 20th manifestation and sees thousands of 'neo-hippies' gather in Amsterdam to sample the entries, which can be inhaled using bongs, hookahs and pipes, or ingested in cakes, muffins, lollypops and chewing gum.

PRETTY AS A PICTURE – ART IS LAID BARE AT THE WORLD BODYPAINTING FESTIVAL.

★ WORLD BODYPAINTING FESTIVAL, AUSTRIA

Visitors admire the canvases as much as the art on display during this week-long event in the quaint mountain town of Seeboden. Every summer a wildly enthusiastic crowd of 20,000 spectators marvels at magnificent creations by more than 180 artists from 40 nations. You can visit specialist exhibitions, or attend workshops in body and face painting, special effects, henna, hair design, photography and digital artwork. Accompanied by raucous applause, the closing ceremony features presentation of the World Bodypainting Awards. Wherever you look, the scenery is certainly worth celebrating.

RE THAN 500,000 PILGRIMS E SUB-ZERO CONDITIONS AND ACHEROUS MOUNTAIN PATHS ON AMARNATH TREK.

★ AMARNATH YATRA, INDIA

It's been said that the Himalayan *yatra* (pilgrimages) are the world's oldest organised travel system. Every year at the end of summer, during the Hindu holy month of Sravana, thousands of pilgrims brave steep, high-mountain passes to visit an incredible natural shrine to the god Shiva at the remote Amarnath cave. Situated in a narrow gorge at the end of Lidder Valley, at an elevation of 3888m, Amarnath is 45km, a four-day return trek, from the nearest town, Pahalgam. The state government provides security and tented rest areas for those making the journey to one of Shiva's most inaccessible Himalayan abodes.

Bluelist 2006 gave readers an opportunity to do some **bluelisting** of their own on the Bluelist site – and at the same time, be in the running to win a trip to Shanghai, travelling with a Lonely Planet author. Have a read, be inspired and go to **www.lonelyplanet.com/bluelist** for a chance to win your own authoring adventure.

#39. BLUELIST ONLINE
⭐ WINNERS' LISTS

HOW TO GET THERE WITHOUT REALLY GOING THERE
Jeanette Scott

✪ COSTA DEL SOL, SPAIN = ENGLAND
Rainy days, warm beer, Prince Phillip. It's little wonder Brits head to Spain's Andalusian coast to make the Costa Del Sol the real 'Little Britain'. Say *hola* to fish and chips, bangers and mash, and beer bellies hanging over Union Jack shorts.

✪ LONDON, ENGLAND = INDIA
Nearly renamed 'Punjab-town' for its enormous Indian population, Southall, in the London borough of Ealing, is still known as Little India. It's a great place to try chicken tikka masala, Britain's favourite dish. Not a real curry, more a British take on the dish, but 23 million portions can't be wrong.

✪ SAN FRANCISCO, USA = CHINA
Thousands of Chinese immigrants flooded into America hoping to cash in on the Californian gold rush in the 1800s. They didn't make millions, but they did make a sizeable Chinatown in San Francisco. The area's sensory delight draws more visitors than the Golden Gate Bridge.

✪ MELBOURNE, AUSTRALIA = GREECE
No, Melbourne not the Med, but it is the globe's second-biggest Greek city, after Athens. Souvlaki, moussaka and cries of *yamas* (cheers) centre on Melbourne's Lonsdale St. The ancient Greek gods never foresaw little Greece ending up in the land of kangaroos and tinnies.

✪ BOSTON, USA = IRELAND
The capital of Irish America is in Massachusetts. St Patrick's Day in March is the time to be there when the city is awash with green for days of drinking and partying. South Boston is the place for the good ol' fashioned Irish craic.

✪ DÜSSELDORF, GERMANY = JAPAN
Düsseldorf has Europe's largest Japanese community, and it's home to a thriving Little Tokyo. Many Japanese businesses operate out of this northwestern German city. At the end of a hard day at the office, there is a plethora of karaoke bars where you can wail the night away.

✪ SÃO PAULO, BRAZIL = JAPAN
Strange but true, São Paulo has the world's biggest Little Tokyo. The city is better known for football, festivals and skyscrapers than sushi, but more than one million Japanese *paulistanos* populate the Liberdade area.

✪ NEW YORK CITY, USA = THE WORLD
No other city on earth can boast such a blend of ethnicities, a hotchpotch of culture, a jumble of nationalities. And no Bluelist on how to get there without really going there could be complete without the Big Apple. A true melting pot of the world.

BEST PLACES TO PEOPLE-WATCH
Jim Doherty

✪ WASHINGTON SQUARE PARK, NEW YORK CITY
Station yourself on a green bench and observe the odd but delightful mix of the princes and paupers of New York converging on this park in Greenwich Village. Particularly fascinating is watching homeless men defeat any and all takers on the park's chessboards.

✪ PARQUE DEL BUEN RETIRO, MADRID
Find a spot near the large pond in the centre of this park to watch romance bloom all around you. But be warned, gratuitous public affection has become a kind of obsession among Spain's youth – although half the fun is watching the older generation gasp in horror.

✪ THE LOUVRE, PARIS
In a museum where there are as many languages spoken as at the UN, watch cultures clash as the French raise their noses, Americans raise their voices and hundreds of Japanese tour guides raise their umbrellas to the disdain of everyone.

✪ TANGIER, MOROCCO
Every day, on the exact same path, at the exact same time, hundreds of foreign tourists take guided tours through this port town, a stone's throw from Europe. Watch as street vendors aggressively prey on unsuspecting visitors and their wallets.

✪ SOUTH BEACH, MIAMI
Perhaps this qualifies more under ogling rather than watching. Regardless, upon arrival, you can observe the palpable divide of who belongs on the beach perfecting their tan and who does not. More than likely, you belong to the latter.

✪ RED LIGHT DISTRICT, AMSTERDAM
There is little that's seedy about this area anymore, as sleaze has begrudgingly become a most unusual but extremely effective tourist draw. The disparity between the unfazed locals and the shocked and awed tourists is sheer entertainment.

✪ SPEAKER'S CORNER, LONDON
This monument to free speech in Hyde Park gives you the opportunity to hear speeches that range from inspiring idealism to crackpot insanity. Watch the very amusing dialogue between the speakers and hecklers, or feel free to enter the fray.

WORLD SENSES: SMELLS
Izzie Robinson

✪ CLOVES ON PEMBA, TANZANIA
Pemba, north of Zanzibar, is the world's biggest producer of cloves. With its distinctive strong aroma, this famous spice can be smelt all over the island as families dry the buds on mats outside their houses.

✪ TROPICAL RAIN
That heavy, earthy smell, especially good on your first night in the tropics. Best appreciated from under the shelter of an overhanging roof…

✪ RAFFLESIA FLOWERS, SUMATRA & BORNEO
The largest flower in the world, which is found in the jungles of Sumatra and Borneo, has the odour of rotting flesh. Not exactly the nicest smell on earth, but impressive even so. The flowers are hard to locate and only last a few days.

✪ CIGARS, CUBA
The definitive Cuban product. Sit outside a side-street café, letting the smell of cigars and the big-finned cars take you back to the '60s.

✪ YELLOWSTONE GEYSERS, USA
The geothermal wonders of Yellowstone helped to make this the world's first national park. Geysers are formed when water is warmed underground by rocks heated in turn by magma. The smell is caused by hydrogen sulphide – don't breathe too deeply!

✪ VANILLA PODS, MADAGASCAR
Originally from Mexico, Madagascan vanilla is sold worldwide. The pod comes from the vanilla orchid plant, which is converted into the cooking product we know via a complicated process. Northeast Madagascar is where sweet vanilla can be smelt as it is tied in bundles.

✪ COFFEE, ITALY
Wake up to the scent of freshly ground coffee floating through your window. Italy seems to have almost as many variations of coffee as pasta, and although most of it comes from South America, this really is the place to enjoy it.

✪ NIGHT-FLOWERING JASMINE, INDIA
Night-flowering jasmine has an exotic fragrance that's as strong as it is alluring; this is not a smell for those with bad allergies. It's used in Spain to deter mosquitoes, but elsewhere people use it for more aesthetic reasons. In India the flowers are woven into the hair as fragrant decoration.

✪ DURIAN, THAILAND
Durian, the 'king of fruits', is highly rated by Southeast Asians. This distinctive-smelling fruit has been described as 'tasting like heaven, smelling like hell'. Banned from many hotel premises, its incredible perfume is worse than garlic – beware the durian breath!

✪ PERFUME MARKETS, OMAN
Desired by Roman emperors and deemed worthy of Jesus, frankincense is the name given to the resin of the *Boswellia sacra* tree. Oman is one of the few places it grows. Small crystals, ideally clear or pink, are burnt to create the singular aroma.

INTERESTING OUTDOOR TOILET EXPERIENCES
Karin Best

✪ GREAT SAND DUNES NATIONAL PARK IN COLORADO, USA
An amazing place for an outdoor toilet experience – sand dunes snuggled against a mountain range. No-one is around and it's so quiet the only thing you can hear are the grasshoppers clicking all over the place. The view is stunning. Just watch out for that wind…

✪ BY A GLACIER IN ALASKA, USA
The glacier is in all its icy glory on one side, the sun shining above you, there's not a cloud in the sky and you're answering the call of nature – all is well in the world. Then you see the kayakers paddling in the waters below you. Oops!

✪ NIGHT ONE OF THE INCA TRAIL, PERU
It's 2am, it's very cold and as you gingerly make your way down the slope to the toilet, disaster strikes! You fall over, cut your knee and can't face going any further. You find the nearest place, squat down and hear a cow mooing close by – what if it tramples on you? Weeing fast and keeping your feet dry is not easy.

✪ COPPER CANYON, MEXICO
Right down at the bottom of the canyon, with the cool, clear river running by you, swatting away the flying insects. Absolutely lovely.

✪ ANYWHERE IN CHINA
Chinese public loos often have no cubicles, just knee-high partitions, and a not-so-terribly-clean trough running through the length of the building over which you squat and go. You'd just much rather be outside.

✪ A SATURDAY NIGHT IN BOURNEMOUTH, ENGLAND
The pubs have shut, there's a huge taxi queue and you're DESPERATE. You run into the woods, relieve yourself, get stuck in mud and lose your shoes. I think that's known as karma.

#40. HOTELS WHERE FAMOUS PEOPLE

HAVE DIED

★ CHELSEA HOTEL, USA

Sid Vicious, bass guitarist of the Sex Pistols, stabbed his 20-year-old girlfriend Nancy Laura Spungen to death in Room 100 of the Chelsea Hotel in New York City on 12 October 1978. Less than a year later, Sid was dead as well, at the age of 21 from a deliberate heroin overdose. The Chelsea has had many other rock'n'roll appearances including featuring in a classic Leonard Cohen song. Dylan Thomas would also have died at the Chelsea Hotel, after his famous '18 straight whiskies' binge, but he was taken to hospital in time to die there, rather than at the hotel.

★ HÔTEL D'ALSACE, FRANCE

On 30 November 1900, Oscar Wilde died in Room 16 of the Hôtel d'Alsace on Paris' rue des Beaux Arts. Gazing at the awful wallpaper, Wilde supposedly uttered his last words, 'well one of us had to go'. He was reputed to have left a large bill at the hotel and the comment that 'I'm dying as I have lived… beyond my means'. Wilde was 46 years old, his health broken after a spell in Reading jail; his death was caused by cerebral meningitis after an operation for an ear infection. Today, now renamed as L'Hôtel, this luxurious establishment is a much more up-scale place than it was in the time of the author of *The Picture of Dorian Gray* and *Lady Windermere's Fan*.

★ LORRAINE MOTEL, USA

Memphis' Lorraine Motel is now the National Civil Rights Museum. No question about it, the museum is a powerfully moving experience. It winds its way through a series of exhibits in the gutted and rebuilt old motel to finally emerge in Room 306, from which Martin Luther King Jr stepped to his death, shot by a racist sniper on 4 April 1968. King was 39 years old. Four years earlier, King won the Nobel Peace Prize; in 1977, he was posthumously awarded the Presidential Medal of Freedom.

★ ST FRANCIS HOTEL, USA

Prohibition or not, there was plenty of alcohol at the party that silent-movie star Fatty Arbuckle put on in Room 1220 of the St Francis Hotel in San Francisco. At some point in the proceedings on 5 September 1921, starlet Virginia Rappe suffered a ruptured bladder, which led to her death a day later; a friend subsequently alleged that Fatty had raped her. Fatty really was fat, tipping the scales at around 140kg; was the starlet's death the result of his weight when he raped her? And in fact did he rape her at all? Although Arbuckle was tried for murder, he was subsequently acquitted. However, the scandal wrecked his career.

★ SHELTON HOTEL, USA

Playwright Eugene O'Neill, who wrote *The Iceman Cometh* and *A Long Day's Journey into Night*, was 65 years old when he died, broke and unhappy, in Suite 401 of the Shelton Hotel in Boston on 27 November 1953. His last words were 'I knew it. I knew it. Born in a hotel room – and God damn it – died in a hotel room.' He had been born in a Broadway hotel room in New York, the son of an Irish-American actor. The hotel is now Shelton Hall, a student residence for Boston University.

★ LANDMARK HOTEL, USA

Janis Joplin was 27 years old and recording her classic rock album *Pearl* when she died of a heroin overdose on 4 October 1970. She died in Room 105 of Hollywood's Landmark Hotel, now renamed as the Highland Gardens Hotel. The singer had finished her last recordings three days earlier; among them were the song 'Mercedes-Benz' and a birthday greeting for John Lennon. Jimi Hendrix had died just two weeks earlier; he was also 27 years old.

★ AMBASSADOR HOTEL, USA

Soon after midnight on 5 June 1968, Robert F Kennedy was gunned down by Palestinian-born Sirhan Sirhan as he left the Ambassador Hotel's Embassy Ballroom via the kitchen area; he died a day later in hospital. Located at 3400 Wilshire Boulevard, the Ambassador was a true Hollywood hotel, used for Academy Award presentations in the 1930s and 1940s and the backdrop for many movies, most notably *The Graduate* where it appeared as the Taft. The hotel closed in 1989, but even as an empty building it made many movie appearances; scenes from *Pretty Woman*, *Forrest Gump*, *LA Story* and *Apollo 13* were all filmed here.

CHIP SIMONS | GETTY IMAGES

On the door sign: **PLEAS DO NO DISTUR[B]**

If you do not wish to be disturbed, hang this knob outside your door. Be sure to remove... IMPORTANT - If you do not wish to be disturbed... calls, please notify the Operator. Advise the... you will again accept telephone calls

✪ RITZ-CARLTON HOTEL, AUSTRALIA

Michael Hutchence, the lead singer from Australian rock band INXS, hanged himself with a leather belt in Room 524 of Sydney's Ritz-Carlton Hotel on 22 November 1997. The room cleaner found the body of the 37-year-old hanging behind the door the next morning. Hutchence is remembered for singing INXS classics that became anthems of the late '80s and '90s, such as 'Need You Tonight', 'Never Tear Us Apart' and 'Suicide Blonde' – and for highly publicised relationships with celebrities including Kylie Minogue, Helena Christensen and Paula Yates.

1

✪ HÔTEL RITZ, FRANCE

Fashion designer Coco Chanel was 87 years old when she died at the Ritz Hotel in Paris on 10 January 1971; she had been living at the hotel for 30 years. Born Gabrielle Bonheur Chanel, the designer was raised by aunts after her mother died when she was 12 (some sources suggest she was aged 6) and her father abandoned her. Coco, who never married or had children, started a fashion house that became one of the largest in the world. Another style icon linked to the Ritz was Princess Diana, who left the hotel by car for her appointment with death in 1997.

2

✪ CHATEAU MARMONT, USA

Hard-living film star John Belushi (who featured in *Animal House* and *The Blues Brothers*) was 33 years old when he died of a heroin and cocaine overdose on 5 March 1982 at the Chateau Marmont. He was staying in Bungalow 3 at the extremely fashionable Sunset Strip hotel in Los Angeles. Robin Williams and Robert De Niro are both said to have visited him at the bungalow on the night he died, when the star had been partying hard. Another of the Marmont's celebrity deaths was Helmut Newton, who was driving out of the hotel in 2004 when he died.

3

SPECIAL FEATURE

BY PIERS PICKARD

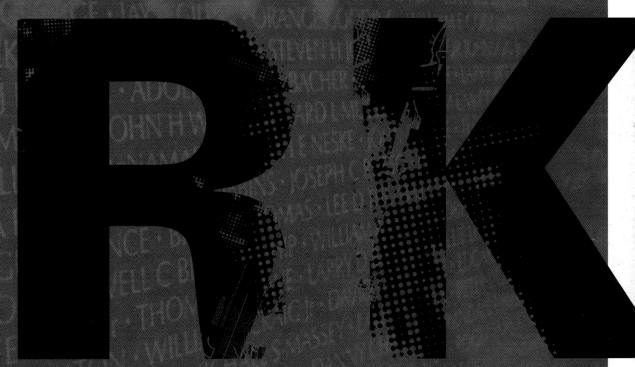

DARK TOURISM

TOURISM

TRAVEL TO SITES ASSOCIATED WITH
DEATH, DISASTER + DEPRAVITY »

DARK TRAVEL IS HERE.

And whether you care to admit it or not, you're a dark tourist.

Would you consider visiting Auschwitz-Birkenau to see for yourself the evil that humans are capable of? Do you admire the volunteers who flew out to the areas affected by the tsunami in 2004? And if you were in New York, wouldn't you want to see Ground Zero to decide for yourself what changed that day? If the answer's no, dark tourism has other forms that you might not be able to deny. If you've never dreamed of visiting the Taj Mahal, the Pyramids of Giza or the ruins of Pompeii, then you can say that really, you've no interest in poking around other people's graves.

The question isn't are you dark. The question is: how dark are you?

The term 'dark tourism' was coined in 1996 by Professors John Lennon (no relation, apparently) and Malcolm Foley to describe what they first identified as a travel trend – tourism to sites associated with death, disaster and depravity. Lennon, who describes himself as a die-hard

dark tourist, says that the number of travellers who fit this definition is growing exponentially. When they invented the term, Ground Zero didn't exist, Rwanda was reeling from what its people had done to each other, and Cambodia's Killing Fields were still a dangerous place to visit. Since then, visitor numbers to dark attractions have rocketed – Auschwitz-Birkenau saw an astonishing 37% growth in overseas visitors in 2004 alone.

But if dark tourism sounds shocking when you first hear about it, at its mildest it's plain harmless – a Sunday stroll around Père Lachaise cemetery in Paris to see the graves of Oscar Wilde and Jim Morrison; attending a memorial service at Gallipoli in Turkey; or visiting Mt St Helens National Volcanic Monument in the US. In many forms, almost everyone would agree that it is good – visiting memorials reminds you what horrors humanity is capable of, makes you remember why certain values are important. And travelling to a place that has been recently devastated – so long as it is done responsibly – is beneficial to the host community, as well as to you.

However, if one end of the dark scale is actually pretty white, there's certainly a black side to shy away from, where voyeurism and self-gratification live. Just like every other form of travel, if you do dark tourism badly, you'll hurt people and places. There will always be those who get a kick out

WITH A FEROCITY UNSEEN IN THE INDIAN OCEAN SINCE KRAKATAU IN 1883, THE 2004 TSUNAMI MADE CLEAR THE POWER OF NATURE.

of watching the suffering of others or foist themselves on grieving societies who aren't ready to support them.

In between, of course, there are shades of grey. And it's here that things get more complicated. Lennon believes that even when visiting sites that are popularly

DARKOMETER – HOW DARK ARE YOU?

OPAQUE – you visit sites at which evidence of death has been assembled – museums like the Smithsonian. By definition, you're just about a dark tourist, but then so are most people.

DARK – you travel to re-enactments of death or destruction – battle re-enactments. It's a minority interest, but it definitely makes you dark.

DIE-HARD DARK – you go to memorials and interment sites – monuments to death and graveyards like Rwanda's Gisozi Genocide Memorial. You take your dark seriously.

PITCH BLACK – you visit actual sites of death, but a respectful amount of time after it has happened – places like Auschwitz and the Killing Fields. This is the darkest level that is acceptable.

TOO DARK – some people travel to watch death – public hangings, whippings and executions. Likewise, some people travel to sites that still haven't recovered from catastrophe and are not yet ready for travellers. Neither of these have any justification.

| opaque | dark | die-hard dark | pitch black | too dark |

something we crave to understand. This need to move away from the world of everyday living and connect with something new is exactly the same motive that drives people to travel, so it's no wonder the two go hand in hand. Lennon calls both an exploration of 'alterior territory'.

But while he acknowledges the huge growth in dark tourism at the moment, he doesn't see it as anything new. He cites religious pilgrimages, public hangings, Roman gladiatorial games and Victorian morgue tours as examples of dark tourism. 'It has always been interesting to people,' he says. 'The British nobility actually paid to watch the Battle of Waterloo in 1815.'

What does surprise him, though, is the speed at which sites are recovering from their problems and commodifying them. He mentions examples all over the world: guided walks around Sarajevo, taxi tours of Belfast, Ground Zero, the Rwandan massacre sites, Katrina tours of New Orleans. He sees this as a reaction to modernity and the feeling that the world isn't becoming a better place, that the horrors are still continuing.

After all the analysis though, Lennon is a committed dark tourist himself. His next trip is to Cambodia to visit the Killing Fields. His main motivation, he says, is pretty simple. 'It's about the dark side of human nature. It's in all of us, and it fascinates us.'

perceived to be good and educational, no-one's motives are completely pure. He thinks that places like the Smithsonian museums in Washington DC are dark – 'see how much space is given to death' he enthuses – and he calls London's Imperial War Museum 'a tank-stroker's paradise'.

Lennon and his colleagues think that behind the drive to get educated, the wanting to help, and the undoubted good effects these produce, lies a simple need: people want vicarious contact with death and violence. Much of society is now so far removed from human mortality that death has become

RE-ENACTMENTS AT GALLIPOLI SERVE AS A REMINDER OF THE SENSELESS LOSS SUFFERED BY ANZAC AND TURKISH FORCES IN WWI.

THE 1996 ERUPTION OF THE SOUFRIERE HILLS VOLCANO LEFT MONTSERRAT BARREN; TOURISM IS JUST BEGINNING TO RECOVER.

AT THE SMITHSONIAN, THE *ENOLA GAY*, HARBINGER OF THE ATOMIC ERA, REMINDS THE WORLD OF THE BOMB IT DROPPED ON HIROSHIMA.

WHITE CROSSES MARCH ENDLESSLY ACROSS THE AMERICAN CEMETERY IN NORMANDY, FRANCE, A STARK REMINDER OF THE TRAGIC LOSSES IN WWII.

AROUND 40,000 US SERVICE PERSONNEL WERE KILLED DURING THE VIETNAM WAR. THE WALL OF NAMES AT THE VETERANS MEMORIAL IN WASHINGTON COMMEMORATES THE LOSS.

who cannot remember the past are condemned to repeat it'.

Many of the sites of the last century's worst atrocities have been turned into places travellers can visit. And even if you couldn't describe them as fun, they still form an essential part of many people's itineraries.

But while you can feel justified in confronting humanity's darkest moments and educating yourself as to exactly what happened and why, the very existence of these places raises some difficult issues.

While opinion is almost unanimous that somewhere like Auschwitz-Birkenau should be preserved, many people find

some of the exhibits ghoulish and unnecessary: the room filled with the hair of 40,000 people; the display of babies' clothes; the fact that the canisters of Zyklon B on display are the actual ones used on hundreds of people. Is all that really necessary, or is it there just to indulge people's taste for the dark?

An even tougher question is to try to work out what spin is being put on the facts. Until 1989, when Poland freed itself from the Soviet Union, Auschwitz-Birkenau was wholly dedicated to the memory of the Poles and Russians who died there. Little mention was made of the Jewish Holocaust, as it didn't suit the Communist ideology of

LEST WE
FORGET.

'THOSE WHO CANNOT REMEMBER THE PAST ARE CONDEMNED TO REPEAT IT'
George Santayana, philosopher

Churchill, for all his good intentions, got it wrong.

'We must draw a veil over all the horrors of the past,' he proclaimed after WWII. You can see why – the wounds seemed too fresh, the horror unspeakable.

But on the other side of the Atlantic, American philosopher George Santayana was of a different opinion, one which has become almost universally accepted. He warned that 'those

ONE PICTURE IS WORTH A THOUSAND WORDS – AT RWANDA'S GISOZI MEMORIAL IN KIGALI, MILLIONS OF WORDS ARE REPRESENTED.

the time. Lennon's concern is that things like this can easily happen when big, complex issues are given an oversimplified – or just plain wrong – interpretation.

'At all these sites – Auschwitz, the Smithsonian, the Killing Fields – you do the three-hour tour and that's the only history you get,' he says. 'Is that really enough? My worry is that it doesn't say how, for example, Cambodia got to a situation where 25% of the population could be wiped out. That event didn't happen in isolation.'

Lennon is well aware that some education is better than none, but he encourages travellers to be as well informed as they can be. 'I can't be pious and say that you have to read six history books before you go anywhere. But it's too important to leave it to the curators to interpret. Read as much as you can.'

The most infamous recent example of a site struggling with its own identity has been Ground Zero in New York. Within months of the attacks, you could buy Ground Zero T-shirts, DVD montages of the disaster, even Osama bin Laden toilet paper. The New York authorities knew they had to let the site be used by the huge numbers of dark tourists who flocked there, but were careful not to be seen to capitalise on the grief of others; a group of victims' families had already branded the merchandise sellers and their customers 'unbelievably sick'. And this is why dark tourism is a contentious issue: people interpret the same site in different ways. Some thought of visiting Ground Zero as an important part of a city's grieving process, where others saw only the commodification of death and disaster for the sake of a few tourist dollars.

Lennon takes a pragmatic approach to the role of such sites. 'For a die-hard dark tourist like me, these places are fascinating. But at the end of the day, they're still not stopping the atrocities happening.'

MEMORIALS

✪ ROBBEN ISLAND
It wasn't just Nelson Mandela's unwanted home for 27 years – Robben Island had been used to bully and oppress political troublemakers for almost 400 years, yet now it is a symbol of triumph over apartheid and oppression.

✪ KUTNA HORA
The small chapel in Sedlec, Czech Republic, is decorated with the bones of more than 40,000 people. There were no horrors committed here – it is an ossuary. Creepy, but irresistibly beautiful.

✪ TAJ MAHAL
The Taj is a moving memorial for all the right reasons. It's about a man missing his wife. Emperor Shah Jahan was so bereft when his beloved Mumtaz Mahal died that he constructed the most beautiful building in the world to house her body.

✪ GROUND ZERO
Controversial, laden with meaning and enduringly popular – it's the most-visited building site in the world. It'll be another five years before the Freedom Tower is completed, but you can watch its foundations being laid already at the site of the World Trade Center.

✪ ACTUN TUNICHIL MUKNAL
Trek through the Belize jungle, enter a cave, swim through a pool, step over the skeletons, dodge the fruit bats, and you might get to see the skeleton of a young Maya woman, possibly a princess, half embedded in sparkling calcite.

✪ GALLIPOLI
The cove in Turkey where 200,000 Allied lives and even more Turkish lives were lost becomes the scene of a huge memorial service on 25 April every year.

✪ AUSCHWITZ-BIRKENAU
If you can stomach it, take the longer tour that also visits the huge camp of Birkenau, built when the gas chambers and crematoria of Auschwitz could no longer deal with the numbers of people being sent there.

✪ JALLIANWALA BAGH
To gain an understanding of what made India the place it is today, go to Amritsar to the spot where British troops, without warning, blocked off a square before firing 1650 rounds into a crowd of 5000 peaceful protesters.

✪ SON MY
It is the setting that makes the Son My Memorial so moving. As you walk through rice paddies and vegetable gardens, it is difficult to believe that this is where hundreds of Vietnamese villagers were slaughtered, beaten and raped by American troops.

✪ TUOL SLENG
S-21, the old schoolhouse used as the Khmer Rouge torture centre in Cambodia, is a memorial to the atrocities that left 1.7 million dead. The controversial map made of skulls and bones was deemed too macabre and has now been replaced.

NIC DUNLOP | PANOS

FROM 1975 TO 1979, 25% OF THE CAMBODIAN POPULATION LOST THEIR LIVES. BONE-LITTERED MEMORIALS ATTEST TO THE HORROR.

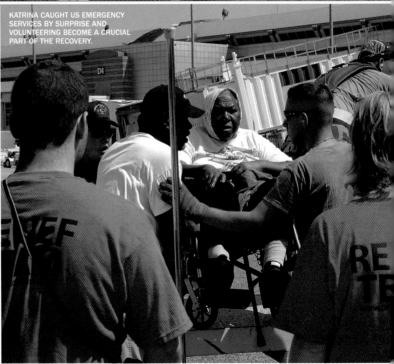

WITH MORE THAN THREE MILLION PEOPLE LEFT HOMELESS AFTER THE EARTHQUAKE IN PAKISTAN, INTERNATIONAL AID ORGANISATIONS SWUNG INTO ACTION TO ASSIST WITH TEMPORARY SHELTER.

PAULA BRONSTEIN | GETTY IMAGES

PAUL PIAIA

KATRINA CAUGHT US EMERGENCY SERVICES BY SURPRISE AND VOLUNTEERING BECOME A CRUCIAL PART OF THE RECOVERY.

MEDICAL AID WORKERS ARE HIGHLY SOUGHT AFTER IN DISASTER-STRUCK AREAS, AS ARE OTHER SKILLED VOLUNTEERS.

WESLEY BOCKE | PHOTOLIBRARY

HURRICANE KATRINA REINFORCED THE IDEA THAT ORDINARY VOLUNTEERS COULD BE OF REAL SERVICE IN A HUMANITARIAN CRISIS.

without saying that volunteering is of huge benefit to the host community. But it can also be an incredibly rewarding experience for the traveller. It may be hard, even harrowing, but Piaia thinks it is definitely worth it.

'It sounds corny, but you see the good side of humanity,' he says. 'People came from all over the world, slogging their guts out for 12 hours a day unpaid. The locals knew it, and appreciated it. You couldn't go five minutes without someone stopping you to shake your hand and thank you.'

So what's the link with dark tourism? Lennon believes there may be one. While he doesn't question the good work relief volunteers are doing, he is curious as to what drives them. 'When I was a boy, I dreamed of being a hero at a car crash,' he explains. 'But one of the reasons was so I could see the car crash.'

by complex, often conflicting, emotions and that many factors fed into his choice to help the earthquake victims. He's someone who wanted to make a difference to the suffering of those less fortunate than himself. But he's honest about some of the darker sides of this 'tourism'.

And when he got home, he was surprised by the reaction he got from people he met. 'When I came back, everyone's first question was "did you see dead people?" That was the thing they all wanted to know.'

Piaia doesn't have a problem with this. His experience in Pakistan was absolutely positive. And now he's home, he raises money and awareness for Australian Aid International (AAI), the charity he travelled with, until they need him to head overseas again. If you ask him what he has taken from the experience, he gives a typically honest answer.

'When you get back home, people ask you what the experience has meant to you. You can tell they want you to say that you feel sad.

AID & RELIEF
VOLUNTEERING.

When a cataclysmic earthquake flattened northern Pakistan on 8 October 2005, Paul Piaia was more than 11,000km away in Melbourne, Australia. He didn't know anyone in Kashmir, had no links with the disaster. Yet within nine days he was there as voluntary support to a doctor, trekking to stricken mountain villages that the big charities could not reach.

Piaia is one of a growing number of travellers who want to give up their holidays to volunteer abroad. Now that people can watch disasters unfold in real time from their own living rooms, those far away places don't seem so far away after all. People like Piaia are looking to do something positive with their holidays and volunteering can provide the perfect opportunity.

Done responsibly through a reputable charity or NGO, it goes

OVERSEAS VOLUNTEERING IS A GROWTH AREA, BUT IS IT REALLY JUST ANOTHER FORM OF DARK TOURISM?

Surprisingly, Piaia is quick to agree. 'Motive one was to help people, there was never any doubt in my mind about that. But things are never that simple. By the time you get down to about motive five …yes, I wanted to know how I'd cope with death and tragedy. Part of me wanted to see it.'

Piaia doesn't think of himself as morbid or voyeuristic. He is keen to point out that people are driven

IT WAS THE 2004 TSUNAMI THAT CHANGED VOLUNTEERING FROM SOMETHING YOU DO AT HOME TO SOMETHING YOU DO ON YOUR TRAVELS.

But my attitude is that I did what I could.

'If we had saved one life, that would have been enough. As it was, we saved at least 100.'

Paul Piaia volunteered with AAI (www.aai.org.au), a not-for-profit NGO that seeks to provide health care in remote or dangerous regions. AAI is always looking for suitable volunteers or donations.

TASTELESS,
BUT FUN.

So now, if you visit Stalin World, you'll find yourself surrounded by barbed-wire fences and guard towers. You'll tread wooden walkways built to resemble those in the Siberian gulags where 360,000 Lithuanians were sent. You'll ogle 86 Soviet statues arranged by theme; 'totalitarian' contains the big hitters Lenin, Stalin and Marx, while other themes include pithily named 'terror' and 'death'. After that, you should pop into the museum of Soviet memorabilia and maybe round the trip off with a look around the zoo. Oh, and don't forget the shop – you can buy souvenir vodka glasses with pictures of Stalin on them. Kids love the place.

Actually, it's not supposed to be a sick joke. Or at least it's not just supposed to be a sick joke. Malinauskas' idea is that if the

try. There are Jack the Ripper tours around London, the cult of Elvis at Graceland and the celebration of blood and guts at the Colosseum in Rome. At the Titan Missile Museum in Arizona, the tour ends in the control room, where the group goes through the sequence of steps necessary to launch a nuclear bomb. One lucky member of the group, often the youngest, then has the privilege of pressing the big red button.

At Johor Baru prison in Malaysia, travellers are offered the chance to stay overnight and experience the joys of prison food and no toilets. If that sounds like too much, they can visit during the day and watch a caning demonstration being performed on a life-size mannequin. Supposedly, it's educational.

The proliferation of these kinds of attractions is a new phenomenon. The Texas School Book Depository lay untouched for two decades before a local group decided to turn it into a memorial to JFK's life and death. Now the renamed Sixth Floor Museum at Dealey Plaza is Dallas's biggest tourist draw.

But even if all this seems relatively harmless, there are still a few questions to be asked. In 1995, the Inter-American Development Bank dubbed Bolivia's Yungas Road the most dangerous in the world. Immediately, local adventure operators wheeled out some mountain bikes and a set of capital letters, and the newly christened 'Most Dangerous Road in the World' became a renowned mountain-bike route. Travellers who give it a go know what they are letting themselves in for, but there is an obvious catch: the road really is dangerous. Blind bends, trucks, cliffs and a 3600m descent mean that there are deaths every year. But really, it's the deaths that are selling the trips – if it wasn't the Most Dangerous Road in the World, would it still be so popular?

SIMULATING AN ICBM LAUNCH IS A MAD WAY TO RELIVE THE PAST AT THE TITAN MISSILE MUSEUM IN ARIZONA.

FASTEN YOUR SEAT BELT FOR A TRIP DOWN THE MOST DANGEROUS ROAD IN THE WORLD, IN YUNGAS, BOLIVIA.

Not many people have heard of Grutas Park in Lithuania. Even if you call it by its more popular nickname, Stalin World, it is still comparatively unknown.

Which is strange, because Grutas Park is one of the weirdest places on the planet. Viliumas Malinauskas, the Lithuanian tinned-mushroom mogul and ex-wrestler who opened the park in 2001 (on April Fool's Day, of course) announced that its goal was to 'combine the charms of a Disneyland with the worst of the Soviet gulag prison camp'.

Lithuanians can laugh at the Soviets after 40 years of abuse, fear and deportation, they are probably facing their fears. It may be weird, it may be tasteless, but a lot of people love it, and visitor numbers are already approaching a quarter of a million a year.

But the existence of Stalin World shouldn't come as too much of a surprise. The world is full of places that are often tacky, sometimes weird and almost always in slightly dubious taste – but that are too much fun not to

IF THE KING IS ALWAYS ON YOUR MIND, LIGHT A CANDLE FOR HIM DURING ELVIS WEEK AT GRACELAND, MEMPHIS, USA.

CANING IS THE PUNISHMENT IN MALAYSIA FOR AROUND 40 CRIMES – WITNESS THE TERRIBLE WRATH ON A TOUR OF A FORMER PRISON.

YAHWEN HO | TREK EARTH

TOO GOOD TO MISS...

✪ GRACELAND

Most kings live in a castle, but Elvis had a home. Big things are afoot at Graceland after its sale in February 2006 to the entertainment company that owns American Idol. Expect more jumpsuits, a bigger Heartbreak Hotel and lots more visitors. Uh-huh.

✪ TITAN MISSILE MUSEUM

Tucson, Arizona proudly presents 'the only ICBM site in the world with a Titan II missile in the launch silo'. Wow! Step back into the '60s at this dinosaur of the Cold War and press the big red button yourself.

✪ PÈRE LACHAISE

Not many cemeteries have their own website and not many graves have their own security guard. But Jim Morrison's grave at Père Lachaise does. Actually, it's pretty grotty, so check out those of Maria Callas, Oscar Wilde or Chopin instead.

✪ GRUTAS PARK

Send the kids off to a gulag for a great day out mocking Soviet oppression in Stalin World, Lithuania. Almost seems too good to be true.

✪ COLOSSEUM

In one 117-day killing spree, Roman Emperor Trajan pitted 9000 gladiators and 10,000 animals against each other. That's got to get him a big thumbs down.

✪ COLDITZ

Head to Colditz and enjoy your visit. The most infamous POW camp in Germany is available for children's birthday parties, and rumours are that a youth hostel may open soon. Chances of doing a runner without paying are slim, though.

✪ SIXTH FLOOR MUSEUM

Relive every minute of JFK's final journey through Dealey Plaza in Dallas. You can't look out of the exact window Oswald used, but you can go to the same spot on the floor above and see for yourself if the shot was really possible.

✪ JACK THE RIPPER TOURS

Follow a trail of bloody murders through the streets of Victorian London. For maximum effect, book in winter when the streets will be dark and, if you're really lucky, foggy.

✪ VILNIUS KGB PRISON

Guides are always good, but as you look round the former KGB headquarters in Vilnius, Lithuania, you might notice your guide seems to know more than you'd expect. He should – he's a former inmate.

✪ MOST DANGEROUS ROAD IN THE WORLD

Actually, the 45km route from the Andes down to the Amazon Basin is OK for mountain-bike beginners. But take it very slowly, give the trucks plenty of space, and CHECK THOSE BRAKES.

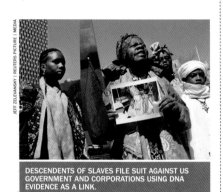

DESCENDENTS OF SLAVES FILE SUIT AGAINST US GOVERNMENT AND CORPORATIONS USING DNA EVIDENCE AS A LINK.

ROOTS
TOURISM.

only by what she learned, but by how much it meant to her.

'It was easy to imagine what it must have felt like to be plucked from your village then thrown down there,' she says. 'It was dark, cold and horrible – a very, very scary place.'

The experience affected her profoundly. 'I felt really angry. How could one set of people treat another set of people like that? I left feeling extremely sad.'

When you speak to people like Rowe, the justification for preserving places of horror like Elmina becomes self-evident. She has been learning more and more about West Africa and the slave trade ever since. She's even considered DNA testing to find out exactly where her ancestors came from. Talking to her, you realise that dark tourism can be a powerful force in creating a sense of identity in people.

For Rowe, that trip to Ghana has changed her sense of who she is today. 'It made me realise that the Caribbean wasn't where I was truly from,' she says. 'The Caribbean was just a transitional place. I'm a West African descended from slaves – I am descended from Africa.'

Lila Rowe is a Londoner, born and bred. Her parents came there from Jamaica in the '60s. So really, she has no direct physical links to West Africa. But Rowe knows, as someone of Jamaican parentage, that she must be descended from West African slaves. When she visited Ghana with a friend a few years ago, she took the chance to visit Elmina Castle, the notorious Portuguese fortress and prison that was once the centre of the Portuguese slave trade.

Rowe is not alone. Increasing numbers of black Americans and Europeans are heading to West Africa to find out what their ancestors went through. Rowe didn't know much about the slave trade until she went to Elmina. When she did, she was shocked not

SUNSHINE AND PALM TREES BELIE THE SLAVE-TRADE PAST OF ELMINA CASTLE, GHANA.

CHOOSE YOUR DARK DESTINATION
WISELY. DON'T TRAVEL WHERE
PHYSICAL AND EMOTIONAL WOUNDS
HAVE NOT YET HEALED.

TOO DARK – DON'T TRY THIS.

So, you've come over to the dark side. You're one of us now. Here's a quick check list of the dark tourism you should be shying well away from.

PUTTING YOUR LIFE AT RISK

Going somewhere a bit edgy is not the same as going somewhere where you're putting your life in real danger. Central Iraq, southern Afghanistan, parts of Somalia – there are always places in the world that are simply too dangerous for travellers. The best resource for finding out where is safe is your government.

DISRESPECTFUL VOYEURISM

Dark tourism becomes disrespectful when you're doing it purely for kicks and it impinges on the grief or suffering of others. So, watching executions or corporal punishment

is of course out. Travelling to areas that have been devastated by war, famine or natural disaster while people are still grieving is not on if you're doing it for no reason other than to have a good look around and indulge your own pleasure. Watching Hindu funeral ceremonies, where corpses are burnt by the river amid their grieving relatives, falls into this category if the relatives feel their grief is being intruded upon.

GOING BACK TOO EARLY

Places take time to recover from disasters. And when they are still in the early stages of recovery, your presence might not be welcome. Travellers should be careful not to put extra strain on places that are already stretched to provide locals with basic needs like food, water and shelter.

MORAL ISSUES

Some dark tourism destinations may have regimes you disagree with. Author and BBC presenter Simon Reeve has visited many of the world's most difficult places making programmes like *Holidays in the Danger Zone*. For Reeve, the key is to be well informed. 'You have to check the current situation in your destination before you travel and decide if you want to be part of it. Nagorno-Karabakh, for example, is a stunning area of the Caucasus that is recovering from terrible conflict. The people are friendly and welcoming, they serve great vodka, and the mountains will make your jaw drop. But Muslim Azeris and Christian Armenians used to live together in Karabakh. Then the Muslims were pushed out during the war. Until that situation is resolved it's not somewhere I would want to visit.'

Back in the '60s, getting stoned in Afghanistan meant wearing a kaftan, growing your hair, and saying 'man' a lot. In the '90s, however, it meant having members of the Taliban throw rocks at you.

The point is, places change. Anyone who says there's nowhere left to explore in the world clearly hasn't read a newspaper or turned on a TV. Today's hot spot is tomorrow's travel mecca, as places such as Vietnam, Croatia and South Africa can attest.

For the traveller, this throws open some interesting opportunities. If you're savvy, you can spot the places that are emerging from their troubles and – when the time is right – be one of the first travellers back in. Do that, and everyone's a winner: you get to discover a country that hasn't been trampled by tourist hordes, and they get your dollars when they most need them. It's called phoenix tourism and it's something you can feel very good about.

Why? First of all, there are the destinations. For a traveller, there's nothing more exciting than visiting somewhere that is a big blank on the map. This is travel at its most cutting edge. There's no tourist trail to follow, no comfortable rut to slip into. You've got to make it up as you go along.

The benefits are huge. You'll get authentic interaction with the local population, rather than seeing everything through the tired filter of a well-established tourist infrastructure. And apart from a warm glow and an unusual stamp in your passport, you should find that phoenix destinations are by definition pretty cheap.

Author and BBC presenter Simon Reeve (whose website is www.shootandscribble.com) has specialised in travel to the world's more obscure destinations and is a big fan of phoenix tourism. According to him, there are feel-good benefits after your trip, too. 'You're a trendsetter, going somewhere which is still a bit edgy. Let's be honest, it gives you a great story to tell when you get home.'

Reeve sees phoenix tourism as a very responsible form of travel. Without a well-established

PHOENIX
TOURISM.

PHOENIXES.

✪ RWANDA
Surprisingly, Rwanda is a country full of hope. The wounds will be a long time healing, but things are looking up. Travellers are once more coming to see the mountain gorillas and many visitors are now making the Gisozi Genocide Memorial in Kigali part of their trip.

✪ MONTENEGRO
If you think Croatia is becoming just another Mediterranean tourist honey pot, head one country south to Montenegro. Here, mile-high mountains drop straight into the blue waters of the Adriatic, and you'll have the place to yourself.

✪ SIERRA LEONE
After a decade of horrific civil war ended in 2002, Sierra Leone has limped towards recovery. By the end of 2005, the country was stable enough for the UN to leave. In 2006, intrepid travellers started exploring. They found friendly people, amazing beaches and surprisingly diverse national parks.

✪ UGANDA
Uganda has a diversity of natural beauty to rival that of Tanzania and Kenya. And now that relations with DR Congo and Rwanda are improving, this year promises fantastic safari opportunities without the hordes of zebra-striped minibuses.

✪ CHERNOBYL
The radioactive exclusion zone in northern Ukraine is now open for tours. Thinking of going? At www.kiddofspeed.com, read the extraordinary blog of Elena, a local biker who enters the contaminated wasteland to indulge her passion for speed, and you just might want to go there.

tourist industry, your money will be going straight into local communities, rather than into the pockets of tourism fat-cats. Just as importantly, it will reassure the country you're visiting that the outside world hasn't forgotten about them – that they still matter, that foreigners still want to come and see what they have to offer.

Reeve has seen these benefits on the ground and knows that as soon as people have an economic reason to protect their environment, they will. He says, 'when you're paying a local for a meal or a bed for a few weeks it encourages people to protect and preserve their wildlife and heritage, rather than eating local fauna for food or destroying

ancient buildings to rebuild their homes.'

For some countries, the ashes they have risen from even help their future as a travel destination. South Africa has always had a wealth of wildlife and natural beauty, but now it has a new attraction: apartheid tourism. Robben Island, where Nelson Mandela spent 27 years in prison, has become a symbol of victory over oppression, while Soweto township tours are lifting previously poor areas out of poverty and providing much-needed employment.

Phoenix destinations are where dark tourism meets the whitest morals. For you, it means a guilt-free trip that celebrates everything that is good about travel. It may be dark, but for those you're visiting it might seem like a first glimpse of light.

LIFE IF STILL TOUGH FOR MANY IN SOWETO, SOUTH AFRICA, BUT PHOENIX TOURISM MAY BE STARTING TO MAKE A DIFFERENCE.

PLACES YOUR GRAN MIGHT NOT WANT YOU TO GO.

✪ LIBYA

Gaddafi is still there, writing his poetry in the desert. Despite that, Libya is enjoying a modest tourism boom, as travellers discover the best Roman ruins in the Mediterranean and a populace who are keen for contact with foreigners.

✪ CROATIA

The tourism flagship of the new Eastern Europe, it is difficult to remember that Croatia was a warzone as recently as 1995. In the noughties, it has been 'this year's hottest secret beach destination' in the glossies so many times now you wonder if anyone but your gran is still not in on the 'secret'.

✪ VIETNAM

If it wasn't for sites like the Cu Chi tunnels, the demilitarised zone (DMZ) and the preserved corpse of Ho Chi Minh himself, you'd never know that market-

driven, fertile Vietnam had ever been at war. These days, it's one of the friendliest places on the planet.

✪ NICARAGUA

Noriega and Reagan are long gone. So visit Central America's largest country where you'll find Spanish colonial towns, galleons entombed in coral, and big, black volcanoes. It's like Costa Rica, except you won't trip over the ecotourists.

✪ NEW ORLEANS

Even with the efforts being made to get the Big Easy's economy afloat (rather than the houses), visitor numbers are still well down compared to pre-Katrina. But all the city's traveller drawcards are up and running, making this a great year to visit.

AROUND THE NEXT BEND »
Most tourists want to do little more than spend their precious holiday time sitting on a beach in Spain or Florida. But you can do that when you retire.

Instead why not get off the beaten track and start exploring places that are just a bit more remote, and sometimes even a little bit risky.

Travelling off the map, to destinations like some of those featured in the next pages, will do wonderful things for your understanding of the planet and its diverse cultures. It will enlighten you about the difficult reality of life in far-flung corners of the world, and can make you feel very fortunate to be carrying a passport that means you can leave.

Your conscience can also benefit. You probably don't want to spend your cash filling the coffers of a big, bland hotel chain. So instead, spread a bit of wealth around some of the poorer parts of the world, and put money directly into the hand of a welcoming guesthouse owner in Somaliland or Cartagena.

Personally, I find journeying through more obscure parts of the world to be the most rewarding type of travel.

In the ancient Uzbek city of Samarkand, a taxi driver I will call 'Ismail', moonlighting from his job as a doctor, told me tales of torture committed by the police, of horrific beatings and the quashing of political opposition.

I found his stories upsetting, but it would have been wrong to enjoy the glory and history of Samarkand without understanding what life is like in modern Uzbekistan. My chat with the doctor, coupled with endless meals and stories shared with other locals during a trip around the country, encouraged me to care about Uzbekistan in a way reading books about the place never could.

I consider myself extremely lucky to have visited a handful of places on this list. In Gabon,

a corrupt but beautiful country, President Bongo has converted huge areas of land into protected national parks. I headed along the equator to the village of Makougue, where locals have been ordered to stop hunting food in the nearby forests. Bongo's move was great for the wildlife, but villagers in Makougue still need to eat. Paying to watch them perform their traditional dances helps the community to survive.

My personal favourite on the list is Somaliland. With little help from the outside world, the inspirational locals are building a functioning democratic country with a police force, an army and traffic lights. Most people have two jobs to make ends meet; the foreign minister doubles as a midwife.

The stability of Somaliland sits in stark contrast to neighbouring Somalia, which has suffered endless conflict. The Somali capital of Mogadishu is anarchic and exceptionally dangerous. In the main market in Mogadishu I bought myself a Somali diplomatic passport from a man called Mr Big Beard. Ironically, Somalia has a seat at the UN, while Somaliland remains an unrecognised state.

Like many of the places presented in the GoLists, a visit to Somaliland should stretch your senses and feed your brain. You won't get that sitting on a beach in Benidorm.

– Simon Reeve

Simon is a British author and broadcaster. He's travelled to scores of official and unrecognised countries, and around the Caucasus, Central Asia and the Arabian peninsular for a series of BBC television documentaries. His latest journey took him around the equator.

SIMON'S TOP FIVE PLACES TO VISIT IN 2007

- WESTERN SAHARA. One of the most sparsely populated territories in the world, this used to be a sovereign state but in recent decades has been fought over by most of its neighbours, and has now been swallowed by Morocco. The town of El Aaiún is the colonial capital, and there are also settlements at the kasbah and mosque of Smara. Nomads raise camels, goats and sheep, and eat cheese made from the whey of soured camel's milk. Meanwhile, rebels and Moroccans fight over the vast phosphate deposits at Bu Craa.

- MONTENEGRO. People keep telling me this largely forgotten, former Yugoslav republic is one of Europe's best-kept secrets. With 290km of glorious Mediterranean coastline and some of the cleanest beaches in the Med, Montenegro apparently also offers a dramatic interior – a landscape of peaks, canyons and valleys, populated by brown bears, boar and wolves.

- COSTA RICA. I've spent the last couple of years travelling around some of the most difficult and dangerous countries on the planet, so it's about time I went to the place described by a friend as 'probably the best country in the world'. The rest of Central America might be chaotic, but Costa Rica sounds like pure heaven.

- LUANG PRABANG, THE 'JEWEL OF INDOCHINA'. The Buddhist temples and French colonial houses of this ancient royal city, situated at the junction of the Mekong and Khan Rivers in northern Laos, were falling apart by the 1990s. But a decade-long initiative by Unesco has restored the city, while apparently still preserving its ramshackle charm.

- ETHIOPIAN HIGHLANDS. High plateaus, rugged mountains and the source of the Blue Nile. The land is dotted with ancient rock-hewn churches, medieval castles and obelisks from a culture dating back more than 3000 years.

COUNTRIES ON THE RISE »
Our top country picks for the year ahead.

- FINLAND. A cool zone of design and fashion in Helsinki, surrounded by remote wilderness areas...Finland is a breath of fresh air on a European adventure (p156).

- ROMANIA. Explore majestic castles and medieval towns, then get back to nature for great hiking and cheap skiing in the 'undiscovered' former Eastern Bloc (p154).

- GABON. Well and truly off the beaten trail, this stable country is a wildlife watcher's dream, shedding a little light on some of the 'dark continent' (p158).

- JORDAN. History surrounds you in Jordan, from the cultural to the archaeological. More than ever, it's time to visit the Middle East and make some personal inroads that venture past media representations (p164).

- LAOS. There's much still to explore all around Laos, but don't miss the developing energy of Vientiane and the timeless charm of Luang Prabang (p166).

- MADAGASCAR. Displaying its famously unique array of fauna and a melting pot of cultures, Madagascar is something of a hidden gem sitting beside the mass of Africa (p168).

- NAMIBIA. Wedged between the Kalahari and the southern Atlantic, Namibia has deserts, seascapes, bushwalking and boundlessness, all in good measure (p174).

- NORTHERN IRELAND. Having moved on from more turbulent times, Northern Ireland is looking to engage at all levels, and it's a great place to make local connections on the road (p180).

- ECUADOR. Experience vibrant indigenous cultures, well-preserved colonial architecture, otherworldly volcanic landscapes and dense rainforest – all packed into the smallest country in the Andean highlands (p182).

- TURKMENISTAN. The most curious of the Central Asian republics, Turkmenistan might be described as a lunar landscape with craters of cultural activity – and one which sees very few travellers (p196).

✪ GO LIST.

ALASKA HIGHWAY

POPULATION 65,000 ✪ **VISITORS PER YEAR** 320,000 ✪ **LANGUAGE** ENGLISH, VARIOUS NATIVE AMERICAN LANGUAGES

✪ **UNIT OF CURRENCY** CANADIAN DOLLAR (C$), AMERICAN DOLLAR (US$) ✪ **COST INDEX** SALMON-BAKE DINNER, C$22-31 (US$20-28); ONE-HOUR

FLIGHTSEEING TOUR, C$167 (US$150); WHALE-WATCHING CRUISE, C$134 (US$120)

A DAMNED FINE ADVENTURE

The Alaska Highway is North America's epic road trip. The route got its start in WWII as a tortuous, mud-splattered military track to the far-flung Alaskan Front. More than six decades later, though tamed and paved, the so-called Alcan is still the sole year-round road through the northwestern hinterland – and still the best damn adventure you can have while sitting down.

The highway starts in the foothills of Canada's Rocky Mountains, in Dawson Creek, British Columbia (BC), and undulates its way across the peak-riddled top of that province, through the big-sky reaches of the fabled Yukon Territory, and into the wild heart of Alaska, reaching its terminus at Delta Junction after 2288 glorious kilometres.

It's certainly possible to drive the Alaska Highway in three or four days. Only the jaded or criminally insane, however, would opt for less than a week. The reason? The Alcan is not just a drive – not just a vehicular expedition, even – but a sort of pilgrimage, from the teeming, domesticated south to a vast and humbling realm beyond mass culture, where the woods and wildlife are still in charge. It's a trip that could change your life, so savour it.

RECENT FAD

✪ RVing. Yep, the stodgy old motorhome – thousands of which ply the Alaska Highway from May to September – is no longer just for wanderlusty geriatrics. Sales are skyrocketing among the young, who've discovered what their grandparents long knew: that recreational vehicles meld the comforts of home with the freedom of the open road. And if you can't afford to buy one, numerous outfits along the Alcan will rent you that Winnebago, whether it be for a day or a month.

FESTIVALS & EVENTS

✪ The Watson Lake Music Festival, held in the Yukon in late May, brings big-name Canadian rock, hip-hop and punk bands to the middle of nowhere.

✪ Whitehorse's Yukon International Storytelling Festival in mid-August features a pan-national line-up of musicians, performers and, of course, storytellers.

✪ In mid-June, the Kluane Chilkat International Bike Relay in Haines Junction, Yukon, sees more than 1000 cyclists pedalling 241km from the Yukon mountains to the coast.

✪ Golden Days, held in Fairbanks in late July, fills the streets with folks in Wild West get up,

WHAT'S HOT ✪

The most popular stop along the Alcan is literally hot. Liard Hot Springs, two hours south of the Yukon border in northwestern BC, burbles year-round at between 42°C and 52°C. Blessedly, these waters have escaped Disneyfication and are protected in a territorial park, retaining their natural beauty amid a lush spruce forest. Accessed by a short boardwalk from the parking lot, the 'alpha' pool is shallow and often thronging with bathers. Less than a kilometre beyond, the deeper 'beta' pool is more peaceful; despite signs to the contrary, this pool has a reputation for being clothing-optional. In summer, the adjoining camping ground fills up fast.

BEASTS OF BURDEN COME IN ALL SHAPES AND SIZES ON THE ALCAN.

commemorating the discovery of gold in interior Alaska.

- The World Eskimo Indian Olympics in Fairbanks, also in late July, brings together aboriginal people from across the north in an athletic and cultural celebration.

LIFE-CHANGING EXPERIENCES

- Reeling in wild-run salmon from a roadside river, cooking them over a campfire and communing with your inner carnivore.

- Pulling over on a lonely stretch of highway, taking a pee by the road shoulder and realising you're being watched…by the 10th black bear you've seen that day.

- Scrambling up an unnamed peak and, from the summit, being beckoned by a hundred other unnamed peaks beyond it.

- Whoopin' it up in a frontier saloon beside swear-to-God prospectors and real-live can-can girls.

- Witnessing – holy shit, can that be? – a wolverine.

WHAT'S NOT HOT

- Sadly, to visit Liard Hot Springs from the south you must go through Fort Nelson, a sprawling oil, gas and lumber boomtown, jammed with fast-food joints and overrun by jacked-up monster trucks. On the upside, it makes a wonderful whooshing sound as you drive by.

RANDOM FACTS

- Watson Lake, Yukon's 'signpost forest,' which was begun in 1942 by a homesick US soldier who posted a sign noting the mileage to his hometown, now boasts more than 60,000 signs from around the world.

THINGS TO TAKE

- A good, full-sized spare tyre. That donut in your trunk won't cut it.

- Mosquito repellent – or risk being eaten alive.

- Bear spray – same reason as above.

- *The Milepost Guide*. It claims to be 'the bible of North Country travel'.
— *Aaron Spitzer*

★ GO LIST.

ANTARCTICA

POPULATION 1000-4000 SCIENTISTS & SUPPORT STAFF ✪ **VISITORS PER YEAR** MORE THAN 28,000 ✪ **CAPITAL** NONE ✪ **LANGUAGE** NO OFFICIAL LANGUAGE

✪ **MAJOR INDUSTRIES** SCIENTIFIC RESEARCH, TOURISM ✪ **UNIT OF CURRENCY** NONE ✪ **COST INDEX** 20-DAY CRUISE, AU$10,500 (US$8000); SEA KAYAKING,

AU$500 (US$370); RESEARCH BASE GYM, FREE; VISITOR ENVIRONMENTAL IMPACTS, INCALCULABLE

A SNOW-WHITE LITMUS TEST

The last great wilderness on earth, Antarctica was to explorers of the early 20th century what space travel is to people today. Inhospitable and seemingly unknowable, it's taken decades of technological advancements, physical endurance and bloody-minded determination to tackle this awe-inspiring continent. Antarctica is more than a destination of dazzling extremes (the earth's driest, coldest, harshest land); it's a massive snow-white litmus test, revealing humankind's ability to peacefully cooperate or quietly and short-sightedly destroy. While seven nations have historic claims on parts of the continent as national territory, more than 40 nations are party to the Antarctic Treaty of 1959, to cooperate to protect Antarctica for the next generation. There's hope for the future in that statement alone.

Time has been quite literally frozen in this once-mythic southern land. Researchers are now uncovering the secrets of the planet's earliest millennia here, to help us better understand our impact on earth and make predictions about what's around the corner. Not long ago, this continent was characterised as 'the slumbering giant of climate change'. Today some scientists think the giant has woken and radical steps need to be taken immediately or we'll all regret the consequences. Global warming and the introduction of alien species to this pristine environment are the top-two concerns on the global agenda. In 2007 and 2008, there will be renewed efforts to measure and combat change before it's too late.

DEFINING ✪ EXPERIENCE

Since explorers first landed here, it's been a feature of Antarctic travel that planned itineraries often change at the last minute: this continent of ice, rock and extreme weather is completely unpredictable.

FOOTPRINTS IN THE SNOW

Tourism to Antarctica has grown exponentially over the last decade and is now one of the continent's major industries along with science and fishing. For those who travel here, the experience is described as nothing short of amazing. This is one of the major arguments put forward by tourism operators: by 'sharing the awe' we'll guarantee the future protection of Antarctica. Before you book to make it there yourself, ensure your tour operator is a member of the International Association of Antarctic Tour Operators (IAATO; www.iaato.org). Member operators adhere to strict requirements in the Antarctic Treaty guidelines including inspections and briefings before, during and after trips.

Some operators offer 'flight-seeing' voyages but this begs the question, what's the point? The experience of being there, touching the land, climbing mountains of ice, walking in snow up to your waist, kayaking glassy seas and listening to the sometimes disgruntled call of wildlife is what a once-in-a-lifetime-only-for-the-lucky-few Antarctica trip is made of. The rest of us will have to be

CATCH A WAVE FROM A LOCAL AS YOU TOUR PAST ANTARCTICA'S SUBLIME ICEBERGS.

content to exercise our imaginations, peruse *National Geographic* and enjoy documentaries such as Luc Jacquet's 2005 *March of the Penguins.*

RECENT FAD
- Most tourism operators include sea or wildlife experts in their crew, increasing the educational value of cruises and lending a slightly scientific cachet to the experience.

FESTIVALS & EVENTS
- Two major events this year will look at the future of study and tourism in Antarctica.
- March ushers in International Polar Year 2007–2008, the biggest internationally coordinated research effort for 50 years. Thousands of scientists from 60 countries focus their attention on the polar regions, providing the most comprehensive record of the region ever obtained.
- The International Symposium on Antarctic Earth Science (ISAES) convenes every four years and brings together around 400 scientists from more than 35 countries. The symposium in August and September 2007 at the University of California (Santa Barbara) will address major topics in Antarctic science.

LIFE-CHANGING EXPERIENCES
- Being approached by a small colony of curious penguins who have no fear of humans.
- Shooting whales, penguins, albatross, snow petrels and seals – with your camera, of course!
- Being silenced by the awesome beauty and majesty of icebergs the size of office towers.
- Rolling naked in the snow then hitting the sauna, thus entering the famed Antarctica 300 Club.

HOT TOPIC OF THE DAY
- The three fastest warming regions on the planet in the last 50 years were Alaska, Siberia and parts of the Antarctic Peninsula, where the average temperature increased by 2°C to 3°C. In 2002, significant areas of ice shelf disintegrated.

RANDOM FACTS
- Most tourist trips are by ship, last two weeks and take place in summer (November to March) when there's about 20 hours of light a day.
- Researchers living on Antarctica have developed their own jargon for everything from snacks frozen by the cold to someone who's been there too long.
- No documentation or visas are required to visit – compare that to passing through US customs…
- Unsurprisingly, most tourists are from the world's wealthiest countries: US (more than 40%), Britain (14%) and Germany (11%).

MOST BIZARRE SIGHT
- Boat wrecks and rotting wooden stations abandoned by the earliest settlers here.

– Tasmin Waby

✪GO LIST.

BROOKLYN, NEW YORK, USA

POPULATION 2.5 MILLION ✪ **VISITORS PER YEAR** FAR FEWER ✪ **LANGUAGE** ENGLISH ✪ **UNIT OF CURRENCY** US DOLLAR (US$) ✪ **COST INDEX** A SLICE OF BROOKLYN PIZZA TOUR, US$55; PARK SLOPE B&B PER NIGHT, US$150-250; BLEACHER TICKET FOR BROOKLYN CYCLONES GAME, US$6; CYCLONE ROLLER COASTER, US$6; PINT OF BROOKLYN LAGER, US$5

WELCOME BACK

Brooklyn's *booming*. Any New Yorker worth their street cred knows the new downtown lies just across the East River, over the stately 19th-century bridge sharing its name with its home borough, Brooklyn, the USA's biggest city-within-a-city.

Long sold by Hollywood as home to WWII-era doughboys with thick accents and comic timing, Brooklyn has ridden the New York City renaissance to new prominence. As Manhattan real-estate prices in the 1990s skyrocketed beyond normal budgets, artists, hipsters, yuppies, workers, families, students and emigrants seeking space and rent relief looked east to the borough that made John Travolta famous. By fate or fortune, a cultural movement emerged, and now Brooklyn stands proud as the hippest part of New York City.

A NATION OF MILLIONS

Brooklyn sports an awesome range of activities. *De rigueur* cultural activities? Head for the huge Brooklyn Museum and avant-garde Brooklyn Academy of Music. Heaping green space? Try Prospect Park, designed (and preferred) by Frederick Olmstead of Central Park fame. Raucous bars and live music? Williamsburg's got you covered. Water views? Coney Island beaches and Brooklyn Waterfront Park fit the bill.

Beyond the sights, Brooklyn remains a borough of strikingly multiethnic neighbourhoods. Here you'll find outposts of Hassidic Jews, West Indians, Russian emigrants, Africans and African-Amerians, Koreans,

Japanese, Pakistanis, Italian grandmothers and Indiana farm boys. They convene on summer days at Coney Island, the classic NYC beach experiencing a renaissance of its own.

DEFINING EXPERIENCE

✪ After biking back across the Brooklyn Bridge, canvassing DUMBO (Down Under the Manhattan Bridge Overpass) art galleries, the Williamsburg Bank building and Empire-Fulton Ferry State Park's jaw-dropping Manhattan views, it's time to munch Jacques Torres chocolate, model Triple Five Soul streetware and knock back some Brooklyn Lagers while blasting Asteroids at Barcade in Williamsburg.

RECENT FAD

✪ Buying in. Manhattan's real-estate surge has forced would-be homeowners to scour emerging Brooklyn neighbourhoods for that most elusive of New Yorkers'

HOT TOPIC ✪ OF THE DAY

The Brooklyn Nets. Ground Zero for Brooklyn's gentrification wars is the ambitious or dastardly (depending on who you talk to) plan to transplant the NBA's New Jersey Nets basketball team to Brooklyn as the centrepiece for a massive, 15-building redevelopment of the forlorn Atlantic Railyards. On the plus side is pro sports' return to the borough to bury the ghosts of the Dodger's abandonment. On the minus, it's a land grab scam that'll boot out tenants and further Wal-Martify NYC. Stay tuned.

EVERYTHING'S COOL IN BROOKLYN – TRY A DIP WITH THE POLAR BEARS.

desires: an affordable, well-built condo or duplex or brownstone with original fixtures, hardwood floors, a backyard, near good markets, schools and subway lines. An elevator's a plus; and the closer to midtown, the better.

FESTIVALS & EVENTS

- Take the ceremonial plunge into frigid Atlantic waters with scores of similarly waterlogged freaks, for the Coney Island Polar Bears First Dip on New Year's Day.

- Rooftop Films, from June to September, screes foreign, indie, experimental and documentary films and music videos at rooftop locations around Brooklyn.

- June's Mermaid Parade on Coney Island sees fairies, freaks and geeks don their best aqua-themed attire to celebrate individuality, personal style and summer.

- Also on Coney Island is Nathan's Famous Hot Dog Eating Contest on 4 July. It's foul enough watching eaters compete in this gorge-a-thon outside the city's famous wienery, but do they really have to chase them with milk?

- Welcome the start of fall at September's Atlantic Antic, a mile-long street fair.

LIFE-CHANGING EXPERIENCES

- Crossing Brooklyn Bridge and imagining how the Manhattan skyline looked before 9/11.

- Passing out on the BDF train after a big night out, then waking on Coney Island to see the sun rise over the Atlantic.

WHAT'S HOT

- The Bronx. Is the warehouse-laden former Fort Apache the New Brooklyn in the making?

WHAT'S NOT

- Jersey. Sorry, ma.

RANDOM FACTS

- With its 2.5 million residents, Brooklyn would be the fourth largest US city if it hadn't been folded into NYC in 1898.

- Walt Whitman wrote *Leaves of Grass* here, but the modern-day bard of Brooklyn is Jonathan Letham, whose novels *The Fortress of Solitude* and *Motherless Brooklyn* serve as late 20th century time capsules.

MOST BIZARRE SIGHT

- Takeru Kobayashi of Japan, the Tiger Woods of competitive food consumption, outchomping challengers and hoisting trophies at Nathan's Famous Hot Dog Eating Contest.

CLASSIC RESTAURANT EXPERIENCE

- The scene's the thing at Alma on Columbia St, the hip, split-level Mexican eatery with more than boutique tequillas and absofuckinglutely unreal views of Lower Manhattan. On a glowing spring day, there's no better place to see and be seen in NYC.

– Jay Cooke

★ GO LIST.

CENTRAL BULGARIA

LANGUAGE BULGARIAN ◦ **MAJOR INDUSTRY** FARMING ◦ **UNIT OF CURRENCY** BULGARIAN LEV (LV) ◦ **COST INDEX** BOTTLE OF LOCAL

BEER, 1 LV (US$0.60); BANITSA (CHEESE PASTRY), 0.75 LV (US$0.50); MEAL IN VELIKO TÂRNOVO, 6 LV (US$4);

TRAIN JOURNEY FROM THE BLACK SEA, 12.50 LV (US$8)

BACK BEYOND THE BEACHES

In visitor numbers, Bulgaria beats all other Eastern European countries, but this statistic is misleading given that the vast majority of these arrivals are package tourists making the most of the cheap prices and great beaches on the Black Sea. Get back from the heaving coastline and find the bucolic, delightful world of central Bulgaria, still only known to a trickle of back-packers. The attractions are largely visual – the pastoral Stara Planina mountains, the beautiful villages of Koprivshtitsa, Kotel and Arbanasi, the dramatic Shipka Pass and one of Eastern Europe's best-kept secrets, the ancient Bulgarian imperial capital of Veliko Târnovo.

MOST BIZARRE SIGHT ★

Check out the powerful frescoes of Zahari Zograf at Troyan Monastery. His detailed renderings of hell and exactly what goes on there are still terrifying today; imagine what the reaction would have been in the 19th century when the frescoes were first painted.

HISTORY, HISTORY, EVERYWHERE

Don't know anything about Bulgarian history? You're about to learn. Central Bulgaria is the heartland of the country's independence movement, where its ancient capital was based during the medieval Bulgarian empire and where many of its towns are overflowing with history from the time of the Ottoman occupation, which only ended in the late 19th century. You'll hear about Russian heroism and Turkish brutality, and become familiar with a slew of local names from Levski to Kableshkov if you visit the revolutionary towns of Karlovo, Shipka and Koprivshtitsa.

If you get bored with history, head for the mountains. The Stara Planina (literally 'the old mountains') have beauty in bucketloads, and there's great scope for hiking and climbing as well as skiing in the winter months. Finally, don't miss the great monasteries of the region: Troyan, Dryanovo and those at magical Arbanasi.

DEFINING EXPERIENCE

✪ Travelling through the magical, Wagnerian scenery of the Shipka Pass, high in the Stara Planina mountains and visiting the stunning memorial church to the thousands of Russians who lost their lives fighting for Bulgarian independence in the 19th century. The trip combines history with utterly amazing scenery. Don't miss it.

FESTIVALS & EVENTS

✪ The best festival to come to in Bulgaria is the International Folk Festival, held in Koprivshtitsa every five years. Sadly the next one is not until 2010, but it's worth the wait. A truly spectacular assembly of Bulgarians from all over the country and beyond demonstrates the music, singing and dancing that has rung out between the mountains here for centuries.

✪ Koprivshtitsa hosts two other impressive annual festivals: the

IN VELIKO TÂRNOVO, CASTLES AND CLUBS
SIT SIDE BY SIDE IN A MODERN FAIRY TALE.

Folklore Days Festival in mid-August, a smaller folk festival, equally full of song and dance; and the Re-enactment of 1876 April Uprising, a massive battle reconstruction of the uprising that was instrumental in seeing Bulgarian statehood come about, usually held in the first days of May.

LIFE-CHANGING EXPERIENCE
✪ Seeing the astonishingly lovely setting of Veliko Târnovo, high above the rushing Yantra River. The peaceful location, surrounded by gorges and mountains, and the beauty of the town itself with its ancient churches and massive 15th-century Tsarevets Fortress, are unforgettable. Moreover, it's full of students, and the cafés, bars and clubs are busy all night in the summer when studying is the last thing on anybody's mind.

RANDOM FACTS
✪ The town of Gabrovo holds a House of Humour & Satire, as its inhabitants have been the butt of jokes in Bulgaria for years, being stereotyped as tight-fisted.

✪ Veliko Târnovo is famous for its sound and light show, put on every night in summer when the story of the rise and fall of the Bulgarian empire is told in flashing lights (rather incomprehensibly it must be admitted) to the beat of Jean Michel Jarre–esque techno.

DEFINING DIFFERENCE
✪ The central Bulgarian region looks in on itself, rather than outward like its neighbours, European Sofia, the Turkish-influenced South or the ultrawestern Black Sea coast. Here, traditions have remained unchanged for centuries, and buildings, the way of life and the spirit of the people reflect this past; it's a region that is at once deeply hospitable and fiercely proud.

– *Tom Tomaszewski*

BLUELIST // ONLINE

✪ LOO WITH A VIEW
Travelling to Bourgas, I was surprised to see a Turkish toilet on the train. I was even more surprised to see the track rushing beneath me. My female friends claimed the first time they didn't pee on themselves on the train as a religious experience.

✪ SIDE ORDER OF HEADACHE
When the first Subway sandwich shop opened in Sofia, word spread quickly through the expatriate community. Soon after it opened, a friend went downstairs to use the toilet. As she got up, a piece of tile fell off the wall and landed on her head.

// KEVIN ELLIOTT

✪ CHRISTMAS CLAYPOT
Kapama is a Christmas speciality from Bansko. All kinds of meat, sausages and stuffed vine leaves in a claypot, sealed with dough and left through the night on a low fire. What else can you ask for?

// DXBSTUCK

★ GO LIST.

NORTHEAST CAMBODIA

POPULATION 150,000 ✪ **UNIT OF CURRENCY** CAMBODIAN RIEL (R), US DOLLAR (US$) OR THE GOOD OLD BARTER SYSTEM ✪ **LANGUAGES** JARAI, KHMER, KREUNG, PNONG, TOMPUON ✪ **COST INDEX** AIR-CON HOTEL ROOM PER NIGHT, 40,410R (US$10); CAN OF ANGKOR BEER, 4040R (US$1); ELEPHANT RIDE, 80,820R (US$20); BOAT TRIP, 40,410R (US$10) ✪ **CAPITALS** SEN MONOROM (MONDULKIRI), BANLUNG (RATANAKIRI)

TEMPLES SCHMEMPLES!

Cambodia has reinvented itself in recent years. Once synonymous with Pol Pot and the genocidal Khmer Rouge, the country is no longer scaring people away, but drawing them in ever-increasing numbers to the magnificent temples of Angkor. But just as Angkor is more than its wat, so too is Cambodia more than a land of old ruins. The capital is cooking and the beaches are red-hot; but where it's at for thrill-seekers this year is the wild northeast of Cambodia, the untamed mountain provinces of Mondulkiri and Ratanakiri.

The landscape breaks the Cambodian mould of swaying sugar palms and shimmering rice paddies. Mondulkiri is a land of rolling hills and pine groves, much more New Zealand than Cambodia. Further north, Ratanakiri is king of the jungle, with the massive Virachay National Park virtually unexplored by outsiders. The mountains provide shelter for myriad minority peoples; the chance to experience their traditional lifestyle is not to be missed. Pnong villagers in Mondulkiri extend the hand of friendship to outsiders and a ride on one of their elephants through the jungle is no circus. The Kreung of Ratanakiri build towering stilt houses for young couples to nurture budding romances, although the staircase might prove a challenge after a night on the rice wine. The Jarai bury their dead in forest cemeteries and carve effigies of the deceased, their haunting eyes staring out of the dark recesses of the jungle.

Waterfalls, lakes and rivers are a major lure. Bou Sraa is a double-drop dream, plunging from a hillside in Mondulkiri into a deep, jungle-clad gorge below. Boeng Yeak Lom in Ratanakiri is the perfect crater lake and nature's ultimate swimming pool in the northeast. Legend has it that a giant created it, but apparently giants were behind most hills and lakes in Cambodia; geologists believe it was a meteor strike. When it comes to rivers, there is none more evocative than Tonlé Srepok, which allows you to follow in the footsteps of Colonel Kurtz in *Apocalypse Now*.

IT'S DEFINITELY NOT THAILAND

If you crave 'awfentic' experiences with minority peoples, where you are the 'first foreigner' to visit the village, in the last 10 minutes at least, then head to northern Thailand and share it with millions of others. If you want the real Asia, an older Asia, where the rhythms of life play out as they have down the centuries, then succumb to the charms of northeast Cambodia. The roads are rough, but they won't be for much longer. This makes the northeast so now that you'll need to book a ticket today.

DEFINING EXPERIENCE

✪ Saddle up an elephant for a roller-coaster ride through the jungle

DEFINING ✪ DIFFERENCE

Thankfully, the climate. Lowland Cambodia can be as steamy as a sauna, and the thermometer goes into overdrive around April. The northeast is usually about 10°C cooler, making for glorious days and balmy nights.

TICK OFF ANGKOR THEN HEAD TO MONDULKIRI'S PNONG VILLAGES FOR A DIFFERENT KIND OF CROWD.

to a perfect horseshoe waterfall where you can play Tarzan or Jane and plunge into the crystal-clear waters from a vine.

FESTIVALS & EVENTS

- ❂ Celebrating the annual rice harvest is one party not to miss, as it means the village can brew more rice wine. The party season usually runs from around October to January. Copious amounts of rice wine are drunk, but the uninitiated should proceed with caution. While some of the hooch tastes like light cider, the better brews are as strong as absinthe. Sip rather than swig, as a rule.

- ❂ Weddings are the other major social event in the northeast. Nothing like a Khmer wedding, a minority betrothal still involves a lot of sacrifice and, surprise, surprise, a lot of rice wine. The sacrifices usually grow in size as the wedding progresses: rat, chicken, pig and finally buffalo. If it's too graphic for you, forget it all in an instant as you join the celebrating families in consuming every last drop of rice wine in town.

HOT TOPIC OF THE DAY

- ❂ Land rights for the minorities. Basically they don't have any, as they have held their lands communally for centuries and many practise slash and burn agriculture. Now, some unscrupulous lowland Khmers are moving in and practising a slash and burn of their own, including destroying vast tracts of forest for plantations and wiping out any sort of legal documents when acquiring the land.

MOST BIZARRE SIGHT

- ❂ 'There's gold in them thar hills!' The goldmines of Mimong in central Mondulkiri are a flashback to the Yukon, as prospectors from all over Cambodia flock here to try their luck. DIY mine shafts, rickety carts on frayed ropes and shifting soils – this is not gold-panning for beginners.

– Nick Ray

BLUELIST // ONLINE

❂ THE ROAD LESS TRAVELLED

Motorbiking through Cambodia is a wonderful way for the adventurous to see the country. Wooden bridges, potholes, unpaved roads, gravel, rumble and even being ferried on fragile slim boats. But also pastoral landscapes, children on cows and lotus ponds.

// KLXR250

❂ IT'S NO YOLK (WINCE)

Vegetarian in Cambodia. If tempted by the Ferrero Rocher–style heaps of hard-boiled eggs on display, beware. My yolk had feathers. Hard-boiled chicks are a Khmer delicacy and try as one might, they resist even the toughest of toast soldiers.

// UNCLEMEAT

❂ SIEM REAP, CAMBODIA

The people of Cambodia are finding hope in a new life. Whether it's the túk-túk driver or the eight-year-old street vendor (who inevitably knows the capital city of your country), you won't have to look far to find that smile of hope!

// KEITH BAKER

CARTAGENA, COLOMBIA

POPULATION 1.1 MILLION ⊙ **VISITORS PER YEAR** 150,000 ⊙ **LANGUAGE** SPANISH ⊙ **UNIT OF CURRENCY** COLOMBIAN PESO (CP)

⊙ **COST INDEX** CUP OF COFFEE, 2000CP (US$0.80); DORM BED PER NIGHT, 6600CP (US$3); ONE-HOUR TOUR IN A HORSE-DRAWN CARRIAGE,
33,000CP (US$15); INTERNET ACCESS, 2000CP (US$0.80)

AFTER THE STORM

It was really only a matter of time. After years of languishing in tourism purgatory thanks to Colombia's civil war and failing security, the gorgeous city of Cartagena is quickly resuming its place as a top South American cultural attraction. Visitor numbers increased by 40% in 2005, filling up hotels, beaches and the cobbled, bougainvillea-shrouded streets. The fact that Cartagena was selected to host the general assembly of the World Tourism Organization (UNWTO) in December 2007 is yet another signal that the city is on the brink of a boom-era.

While plenty of travellers make their way overland to Cartagena, the biggest injection of tourists for 2007 is likely to come from cruise ships. Major ocean liners, such as Royal Caribbean and Celebrity Cruises, which had previously discontinued service to Cartagena due to instability across the country, are returning to the walled city.

But why all the fuss? To state it simply, Cartagena is the continent's most romantic city, filled with the scent of flowers, impossibly beautiful women and picturesque colonial architecture. The ancient, cannonball-battered walls and fortresses have withstood the test of time, and the beaches and islands around the city are a beachcomber's paradise. Most importantly, Cartagena's hot, Caribbean culture still thrives; the best time to see the city in action is during the celebrations surrounding the November beauty contest.

Getting there sooner rather than later means you can still enjoy Cartagena before the tourist bonanza hits its stride.

HOT TOPIC ⊙ OF THE DAY

In Cartagena, vanity ain't no sin. The Miss Colombia contest in November is a widely celebrated event and national holiday. It is completely funded by taxpayer dollars, and schoolchildren are given a two-week holiday when the event arrives. Only one Colombian woman has gone on to win the Miss Universe title, Luz Marina Zuluaga in 1958. She was awarded with a mansion and tax exemption for life.

DEFINING EXPERIENCE

⊙ Falling in love at least a dozen times as you walk through the old city streets, a flower in your hair, an emerald dealer whispering an offer into your ear and a moneychanger trying to rip you off.

FESTIVALS & EVENTS

⊙ Bullfighting season gets underway with the Feria Taurina in January.

⊙ Fiesta de Nuestra Señora de la Candelaria on 2 February honours Cartagena's patron saint. Watch the candle-lit procession at the Convento de la Popa. Celebrations start in late January.

⊙ In March 2007, Festival Internacional de Cine is a film festival with an emphasis on Latin American films and Colombian TV.

⊙ In November, Colombia's national beauty contest, Reinado Nacional de Belleza, is held annually in a very appropriate city. Miss Colombia is elected on

BE A PART OF THE BEAUTY ON DISPLAY
DURING THE MISS COLOMBIA FESTIVAL.

11 November. The festival includes street dancing, music and parades, and is easily Cartagena's biggest festival.

WHAT'S HOT
- The temperature. The average daily high temperature throughout the year is 32°C with humidity usually over 90%. The coolest months are December and January but air-con in your hotel room is a must at any time.

WHAT'S NOT
- Bombings, kidnappings, shoot-ups and other nasty stuff. Since 2002, President Álvaro Uribe has stepped up Colombia's military offensive against left-wing guerrillas and secured many previously dangerous roads and regions. Security in and around Cartagena is better than it has been in years.

RANDOM FACTS
- Cartagena was named after the port of Cartagena in Spain's Muricia region. To differentiate the two, the Colombian version was called Cartagena de Indias (Cartagena of the Indies).
- The Spanish-born monk Pedro Claver, who lived in Cartagena in the early 1600s, was the first person to be canonised in the New World (in 1888).
- Cartagena's old city became a Unesco World Heritage site in 1984.

CLASSIC RESTAURANT EXPERIENCE
- Cartagena is a tourist town, and as such you might as well go with the flow and enjoy its best tourist dining experience. Grab a seat in the Plaza de Santo Domingo at any time of day and enjoy a cool drink. Watch as Cartagena's shady characters and impeccably dressed women promenade past, and have your camera ready for the occasional street dance troupe busking across the plaza. A filling chicken, fish or steak dinner will cost around US$7.

CLASSIC PLACE TO STAY
- Mind feeling like royalty for a few nights? The Hotel Sofitel Santa Clara epitomises luxury and is a must for anyone seeking five-star service and old-world charm. This grand edifice, blending seamlessly into the old city, shows little of its bland history – it used to be the Convento de Santa Clara, dating from 1621, and later served as a hospital. It has since been transformed into a glorious spectacle, written about most famously in *Of Love and Other Demons,* by Gabriel García Márquez, who owned the house across the street. For the ultimate private party, you can rent out the disused chapel.

– *Michael Kohn*

✪ GO LIST.

CORNWALL, ENGLAND

POPULATION 517,000 ✪ **VISITORS PER YEAR** 5.1 MILLION ✪ **CAPITAL** TRURO ✪ **LANGUAGES** ENGLISH, CORNISH

✪ **UNIT OF CURRENCY** UK POUND (UK£) ✪ **COST INDEX** PINT OF BEER, UK£2.50 (US$4.50); SHORT TAXI RIDE,

UK£8 (US$14.70); INTERNET ACCESS, UK£2 (US$3.70)

MYTH HUNTING & MYTH MAKING

While its spectacular coastline, quaint fishing villages and the granite tors of Bodmin Moor account for much of Cornwall's allure, there's no doubting the enduring attraction of its mythological connections. King Arthur, the semihistorical poster-boy of Celtic resistance, is thought to have pegged his tent in this area. From his 'castle' at Tintagel on the county's west coast, to Dozmary Pool (where Bedivere apparently threw Excalibur), Cornwall is saturated with Arthurian 'history' – and locals keen to profit from it.

Don't make the mistake of thinking Cornwall's best days are lost in the mists of time. Today, it offers an array of attractions for local and international visitors: the Eden Project; Tate St Ives; the Lost Gardens of Heligan; Jamie Oliver's Fifteen Cornwall; vibrant festivals; plus the highest concentration of organic and traditional food producers in the UK – something Brits are particularly keen to enjoy these days.

RECENT FAD ✪

Puffin-spotting. Sadly, these characterful creatures are extremely rare in this part of the country, long renowned as a haven for seabirds. Those equipped with binoculars can still spot them nesting in the cliffs near Padstow or Boscastle, while other birds, including kittiwakes, razorbills and guillemots are more plentiful.

SAVOURING THE CORNISH PASTY

Cornwall is one of those oddities that the British seem to specialise in. Officially the poorest county in the UK, it's a place of arresting beauty blessed with cultural and historical riches immodest even by British standards. The 'Duchy' (as some call it) first entered the historical record as the centre of tin mining, an industry that remained of primary importance until the 20th century. In Roman times, Cornwall was Celtic, and many, including Mebyon Kernow (or the 'Sons of Cornwall', the major political party of Cornish home rule) insist that it still is. It is recognised by the Celtic League as one of Europe's six Celtic nations, and moves to revive the practically defunct Cornish language have been made.

Cornwall is also associated with the natural splendours of coastal reserves such as Pentire and West Penwith, smuggling, pasties, a unique local culture and celebrity restaurateur Rick Stein. The region has become a favourite holiday destination for the natives – always a good indication of a place worth going!

DEFINING EXPERIENCE

✪ Getting cut off by the tide at St Michael's Mount. This otherworldly island is one of Cornwall's compulsory attractions. Linked to the mainland by a causeway that disappears at high tide, it's an impossibly picturesque jumble of stone buildings and cobbled streets capped by a Benedictine priory and a castle inhabited by the same family for more than 300 years.

MEGALITHS AND MYTHOLOGY FIND
FERTILE GROUND IN CORNWALL.

FESTIVALS & EVENTS

- Golowan Festival is an ancient Cornish celebration revived recently in Penzance, where it marks the arrival of midsummer. The 10-day celebration, named from the Cornish for 'Feast of John', culminates in Mazey Day, when festivities take over the centre of this charming town.

- Held annually over the August Bank Holiday weekend, the Cornwall Folk Festival is a laid-back showcase of local and international folk talent that's been going since the early 1970s.

- St Ives September Festival, known until 2004 as the St Ives Fringe Festival, is a celebration of music and performance that occupies the Cornish capital of polygamy each year in, you guessed it, September.

RANDOM FACTS

- Paw prints, mauled livestock and the discovery of a large feline skull have all fuelled speculation over the existence of the 'Beast of Bodmin Moor', reported in most sightings to resemble a great cat.

- Such is the omnivorous reputation of Cornwall's pasty-makers that legend has it the devil feared to cross the River Tamar in case he ended up in one.

- Cornwall's holy wells were probably pagan wishing-wells rededicated to saints when Christianity was firming up its hold on the populace.

MOST BIZARRE SIGHT

- Helston Furry Dance. Held annually in Helston on 8 May (except when this falls on a Sunday or Monday), the Furry Dance is a ritual with origins receding into prehistory. In its modern incarnation, male and female dancers don top hats, tails and elaborate dresses, and dance in and out of greenery-strewn houses, chasing out the spirits of darkness and ushering in the spring.

– *Tasmin Waby*

BLUELIST // ONLINE

● 'UMBLE CRISPS
Nowhere else is the simple spud treated with such reverence than in the UK. Beef and horseradish, cheese and chutney, lamb and rosemary… If Camilla came in a flavour, she'd be sprinkled on them too.

// MAGGIEMC

● TALK ABOUT THE WEATHER
If you really must speak to the natives, this is a safe bet. Please note however that the weather is always wrong, too hot, too cold, too wet, too dry etc. A bit of mutual misery is the best way to bond with the average Brit.

// MOKOB204

● ON THE PLANE TO THE UK
Fifteen minutes into flight mother zips child's penis up in zipper. Kid screams so high dogs in hold have hearing loss. So does everyone else. Never knew children could scream and breath at same time. Child will become famous falsetto later in life.

// SEIJAKU

⭐ GO LIST.

DANUBE DELTA, ROMANIA

POPULATION 300 BIRD SPECIES, 150 FISH SPECIES ✪ **AREA OF WETLAND** 4187 SQ KM (3446 SQ KM OF WHICH ARE IN ROMANIA) ✪ **GATEWAY CITY** TULCEA

✪ **LANGUAGE** ROMANIAN ✪ **UNIT OF CURRENCY** ROMANIAN LEU, BUT PRICES QUOTED IN EURO (€) ✪ **COST INDEX** CUP OF COFFEE, €0.60 (US$0.75);

FULL-DAY ROWBOAT TOUR WITH A LOCAL FISHERMAN, €51 (US$64)

SECOND-CLASS CITIZENS

Humans take note; water, fish and birds call the shots in the Danube Delta. If a megalomaniac like Nicolae Ceauşescu couldn't tame it, neither can you. However, being subservient to nature is rarely more marvellous than in this boisterous rampage of marine life, where almost 30 different ecosystems have been counted. This is Europe's second-largest delta and its youngest and least-stable land. After surging through 10 countries, the Danube discharges an average of 6300 cubic metres of water per second into the Black Sea, making the delta region a constantly evolving landscape.

> **HOT TOPIC ✪ OF THE DAY**
>
> The burgeoning tourism industry: how to maximise it, while minimising ecoimpact.

Tourism in the delta region is still comparatively minor, as it's over-shadowed by the wonders in nearby Transylvania. But, with Romania's anticipated 2007 EU entry, breathless development has ensued. Hotels, tourism agencies and even restaurants all have private boats and packages for delta tours. Alternatively, three- and four-star boat hotels ('boatels') offer the option of trundling along the major arteries without retreating to terra firma at night. Yet the minor waterways are where true delta immersion occurs. Hitching a ride with fishermen or hiring a small boat to explore these areas is indisputably one of the area's greatest pleasures.

The Danube Delta is protected under the Danube Delta Biosphere Reserve Authority, set up after the 'ecological disaster' (read: Ceauşescu) that befell it during crackpot attempts to transform it into an agricultural region. Now there are 18 protected areas, making up 506 sq km (8.7% of the total area), including a 500-year-old forest. The delta was added to Unesco's World Heritage list in 1991.

FOLLOW THAT FOWL!

Stewing halfway between the North Pole and the equator, the Danube Delta is a convenient migration hub on the itinerary of thousands of birds travelling to and from Mongolia, Siberia, India, Africa and China. From mid-April to mid-May and in late October, half the world's population of red-breasted geese pile in. Long-tailed ducks, whooper swans, black-throated divers and clouds of white storks are equally abundant at these times. Europe's largest white pelican and Dalmatian pelican colonies are also here, along with 60% of the world's population of pygmy cormorants, and protected species such as the roller, white-tailed eagle, great white egret, mute swan, falcon and bee-eater.

Protected zones shield the largest bird colonies. Large green signs in most villages show visitors where these zones are and what birds can be found there. While there are 65 observation towers dotted throughout the delta, bird-watchers usually congregate around Lake Furtuna, Murighiol, the brackish areas around Lake Razim and Lake Babadag, and Histria.

STRAP ON YOUR SEA LEGS FOR A JOURNEY BETWEEN THE BLUE WATER AND THE BLUE SKIES OF THE DANUBE DELTA.

DEFINING EXPERIENCE

- Creeping through delta backwaters in a rowboat, fishing lines out, while thousands of pelicans go about snatching up your prey.

RECENT FAD

- Luxury resorts. Investors are targetting people who like their nature plush and comfortable. Existing resorts are joining in; but, in their glee to match competitors' steep prices, some have forgotten to include the 'luxury' part.

FESTIVALS & EVENTS

- Each August, Sfântu Gheorghe hosts what is probably the world's most remote film festival. Check www.delta-resort.ro for info.
- Also in August, Tulcea hosts the annual International Folk Festival of Danubian Countries, with local songs, games and activities.
- In December, Tulcea is the site of a winter carnival where you can drift between delta wintertime customs with a cup of hot mulled wine.

RANDOM FACTS

- The Lipovan people (13% of the region's population) are descendants of the Old Believers who left Russia in 1772 to avoid religious persecution. Following their faith, they're perhaps Romania's only group of non-smokers.
- The delta's ever-changing topography is shown by the Sfântu Gheorghe lighthouse. Built by the sea in 1865, it now stands 3km from open waters.

MOST BIZARRE SIGHT

- The gigantic metal aeolian windmill standing north of Sfântu Gheorghe's beach. This monstrosity, a classic Ceauşescu blunder, worked for all of two months before breaking down. Whether it's the largest metal aeolian windmill on the planet isn't clear, but it's almost certainly the world's largest *rusting* metal aeolian windmill.

REGIONAL FLAVOURS

- A delta staple is *bors de peşte* (fish and vegetable soup). Although locals dip into the Danube's polluted waters to make tea and soup, you cannot drink it 'raw'. That said, fresh fish in restaurants is fine, but visitors to private homes may suffer upset stomachs after eating fish that hasn't been cooked enough.
- Sfântu Gheorghe is one of the best villages to taste traditional cooking; but the black caviar for which the village is famed is a delicacy reserved for religious feasts.

THINGS TO TAKE

- Binoculars, mosquito repellent, 'wet' and 'dry' shoes, and an antidiarrhoeal agent.

HOT TIP

- Entrepreneurs take note; the 'boatel' industry was going through a lull at the time of writing, with no-one standing ready to fill the void.

– Leif Pettersen

★ GO LIST.

FINLAND

POPULATION 5.2 MILLION ✪ **VISITORS PER YEAR** 5 MILLION ✪ **CAPITAL** HELSINKI ✪ **NUMBER OF REINDEER** 230, 000

✪ **LANGUAGES** FINNISH, SWEDISH, SÁMI ✪ **UNIT OF CURRENCY** EURO (€) ✪ **COST INDEX** HALF-LITRE OF BEER IN A BAR, €5 (US$6.40); HOTEL DOUBLE/DORM PER NIGHT, €95/15 (US$121/19); SHORT TAXI RIDE, €10 (US$12.70); INTERNET ACCESS PER HOUR, FREE-€3 (US$3.80); SAUNA, FREE-€10 (US$12.70)

'JUST LAKES & PINE FORESTS'

What was once an insult now sounds like a compliment, as ever-more people search out some of Europe's most remote wildernesses for the outdoor activity, or postsauna inactivity, that they offer. Not that it's true anyway; anyone half-interested in design or music trends has an eye on Helsinki these days, and the country is increasingly an IT powerhouse. For years, the USSR next door was a powerful incentive for invisibility, and blonder, more confident Sweden hogged the social democratic headlines. Now, however, more people are appreciating what this complex and idiosyncratic country has to offer.

THE MYTH OF THE TWENTY-BUCK BEER

The euro has led to a price rise in places like once-cheap Spain and Italy, but a sigh of relief has been heard from Helsinki. For years, Finland lived with the stigma of being expensive. Travellers' tales were exaggerated, Chinese-whispers style, until spectres of backbreaking beer bills and bankbreaking hotel room rates seemed to loom over Europe's northeast. This was never really the case; but now Finland is fairly affordable by western European standards, and, happily, accommodation prices almost halve in summer.

25 DEGREES... ABOVE OR BELOW?

And what a summer it is. Who'd have thought it, being so far north? It's a golden, sunny season when Finland bursts into life with an explosion of festivals, good cheer and optimism. It's a time when the towns are buzzing, but it's also a time to head forestwards to absorb beautiful lakescapes from the deck of a wooden cottage.

> ### MOST BIZARRE SIGHT ★
>
> Ice-fishing. It's 20°C or more below zero, and the Finns are perfectly content to sit by a hole in the ice for hours with only a bottle of vodka for company...

But it's not all midnight sun. While winter tourism in Finland was once just a visit to Santa's tacky grotto, it's now an exciting time to visit the country. You won't get much sun, or even any daylight in parts, but this is the time to go sleighing across the awe-inspiring Lapland wilderness, pulled by a team of huskies or reindeer. Then there's snowmobiling, skiing, ice-fishing, and the chance to see the humblingly magnificent northern lights.

DEFINING EXPERIENCE

✪ Swishing through Lapland on a sleigh pulled by your own team of huskies. The destination? A rural wooden cabin where you'll barbecue reindeer sausages before sweating in the sauna and rolling naked in the snow under the glory of the northern lights.

RECENT FAD

✪ Finns are proud to have invented the burgeoning sport of Nordic

BREAK THE ICE IN FINLAND WITH FANTASTIC FISHING TALES.

walking, which essentially involves strolling around with a pair of ski sticks for a more complete exercise experience. More challenging is the skating version, Nordic blading, where some impressively high speeds can be attained.

FESTIVALS & EVENTS

- After triumphing in 2006, Finland will stage the Eurovision Song Contest Final in Helsinki on 12 May 2007.
- In a country of bizarre festivals, it's hard to beat the Wife-Carrying World Championships, in Sonkajärvi, in June 2007.
- Held in July 2007, the Savonlinna Opera Festival is perhaps Finland's premier festival, with opera in a stunning castle setting.
- The World Masters Orienteering Championships take place in Kuusamo, from 7 to 14 July 2007.
- Oulu hosts the Air Guitar World Championships in September 2007. Unmissable.

LIFE-CHANGING EXPERIENCES

- Hiking one of the country's awesome trekking routes, and coming face to face with an elk.
- Picking yourself a feast of delicious Arctic cloudberries in early summer.
- Spending a few days in a lakeside cottage, with a proper wood-fired sauna.
- Singing a sleighing song as a team of reindeer or huskies pull you across Lapland.
- Learning about the Sámi reindeer herders of Finland's far north.
- Grabbing a canoe, and heading out to spot a rare freshwater seal.
- Taking a snowmobile safari through the pine and birch forests.

HOT TOPIC OF THE DAY

- Russia. While Finnish companies are taking advantage of traditionally close ties with the Bear, many Finns are worried about an increase in

organised crime, masterminded by Russians.

RANDOM FACTS

- Finns drink more than 10kg of coffee each a year, more than double the Italian rate of consumption.
- A traditional part of the sauna is lightly beating yourself with a spray of birch twigs, which cleanses the skin and aids circulation.
- Finland's elk population is more than 100,000. They constitute a serious traffic hazard.
- Only 4% of Finns attend church regularly, one of the lowest rates in Christendom.
- In Nuorgam, in the far north, there are 72 consecutive days of uninterrupted daylight in summer.

– Andy Symington

GABON

POPULATION 1.4 MILLIO N ★ **CAPITAL** LIBREVILLE ★ **LANGUAGES** FRENCH (OFFICIAL), FANG, BAPUNU, GESHIRA, BANJABI &

OTHER LOCAL LANGUAGES ★ **UNIT OF CURRENCY** CENTRAL AFRICAN FRANC (CFA) ★ **COST INDEX** LOCAL STREET FOOD, 1540CFA (US$3);

BUDGET SINGLE ROOM, 6150CFA (US$12); INTERNET ACCESS PER HOUR, 1025CFA (US$2)

GETTING LOST IN GABON

Tucked away in a scantly travelled part of Africa is Gabon, a country rich in oil, animals and, now, national parks. The country's history is deeply entrenched in oil, so the decision to turn 10% of its land into national parks shocked even the most hardened cynics. However, don't be completely suckered by the spiel: the economy is still fuelled by trade in oil and timber, which had made Gabon one of the wealthiest nations in Africa. It's also one of the most stable, and President El Hadj Omar Bongo has governed for more than 40 years.

REWARDS APLENTY FOR TRAVELLERS

The lure of the jungle is omnipresent in Gabon; the country hides thousands of species of animals in its dense, tropical foliage. In fact where else in the world can you gaze at western lowland gorillas sunbaking on white-sand beaches, swim with turtles, dolphins or whales or watch hippos frolicking in the surf?

Gabon is a wildlife-watcher's dream, so head to one of the 13 national parks to get your fill. But it also offers amazing laid-back experiences in the coastal towns and villages. You'll be welcomed with open arms, as long as one of those arms is holding an icy-cold drink and you have a smile on your dial. The Gabonese are a friendly lot, fond of a beer and a chat with anyone. And they'll be more than willing to show you first-hand all the delights Gabon has to offer.

Gabon is a country that rewards your patience. The longer you can stay and explore, the less likely you'll want to leave.

FESTIVALS & EVENTS ★

In every village and town in Gabon, 17 August is celebrated with great fervour and joy, the date commemorating Gabon's declaration of independence from France in 1960. Head out into the country to witness the best partying with your own eyes.

DEFINING EXPERIENCE

★ Wandering dense jungle paths to the sounds of hundreds of monkeys canoodling, while you can just hear the distant sound of the surf pounding the shore. Gabon's 13 national parks provide the ultimate opportunity for wildlife-watching, and Loango National Park (or as *National Geographic*'s Mike Fay calls it, 'Africa's last Eden') is the place to be. The park covers 1550km of beach, savanna, forest and mangroves and is home to vast amounts of fauna. The bright lights of home will seem like they are on another planet when you are ensconced in the beauty of the park and its inhabitants.

LIFE-CHANGING EXPERIENCES

★ Attending mass in Gustav Eiffel's 1885 cast-iron church smack-bang in the middle of the jungle in the small town of St Anne.

★ Cruising in a houseboat on the blood-red Mpvie River with

LOVED SWIMMING WITH DOLPHINS? DON'T TRY SURFING WITH HIPPOS IN GABON.

thousands of animals staring at you from the lush banks.

- Hiding behind some bushes while a herd of stoned elephants staggers and sways its way past.
- Kayaking along the coast from Point St Catherine, spotting turtles, dolphins and whales as you paddle.

RANDOM FACTS

- Gabon is home to what could be called the world's biggest white elephant, the Hotel InterContinental. It was built to accommodate wealthy foreign conference attendees in Libreville, but now stands empty aside from the occasional army regiment.
- Lambaréné in southern Gabon was the final home of Albert Schweitzer and houses his once-innovative hospital.
- Although Gabon is made up of more than 40 ethnic groups, it is the most stable country in the region.

REGIONAL FLAVOURS

- Late-night party people travelling in Gabon should seek out *kola* nuts or *iboga* to keep their fires burning. Both are renowned for giving you the get-up-and-go you need to dance all night. But, watch out with *iboga* as it's actually a mild hallucinogen used in adolescent initiation ceremonies. *Kola* nuts too, have their downside, as they taste terribly bitter (best washed down with a beer). Don't let the flavour stop you; sharing these nuts with someone is a sign of respect and friendship in Gabon.

– *Kate McLeod*

BLUELIST // ONLINE

HOW TO STAY ALIVE ON SAFARI

Predators can only see in mono so never wear black or white on safari. Always keep your tent zipped, unless you want to become takeout. Never look a leopard in the eye and don't run from a black mamba. Lions can swim and hippos aren't cuddly.

// GLOBALB

BEST PLACES TO BREAK THE SEAL – IN A FIELD FILLED WITH MONKEYS

Being the only woman out of seven passengers and a chauffeur in West Africa, it may be difficult to get any of them to agree and stop for a bathroom break (not like there is any toilette around anyway)…

// MARIANNEQUIQUI

ELEPHANTS IN YOUR CAMP

I had just fallen asleep when I was awakened by the sound of an elephant eating the thatch off the roof of my cabin.

// CHELLYBELL

⭐GOLIST.

ILHA DE SANTA CATARINA, BRAZIL

POPULATION 370,000 ✪ **LANGUAGE** PORTUGESE ✪ **MAJOR INDUSTRIES** TOURISM, FISHING ✪ **UNIT OF CURRENCY** REAL (R$)

✪ **COST INDEX** MIDRANGE HOTEL DOUBLE PER NIGHT, R$100-150 (US$45-68); GLASS OF BEER, R$2 (US$.91)

BRAZIL, BUT BETTER

Many of us dream of escaping to Rio de Janeiro, but what destination tops the get-away lists of Rio natives themselves? Ask around the sands of Ipanema, and most people will mention Ilha de Santa Catarina, an island that sits just off Brazil's southern Atlantic coast.

REGIONAL FLAVOURS ⭐

It's no surprise that seafood rules menus on Santa Catarina. Cultivated beds yield Brazil's very best oysters, while the open seas offer up wonderful shrimp and *tainha*, or grey mullet. The latter is prized for its delightful white flesh, which manages to be both rich and light, mild and distinctly flavoured. In May and June, many beaches are closed to surfers so fishermen can do their work unencumbered.

When Brazilians speak of Ilha de Santa Catarina they do so with an air of wistfulness, as if the few hundred metres that separate the island from the mainland also insulate it from all that ails their country – the drugs, *favelas* (slums or shantytowns) and violent crime. And yet Brazilians need sacrifice very little for their peace of mind, because in not much more than 400 sq km, Ilha de Santa Catarina packs in nearly all that is good about Brazil.

Indeed, the island is a fine recapitulation of the entire country, with a few bonuses thrown in. Famously picky about their beaches, Brazilians reserve high praise for many of the island's 42 beaches, which range from cliff-hugging prayer rugs to long arcs of sand. A spine of mountains, luxuriant with the flora and fauna of the Mata Atlántica (Atlantic rainforest), runs the length of the island. Near the island's centre, the peaks drop precipitously to the stunning, saltwater Lagoa da Conceição – a Swiss lake transported to warmer climes. Just to the north of the lagoon begins a forest of rare, protected pines, while to the east sand dunes, some of them hundreds of metres high, create an almost lunar landscape. And on the western shores, whitewashed fishing villages seem to have been imported wholesale from the Azores Islands.

GO NOW OR FOREVER HOLD YOUR PEACE

With its shallow bays, the northern half of the island features Brazil's southernmost beaches that manage to be both tropical and family-friendly, hence the poured-concrete hotels and large summer crowds from Argentina and Paraguay (think South Florida with a hilly backdrop). Lagoa da Conceição, the island's navel, also grows crowded with motorboats and holidaymakers. Both spots are more than pleasant, but they may not be the kinds of places you'd travel great distances to see.

But the wilder southern half of the island is another story. Even in the height of summer, fishermen seem to outnumber travellers, and there are still beaches that, at the price of a vigorous hike, you can have entirely to yourself. With narrower roads, higher peaks, and more challenging surf, this area has been largely overlooked by developers.

But things are bound to change, as there are plans to build a new road

YOU'LL NEED A BOAT, BUT FINDING YOUR OWN PRIVATE BEACH IS SURELY WORTH IT.

linking the southern half of the island with Florianópolis (the provincial capital, on the island's eastern shore) and its airport; developers are salivating at the prospect. To enjoy the still largely unspoiled pleasures of southern Ilha de Santa Catarina, the time to go is now.

So what is there to see? The long, curving Praia da Armação is a surfer's delight. From the beach's southern end, catch a boat to Ilha do Campeche, an ecological reserve offering a paradisiacal beach, good snorkelling and a short, cross-island hike to see Stone Age etchings. Further south, the village of Pântano do Sul, still mainly inhabited by fishermen of Azorean descent, looks onto a half-moon beach ringed by mountains. Most extraordinary, though, are hikes to the stunning beaches that can be reached only by foot, including Lagoinha do Leste, Saquinho and, at the very tip of the island, Naufragados. Even after the new road is built, these beaches will remain only for the determined, if not the intrepid.

DEFINING EXPERIENCE

✪ After a morning of snorkelling in the turquoise waters around Ilha do Campeche, return to the mainland for a challenging afternoon hike to the remote beach at Lagoinha do Leste with its own, private waterfall. Finally, head to the village of Pântano do Sul to feast on a freshly caught *tainha* – a celebrated local fish that is encrusted in salt and grilled until golden brown.

FESTIVALS & EVENTS

✪ It may not be as lavish as celebrations in Rio or Bahía, but Carnaval on Ilha de Santa Catarina is still a raucous, nonstop, four-day party. In Florianópolis there are Rio-style spectacles in the city's *sambodromo* (parade grounds). In addition, streets are closed to traffic and each neighbourhood holds its own, more informal block parties. Festivities often spread out to the island's beaches as well.
– *Robert Landon*

BLUELIST // ONLINE

✪ INTESTINAL, HUM, DAMAGE?

Feijoada, vatapá, caruru, bobó, churrasco, red pepper, *acarajé, moqueca,* fried shrimps on the beach, *coalho* cheese, 'veggie' snacks. Too much for you to handle? Most tourists don't think so, at least not at the time, but later in the toilet.
// FILLIP_BARINI

✪ SOUTHERN LOVE

Blondes in ballooned pants eat chicken hearts from a spit near violet wine valleys. In between chews, they gush over Ocktoberfest, in Portuguese. Welcome to Brazil. The south, often overlooked by the tourist, is full of beauty and surreal mystery.
// JENSSPELKOMAN

✪ SURVIVING PANTANAL

Many don'ts here: don't drink rum 'til midnight then go looking for anacondas; don't get your period then wash your messed-up shorts in alligator-infested swamps; and DON'T put your head in a gator's mouth just because your guide says it's asleep.
// TEZZACOOPS

★GOLIST.

NORTHEAST INDIA

POPULATION 37.5 MILLION ✪ **CAPITALS** ITANAGAR (ARUNACHAL PRADESH), DISPUR (ASSAM), IMPHAL (MANIPUR), SHILLONG (MEGHALAYA),

AIZAWL (MIZORAM), KOHIMA (NAGALAND), AGARTALA (TRIPURA) ✪ **LANGUAGES** HINDI, ENGLISH, BENGALI, ASSAMESE, KHASI, MANIPURI, MIZO, KOKBOROK

✪ **UNIT OF CURRENCY** INDIAN RUPEE (RS) ✪ **COST INDEX** BUDGET HOTEL PER NIGHT, RS 200 (US$4.30); ROADSIDE SNACK, RS 5 (US$0.10)

WHEN INDIANS THINK 'EXOTIC'...

It may not have the sizzle of Rajasthan or the cool factor of the Himalaya, but India's most far-flung corner is popping up on more and more southern Asian itineraries. The last and remotest part of India to be assimilated into the country, the northeast speaks different languages, eats different food, dresses in different clothes and sports a significantly different attitude from the rest of the nation. A visit to this region means exposure to a veritable cultural smorgasbord, including tribal and Buddhist traditions that are hard to find in the west of the country.

REGIONAL FLAVOURS ✪

Food in the northeast is quite different from the Indian food you might be familiar with. The Khasi people have their own distinctive cuisine, using lots of meat and delicate spices, while the Naga hill tribes offer such delicacies as curried dog meat and insect grubs.

JUST FOR YOU

Because travel to the region is still relatively difficult (foreigners need a permit to go anywhere outside Assam and Meghalaya), there's still a trailblazing feel to exploring the northeast. Incredible sights like Guwahati's Kamakhya Mandir temple (where Shiva's wife's genitalia supposedly fell to earth), the rhinos of Kaziranga National Park and the mighty waterfalls of Cherrapunjee still feel pristine and untainted by globalisation and commercialism. It's easy to travel for weeks in the northeast and not meet another foreigner.

CAVEAT VOYAGER

The seven states that make up the northeast are a world apart from 'mainstream' India, although migrants from the rest of the country as well as immigrants from neighbouring Bangladesh are gradually diluting – or adding to (depends on who you ask) – the region's unique cultural tapestry. This situation makes for an interesting, and often unstable, political climate. Be sure to check with authorities and trustworthy sources before planning any independent trips.

DEFINING EXPERIENCE

✪ Spotting a one-horned rhino, sharing snacks with langur monkeys at a Shiva temple, and chatting up a local chieftain for permission to visit his village – all while getting rained on nonstop.

FESTIVALS & EVENTS

✪ Held in January, the Brahmaputra Beach Festival sees Guwahati burst at the seams with an array of elephant races and adventure sports.

✪ March in Mizoram sees Chapchar Kut, when tribal dances and other celebrations are held for the end of the annual forest clearance.

✪ During Ashokastami Mela (early April), Shaivite pilgrims bathe in a sacred stream among the ancient sculptures at Unakoti, Tripura.

BIG SPEARS AND BRIGHT SHAWLS ARE THE HALLMARKS OF THE ANGAMI PEOPLE OF NAGALAND.

- Shad Sukmynsiem, also held in April, is the Khasi Thanksgiving festival; it's celebrated with three days of dancing in traditional costume.

- Buddhist dances are on display during Buddha Mahotsav, held in October in Tawang Gompa, Arunachal Pradesh.

- Nagaland's biggest annual event is the Hornbill Festival. During December dance troupes from all the main tribes perform in the Kohima marketplace and Naga food and handicrafts are on sale.

HOT TOPIC OF THE DAY

- In the northeast states, regional violence is a problem. Separatist factions abound, often warring against each other (for example, in diminutive Tripura, literally dozens of factions fight for or against the establishment of an independent tribal state). Because of the area's unique past – it was never part of Mughal India or affiliated with the Hindu kingdoms to the west – assimilation into India has been troubled historically. Those issues last into the present, and the troubles affect travellers to varying degrees depending on the state and area.

RANDOM FACTS

- The Khasi people of Meghalaya are known for their matrilineal system of inheritance, in which all property and titles are passed down from mother to daughter through the generations.

- The Naga were once feared head-hunters. Today, Naga warriors wear pendants, known as *yanra*, that depict severed human heads. Don't mess with Naga men or women – both traditionally carry a machete-type weapon known as a *dao*.

- 'Meghalaya' means 'abode of the clouds' and 'Manipur' means 'jewelled land'.

- Mizoram is the only Indian state to be ruled by a tribal government.

- Meghalayans are obsessed with bows and arrows and routinely hold archery competitions.

MOST BIZARRE SIGHT

- In 1930 the maharaja of Tripura ordered a palace to be built in the middle of Rudrasagar Lake. Today, the Water Palace of Neermahal is waterlogged, too big for the tiny island it occupies, and slowly but surely falling into ruin. Take a wander through its halls and stately rooms before it's too late.

LOCAL LINGO

- Northeast India is awash with regional languages and dialects, and intertribal communication is generally rendered in the lingua franca of the state. Assamese is closely related to Hindi and Bengali, but the Khasi language of Meghalaya is more akin to Cambodian Khmer. Manipuri, Mizo and Kokborok are from the Tibeto-Burman language group.

– *Vivek Wagle*

★ GO LIST.

JORDAN

POPULATION 5.9 MILLION ○ **VISITORS PER YEAR** 1.6 MILLION ○ **CAPITAL** AMMAN ○ **LANGUAGES** ARABIC, ENGLISH ○ **MAJOR INDUSTRIES** TEXTILES, PHOSPHATE MINING, FERTILISERS ○ **UNIT OF CURRENCY** JORDANIAN DINAR (JD) ○ **COST INDEX** CUP OF TEA, JD0.40 ($US0.50); MIDRANGE MAIN MEAL, JD3-6 ($US4-8); MIDRANGE ACCOMMODATION PER NIGHT, JD18-70 ($US26-100); AMSTEL BEER, JD2.50 ($3.50); FALAFEL STREET SNACK, JD 0.25 (US$0.30)

JOINING SOME ILLUSTRIOUS COMPANY

Those seeking the quintessential Middle Eastern experience – the romance and adventure that is, not the war zones and squabbling – should make Jordan high on their list of priorities. This is the land where Jesus was baptised, Moses died on the doorstep to the Promised Land, the Prophet Mohammed traversed, Cleopatra indulged in a Dead Sea spa, the legend of TE Lawrence (of Arabia) was born and where Indiana Jones laid his hands upon the Holy Grail. Aside from merging fact into fiction, these figures evoke the mythical appeal of Jordan. It won't be long before Jordan is recognised by the masses as a classic Middle Eastern travel destination alongside Egypt and Israel.

FESTIVALS & EVENTS

The Jerash festival, with its backdrop of the flood-lit colonnaded streets, plazas and theatres of the city's ancient roman ruins, takes place in July and August. This two-week cultural and arts festival showcases performers from all over the world in events including music, opera, dance, plays and poetry.

SHOCK TO THE SYSTEM

Jordan is still the safest country in the region, though this position is held tenuously after the terrorist bombings in Amman in November 2005. The incident left the peaceful nation devastated and deeply shocked, and outraged residents took to the streets in their hundreds of thousands in protest. Travellers should not be deterred from heading to Jordan because of safety concerns (unless you're worried about how to cross the busy streets in downtown Amman), but the volatile political climate in neighbouring Iraq, Israel and Syria means that caution should be exercised in border regions.

OLD WORLD MEETS NEW

As Jordan moves through the 21st century, nowhere in the world will you witness a more fascinating juxtaposition of ancient and modern cultures.

The total picture comes together while paragliding over the desert scenery where Lawrence of Arabia made a name for himself, enjoying a few stiff drinks in a bar set in the now 'classy' 2000-year-old Nabataean rock tomb, or cheering on chariot races and choreographed gladiator battles (starring ex-Jordanian Army Special Forces) in the 1500-year-old Roman hippodrome.

However, it's through the people of Jordan themselves that you can observe the clash between ancient and modern. The middle and upper classes have become increasingly westernised in their outlook, embracing mall-mania in Amman, mobile phones and Starbucks. These fashions stand in direct opposition to the country's traditional conservative culture and the seminomadic lifestyle of the Bedouin. But one thing shared by all Jordanians is their legendary hospitality, which you'll encounter wherever you go. For many this is the lasting impression of the country.

PACK A HAT AND A
WHIP AND PUT A LITTLE
INDIANA JONES INTO YOUR
EXPLORATION OF PETRA.

DEFINING EXPERIENCE

☼ Stepping out into daylight after walking through the narrow 1km-long Siq to reveal an awe-inspiring first glimpse of Petra's Treasury façade, carved into the rose-red rock. The 2000-year-old ancient Nabaetaen city of Petra is widely agreed upon as the country's must-see sight, and is legitimately deserved of the overused 'eighth wonder of the world' tag.

RANDOM FACTS

☼ Jordan has no significant oil resources of its own and relies heavily on oil imported from Iraq and Saudi Arabia.

☼ The current monarch, King Abdullah II, and his father the late King Hussein were both known to go undercover disguised as taxi drivers, and Abdullah even as a TV reporter, to gauge current opinions on the issues and problems facing ordinary citizens.

☼ Besides attracting tourists to its archaeological ruins, Jordan actively promotes itself as one of the world's hottest 'medical tourism' destinations, for those who travel for affordable high-standard medical treatment.

☼ Only 5% of Petra has been excavated.

☼ Jordanians are extremely hospitable, so much so that if you express excessive admiration for an item in their home they might give it to you!

☼ Jordan's deserts make up 80% of the country's land, yet support only 5% of its population.

– Trent Holden

BLUELIST // ONLINE

☼ BEDOUIN TEA PARTY

Trudging up the many stairs to the monastery is a necessity for any visitor to Petra, however the experience is not complete without tea amongst the Bedouin. They know Petra better than anyone else and might show you some of its most coveted secrets.

// JAMIEFOLEY

☼ PETRA ADVENTURE

Live like a Nabatean Arab. Grab a stallion and ride to the entrance of the Siq, then walk the long, narrow walled canyon that opens onto the huge rose-red Al-Khazneh, known as the Treasury and seen in the Indiana Jones movies.

// CTKING

☼ WADI RUM PICNIC

We left all places with names and went into the desert Wadi Rum, land of 'God Without Man'. Found some shade amongst vast panoramic rock structures popping out from Dali's paintings and had our picnic lunch, served with freshly brewed Arabian tea.

// LAIPUILIM

☆ GO LIST.

SOUTHERN LAOS

LANGUAGE LAO, PLUS SEVERAL MINORITY LANGUAGES ☼ **MAJOR INDUSTRY** AGRICULTURE, COFFEE, LOGGING

☼ **UNIT OF CURRENCY** LAO KIP ☼ **COST INDEX** CUP OF LAO COFFEE, 3000 KIP (US$0.30); 660ML BOTTLE OF BEER LAO, 6000 KIP (US$0.50);

GUESTHOUSE DOUBLE PER NIGHT, FROM US$4; 100CC MOTORBIKE HIRE PER DAY, US$10

IN THE JUNGLE

After years of being overlooked in favour of the mystical charms of Luang Prabang, the mountainous jungles, rivers and cool plateaus of southern Laos are fast becoming a must-see destination for any self-respecting backpacker heading into Indochina. And with the opening of a new border to central Vietnam in mid-2006, it's easier than ever to reach what was until recently about the most remote place in the region. Which is, of course, a mixed blessing. Fortunately, 'rising visitor numbers' is a relative term and 'mass tourism' is a phrase that's a fair way from being regularly used in the same sentence as 'southern Laos'. So you've still got time to really appreciate what the region is all about – getting off the beaten track – if you get here soon.

Fortunately the notoriously slow-moving Lao government has, with gentle encouragement from numerous foreign NGOs, begun to embrace tourism as a legitimate way of earning much-needed foreign cash (particularly handy when you consider that US dollars act as the de facto currency here). Even better, the authorities have embraced the idea that bona fide sustainable activities are the way to go. A good example is the Katang villagers in Dong Phu Vieng National Protected Area (NPA), who now welcome only as many travellers as their jungle village can handle without spoiling their traditional way of life and relationship with the forest spirits.

> ### DEFINING ☼ EXPERIENCE
>
> Sitting on the roof of a boat slowly descending the mighty Mekong, with locals and domestic animals gibbering away alongside, eating sticky rice and skewered crickets while drinking Mirinda laced with *lào-láo* (rice whisky) from a sandwich bag.

FOLLOW THE HO CHI MINH TRAIL

Apart from ecotourists, volunteers and backpackers seeking out herbal fruit shakes, southern Laos is attracting cultural tourists keen to see the fantastic Wat Phu Champasak, and a small but growing number of war tourists here to check out the Ho Chi Minh Trail. Included among the latter are aging Vietnamese who last 'toured' southern Laos on very long, very dangerous walking trips in the '60s and '70s. These days much of the trail has returned to the jungle, but almost all of the rugged tracks running from north to south within 100km of the Vietnam border were part of the trail at one point or another. Most of the war-junk – including countless unexploded bombs – has been recovered and scrapped, but a few rusting reminders are worth the trip. Highlights include the American tanks near Ban Dong and the menacing-looking Russian surface-to-air missile still on its launcher, nestled under a tree in deepest Attapeu Province.

FESTIVALS & EVENTS

☼ Bun Wat Phu Champasak, held in March at the Unesco World Heritage–listed Khmer temple site

UNESCO-LISTED *AND* PLENTY OF BREATHING SPACE? WAT PHU CHAMPASAK IS ALMOST TOO GOOD TO BE TRUE.

at Wat Phu overlooking the Mekong River in Champasak, is a Buddhist celebration embellished with secular delights such as elephant races, boat races, comedy acts, dancing in makeshift nightclubs and – no surprise here – copious consumption of Beerlao and *lào-láo* (rice whisky).

- Held around the first week of May, Bun Bang Fai is the appropriately named rocket festival, celebrated with particular gusto in the south, with a homemade combination of fireworks (bamboo rockets), firewater (the *lào-láo*) and unfeasibly large wooden phalli. It's all designed to bring on the rains, though we're not entirely sure where the phalli fit in.
- Bun Nam, a lively boat racing festival, follows directly after the Awk Phansa festival in late October; dates vary from town to town.

LIFE-CHANGING EXPERIENCES

- Spending the night in the jungle in your role as volunteer surveying wildlife in the region's national protected areas.
- Following Katang villagers through the jungle in Dong Phu Vieng NPA in search of mushrooms, roots, berries, frogs, insects and, if you're lucky, snakes to add to that night's dinner menu.
- Sucking down a 'happy shake' while swinging in a hammock as the sun sets over the countless islands of Si Phan Don – although this might be better described as mind-altering rather than life-changing.

REGIONAL FLAVOURS

- You can expect the unexpected on your dinner plate (or banana leaf) in southern Laos. Among the specialties are myriad insects and arachnids that come roasted or fried and are most commonly found when shoved in your face by overzealous saleswomen as you sit in the back of a *sǎwngthǎew* (a truck-cum-bus).

– *Andrew Burke*

✪GOLIST.

MADAGASCAR

POPULATION 18.6 MILLION ✪ **VISITORS PER YEAR** 200,000 ✪ **CAPITAL** ANTANANARIVO ✪ **LANGUAGES** MALAGASY, FRENCH

✪ **UNIT OF CURRENCY** MALAGASY ARIARY (MGA) ✪ **COST INDEX** A CUP OF COFFEE, MGA1600 (US$0.75);

MEAL AT A ROADHOUSE, MGA 27,700 (US$12.70); MIDRANGE HOTEL, MGA 47,100 (US$21.60)

THE EIGHTH CONTINENT

Madagascar is a stew of an entirely different flavour. Suspended between Africa and Asia, geographically isolated for 160 million years and influenced by traders, slavers, pirates and missionaries, it is unlike any other place on earth. Everyone knows about lemurs, but few know that no less than 80% of the island's plant and animal species are unique to the island, including a now-extinct pygmy hippopotamus whose ancestor crossed the 400km Mozambique Channel! Such is its natural diversity, Madagascar is known to ecologists as 'the eighth continent'. And the Malagasies are no less surprising: recent genetic studies suggest that the original inhabitants, a mixture of groups from Borneo and East Africa, arrived here as recently as 1500 years ago. Since then, Madagascar has attracted the colonial and mercantile attentions of Arabs, Portuguese, British and French, absorbing influences from each while forging an entirely distinct national identity. The result is a bouillabaisse of natural and cultural wonders guaranteed to rouse even the most jaded traveller.

RECENT FAD ✪

Razor theft in the crowded streets of Tana. Sadly, crime is on the up in the Malagasy capital, and lightning-quick slashing of bags is one of the preferred methods of relieving tourists of their cumbersome belongings. Don't be unduly alarmed, but do keep your wits about you.

THE MALAGASY MOSAIC

'Madagascar' is a relatively recent entity. Throughout its recorded history, the island, the largest in the Indian Ocean, has been divided between as many as 36 different tribal groups. Some of these, such as the Sakalava and their successors the Merina, managed to dominate their neighbours for a time, but it was not until the island became a French protectorate in 1885 that political unity was achieved. This isn't to suggest that Malagasies have enjoyed harmony ever since. More than 100,000 died trying to shake off French suzerainty after WWII, and the burning of the Rova palace in the capital Antananarivo (just call it 'Tana') in 1995 has been blamed on the *côtiers* (coastal tribes) resentful of the power enjoyed by the Merina. There's no need to be concerned however, Madagascar has been relatively peaceful since gaining full independence in 1960, and from the bungalows of Île Sainte Marie to the rainforest of Montagne d'Ambre, you'd be hard pressed to imagine it being anything but tranquil.

DEFINING EXPERIENCE

✪ The practice of *famadihana,* or turning over the dead, pretty much sums up this nation's uniqueness. The custom sees corpses of ancestors exhumed, wrapped in fresh shrouds and reburied, after family members fill their loved one in on the gossip of the last 12 months. It's indicative of the connection between life and death in indigenous Malagasy religion. And as befits Madagascar's creolised culture, a Catholic priest is sometimes invited to participate.

JOIN VERREAUX'S SIFAKA IN WIDE-
EYED WONDER AT THE STRANGE AND
DIVERSE WILDLIFE ON OFFER.

FESTIVALS & EVENTS

☼ *Hira gasy,* Madagascar's indigenous form of entertainment, dates from the late-18th-century rule of King Andrianampoinimerina. On many Sundays in Malagasy villages, performers, sometimes wearing approximations of French colonial dress, sing about social themes such as farming and marriage.

☼ Each Friday, much of Tana is taken over by the Zoma (Friday) market, a sprawling forest of stalls selling everything from exotic food to spare parts for the French cars that are the legacy of the colonial past.

RANDOM FACTS

☼ Queen Ranavalona, the 'Modern Messalina' who ruled from 1828 to 1861, is best remembered for exterminating most of her family and violently persecuting Christians and foreigners.

☼ During Ranavalona's reign, royal justice was often administered by *tanguin* ordeal: the accused was forced to eat an emetic poison, and his or her vomit was then examined to establish guilt.

☼ 90% of Malagasy vocabulary is shared with Maanyan, a language of southern Borneo, despite the fact that the Malagasies' ancestors left Borneo nearly two millennia ago.

☼ The Malagasy ariary is one of only two nondecimal currencies in the world – it is based on multiples of five.

MOST BIZARRE SIGHT

☼ Verreaux's sifaka, the dancing lemur of southwest Madagascar, is as unforgettable as it is rare. Although endangered, this tree-dwelling prosimian can be sighted in national parks such as Berenty and Isalo. In the open, you can't miss it. Adapted to life in the trees, this lemur is forced to hold its forearms aloft and 'dance' across the ground in a series of sashaying leaps. Swing those hips!

 BLUELIST // ONLINE

☼ LEMURS

The largest species of lemur, indri indri, wakes up at 10am and yells from the tree tops. In Berenty the ringtails are matriarchal. Don't feed the poor male or he'll be henpecked. Females appreciate a banana and will hold your hand politely in their delicate simian paw.

// HOLLYBRECON

☼ MAHAJANGA PROMENADE

The Malagasy teenagers sing and dance along the boulevard, completely oblivious to the majesty of their backdrop: the meat cooking on the grills of street vendors, the palm trees swaying in the breeze and the sun saying a final farewell.

// AMFOSKET

☼ MORE EXCELLENT DIVING

Go with the friendly South African diving operator, Richard, to his little paradise up the coast at Salary. Sand of white shells, corals everywhere and a shipwreck from the 20th century.

// JONASO

⭐ GO LIST.

MALUKU, INDONESIA

POPULATION 2 MILLION ✪ **CAPITALS** KOTA AMBON (MALUKU PROVINCE), KOTA TERNATE (NORTH MALUKU PROVINCE) ✪ **LANGUAGES** BAHASA INDONESIA

PLUS AROUND 130 LOCAL LANGUAGES AND DIALECTS ✪ **MAJOR INDUSTRIES** FISH, SPICES, TIMBER, OIL ✪ **UNIT OF CURRENCY** INDONESIAN RUPIAH (RP)

✪ **COST INDEX** CUP OF COFFEE, 2500RP (US$0.25); BEER, 25,000RP (US$2.70); INTERNET ACCESS PER HOUR, AROUND 10,000RP (US$1.10)

PEACE BREAKS OUT IN PARADISE

Today few places are as warm-heartedly welcoming as the utterly unspoilt islands of Maluku. Yet just seven years ago, they were gripped by an appalling wave of intercommunal fighting. This 'accident' (as the Christian-Muslim violence is euphemistically known) calmed down very rapidly once radical *agents provocateurs* departed. Until 2004 visiting the region required permits, and all the burnt-out buildings were hardly the kind of picture-postcard image most tourists would come for. Since then, however, reconstruction has been remarkably swift. And those war ruins that do remain have mostly been gobbled up by humidity and tropical weeds. The mood is suddenly remarkably optimistic.

TRULY UNDISCOVERED DESERT ISLANDS

Improved air links with Jakarta and Makassar make it possible (if a little rushed) to visit Maluku within the one-month allowed by Indonesian visas-on-arrival. So, with permit requirements now dropped, Maluku is open for business. No, it's not party central. Even the area's finest beach (Pasir Panjang) has only a couple of guesthouses hidden in waving palms at either end of the perfect flour-white sand that stretches 3km, and even these aren't usually full. But hurry to savour the starlight, mesmerising sea sounds and fabulous snorkelling before the rest of the world finds out.

DEFINING EXPERIENCE

✪ Snorkelling some of the world's finest and most easily accessible coral gardens backed by kilometres of picture-perfect white-sand beaches, over which palm trees bend for your photographic delectation.

✪ Savouring a dinner of superfresh fish with a unique nutmeg-fruit garnish and perhaps a cold beer (if you know where to look).

RECENT FAD

✪ Osama bin Laden T-shirts and Saddam Hussein portrait-graffiti. Just for fun.

FESTIVALS & EVENTS

✪ Most of Maluku's tourist-oriented events came to a halt with the troubles. In 2007 tourist authorities plan to kick-start several festivities but you should double-check before planning your itinerary.

✪ July's Darwin–Ambon sailing race is a classic that switched routes to Darwin–Bali then Darwin–Kupang during the fighting. Ambon authorities hope to reclaim the event in 2007, but this is yet to be confirmed.

HOT TOPIC OF THE DAY ✪

The 'hijacking' of *sasi* in the Kei Islands. Traditionally a *sasi* is a kind of spell to prevent trespass. Only a palm frond physically blocks your way, but superstitious locals would never dare to cross a *sasi* line. Recently some savvy Kei Islanders have turned this to their advantage. A *sasi* appeared on the only bridge between the main two islands, making a bonanza for boatmen; its ceremonial removal incurred a big fee. The idea caught on. The latest *sasi* protection racket was to block the access path to Tual's government offices! Whatever next?!

FORGET DELAYED BUSES AND JAM-PACKED METROS: BOARD THE BOAT FOR MALUKU.

The Belang Races are held in Dullah on the Kei Islands in October. Competition is between traditional *kora-kora* (war canoes) with multiple paddlers in colourful costumes. The event is tentatively scheduled to restart in 2007.

Sasi Lompa Festival takes place in Haruku village in November. It's a curious, widely renowned celebration of the end of the annual prohibition on catching flying fish.

Ramadan will run from 12 November to 9 December 2007, moon obliging. Beer will be harder to find than usual, and in much of North Maluku, getting lunch will become a somewhat cloak-and-dagger affair.

DO MENTION

Your understanding that most of the 1999–2002 violence was stirred up by outsiders for arcane political reasons.

DON'T MENTION

That you'd like to photograph remaining civil-war wreckage. Listening to people's stories is one thing but taking unflattering pictures might get you suspected as a troublemaker or a journalist (just as bad).

RANDOM FACTS

The Maluku Islands were the original Spice Islands. The whole of European colonialism started as a dash to get those spices for cheap.

In colonial times the Brits and Dutch agreed to swap a pair of islands. The British gave Pulau Run in the Banda group. In return they got a 'useless piece of swamp' in North America: Manhattan.

MOST BIZARRE SIGHT

Cengeh Afo on Ternate. It's touted by tourist brochures as the world's biggest clove tree. Hardly a great attraction you might think, but worse, the tree actually fell down many years ago. Saucily, there's now a new and much smaller clove tree marked Cengeh Afo on the path to the (almost disintegrated) original. Don't waste your time!

REGIONAL FLAVOURS

Kenari nuts taste like creamy almonds and make uniquely delicious cookies.

Nutmeg is not just a spice. The fruit's outer flesh is sun-dried as a snack or cooked to make a delicious accompaniment for fish meals.

Cassava is a local staple in the Kei Islands but rarely appears in restaurants.

– Mark Elliott

★ GO LIST.

LA MOSQUITIA, HONDURAS

POPULATION 67,000, PLUS 500 MILLION MOSQUITOES ◌ **CAPITAL** PUERTO LEMPIRA (GRACIAS A DIOS DEPARTMENT) ◌ **GATEWAY CITY** PALACIOS

◌ **LANGUAGES** SPANISH, ENGLISH, MISKITO, PECH, GARÍFUNA, SPANGLISH ◌ **MAJOR INDUSTRY** LOGGING (ESPECIALLY ILLEGAL LOGGING)

◌ **COST INDEX** *COLECTIVO* (SHARED TAXI) LAUNCH FROM PUERTO LEMPIRA, US$3-7; FIVE- TO SEVEN-DAY GUIDED TRIP, US$350-400

RISING UP

Central America is on everybody's agenda – and goddamnit, it's crowded as hell.

Nearly every country in the region is nearing the magic one-million-annual-visitors mark, or blowing through it, as is the case for Costa Rica and Guatemala. But poor old Honduras retains its backwater status with only around 700,000 visitors annually. And Honduran Mosquitia – with its creepy crawlies, lack of roads (there are none in or out, so hope you are good with a paddle) and lack of developed tourist infrastructure – is one of the least-visited places left in the region.

It's a wild, wild world. The tropical region, which extends past the border into northern Nicaragua, is home to the largest remaining stand of virgin rainforest in Central America. It's veritably primeval. The roar of howler monkeys mixes with the squawks of macaws and the hungry growl of chainsaws. This is humankind and nature in their raw forms: atavistic and hard, mysterious and savage. And it's still there, miraculously hanging on to the strings of survival.

So why go there? For the same reason you started travelling, to get off the beaten track. La Mosquitia lets you explore uncharted territories such as the 815,000-hectare Biosfera del Río Plátano, and engage with and learn from other cultures, like the region's Miskito, Tawahka, Pech and Garífuna peoples. Which brings up the great conundrum of 21st-century travel. How do we preserve culture and nature in a region as untrammelled as La Mosquitia? The answer comes out in shades of grey. One thing is certain, given the fact that rampant illegal clearcutting continues – despite much of the region being protected as a biological reserve – perhaps tourism is the best way to save this little overgrown slice of Eden.

DEFINING EXPERIENCE

◌ For most people in the 'developed world', La Mosquitia evokes images of Charlie Fox, played by River Phoenix, climbing through the jungle, 'under the bam, under the boo', and dreaming about what it'd feel like to kill his father, played by Harrison Ford, in the 1986 classic The Mosquito Coast. The Peter Weir flick was based on Paul Theroux's book; but trust us, the book was much better.

◌ For most residents of La Mosquitia, the defining experience of the last few years was the rat plague of 2005. The rats razed entire fields and left many locals starving. But the people that live in this area come from hearty stock – hurricanes,

HOT TOPIC OF THE DAY ★

People from other parts of Honduras and Nicaragua are moving en masse to the region to cut down, dig out, shoot and trap every last one of the region's resources. Illegal logging remains rampant, and the UN is vacillating on removing World Heritage status from the region. Will tourism save the day and this vast swath of rainforest? Honestly, most locals are more concerned with their next meal than with preserving the rainforest, and who can blame them.

plagues and scarcity are everyday realities here – and they're bouncing back with vigour, hope and unwavering strength of spirit.

RECENT FAD

☺ Paying more for your trip. This is not a new idea, but it's a great one. Those extra lempiras go a long way in creating a sustainable tourism culture in the region. So splurge a little bit on that 10-day guided trip; the incredible guides can find wildlife you would never even notice, and the cash infusion will hopefully encourage Honduras to protect this diverse region from poaching and illegal logging.

LIFE-CHANGING EXPERIENCES

☺ Hitting your fifth day on the river makes you feel a little like a Victorian explorer, Jack Kerouac, Bungalow Bill and Captain Kirk, all at the same time. We suggest leaving the pith helmet and ray-gun at home.

MOST BIZARRE SIGHT

☺ If you ever find Central America's most legendary lost city, La Ciudad Blanca, please drop us a line. Since Hernán Cortés rumbled through the region in 1526, explorers and treasure hunters have been searching out the White City. It's reputedly the birthplace of the Aztec god Quetzalcoatl, and the city's inhabitants supposedly eat off plates of gold. Did we mention that this is also a malarial zone, and that malaria is often marked by fevers and hallucinations?

LOCAL LINGO

You're really better off with English than local languages like Miskito or Garífuna in this region, but here are a few Miskito phrases to get you started anyway. It always brings a smile.

☺ hello/goodbye *naksa/aisabi*
☺ yes/no *ow/apia*
☺ please/thank you *plees/dingki pali*
☺ good *pain*
☺ bad *saura*

☺ friend *pana*
☺ How are you? *Nakisma?*
☺ Does anyone here speak Spanish? *Nu apo ya Ispel aisee sapa?*
☺ How much is it? *Naki preis?*
☺ What's your name? *An maninam dia?*
☺ My name is (Jane). *Yan nini (Jane).*
— Greg Benchwick

★GOLIST.

NAMIBIA & BOTSWANA

POPULATION 2 MILLION (NAMIBIA); 1.6 MILLION (BOTSWANA) ✪ **VISITORS PER YEAR** 700,000 (NAMIBIA); 900,000 (BOTSWANA) ✪ **CAPITAL** WINDHOEK (NAMIBIA); GABORONE (BOTSWANA) ✪ **UNIT OF CURRENCY** NAMIBIAN DOLLAR (N$); BOTSWANAN PULA (P) ✪ **COST INDEX** BEER, N$7/P6 (US$1); SPRINGBOK BILTONG, N$10/P9 (US$1.40); BUDGET NAMIBIAN SAFARI PER DAY, N$350 (US$50); EXCLUSIVE 5-DAY ELEPHANT SAFARI IN OKAVANGO DELTA P68,750 (US$11,000)

NAMIBIA IN THE SPOTLIGHT

Over the past decade Namibian tourism has survived on word of mouth alone. This is understandable, considering that few can contain their excitement once they've experienced the Namib Desert, the sensational wildlife of Etosha National Park, the ochre smeared Himba tribe or the dramatic landscapes of Spitzkoppe, the Fish River Canyon and the desolate Skeleton Coast. However, Namibia recently witnessed unprecedented international publicity and may well be on its way to rightly becoming one of Africa's premier destinations. How increasing visitor numbers will shape this vast nation over the next decade is still up for debate, but if you visit in 2007 you'll see the 'before picture' and still feel like you have the run of the place.

MOST BIZARRE SOUND ✪

If walking alone along the arcing crest of an almighty Namib dune wasn't already special enough, the sands actually sing too. The weight of each step causes the sands to shift and the subsequent vibrations can sound like anything from gentle humming to the distant sound of WWII bombers.

DIAMONDS – BOTSWANA'S BEST FRIEND?

With diamond mines making Botswana one of Africa's wealthiest nations, the country has turned its back on mass tourism and its associated environmental downfalls. Instead, rigorously controlled low-impact safaris and stunning ecolodges comfortable enough for the Beckham clan dot the enthralling landscape and make Botswana the African playground of those on a first-name basis with Benjamin Franklin. If you're exploring Africa on the cheap, the town of Maun continues to be the best place to get a taste of the outstanding Okavango Delta.

While some diamond money is now being used to run HIV/AIDS programmes and to provide medication to Botswana's population, the mines are not benefiting the entire population. Almost 46% of Botswana still lives in poverty and numerous bushmen have been forcibly evicted from their Kalahari Desert homeland to make way for diamond concessions.

DEFINING EXPERIENCE

✪ Losing your senses (and a few belongings) while barrel-rolling down a 340m-high dune at Sossusvlei in Namibia, or taking sensations to a new level while floating through Botswana's wildlife-laden Okavango Delta in a traditional dugout *mokoro* (canoe).

RECENT FAD

✪ Brangelina (that's Brad Pitt and Angelina Jolie for the recluses among us). The two Hollywood stars recently and oh-so-famously holed up in Namibia to bring their love child, Shiloh Nouvel Jolie-Pitt, into the world. Although the eventual departure of the beautiful trio brought peace (and some local celebrations) to the nation, the hype may have outed the bounties of Namibia, which until then were some of Africa's best-kept secrets.

FESTIVALS & EVENTS

✪ The annual Maitisong Festival in Gaborone is Botswana's largest

LOOKS LIKE MARS, FEELS LIKE AFRICA – THE NAMIB DESERT IS OUT OF THIS WORLD.

celebration of the performing arts. The 2007 festival (31 March to 8 April) features an outdoor programme of music, theatre, film and dance as well as an indoor programme highlighting some of the top performing artists from around Africa.

○ True to its partially Teutonic background, Namibia's capital, Windhoek, plays host to Africa's largest Oktoberfest, complete with *lederhosen* (leather trousers), German polka and steins upon steins of sweet, delicious beer. And don't forget the sausages!

LIFE-CHANGING EXPERIENCES

○ Getting lost in the view of the Namib Desert's vibrant red sands flowing into the cool Atlantic while skydiving near Swakopmund.

○ Knowing that there is nothing but grass between you and 2000kg of suspicious rhino while on an ecowalking safari in Namibia's Damaraland.

○ Setting out on a safari in one of Africa's most pristine (and exclusive) wildernesses at Botswana's Moremi Game Reserve.

○ Marvelling at the ancient San rock art scattered amid the mystical Tsodilo Hills in Botswana.

RANDOM FACTS

○ The golden wheeling spider *(Carparachne aureoflava)* found in Namibia's dunes escapes its prey by contorting its legs into a ferris wheel-like structure and cartwheeling down the dunes at breakneck speeds.

○ The Okavango Delta contains 95% of all Botswana's surface water.

○ Once a vehicle enters one of Botswana's diamond mines, it's *never* permitted to leave as a precaution against smuggling.

○ Due to a 37% HIV/AIDS infection rate in Botswana, life expectancy is less than 34 years for both men and women (the world's second lowest).

– *Matt Phillips*

BLUELIST // ONLINE

○ WALK WITH THE SMALL MEN OF THE BUSH

The experience of a lifetime… Walk, hunt, sing, dance and laugh with the last generations of Southern Africa's early inhabitants, the Bushmen, in Namibia's remote Tsumkwe District.

○ EXPLORE THE MAKGADIKGADI PANS

The 'nothingness' of this vast expanse in the Kalahari Desert will overwhelm you with a sense of wonder and awe. You will feel one with Africa and with all those wandering peoples, old and new, who were taken by its mesmerising power…

○ FIND DR LIVINGSTONE

Follow Dr Livingstone's tracks up to the 'smoke that thunders', the Victoria Falls. Discover the history of his explorations and read his original diaries in the very interesting museum at Livingstone, on the Zambian side of the Falls.

// NDLOPPU

⭐ GO LIST.

NEW MEXICO, USA

POPULATION 1.8 MILLION ⊙ **VISITORS PER YEAR** 10 MILLION ⊙ **CAPITAL** SANTA FE ⊙ **LANGUAGES** ENGLISH, SPANISH, NAVAJO

⊙ **MAJOR INDUSTRY** MINING ⊙ **UNIT OF CURRENCY** US DOLLAR (US$) ⊙ **COST INDEX** BOTTLE OF CORONA, US$3; ALIEN KEY CHAIN, US$3;

MIDRANGE HOTEL ROOM PER NIGHT, US$80-100; SHORT TAXI RIDE, US$8; INTERNET ACCESS, US$6

MORE THAN FLYING SAUCERS

Unlike any other state licence plate, the New Mexico plate says 'USA', a reminder that it's indeed part of the contiguous 48 states. As a visitor, there will be times when you won't quite believe it.

Pimped-up lowriders and 400-year-old adobe buildings, solar-powered earth ships and the world's most prominent UFO site, trendy mountain ski resorts and the world's largest cave systems – these are just a few things that make New Mexico unique and popular. However, the New Mexico Tourism Department isn't taking anything for granted. Its mission for 2005 to 2010 is to 'market New Mexico as an enchanting destination to the world'.

BEEP! BEEP!

If you want to get the most out of New Mexico, you need a car, the speed of a roadrunner and a good route. Albuquerque is the main hub city, and along with Santa Fe and Taos, completes the triumvirate of New Mexico travel. Those who venture further choose to head either to northwestern New Mexico, which is dominated by Navajo lands and people, and the mysterious Chaco Culture National Historic Park; or hit roads-less-travelled in southwestern New Mexico, where the Gila National Forest offers untrammelled hiking trails and remote cliff dwellings. Southeastern New Mexico boasts the world's largest gypsum dunes at White Sands National Monument.

HOT TOPIC ⊙ OF THE DAY

Recent interest in rescuing local produce and traditional farming methods from agribusiness' genetically modified clutches has resulted in rich pickings at farmers markets across the state. However, it hasn't been easy for the New Mexico Farmers' Marketing Association; in 2006 Governor Richardson vetoed US$135,000 of funding, which was a blow to the association and to small-scale farmers in the state.

DEFINING EXPERIENCE

⊙ Tramping around adobe structures in the heat of the day with a bulky piece of local art that you bought after a few margaritas, drunk at high altitude.

RECENT FAD

⊙ There's always been something spiritual about New Mexico, but more and more visitors are now heading to the state to find their inner selves in the desert or tap into hidden energies in the spa. You can bake yourself like a pot with some of the clay masks in these parts.

FESTIVALS & EVENTS

⊙ The biggest event in Native America is the Gathering of Nations Powwow, held from 26 to 28 April in Albuquerque. Folks come from all over the continent for a week of dancing, drumming, art shows and the Miss Indian World contest.

⊙ The 16-day Santa Fe Indian market, sponsored by the Southwest Association for Indian Arts, takes place the weekend after the third Thursday in August and packs the Santa Fe plaza with the finest Native American artisans from all over North America.

GET A FRESH PERSPECTIVE ON NEW MEXICO DURING YOUR HOT-AIR BALLOON RIDE.

- More than 700 balloons fill the sky during the incredible Albuquerque International Balloon Fiesta, held in October.

- Zozobra, held in the second week of September in Santa Fe, is effigy-burning fun, where all bitterness is burnt away in the inferno.

LIFE-CHANGING EXPERIENCES

- Sitting out in the precious predawn and postdusk moments at White Sands National Monument.

- Horse-packing into the wilderness to help improve wildlife habitats with New Mexico Volunteers for the Outdoors.

- Witnessing the exodus of Mexican free-tailed bats from the caves at Carlsbad Caverns National Park.

WHAT'S HOT & WHAT'S NOT

- Hot-air balloons are in.
- UFOs are out.

RANDOM FACTS

- Santa Fe is the oldest state capital in the US.

- The Roswell Incident celebrates its 60th anniversary in 2007.

- Smokey Bear, of wildfire-prevention fame, was born in New Mexico.

- Española is often called the 'Lowrider Capital of the US'.

MOST BIZARRE SIGHT

- The burning of the 15m-tall Zozobra or 'the gloomy one' at the annual festival in Santa Fe. Traditionally, Zozobra condemns the people's failures and sins, but revellers just shout 'Burn him! Burn him!' and have a party.

DEFINING DIFFERENCE

- For those who sniff that America is a young country, check out New Mexico. It's one of the few places in the US where you can see culture that dates back more than 400 years.

REGIONAL FLAVOURS

- More than balloon fiestas or Pueblo Revival architecture, chilli is the pride of New Mexico. Picked green in September and October or left on the plant to mature to a deep dark red, chillies are a delicacy and a staple of New Mexican dishes. The only question left for you to answer is 'red or green?'

– *Heather Dickson*

★ GO LIST.

NEW ORLEANS, LOUISIANA, USA

POPULATION PRE-KATRINA 485,000; POST-KATRINA 200,000 ✪ **VISITORS PER YEAR** PRE-KATRINA 10.1 MILLION; POST-KATRINA 5 MILLION ✪ **LANGUAGE** ENGLISH

✪ **UNIT OF CURRENCY** US DOLLAR (US$) ✪ **COST INDEX** CAFÉ AU LAIT & BEIGNETS AT CAFÉ DU MONDE, US$4.50; FRENCH QUARTER HOTEL DOUBLE PER NIGHT, US$150-250; COVER CHARGE FOR REBIRTH BRASS BAND AT TIPITINA'S, US$10; MUFFALETTA (HUGE SANDWICH) AT CENTRAL GROCERY, US$$7-10

BACK TO THE BIG EASY

Down in New Orleans, they're eating curb-side crawfish, and pinching da heads and sucking da tails again. They're making groceries at the A&P Market, thickening gumbo and taking drinks in go-cups to follow second-line parades. Buck and Emma the otters swim loops anew at the aquarium, while the newly christened National WWII Museum provides an enduring lesson in perseverance.

Brass bands get backed by clattering pins at the Rock & Bowl, where Mid-City returnees get in frames after reframing their houses, or reconnecting at town-hall meetings. On a Friday night at Café Brasil in the Marigny, the Hot 8 Brass Band raises the roof with donated replacement horns, its crowds spilling onto Frenchman St at set breaks to catch up with old pals.

Make no mistake, it's time to visit New Orleans again. And right now, travel to the Big Easy offers plenty more elbowroom than before Katrina became a four-letter word around this town.

YEAH, YOU RIGHT

Attractions in NOLA (New Orleans, Louisiana) are back, enhanced and upgraded. Restaurants that made the city arguably America's top culinary destination serve full menus, but waits are minimal and your table won't be bunk. Bands are gigging (and tickets cheap), festivals in full swing and community radio station WWOZ is back, broadcasting its musical gumbo.

The high-ground neighbourhoods hugging the Mississippi River – the French Quarter, CBD, Garden District, Uptown, Riverbend, Faubourg Marigny and Bywater – have quickly regained their footing. Rebuilding continues in fits and starts city-wide. The May 2006 re-election of Mayor Ray Nagin provided some

stability, and grand redevelopments are in the works. For now, the clamour of revival continues steadily as this unique, eccentric American city rightfully reclaims its must-see status, with added sides of the profound. Check it out, now.

DEFINING EXPERIENCE

✪ Awakening at your French Quarter hotel and shuffling to Brennan's for a breakfast of Sazerac eye-opener, Oysters Benedict and flaming Bananas Foster. Then, sample New Orleans' Funkiest Delicacies on Louisiana Music Factory headphones, jump on a voodoo-infused cemetery tour and patronise Jackson Sq hornblowers and caricaturists. Head Uptown for dinner, then check out the sets by Galactic at Tipitina's and George Porter Jr at the Maple Leaf. If it's Thursday, head to Vaughn's in the Bywater, where trumpeter Kermit Ruffin dishes up a set-break barbecue.

HOT TOPIC ✪ OF THE DAY

Solving crime, fixing schools, rebuilding the tax base, attracting investors, tackling long-standing social and economic inequalities while rebuilding and reinventing New Orleans. Oh, and those Category 5 levees sure'd be nice, mister.

RECENT FAD

✪ Dead-zone tourism. Don't shy from seeing the flooded-out regions that comprised 80% of pre-K New Orleans, where bathtub rings on houses show where floodwaters crested. Areas such as Lakeview, Mid-City, New Orleans East and the Lower Ninth Ward must be seen to truly grasp Katrina's epic fury.

FESTIVALS & EVENTS

✪ In late April, the New Orleans Jazz & Heritage Festival is the grandaddy of US live music gatherings. Jazzfest stands tall as the city's coolest event. Far more than just jazz here, folks.

✪ February's Mardi Gras whips locals and tourists alike into cup-cradling, bead-crazed, parade-chasing maniacs. It wraps up on Bourbon St at midnight on Fat Tuesday.

✪ Southern Decadence, the 'gay Mardi Gras', in early September brings dance parties, DJs and buff chests galore.

✪ In late October, the Voodoo Music Experience in City Park is a Halloween-infused gothic rock music festival, NOLA-style. Think Nine Inch Nails, Foo Fighters, Queens of the Stone Age and the Flaming Lips.

LIFE-CHANGING EXPERIENCES

✪ Wailing 'throw me something, mister!' at passing Mardi Gras floats – and landing a prized hand-painted Zulu coconut in return.

✪ Banging in nails to help rebuild New Orleans, home by home.

✪ Celebrating strangers' nuptials in the Gospel Tent at Jazzfest, the king of American live-music events (late April to early May).

WHAT'S HOT

✪ Ditching the budget and spreading some coin to help folks out.

WHAT'S NOT

✪ Summers spent in a cramped FEMA (Federal Emergency Management Authority) trailer.

RANDOM FACTS

✪ Creole food implies buttery, elegant, French-influenced cuisine; Cajun promises saucier, rustic one-pot country food from the bayou.

✪ *Easy Rider* was right. New Orleans' celebrated necropolises do exist above ground. Seems you can't bury the dead beneath sea level after all.

MOST BIZARRE SIGHT

✪ Staring up at levees holding back the Mississippi River and realising how precarious this city's position always has been and always will be.

CLASSIC RESTAURANT EXPERIENCE

✪ Chef Paul Prudhomme doesn't staff the grills daily anymore, but the Cajun cuisine he pioneered at K-Paul's Louisiana Kitchen remains elaborate and often hot. Signature dishes include blackened twin beef tips, turtle soup and a piping Cajun jambalaya, all served up in a convivial and inviting atmosphere.

– *Jay Cooke*

NORTHERN IRELAND

POPULATION 1.7 MILLION ✪ **CAPITAL** BELFAST ✪ **LANGUAGE** ENGLISH ✪ **MAJOR INDUSTRIES** MACHINERY, ELECTRONIC & TEXTILE

MANUFACTURING, ENGINEERING ✪ **UNIT OF CURRENCY** UK POUND (UK£) ✪ **COST INDEX** PINT OF GUINNESS, UK£2.50 (US$4.50);

MID-PRICE MEAL, UK£10 (US$18); NEWSPAPER, UK£1 (US$1.80)

NORTHERN LIGHTS

There is no better time to see Northern Ireland than now. Freed from the spectre of the gun by cease-fires and political agreement, it's abuzz with life: the cities are pulsating, the economy is thriving and the people, the lifeblood that courses through the country, are in good spirits. Go anywhere in Northern Ireland and you won't be short of someone to talk to.

MOST BIZARRE SPORT ✪

If you enjoy walking, love sport and take any opportunity to have a flutter, then the All-Ireland Road Bowls Championship should make you very happy indeed. This centuries-old tradition involves a 3km stretch of road in the backcountry of Armagh, an iron ball weighing a little under a kilogram, and a bunch of competitors with seemingly Popeye-type arms who hurl the ball underarm along the road. The winner is the one who reaches the end in the least number of throws. It's a bit like golf. Except without the clubs. Or the holes. Or even the greens. It takes place in August.

If you're into history, head to Downpatrick, the burial place of St Patrick. If hiking is more your thing, gear up for the Ulster Way, a walk of more than 900km around Northern Ireland taking in some magnificent vistas along the way, particularly along the Antrim coast; it'll only take you five weeks or so (of course, you don't have to do the whole thing). Or if you like the craic or are a bit of a party animal then check out some of Belfast's coolest pubs and nightclubs; and while you're there, try a Belfast Car Bomb, a lethal concoction of whiskey and Irish cream in a pint of Guinness.

And if it's the sharpness and humour of the Irish you're after, you'll find it here in spades. Quentin Crisp, the English writer and raconteur, highlighted the peculiar wit of the Irish (and you can expect some of this sort of thing when you arrive): 'When I told the people of Northern Ireland that I was an atheist, a woman in the audience stood up and said, "Yes, but is it the God of the Catholics or the God of the Protestants in whom you don't believe?"'

Whatever the weather – and it will probably be bad – there'll always be something or someone in Northern Ireland to put a smile on your face.

DEFINING EXPERIENCE

Putting some fire in your belly and loosening your lips with a drop (or two) of whiskey, otherwise known as *uisce beatha* (ishka ba-ha; water of life), at the world's oldest distillery, Bushmills, in Co Antrim. Suitably fortified and emboldened, take the short ride to the breathtaking sight of the Giant's Causeway. Legend has it that Finn McCool built the causeway to cross the sea to fight the Scottish giant, Benandonner; the Scot pursued McCool back to Ireland, but got scared after the Irishman played a trick on him and ripped up the path as he ran back home with his tail between his legs. Even if you don't believe the legend, you'll still be scratching your head at the unusual shape of the basalt columns. Rocks don't come more fascinating than this.

RANDOM FACTS

✪ The Harland & Wolff shipyard in Belfast (where the *Titanic* was built) boasts the world's largest dry dock.

LISTEN TO THE LEGENDS THEN
WEAVE YOUR OWN TALE FOR THE
UNBELIEVABLE GIANT'S CAUSEWAY.

- CS Lewis, author of *The Chronicles of Narnia,* was born in Belfast.

- Ballymena-born Liam Neeson was a champion boxer before he became an actor. (Judging by the effect he has on women the world over, it behoves all men to go out and take a beating…)

FESTIVALS & EVENTS

- Check out what's hot or what's not at the Belfast Film Festival, which showcases big and small productions from around the world. It's usually held in late March and early April; see www.belfastfilmfestival.org for a full programme.

- From late July to early August, the Celtic Fusion International Musical Arts Festival in Castlewellan, Co Down, promises long summer evenings of Celtic-inspired music, from traditional tunes to Celtic rock. Visit www.celticfusion.co.uk for more information.

- The wee Georgian village of Hillsborough in Co Down is home to the Hillsborough International Oyster Festival, held during late August and early September. It's a celebration of local food and craic, and boasts the World Oyster-Eating Championship. As if all that wasn't good enough, the money raised by the event goes to a local charity.

LOCAL LINGO

English in Northern Ireland can sometimes sound like a different language, so here are a few phrases to help you find your way.

- Am I some pup or what? (I'm feeling rather pleased with myself.)

- Catch yourself on! (Please refrain from talking nonsense.)

- My bangers went. (At the last minute, I decided it was an extremely bad idea.)

- Hasn't a baldy notion. (Lacks the required intellect or know-how to perform a particular task.)

– Cahal McGroarty

BLUELIST // ONLINE

MIND WHERE YOU WHISTLE
Apparently whistling indoors will bring bad luck in Ireland. It goes back to a time when sailors died by drowning. Instead of blaming the sea, the crew would blame those who whistled while in the boat.

// TATOUSOL

FAST & FURIOUS HURLING
Unless you're Irish, you're unlikely to understand the rules of hurling. No matter. Relax with your pint of the black stuff and watch what appears to be a lethal airborne game of hockey, before experiencing the postmatch Irish craic.

// EDWARDWELIAS

GIANT'S CAUSEWAY, NORTHERN IRELAND
Witness some bizarre volcanic formations: somehow, over millennia, thousands of hexagonal columns formed, creating a coastline that looks like something out of Myst. It lies along the most windy, breathtaking coastal cliffs.

// PROVOKETHETHOUGHT

★ GO LIST.

ORIENTE, ECUADOR

POPULATION 548,420 ◎ **LANGUAGES** SPANISH, ACHUAR-SHIWIAR, COFÁN, HUAO TERERO, QUICHUA, SECOYA, SHUAR, SIONA, ZÁPARO

◎ **MAJOR INDUSTRY** PETROLEUM ◎ **UNIT OF CURRENCY** US DOLLAR (US$) ◎ **COST INDEX**: RUBBER BOOTS, US$8; JUNGLE LODGE PER NIGHT, US$75-215;

ROASTED *GUATUSA* (AN AMAZONIAN MAMMAL) KEBAB, US$2

TONGUE-TICKLING ADVENTURE

Call it a by-product of all those reality shows, but this year's jungle visitors favour getting more than their gumboots wet. In 2006, the popularity of remote class IV white-water trips shot up by 50% and many high-end lodges responded to the adventure trend by adding camping in the wild. Total immersion isn't limited to the adrenaline rush. It also means substantive encounters with locals. Tour operators have seen an increase in volunteer tourism and indigenous community visits, which expose the difficult realities beneath the shiny verdigris of the foliage. Sure, the top jungle lodges still offer the coddling comfort of hot showers and sausage breakfasts. But since outboard engines and baseball caps have replaced spears and feathers, visitors searching for something 'authentic' are dipping directly into the lemon ants themselves.

THE COLOUR OF MONEY

The most accessible Amazon Basin–area of any country is vulnerable. Since oil was discovered in Ecuador's Oriente in the 1960s, antiquated extraction practices have wreaked havoc on wildlife and indigenous communities; the most contended case today is rainforest dwellers' US$40-billion lawsuit against Chevron-Texaco for damages 30 times greater than those of the *Exxon Valdez* spill in Alaska. In the meantime, Ecuadorian government policy is trying to rein in foreign exploitation, since 80% of oil profits leak abroad.

Indigenous groups are also clambering to have their say. Some have formed agreements requiring all members to sign off on oil deals. One community traded land to an oil operation for a sustainable lodge that they now run themselves. Even cut-off groups once opposed to tourism are starting to pursue the longer-term benefits of green gold versus black gold.

HOT TOPICS ◎ OF THE DAY

With increasing pressure from logging interests, will the uncontacted Tagaeri Taromenani be able to maintain autonomy in the Intangible Zone?

Will rainforest-dwellers |win the first class action suit on their home turf against a multinational oil company?

DEFINING EXPERIENCE

◎ Running the mile-wide, chocolatey 1930km Río Napo in a motorised public canoe alongside locals travelling 14 hours to the nearest bank, past forgotten villages, foliage-choked shorelines and gleaming oil towers.

RECENT FAD

◎ Shaman encounters and canopy towers. Cleanse your spirit through a sometimes spittle-soaked ritual or scramble to dizzying heights to observe toucans and miniscule pygmy marmosets at eyelevel.

FESTIVALS & EVENTS

◎ The Chonta Festival, held each May in Shuar villages, celebrates harvest and a reincarnated Shuar deity. Dancers encircle the

IT'S NOT ALL WHITE-WATER CHAOS
– TRY THE WATERS OF THE RIO NAPO
FOR A LITTLE MORE PEACE.

brewing chicha (a corn drink) for hours, chanting and stomping to egg on the brew's fermentation. By invitation only. More information can be found in the Macas tourist information office.

- Tena's founding day is celebrated on 15 November, amid a week's worth of live bands and street snacks.

LIFE-CHANGING EXPERIENCES

- Paddling blackwater flooded forest lagoons travelled by ancient hoatzin (pheasant-sized tropical birds) and pink river dolpins.

- Imitating clucks and growls to learn animal names in Shuar from village children.

- Crashing through remote rapids on the jade waters of Río Hollín.

- Sleeping under a thatched roof while the jungle rustles and bumps in the night.

WHAT'S HOT

- The things we've yet to name. With some 20,0000 unknown plant species awaiting discovery, university-affiliated research centres are sprouting up in remote jungle outbacks.

WHAT'S NOT

- *End of the Spear,* a 2006 docudrama recreating the 1956 massacre of five missionaries; Panamanians in poor wigs play the indignant natives.

RANDOM FACTS

- The nine-country Amazon Basin outscales Western Europe; each hectare shelters an average of 200 tree species.

- Hunter-gatherers Tagaeri Taromenani live in a self-imposed Intangible Zone off-limits to all outsiders.

- The trans-Andean oil pipeline sucks 400,000 barrels of petroleum out of the Oriente daily.

- Indigenous individuals consume up to 6L per day of *chicha.*

MOST BIZARRE SIGHT

- A shaman clad in a polo shirt and parrot-feather headdress.

DEFINING DIFFERENCE

- The Oriente contains just 3% of Ecuador's population and almost half of its territory, a treasure-trove teeming with emerald rainforests, ancient cultures and a staggering biodiversity that dwarfs that of Ecuador's renowned Galápagos Islands.

REGIONAL FLAVOURS

- Millennial staples include fish, chonta palm and yuca, but *chicha* is the Oriente's most indispensable refreshment. Women make it by masticating yuca or chonta palm and spitting it into bowls to ferment. The resulting brew is yogurtlike and vitamin-packed.
– *Carolyn McCarthy*

★ GO LIST.

NORTHERN PATAGONIA, CHILE

POPULATION 103,320 ✪ **LANGUAGE** SPANISH ✪ **MAJOR INDUSTRIES** FISHING, LIVESTOCK ✪ **UNIT OF CURRENCY** CHILEAN PESO (CH$)

✪ **COST INDEX**: PUERTO MONTT–CHAITEN FERRY, CH$16,000 (US$31); CARTON OF RED WINE, CH$1300 (US$2.50);

FARMHOUSE B&B PER NIGHT, CH$6000 (US$12)

RAW, RUGGED & REAL

Don't be alarmed by the cowboys strolling around with butcher's knives tucked under their belt loops. Sure, some have scars, but a blade proves handy both to machete trail overgrowth and to cram dinner in the pot. Welcome to rural Patagonia, where the telephone is replaced by broadcast radio messages, horses outnumber cars and time moseys so slowly it damn-near stands still.

HOT TOPIC ✪ OF THE DAY

The weather. Persistent rain means ferries and flights are cancelled, roads wash out, rivers flood, and papa ain't coming home for dinner.

Chile was slow to realise the Wild West appeal of this rugged outback, although it has long attracted eager anglers to high-end lodges. While the area's tough logistics make it prone to exclusivity, there are myriad options for the patient and adventurous traveller. Some eight years ago, a rural economic initiative trained rural settlers in the valleys of Palena and Puelo to become horseback-riding guides using their own horses and to set up B&B accommodation (fresh eggs included). The rustic result is one of the best grassroots tours around, where you can hoof or ride pioneer trails through hidden valleys and get a glimpse of what life was like before the hubbub.

TO SINK OR SWIM

If big business interests get their way, this pristine region won't remain so forever. Chile's salmon-farming industry, second only to Norway's, expands south, bringing with it contaminating waste that eradicates native marine life. Patagonia's rivers are also in grave danger. Spanish electrical company Endesa plans to build mega hydroelectric projects, which would dam several of the region's major waterways, leaving whole pioneer valleys underwater.

The time to see it all while it lasts is precisely now. Road improvements and increased twin-engine taxi flights mean better accessibility than ever.

And, since American conservationist Douglas Tompkins created Parque Pumalín, visits to the region have doubled. But that's still not saying much; your chances of speaking English here are practically nil. Pack your butcher's knife in your check-in luggage on the flight out.

DEFINING EXPERIENCE

✪ Trotting along muddy trails without a care in the world, à la Butch Cassidy.

RECENT FAD

✪ Millionaire environmentalists purchasing large tracts of land for conservation projects.

FESTIVALS & EVENTS

✪ Palena Rodeo, held on the last weekend in January, features the best Chilean *huasos* (cowboys) around flaunting slick skills on the crescent stadium to howling crowds.

✪ Coyhaique Rodeo is a similar event held on a larger scale four

PATAGONIAN COWBOYS ... LOST IN TIME AT THE END OF THE WORLD.

times yearly. Check out www .caballoyrodeo.cl (in Spanish) for dates.

- Every village takes time out for a week of summer revelry, the Fiestas Costumbristas. This means seafood cookouts on the coast or lamb barbecues in the mountains, as well as horse racing and dancing in the soccer field after sunset. Check local municipal tourist information offices for date announcements.

LIFE-CHANGING EXPERIENCES

- Visiting the small farms of isolated pioneers.
- Shooting the scary crystal-cut rapids of the Río Futaleufú.
- Helping out in resource-poor rural schools.
- Hiking the Andes' lush low passes into Argentina.

WHAT'S HOT & WHAT'S NOT

- Basque berets, moonshine cider and sheepskin chaps are in with

the ranch set. Keep it real by leaving your iPod and Blackberry at home.

RANDOM FACTS

- In the 19th century, Patagonia was ruled by French adventurer Orelie-Antoine de Tounens who was made king by the Mapuche; he died penniless after expulsion by the Chilean government.
- Annual rainfall reaches 3300 mm, five times the London average.
- At 40cm the Patagonian pudú is the world's tiniest deer. It scrambles up bamboo stalks and barks when threatened.

MOST BIZARRE SIGHT

- In remote areas with few services, you might be sharing the dinner table with a convivial mix of Chilean army-corps workers, fly-fishing guides and local cowboys.

DEFINING DIFFERENCE

- Fiercely independent and idiosyncratic, the local character

was forged in utter isolation. While pioneers arrived at the beginning of the 20th century, it wasn't until the 1980s that the Carretera Austral linked the region with the rest of continental Chile.

LOCAL LINGO

- Wry references toward hard times on the ranch abound. Phallic fried-bread twists are called *calzones rotos* (busted underwear) and howling winter storms have the whimpy bundling up *más forrado que bola e'carneo* (snugger than a ram's balls).

REGIONAL FLAVOURS

- Summer *asados* (barbecues) feature spit-roasted whole lamb and potatoes. Farmers' fare includes heaping plates of *porotos con riendas* (literally, beans with reins), featuring pasta glazed in lard, bits of leftover meat, squash and legumes.

– *Carolyn McCarthy*

⭐ GO LIST.

PORTLAND, OREGON, USA

POPULATION 530,000 ⚙ **VISITORS PER YEAR** 2 MILLION ⚙ **LANGUAGE** ENGLISH ⚙ **UNIT OF CURRENCY** US DOLLAR (US$)

COST INDEX PINT OF MICROBREW BEER, US$3.50; ROOM AT A HIPSTER HOTEL PER NIGHT, US$75 (AND UP); TAXI RIDE FROM THE AIRPORT, US$30;

MAX LIGHT-RAIL RIDE DOWNTOWN, FREE (OUTSIDE DOWNTOWN, US$1.40-1.70); INTERNET ACCESS UP TO US$6 PER HOUR

BEER. DARN GOOD BEER.

A few years back, when everyone was busy fussing over San Francisco and Seattle, Portland became the West Coast's newest, hip baby. The city's microbrews were its best liquid asset and its smugness was born more out of how much it could dress down than dress up.

Today, Portland, with its special brews and slightly sleazy charm, is gradually drawing in more and more visitors from around the globe. Most want to get there before the secret gets out, and it's still the perfect place for discovering dive bars, backstreet art galleries, and chef-run bistros – and boasting that you got there first. It's also a great base for exploring Oregon's impressive outdoor offerings, which include climbing Mt Hood, windsurfing the Columbia River, skiing above the Timberline Lodge (of *The Shining* fame) and taking ecotours to virgin forests. But, it's worth noting that Portland isn't just a stop-off on a grand tour of the Pacific Northwest anymore. It's got enough appeal to be visited in its own right, and not just for beer drinkers and hipsters.

SORRY, BEER GIVES ME GAS

For those who aren't in the least interested in the latest pale ales and dark porters, Portland has public art, classic architecture, riverfront walks, some rather swanky places to stay, a convenient light-rail system and Powell's City of Books, the largest independent bookstore in the world – taking up an entire block and stocking more than a million books. Portland is also known for some trendy shopping areas such as Hawthorne Blvd and Pearl St.

Oh, and if you need more convincing, Portland has been touted as the 'best city to live in the US', the 'best walking town in America', the 'best cycling city in the US' and the 'number 10 best arts city in America'.

HOT TOPIC OF THE DAY ⚙

Organisers of Portland's Rose Festival are trying to find ways to attract young people to the event without losing the interest of families. By getting this right, they hope that the Rose Festival will continue far into the next century but, with a growing number of beer fests battling for attention, it's going to be hard.

DEFINING EXPERIENCE

⚙ Dashing out of the rain into a brewpub, where your tattooed waitress brings you a menu, listing more than 20 local beers. You mull over this for ages, finally pick a beer, then ask your waitress what she recommends and go for that.

RECENT FAD

⚙ Wi-fi friendly pubs.

FESTIVALS & EVENTS

⚙ The Portland International Film Festival (PIFF) is held every February. Celebrating its 30th anniversary in 2007, the PIFF is the big celluloid event in Oregon, attracting more than 33,000 people – and some celebrities.

⚙ US Navy, Royal Canadian Navy and Coast Guard ships have sailed to Portland for almost 70 years for the annual

OVERDONE IT WITH THE BEER, ARTS SCENE AND STRIP CLUBS? HEAD TO NEARBY MT HOOD FOR A DETOX.

celebration of the Portland Rose Festival in June. Chain your lawn chair to the sidewalk like a local in advance of the parades.

- The Gay Pride Parade takes place in late June. March through town with Dykes on Bikes and 10,000 others during this Pride Northwest parade.
- Showcasing more than 50,000 beers, the Oregon Brewers Festival in late July is one of the best brew fests in the US.

MIND-BLOWING EXPERIENCES

- Tootling around the Willamette Valley, along scenic Hwy 99W. Scaling the dizzy heights of the bar stool after a few fancy microbrews. Wandering through book heaven at Powell's City of Books.

RANDOM FACTS

- Portland has more strip clubs per capita than anywhere else in the US. Howard Hughes' 'Spruce Goose', the world's largest wood-framed airplane, is housed in the Evergreen Aviation Museum, an hour from Portland.
- Portland was almost named 'Boston'.

MOST BIZARRE SIGHT

- 'Keep Portland Weird!' bumper stickers. A group of small-business owners, eager to preserve the city's oddball character got together some years ago to encourage people to frequent local places over malls and chain stores.

MOST UNUSUAL PLACE TO STAY

- McMenamins Edgefield. There's so much at this 15-hectare complex, it's ridiculous. Think quirky hotel, three eateries, six bars, a pitch-and-putt golf course, winery, brewery, distillery, movie theatre, art museum, live-music venue and gardens (with rabbits) all on the premises. Add the McMenamin brothers' unique sense of style and you have a most unusual place to stay.

– *Heather Dickson*

BLUELIST // ONLINE

✪ LAURELWOOD BREWING COMPANY

Off trendy NW 23rd, this is Portland's only organic brewing company. Order a garden salad and some Free Range Red in this converted house, or try their very Oregon Tree Hugger Porter. Family-friendly and cabin-feel atmosphere.

// NICK WUSZ

✪ JIMMY MAK'S

Portland remains the best city on the West Coast for jazz, and has been so for 25 years. Jimmy Mak's Greek restaurant and bar (NW Everett and 10th, 503-295-6542) gets most of the national acts and best local musicians to play here.

// ADREANIEMIEC

✪ PORTLAND ZOO-BOMBERS

On Sundays, Portland bike enthusiasts grab kiddie bikes and go 'bombing' – joyriding down the steep hill from the Oregon Zoo to Washington Park. The law doesn't like it, and in the past the bombers have had their kiddie bikes confiscated.

// KAT DUFFY

PUGLIA & BASILICATA, ITALY

POPULATION 4 MILLION (PUGLIA); 598,800 (BASILICATA) ✪ **CAPITAL** BARI (PUGLIA); POTENZA (BASILICATA) ✪ **LANGUAGE** ITALIAN

✪ **MAJOR INDUSTRY** AGRICULTURE ✪ **UNIT OF CURRENCY** EURO (€) ✪ **COST INDEX** CUP OF COFFEE, €1 (US$1.20); HOTEL DOUBLE, €80-180 (US$100-225);

BOTTLE OF WINE, €12-24 (US$15-30); BOWL OF PASTA, €6-10 (US$7.50-12.50)

THE NEW TUSCANY

You can't have missed all those newspapers articles declaring Tuscany, the darling of the Italian holiday scene, dead and Puglia as its shiny new successor, although you may have raised an eyebrow at the veracity of such a bold statement. For what could the straggling heel of Italy's remote south have that those rolling Tuscan hills don't? For one thing, most of the items on that Tuscan table are harvested here on Puglia's sunny plains. In addition, its 800km coastline has Italy's best sandy beaches, and the Valle d'Itria, southwest of Bari, is a picture of rolling green hills and low-slung dry-stone walls, where vineyards and country lanes preserve an utterly rustic character.

What's more, in April 2005, Bari opened a brand new airport, bigger and better than the poor old portacabin that previously received those intrepid enough to journey south. And with Ryanair flights to the region for as little as UK£20, the regional tourist body anticipates 3.5 million visitors will pass through customs over the next 10 years. Hot footing it onto those planes is a surprising list of star-studded celebrities, who are booking rooms in luxurious spas in the southern sun. When Lord MacAlpine bought his own *masseria* (fortified farmhouse) it was finally official – Puglia really is the new Tuscany.

> ### DEFINING ✪ EXPERIENCE
>
> Spending the morning with a bona fide shepherd turning curds into whey, before sitting down to feast on one of the finest nine-course meals you're ever likely to experience.

THE LAST TRUE WILDERNESS

If Puglia is a land without shadows, then neighbouring Basilicata is defined by its crush of mountains. It is the last true wilderness in Italy, a chaotic landscape of tremendous mountain ranges, dark forested valleys and villages so melded to the rock face that you often can't tell they're there at all. For years, Basilicata was sidelined as the land of *terroni* (peasants), but then Mel Gibson came to town and shot his controversial film, *The Passion of Christ*, in the troglodyte town of Matera. Since then there has been a growing awareness of the region's startling beauty (it's home to Italy's largest national park, the Parco Pollino) and opaque history. So much so that Francis Ford Coppola is currently engaged in renovating the Palazzo Margherita in Bernalda, while his nephew Nicolas Cage is busy developing an experimental centre for visual and musical arts in Metaponto. Even *Hip Hotels* guru, Herbert Ypma, has recently declared Basilicata 'the new place to be'.

BACK IN TIME

But hype aside, what is really luring travellers to southern Italy is the fact that it remains resolutely Italian; untouched, as yet, by the deadening hand of overexposure that affects so much of modern Italy. As George Gissing noted in 1901, the south has an engaging 'tigerish

flavour' – closed, wearied and regretful one moment, warmly human and generous the next. The widely distributed sights, small towns and intimate experiences force visitors to travel outside the usual comfort zone and engage with the landscape and people on a level that is nearly impossible now in the more sophisticaed north. Venture into these parts and you'll be rewarded with an unforgettable experience that will challenge your comfortable preconceptions of just what modern Italy is all about.

RECENT FAD

- Buying a masseria and converting it into an über-chic rustic resort. Lord MacAlpine leads the way with Il Convento di Santa Maria di Costantinopoli.

FESTIVALS & EVENTS

- Le Feste di Pasqua (Holy Week) in Taranto is a time of high emotion, when thousands gather to watch bearers carry statues representing the Passion of Christ.

- Festa di San Nicola is Bari's biggest shindig, celebrating the arrival of St Nicholas' relics in Bari in early May.

- Sagra della Madonna della Bruna is Matera's bizarre festival held on 2 July involving a procession of the Madonna on a papier-mâché float. Once the statue is removed, the crowd tears the float to pieces.

- Jazz in Puglia Festival presents jazz, soul, blues and gospel music in Lecce, in early September.

LIFE-CHANGING EXPERIENCES

- Helping out with the olive harvest at Il Frantoio, Ostuni.

- Sleeping in a Unesco World Heritage cave in Matera's ancient *sassi* (districts).

- Trekking through the alpine meadows and deep river canyons in the Parco Pollino.

RANDOM FACTS

- The average Italian eats 28kg of pasta per year, 80% of which is produced in Puglia.

- Puglia's *trulli* (beehive-shaped houses) may have been conceived as a tax dodge. Built without mortar, they were simply dismantled when the tax collector passed.

- Taranto is allegedly the town where the first cat landed on European soil.

MOST BIZARRE SIGHT

- The skulls of Otranto's 800 martyrs stacked in glass cabinets in a chapel in Otranto's cathedral.

REGIONAL FLAVOURS

- The folk of Puglia and Basilicata eat a lot of *agnello* (lamb) and *capretto* (kid), usually cooked with aromatic herbs or served in tomato-based sauces. Raw fish, like anchovies or squid, marinated in olive oil and lemon juice, is not uncommon. On top of this cornucopia, bread and pasta are fundamental to the southern Italian diet, with per capita consumption at least double that of the USA.

– Paula Hardy

SAN SEBASTIÁN, SPAIN

POPULATION 200,000 ✪ **VISITORS PER YEAR** 500,000 ✪ **LANGUAGES** EUSKERA (BASQUE), CASTILIAN SPANISH

✪ **UNIT OF CURRENCY** EURO (€) ✪ **COST INDEX** *PINTXO*, UP TO €2.50; BOTTLE OF WINE, €5; HOTEL DOUBLE PER NIGHT, €50-70;

SHORT TAXI RIDE, €5; INTERNET ACCESS PER HOUR, AROUND €3

HOW TO ✪ *PINTXO*

Just rolling the word *pintxo* round your tongue defines the essence of this cheerful, cheeky little slice of Basque cuisine. The perfect *pintxo* should have a bouquet of exquisite tastes, distinctive texture and eye-popping appearance – a sort of *pintxo haute couture*, to be savoured in two elegant bites. In San Sebastián especially, Basque chefs have refined the *pintxo* process to an art form. Many *pintxos* are bedded on small pieces of bread or on tiny half-baguettes upon which towering creations are constructed, often melded with flavoursome mayonnaise and then pinned by large toothpicks. Some bars specialise in a seafood genre, while others deal in mushroom delicacies, or simply offer a mix of everything. Match each one with a glass of the delicious *txakoli*, the young white wine of the Basque Country.

CATWALK QUEEN OF THE BELLE ÉPOQUE

San Sebastián (in Basque, Donostia) has been strutting its stuff on the golden shores of the beautiful Bahía de La Concha on Spain's northern Basque coast for a very long time, and it shows no sign of losing any of its poise or its subtle flavour of high camp. After centuries of knockabout French–Spanish conflicts, the city was hoisted into 19th-century stardom as a fashionable watering hole by Spanish royalty dodging the searing heat of the southern mesa. By the close of the century, San Sebastián had been given a superb *belle époque* makeover that has left a legacy of elegant Art Nouveau buildings and beachfront swagger. Matching the swagger ever since has been a stream of blue bloods, fashionistas, celebs, politicos, artists, writers, film stars, fixers, brokers, bankers and the bankable. They join waves of salivating foodies paying homage to San Sebastián's modern metamorphosis as a world capital of culinary excellence, in which the gourmet subculture of the *pintxo* (the Basque tapas) underpins Michelin-starred cuisine. (Thirteen Michelin stars sparkle in the San Sebastián firmament of classy eateries, a galaxy matched only by central Paris.)

As if this was not enough, the atmospheric Parte Vieja (Old Town) is said to have more bars than any other city quarter in the known world, most of them laden with bar-top kaleidoscopes of skewered *pintxos*, every one an irresistible work of art. The city is also exuberantly Basque by nature, with cultural and corporate happenings round every corner.

Get there soon. French big spenders skip across the border from a mere 21km away to get some serious unstraightened nightlife in. The Basque terrorist group ETA's cease-fire announcement in April 2006 is bringing southern Spanish flocking north, so San Sebastián's star seems set to rise even more galactically. Book ahead, bring enough to bankroll some of that gourmet glory, and relax in the knowledge that the fabulous beaches and their fabulous surroundings are free – and that the fabulous *donostiarras* (locals) know how to party.

DEFINING EXPERIENCE

✪ Spending a normal San Sebastián Saturday lunchtime feasting on *pintxos* and *txakoli* (Basque white wine) with friends, followed by a surprise view of photographer Spencer Tunick marshalling 1000 *shudddddering* nudies along Zubiella's beach for one of his multi-stripograms against a background of Zubi's massed

ET A TASTE FOR THE BASQUE COUNTRY,
N A PLATE OR TWO (OR THREE ...).

surfing cadre, while a good-natured local crowd discussed the latest ETA cease-fire and the chances of Biarritz Olympique beating England's Bath City in the rugby semis at San Sebastián's Estadio Anoeta later that evening…

FESTIVALS & EVENTS

- St Sebastián's Day, known as La Tamborrada, is held in January. Groups of drummers thunder through the city's streets.

- Carnaval, in February, sees exuberant, often outrageous processions and celebrations.

- The month-long International Jazz Festival has featured stars such as Van Morrison in 2005 and Bob Dylan in 2006.

- Semana Grande in mid-August sees all sorts of fun and games plus spectacular firework displays.

- Mid-September's International Film Festival is a major showcase for mainstream but essentially ground-breaking films.

CLASSIC RESTAURANT EXPERIENCES

- With three Michelin stars, Arzak, on Alto de Miracruz, takes some beating. Chef Juan Mari Arzak was one of the first Basque chefs to embrace *nueva cocina vasca* (new Basque cooking). Signature dishes include the positively sculptural squid circle, a clever presentation of squid dressed with a sauce with hints of bergamot tea and sarsaparilla, and a final flourish of cocoa and ginger drapery. Prices for a meal can rise to €160.

- If your funds don't stretch to Arzakland, then head for the Parte Vieja's La Cuchara de San Telmo, just off Calle de Agosto 31, by the San Telmo Museum. Here, in an easy-going little bar, chefs Álex Montiel and Iñaki Gulin drum up superb *cocina vasca,* like *tempura de bacalao* (€3), a fine chunk of cod in light batter, and *pato Hembra* (€2.80; just ask for the duck). Feel these dishes melt on the tongue.

– Des Hannigan

BLUELIST // ONLINE

DUENDE

A flamenco dancer is said to 'have *duende*' when the spirit takes his body in sacrifice. He lets her fill him wholly so that the sound of his heels and hands becomes a weapon against oppression and injustice. *Duende* gives and takes life.

// FIRECHILD

DINING ETIQUETTE

Tapas or *pintxos* in Basque places are colourful stacks of finger food fastened together with toothpicks. Ask for a plate to fill up with the tasty treats. Be sure though to hold onto the toothpicks, as this is how you settle up the bill.

UNLUCKIEST NUMBER

Like in the US, in Spain it's believed that the number 13 is very unlucky. Buildings omit this floor number, even people who reside in homes with the number 13 change it to 12A or B. But, unlike in the US, Tuesday, not Friday the 13th is the unluckiest of them all!

// CAREY REED

✪ GO LIST.

SOMALILAND, SOMALIA

POPULATION 3.5 MILLION ✪ **CAPITAL** HARGEISA ✪ **LANGUAGE** SOMALI ✪ **UNIT OF CURRENCY** SOMALI SHILLING (SSH), US DOLLAR (US$)

✪ **COST INDEX** ARMED BODYGUARD PER DAY, SSH 20,100S (US$15); HOTEL DOUBLE IN HARGEISA, SSH 26,850 (US$20)

THE COUNTRY NOBODY KNOWS

It has a parliament. It has a broadly representative government. It has a capital. It has a flag. It has a currency. It has a university. It has an army. It has multiparty elections. But nobody recognises it. Welcome to Somaliland, the country that does not exist and the most bizarre 'state' in the world. The self-proclaimed Republic of Somaliland was formed in 1991 after the collapse of unitary Somalia. Although its leaders desperately struggle to gain formal international recognition, Somaliland is still treated as a pariah by the international community and is not recognised as a separate state by the outside world. The main reason why the world is reluctant to accept Somaliland's independence is that the rest of Somalia does not want it, and its other neighbours are wary. For Somalilandese, this sounds profoundly unfair. 'Why are we treated as outcasts? We have managed to establish law and order in our country – unlike the rest of Somalia, which is totally chaotic and has no proper institutions but is recognised by the UN and the African Union nonetheless,' lament Somalilandese nationals.

True, it has long been a lot more secure than the anarchic south. Somalilandese from the diaspora keep doing their best to influence diplomatic corps in Europe, in East Africa and in North America – in vain. It's certainly unjust.

> ### HOT TOPIC ✪ OF THE DAY
>
> The much sought-after international recognition. When will the international community recognise Somaliland and treat it as a proper country, distinct from the rest of Somalia?

UNCHARTERED TERRITORY

At least Somaliland is a Shangri-la for the savvy travellers who want to break the rules of conventional travel. Want to impress your peers? In the mood for real adventure and absolute discovery? Look no further, you'll find everything in Somaliland. As far as safety goes, Hargeisa is one of the safest cities in Africa, and travellers are more than welcome. The city was destroyed in 1991 during the civil war and has few highlights, but it feels so exotic to be the only foreigner in the streets. It's surprising to see that Hargeisa has all the conveniences a traveller could hope for: good-value hotels with English-speaking staff (Somaliland was a former British protectorate), a couple of tasty restaurants, innumerable Internet cafés, bureaus de change, bus stations, taxis – but no alcohol (it would be too good to be true!).

There's also great potential for archaeology and history buffs. Outside Hargeisa, there's Las Geel, a phenomenal archaeological site that was only discovered in 2003. With hundreds of magnificent rock-art paintings in perfect shape, representing humans and animals, adorning the walls of several interconnected caves and shelters, this is the highlight of any trip to Somaliland. The totally unspoiled

KICK SOME GOALS IN SOMALILAND: HISTORY, BEACHES AND AN INTREPID ADVENTURE ARE ON THE CARDS.

beaches in Berbera come a close second. One day, investors will come and erect resorts here. Or it could be the islands off Zeila, close to the border with Djibouti, which await divers…

Worried about security issues? Rest easy: Somaliland has nothing to do with Somalia. The safety of tourists is taken very seriously here since 'terrorists' from Mogadishu shot several aid workers in 2003 to destabilise the fledgling country, which explains why the local authorities tend to be overprotective with foreigners outside the capital. Therefore, all travellers are assigned an armed bodyguard – US$15 per day is the price to pay for being a special guest.

DEFINING EXPERIENCE
✪ Haggling for the price of an armed bodyguard in Hargeisa.

RECENT FAD
✪ Mobile phones. Somaliland has the cheapest telecommunications system in the world.

LIFE-CHANGING EXPERIENCES
✪ Snorkelling near the islands off Zeila.
✪ Feeling like a *National Geographic* explorer and speculating on Somalia's mysterious past at Las Geel archaeological site.
✪ Enjoying the smug feeling of impressing your peers, 'yes, I've been to Somaliland!'

RANDOM FACTS
✪ The daily cost of a (mandatory) armed bodyguard is US$15 in Somaliland (without meals), compared to US$500 for a gang of armed guards in Mogadishu in Somalia.
✪ As Somaliland is not recognised by the international community, it does not have official banks, but private exchange offices. It's a cash-only economy.
✪ Somaliland claims 10,442,443 goats, 5,571,565 sheep and 5,454,590 camels.

– *Jean-Bernard Carillet*

🖑 BLUELIST // ONLINE

✪ CUTTING THROUGH THE RED TAPE
Try getting a visa for Somaliland when they didn't have a government in the country.

// MISSBYBNES

✪ CAPITAL
Hargeisa, the capital of Somaliland is an oasis waiting to be discovered. Situated in the Horn of Africa this city, which in recent years has undergone major development, has been hidden from the outside world, as a secret waiting to be laid bare.

✪ SOUL FOOD
Paradise, which is what most travellers look for especially in cuisine, can be found in Hargeisa. Forget Jamie Oliver or Gordon Ramsey, Hargeisa provides a wealth of special foods that not only tingle your taste buds but reach the depths of your soul.

// AMINA ELMI

★ GO LIST.

TŌHOKU, JAPAN

POPULATION 9.8 MILLION ✪ **LANGUAGE** JAPANESE ✪ **MAJOR INDUSTRIES** FISHING, RICE PRODUCTION, PETROLEUM REFINING,

ELECTRICAL MANUFACTURING ✪ **UNIT OF CURRENCY** JAPANESE YEN (¥) ✪ **COST INDEX** MIDRANGE MEAL, ¥2500 (US$21);

LOCAL BUS RIDE, ¥220 (US$2); NEWSPAPER, ¥130 (US$1.50); HOTEL DOUBLE FROM ¥9000 (US$78)

GRIM UP NORTH?

Tōhoku is called the Japanese 'deep south' (even though it's up north), a place where Japanese city slickers simply won't go. Not only is Tōhoku reckoned to be full of ghosts but it's also considered a backwater, a less developed, agricultural region habitually treated with suspicion by urban types. So why are we recommending it? Because no one ever said city wankers had to have the last word in anything. But more than that, because Tōhoku is a deeply compelling region, with an absorbing feudal history, abundant natural beauty, and a palpable sense of mystery and adventure seeping through its very strata, like thick, white Japanese mist in winter. English isn't widely spoken in Tōhoku's northernmost tip – the dialect can be impenetrable even to southern Japanese – but it's really not that difficult to get around. You'll find no shortage of friendly locals, keen to debunk the myths about their land, or to mischievously enhance them with a spook story or two.

If you like samurai tradition, then towns like Aizu-Wakamatsu, Tōno, Hiraizumi and Kakunodate will yield potent feudal rituals and reconstructed warrior fortresses. And if you're into the whole outdoors thing, then you'll love the many hiking opportunities and the volcanic regions peppered with sublime *rotemburo* (open-air hot springs). Blissfully, Tōhoku has also birthed some of Japan's most exquisite regional cuisine and is home to a wonderful programme of festivals celebrating Old Japan.

You follow in fine footsteps. Matsuo Basho, feudal Japan's Zen-enlightened haiku master, moaned before a trip north in 1689, 'I may as well be travelling to the ends of the Earth', but by the end of his adventure he was a bona fide convert. Today, his lovingly detailed *The Narrow Road to the Deep North* is the most well-known Tōhoku travel book.

DEFINING EXPERIENCE

✪ Boiling your butt off in a mountainside *rotemburo* as a light drizzle descends. Communal bathing with a group of naked strangers may take some getting used to but it's proven addictive to a nation of many millions, so who are you to resist? Failing that, trek along Tōhoku's spectacular coastlines and around its spectral mountain ranges. When the mist descends like a preternatural revenge scene from a Kurosawa film, Tokyo and the big-city lights will seem a world away.

FESTIVALS & EVENTS

The following are very popular. Book accommodation well in advance.

✪ Aomori's Nebuta Matsuri, held from 2 to 7 August, features parades of colossal illuminated floats accompanied by thousands of rowdy, chanting dancers. Visit www.nebuta.or.jp for information.

✪ In early August, Hirosaki's Neputa Matsuri also boasts illuminated

floats parading every evening to the accompaniment of flutes and drums. Like Aomori's main draw, it attracts thousands of visitors.

- Akita's visually stunning Kantō Matsuri (Pole Lantern Festival), from 4 to 7 August, sees hundreds of men exercising their balancing skills to the beat of traditional drums. Giant poles weighing 60kg and hung with illuminated lantners are balanced on the participants' heads, chins, hips and shoulders. See www.kantou.gr.jp for more.

- Sendai's Tanabata Matsuri (Star Festival) celebrates a Chinese legend about the stars Vega and Altair, who once took human form and were, quite literally, star-crossed lovers. The festival, from 6 to 8 August, is among Japan's biggest, with millions enjoying parades along the main streets, which are decorated with bamboo poles festooned with multicoloured streamers.

- On Sado Island, the Earth Celebration in the third week of August is a three-day music, dance and arts festival, featuring the world-famous Kodo Drummers. International guest performers and Japanese artists offer workshops. Visit www.kodo.or.jp for details.

REGIONAL FLAVOURS

- Real thrill-seekers will want to try *wanko-soba,* Morioka's famous dish that's more competition than meal. It's just buckwheat *soba* noodles with side dishes like raw tuna, fish flakes and shredded chicken, but it's the way that it's presented that is off the planet. You eat bowl after bowl of *wanko-soba,* with the waitress refilling your dish as soon as you've finished. The only way to stop is to slam your lid over the bowl. Be superalert: these ladies are quick, and will give you a refill before you can draw breath. If they do, you have to eat it, that's the rule. The record is 500 bowls. Moriokan hospitality at its finest.

– Simon Sellars

BLUELIST // ONLINE

✪ TOILETS WITH OPTIONS

The toilets and the surprise of sitting down on a prewarmed toilet seat and being given the option of buttons labelled wash, prewash, heavy pots and pans, warm, spray, dry, tickle and one I was never game to try, the 'powerful deodoriser'.

// ANDREW CHARLESTON

✪ SINGLE WOMEN BROOM DODGING IN JAPAN

No, this is not a new sport, but, if you're a single woman in Japan, be sure to dodge any sweeping brooms that you encounter. According to Japanese lore, a single woman who has had her feet swept by a broom will never marry.

// CAREY REED

✪ 'ME' GENERATION

To indicate yourself, it is expected that you point to your nose.

// OAFBUTT

⚙ GO LIST.

TURKMENISTAN

POPULATION 4.5 MILLION ⚙ **CAPITAL** ASHGABAT ⚙ **LANGUAGES** TURKMEN, RUSSIAN ⚙ **MAJOR INDUSTRY** NATURAL-GAS EXTRACTION

⚙ **UNIT OF CURRENCY** TURKMEN MANAT (M) ⚙ **COST INDEX** BOTTLE OF LOCAL BEER, 1050 M (US$0.20); GOOD DINNER IN ASHGABAT, 26,000 M (US$5);

TRADITIONAL HAT, 20,800 M (US$4); INTERNAL FLIGHT, 10,400-26,000 M (US$2-5)

PENGUINS IN THE DESERT

In the past year Turkmenistan has definitely leaped ahead of other eccentric dictatorships and gained an almost unassailable lead. Under President Niyazov, known to the world as Turkmenbashi (the leader of the Turkmen) things have taken a turn for the decidedly surreal in this little-known former Soviet desert republic. Having renamed much of the country after himself, including the capital's airport, the country's chief port and the month of January, in 2006 Turkmenbashi announced his most harebrained scheme yet. He put a stop to all state pensions and sick leave, and later announced a plan to spend US$17 million on building a zoo in the middle of the Karakum Desert. Here, despite the 50°C temperatures, Turkmenbashi decreed that a zoo for polar creatures such as penguins would be built to alleviate their suffering in the wake of global warming. You wouldn't be blamed for asking, is this man bonkers? A trip to Turkenistan then is first of all about soaking up the egotism and human idiocy that allows men like to Turkmenbashi to retain power.

MORE THAN JUST SAND

Turkmenistan is essentially one huge desert with the odd oasis and a green belt of land running around its periphery, but you'd be wrong to think that a personality cult is the sole attraction of this barren place. While you should expect lots of gold statues, vast palaces of marble, water works (Turkmenbashi loves to build extravagant fountains all over the country despite the scarcity of water) and dying palm trees (imported because Turkmenbashi likes them, even though they can't stand the climate here), don't forget the fascinating history of the region, associated with Genghis Khan and Timur (Tamerlane), whose legacies live on in ancient cities and archaeological remains.

DEFINING EXPERIENCE

⚙ Being stopped by road blocks every 50km and generally harassed by a Kafkaesque state that hounds everyone from travellers to its own citizens whenever they try to do anything. Smile for the illiterate teen soldiers, otherwise they may keep you waiting all day by the checkpoint.

RECENT FAD

⚙ Turkmen Russians are leaving in droves for the relative democracy and freedom of Russia. With all civil servants having to speak Turkmen and passing exams on Turkmenbashi's extraordinarily pompous *Rukhnama* (Book of the Soul), who can blame them?

FESTIVALS & EVENTS

⚙ Turkmenbashi simply adores holidays and as a result Turkmenistan has more than most countries. Check out Melon Day (10 July), Carpet Day (last

RICH HISTORY, ODDBALL OBSESSION, EVERYDAY LIFE – A TRIP TO TURKMENISTAN TICKS ALL THE BOXES.

Sunday in May), Drop of Water is a Nugget of Gold Day (6 April), Horse Day (27 April) and Good Neighbourliness Day (7 December). Nothing particularly thrilling happens at any of these, but the names are amusing.

LIFE-CHANGING EXPERIENCE

- You may come to see the oddest and most surreal of countries, but stay to see the awesome ancient cities of Konye-Urgench and Mary, walk in the footsteps of dinosaurs (literally) in the Kugitang Nature Reserve, experience the magnificent Darvaza Gas Craters in the Karakum Desert and don't miss a swim in the Köw Ata Underground Lake.

RANDOM FACTS

- The month of April has been renamed after Turkmenbashi's mother.

- Turkmenistan was mentioned in *The Simpsons* (episode 311, in a song about the merits of walking).

- It is illegal to lip-synch to songs in Turkmenistan.

- According to Turkmenbashi, those who read his fascinating 'Book of the Soul' three times are guaranteed a place in heaven.

MOST BIZARRE SIGHT

- While you could write a whole book about the bizarre sights of Turkmenistan, our favourite is the Walk of Health, concrete staircases that have been built into the side of the Kopet Dag Mountains south of Ashgabat to encourage people to enjoy mountain walking. Taking all possible joy out of a ramble across the hills is one thing, but the Walk of Health serves another function – once a year Turkmenbashi sends all his ministers off on a televised 'fun run' across the mountains in the blistering heat.

– Tom Tomaszewski

⭐ GO LIST.

XINJIANG, CHINA

VITAL STATISTICS ⊛ **POPULATION**: 19.6 MILLION ⊛ **CAPITAL**: ÜRÜMQI ⊛ **LANGUAGES**: UIGHUR, KAZAKH, UZBEK, KYRGYZ, TAJIK

⊛ **MAJOR INDUSTRIES**: AGRICULTURE, ANIMAL HUSBANDRY ⊛ **PER CAPITA INCOME**: Y20,000 ⊛ **UNIT OF CURRENCY**: CHINESE YUAN (Y)

⊛ **COST INDEX**: CUP OF *REAL* COFFEE, Y15 (US$1.87); KEBAB, Y2 (US$0.26)

NEW FRONTIER

The Xinjiang (New Frontier) province, one-sixth of China's territory, possesses unrivalled Silk Road history, a mixed salad of nearly 50 ethnic minorities and a preternaturally lovely geographical palette.

Yet it's also woefully underappreciated. In 1978, when China 'reopened' Xinjiang to outsiders, only 88 hardy foreigners poked around. (OK, the capital, Ürümqi, is known mostly as the answer to 'Which city in the world is furthest from an ocean?', but still…) Thus came Beijing's 1999 start of an infrastructure-building frenzy, part of the ongoing 'Go West' campaign to incite Han Chinese migration and truck out the region's resource wealth. Hopefully tagging along, albeit in a plane or train, would be tourists on a radically rejuvenated Silk Road.

And the results? As of 2007, visitor numbers are predicted to have 'leapt' to 400,000-plus, peanuts compared to the hordes to the (far) east that are taking part in the friendly foreign invasion that is the modern Grand Tour.

This gets the goat of Xinjiang's government, and, happily for tourists who don't mind a bit of a dusty journey (it *is* 4300km from Beijing), this trend is something the leadership is doing its damnedest to correct. Government piggy banks are continually being emptied on infrastructure projects, and more hassle-free borders with Xinjiang's eight neighbouring nations are easing the hardship of travel here…slowly.

Cannes it ain't, but Lonely Planet's new Chinese publishing partner held its opening bash in Ürümqi in 2006. What better barometer of up-and-coming cool is there?

HOT TOPIC OF THE DAY ⭐

Though generally not palpable to travellers, hostility towards Han Chinese (and, shh, a dream of separatism) simmers for many Uighurs, who are now a minority in what was once their homeland. In recent years, bombings were common enough to cause some locals to avoid public buses, and major riots occured outside Ürümqi. Beijing's swift and overwhelming responses, including general round-ups and executions of suspected separatists (long criticised by human rights organisations), have only been ratcheted up to a Big Brother degree since 9/11.

DEFINING EXPERIENCES

⊛ Pick one. Alighting from (falling off) your camel and staggering bow-legged into your yurt for the night; hopping off the bus to stretch as it waits, yet again, for sheep to cross the road; or, in Kashgar's back alleys, munching a kebab and chatting with locals about the Uighur melodrama blaring on the TV.

RECENT FAD

⊛ Living off the land, literally. Horse carts clattering down rural roads and a livestock-dotted landscape are still the rule, yet the majority of herders now dwell in functional if 'unethnic' public housing.

⊛ Sneaking into Tibet, for more and more (fool)hardy backpackers.

FESTIVALS & EVENTS

⊛ Ay Noruz (Festival of Spring) is a late-March blow out when each ethnic group collectively thumbs its nose at winter. Dancing, singing and gastronomic excesses

are the rule, but there's also Uighurs pelting each other with eggs, Kazakhs cleaning the house and men riding beasts everywhere.

- Take part in the Xinjiang Grape Festival to fete the most famed of Xinjiang's amazing fruits, held from June to August in Turpan.

HOT TOPIC OF THE DAY

- The 'lake monster' in Kanas Lake (Hanasi Hu). This 'mythical' beast made headlines in 2005 and 2006, leading to a 60% jump in tourism.

DO MENTION

- How well the person speaks English, a point of pride for many young Uighurs (you may have to lie).
- How much you love those Uighur music videos on your bus (ditto with the lie tip).
- How extraordinary the fruit is here (definitely not a lie).

DON'T MENTION

- Anything about separatism or independence.

RANDOM FACTS

- *Muqam* (Uighur traditional music) has been shortlisted by Unesco as an 'intangible cultural heritage'.
- Since 1950, Xinjiang's wetlands and lakes have shrunk by nearly 50%, due to overpopulation and overuse.

MOST BIZARRE SIGHT

- Kashgar's mind-boggling Sunday market. About 50,000 villagers descend on the town (with a gazillion goats, sheep and horses) for the weekly animal 'test drive'.

HOT TIP

- Non-Han often seem particularly unimpressed by foreigners' prowess in Mandarin, which, to many here, is merely a linguistic symbol of occupation and oppression.
- Meander carefully. Xinjiang has loads of 'sensitive' areas such as Lop Nur, China's nuclear test site, and especially areas bordering Afghanistan and Tibet.

– *Thomas Huhti*

BLUELIST // ONLINE

IF IT MOVES, EAT IT

If the thing slithers, trots, or crawls on 12 legs, you will eat it. Pork is considered a spice. Shock the squares at work with your exotic epicurean risk-taking. The thought of being able to have 'real' Peking Duck again can make one drool.

PEPTO & TOILET PAPER

Your best friends. It is highly recommended to create a workout regimen prior to departure for building up the leg muscles for the inevitable nightmare of using the non-western toilet' (aka, The Squatter). Otherwise, don't stray far from the hotel.

TRAVEL DIPLOMACY

Alone on a sleeper train, my entire car was full of young People's Liberation Army soldiers. They asked me if I liked Richard Nixon. 'Bad man, thumbs down,' they said. 'But he opened relations with China.' 'Good man. Very very good man. The best.' How do you say awkward?

// FITZIE

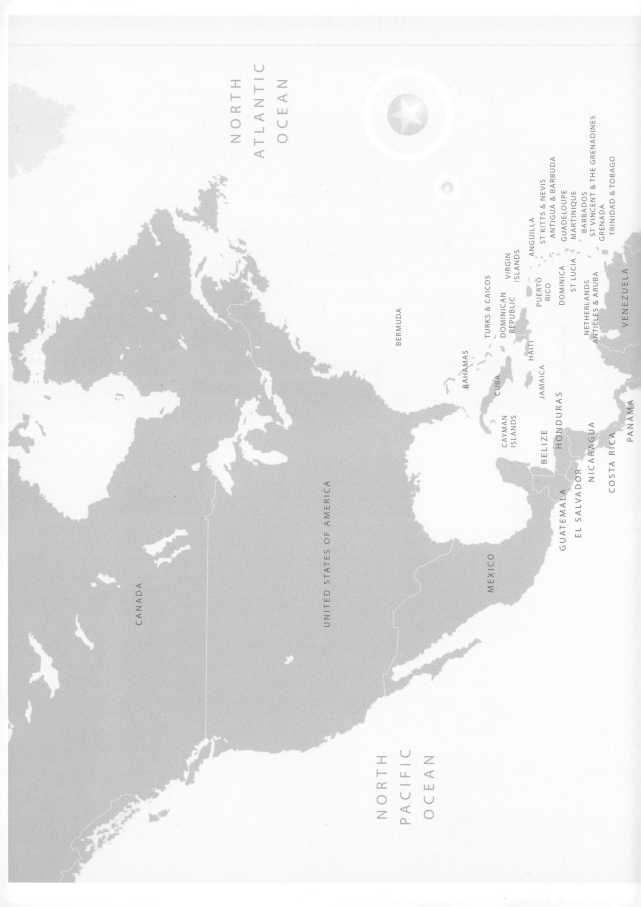

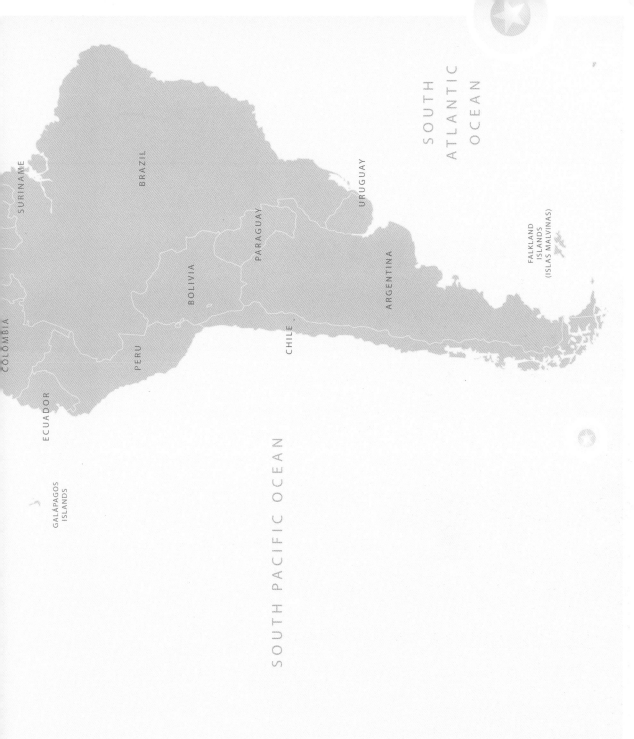

SURINAME

COLOMBIA

BRAZIL

ECUADOR

PERU

BOLIVIA

PARAGUAY

URUGUAY

CHILE

ARGENTINA

SOUTH ATLANTIC OCEAN

FALKLAND ISLANDS (ISLAS MALVINAS)

GALÁPAGOS ISLANDS

SOUTH PACIFIC OCEAN

» AMERICAS

» AMERICAS

ANGUILLA

 ✪ **CAPITAL** THE VALLEY ✪ **POPULATION** 13,480
✪ **AREA** 102 SQ KM ✪ **OFFICIAL LANGUAGE** ENGLISH

On Anguilla, bleached white-sand beaches out-number casinos and fast food chains 33 to 0, and visitors, many of whom fly in on private planes or stay at luxury villas, pay to keep the island sustainably small. In November 2005, the government of Anguilla placed a two-year moratorium on new development projects, continuing on the informal rule that no-one builds anything higher than a coconut tree. The Wallblake Airport's recent runway expansion and a new golf course threaten to upgrade Anguilla's appeal to the masses, but trust the 13,480 residents of this British overseas territory to maintain their island's way of life, where sailors still build their own boats and it's considered rude not to greet passers-by.

ANTARCTICA

See p142.

ANTIGUA & BARBUDA

 ✪ **CAPITAL** ST JOHN'S ✪ **POPULATION** 69,110
✪ **AREA** 443 SQ KM ✪ **OFFICIAL LANGUAGE** ENGLISH

Small wonder Antigua is dubbed the 'wedding island' of the Caribbean. With picture-postcard beaches and glorious tangerine sunsets for a backdrop, whatever happens with the relationship, at least the photos will always look good. Fantasy landscape aside, visitors to this fiercely friendly island are seduced by numerous delights: a wealth of historic remains, a delightfully laid-back atmosphere and the gritty West Indian charm of St John's for starters. Party mode prevails during the Caribbean's biggest sailing regatta in April and summer Carnival, a colour-fest of calypso, floats and rum punch. Remote one-village island Barbuda, with its never-ending beaches and frigate-bird colony, is a haven for bird-watchers, and the rich and famous who secrete themselves away at its few ultra-exclusive resorts.

ARGENTINA

 ✪ **CAPITAL** BUENOS AIRES ✪ **POPULATION** 39.9 MILLION
✪ **AREA** 2,776,890 SQ KM ✪ **OFFICIAL LANGUAGE** SPANISH

Argentina is still sizzling, with around 3.6 million international visitors in 2005. But this big country doesn't feel crowded, and even in bustling Buenos Aires you can find quiet cobbled streets and leafy parks. For true isolation, there are places in Patagonia where you won't see another soul for miles. The government has an ambitious 10-year plan to increase tourism, and it's thinking sustainably to protect its natural treasures. Exchange rates still make Argentina a bargain for most visitors, although happily the darkest economic days are over with its massive debt to the World Bank paid off in 2005. The country is also coming to terms with its past by addressing the horrors of the Dirty War and prosecuting some of the dictatorship's worst crimes. Also uncovered lately, a new dinosaur species, bigger than T Rex, in Patagonia.

ARUBA, BONAIRE & CURAÇAO

 ✪ **CAPITAL** ORANJESAD (A), KRALENDIJK (B), WILLEMSTAD (C)
✪ **POPULATION** 99,470 (A), 14,500 (B), 173,400 (C)
✪ **AREA** 181 SQ KM (A), 285 SQ KM (B), 471 SQ KM (C)
✪ **OFFICIAL LANGUAGES** DUTCH (A, B, C), PAPIAMENTO (A)

Nobody knew exactly where the ABC islands of Aruba, Bonaire and Curacao were located (rumour had it they were somewhere near the 1-2-3 Antilles) until a sun-scrubbed Alabama teenager disappeared while holidaying in Aruba in May 2005, causing a media frenzy. People now know that these islands are located just off Venezuela's coast; they may have even cancelled their vacation to Aruba to protest the Aruban government's reported mishandling of the case, or because the region was walloped by hurricanes in 2005 and the forecasts for 2006 looked equally windy. But the ABCs have withstood the drubbing, with a 2% increase in visitation numbers. Curaçao touts a rich history and culture (a tantalising blend of Dutch, Afro-Caribbean and just a bit of South American influence); Bonaire, the least visited of the islands, has world-class diving; and Aruba is just so damned gorgeous that neither hurricane winds nor media tempests can keep people away.

BAHAMAS

◎ **CAPITAL** NASSAU ◎ **POPULATION** 303,770
◎ **AREA** 13,940 SQ KM ◎ **OFFICIAL LANGUAGE** ENGLISH

An archipelago of more than 700 islands spread across a 1200km arc, the Bahamas snares tourists like sports-fishers around Bimini snap up bonefish. Stellar weather, spectacular shipwreck diving, and countless idyllic, pink-sand beaches (like Harbour Island, among the world's top sand stretches) lure more than seven million visitors annually. A member of the British Commonwealth and a 2007 Cricket World Cup host country, the Bahamas also holds the Junkanoo Summer Festival (a country-wide cultural demo), supports 22 national parks and affords opportunities to travel remotely via overnight mail boats. Don't pack your tent – the Bahamas offers no camping – but do bring some backup sunscreen, and an appetite for Friday fish-fry.

BARBADOS

◎ **CAPITAL** BRIDGETOWN ◎ **POPULATION** 279,910
◎ **AREA** 431 SQ KM ◎ **OFFICIAL LANGUAGE** ENGLISH

Densely populated and developed, Barbados sits atop a coral reef at the eastern edge of the Caribbean, astride the deep Atlantic. Despite a dip in cruise tourism (never bad), Barbados will be bouncing for the West Indies–based 2007 Cricket World Cup, hosting warm-ups, Super 8 matches and the tournament finals. There are plenty more attractions to wave sticks at, such as white-sand beaches, turquoise waters, rum-distillery tours and plantation open houses. The Eastern Caribbean's most popular destination, Barbados ain't exactly undiscovered. But its unique blend of British tradition and African culture affords guests equal shots of horse racing, Afro-Caribbean dance festivals, spicy seafood and soothing spots of high tea.

BELIZE

◎ **CAPITAL** BELMOPAN ◎ **POPULATION** 287,730
◎ **AREA** 22,966 SQ KM ◎ **OFFICIAL LANGUAGE** ENGLISH

Feelin' irie? Belize certainly is. Cruise ships are coming in at a rapid-fire pace, around 850,000 a year. And the good thing about cruise visitors is they seldom visit the off-beat places, leaving more room and space for visitors of the terrestrial kind. And while the world's second-largest barrier reef and the laid-back cays are certainly the centrepiece of any adventure here, inland attractions like the Maya ruins of ancient Altun Ha and the jaguar reserve at Cockscomb Basin make for fascinating cultural and wildlife exploration opportunities. All that, and they speak English, mon.

BERMUDA

◎ **CAPITAL** HAMILTON ◎ **POPULATION** 65,770
◎ **AREA** 53.3 SQ KM ◎ **OFFICIAL LANGUAGE** ENGLISH

People have been losing their way in Bermuda for years. British explorer Sir George Somers was the first, but certainly not the last, to head off course in the western Atlantic doldrums surrounding this tiny British colony, getting shipwrecked on the island in 1609. Years later, some 13,000 international companies have 'set up shop' on the island, creating what many commentators deem one of the world's most prosperous economies. But the funds of these captains of industry always seem to get lost; it seems the Bermuda Triangle is not just good for eating up ships, but also hedge funds and greenbacks. Bermuda is also a great spot for those hoping to get lost from the mundaneness of everyday life. Around half a million US visitors come here every year – some have yet to return home.

BOLIVIA

◎ **CAPITAL** LA PAZ (ADMINISTRATIVE), SUCRE (JUDICIAL)
◎ **POPULATION** 9 MILLION ◎ **AREA** 1,098,580 SQ KM
◎ **OFFICIAL LANGUAGES** SPANISH, QUECHUA, AYMARA

It's been a crazy year for Bolivia. Newly elected President Evo Morales, the country's first indigenous president, pushed forward several leftist reforms, including the nationalisation of the country's vast gas reserves. The CIA's knickers are certainly in a twist over that one, and left-of-centre countries like Cuba and Venezuela are drooling over their new-found bedfellow. So where does this tiny Andean nation go from here? Who knows. The future is so uncertain that you should go there before things change, to see first-hand what a 'country in transition' looks like. While we can't promise stability, we can say that Bolivia is a land of superlatives: it's home to the highest capital » in the world, the 'most native' cultural landscape in the Americas, and the most 'enviro-bio-supercalifragilistic' natural areas on the planet.

BRAZIL

 ⚬ **CAPITAL** BRASÍLIA ⚬ **POPULATION** 188.1 MILLION
⚬ **AREA** 8,511,965 SQ KM ⚬ **OFFICIAL LANGUAGE** PORTUGUESE

'Everyone should move to Brazil for at least a year, to learn how to live life,' mused one Lonely Planet author. Brazilians have the well-deserved reputation of enjoying life, and their country is the birthplace of the samba, the caipirinha and the bikini. But despite that laid-back philosophy, Brazil has become a major political and economic powerhouse in recent years, and has also launched a huge tourism campaign, with the ambitious goal of landing on the top 20 list of most-visited countries by 2007. The plan calls for expansion of key airports and money for ecotourism projects. Budget and mid-range hotel chains are springing up, and discount airline GOL is adding routes at an astounding pace. If you're a sports fan, Rio will be hosting the 2007 Pan American games in July and 500,000 people are expected to attend. If you're not, well, there's never a bad time to go to Brazil.

CANADA

See p30.

CAYMAN ISLANDS

 ⚬ **CAPITAL** GEORGE TOWN ⚬ **POPULATION** 45,440
⚬ **AREA** 262 SQ KM ⚬ **OFFICIAL LANGUAGE** ENGLISH

The Cayman Islands saw an unprecedented 84% increase in the number of tourist air arrivals in 2006. What in the name of all that's holy is going on in the British West Indies? How can an island – already renowned as a top tourist destination – see such an increase in just a year? The answer is simple: nobody came here in 2004 and 2005. Nearly nobody, that is. The island did receive one rather nasty visitor in 2006, a hurricane named Ivan. The storm ripped through the region like a scythe through grass, leaving nearly 70% of the island's buildings damaged. But the offshore bank accounts didn't take a hit during the storm, and the rather robust little British colony was able to

quickly rebuild. On tap for this year are pirate and jazz fests, ecofriendly turtle soup and some of the Caribbean's best dive spots. Ivan has been taken off the island's guest list for good.

CHILE & EASTER ISLAND

 ⚬ **CAPITAL** SANTIAGO ⚬ **POPULATION** 16.1 MILLION
⚬ **AREA** 756,950 SQ KM ⚬ **OFFICIAL LANGUAGE** SPANISH

There's treasure to be found in Chile, literally. In September of 2005, treasure hunters – bet you thought they didn't exist anymore, but they do, and what a job that must be – discovered more than 800 metric tons of gold, silver and jewels on Chile's Robinson Crusoe Island. While the Chilean tourism board and the country's first female president, Michelle Bachelet, are not promising that each and every visitor will find pirated booty on their visit to this long, thin country, they do promise grand adventures at the foot of the heavens in Torres del Paine National Park along with groovy-groupie getaways to the desert enclave of San Pedro de Atacama. And who knows, you just may get lucky and find your own El Dorado. In case you were wondering, the treasure has an estimated value of US$10 billion.

COLOMBIA

 ⚬ **CAPITAL** BOGOTÁ ⚬ **POPULATION** 43.6 MILLION
⚬ **AREA** 1,138,910 SQ KM ⚬ **OFFICIAL LANGUAGE** SPANISH

We said it before and we'll say it again, Colombia's the next big thing in South America. Long considered off-limits due to a violent trifecta of leftist guerrillas, right-wing paramilitaries and drug traffickers from both camps, Colombia has turned around remarkably in the past few years. Kidnapping and homicides are both way down, and more rural and coastal areas are opening to tourism as the safety situation improves. Much of the credit is given to President Álvaro Uribe, one of the few friends of the US in increasingly left-leaning South America. Although foreign tourism increased more than 25% between 2004 and 2005, visitor numbers are still small, so you'll share the white-sand beaches, romantic colonial cities, vibrant artistic capital and rolling coffee plantations with welcoming locals rather than packs of tourists. They'll be here soon enough, so go now.

COSTA RICA

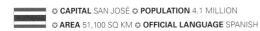 **CAPITAL** SAN JOSÉ ✪ **POPULATION** 4.1 MILLION
✪ **AREA** 51,100 SQ KM ✪ **OFFICIAL LANGUAGE** SPANISH

Seems everybody's going to Costa Rica these days. Nearly 1.5 million people visit there every year, and the numbers continue to grow. In fact, some analysts say the country may draw upwards of four million visitors yearly by 2012. With all those people running around, you'd think it would be difficult to find a beach to yourself. But, by heading into the wilds of giant national parks such as Corcovado and Tortuguero – neither of which have roads connecting them to the 'world' – you can still have a wild experience. And, if that isn't enough, there are beaches, volcanoes, rafting and some really kick-ass surfing.

CUBA

 CAPITAL HAVANA ✪ **POPULATION** 11.4 MILLION
✪ **AREA** 110,860 SQ KM ✪ **OFFICIAL LANGUAGE** SPANISH

¡Viva Cuba! No other country 'sticks it to the man' like this pint-sized Caribbean tiger. Fidel Castro, now 80 years old, continues his antics, regularly grabbing the world stage – not just to embarrass and prod his nemesis to the north, but also to send doctors around the globe on humanitarian missions. Needless to say, the political tit-for-tat between the two countries continues. The US is tightening controls on the trade embargo, and now only about 100,000 Americans risk prosecution yearly to visit the island nation. But the rest of the world seems to have no problem with Cuba, and two million visitors come here annually. Guess it makes sense to go there soon to sip up the contrasts and controls, outright abandon and maybe even a mojito or two. Plans are surely in the works for Disneyland Havana.

DOMINICA

 CAPITAL ROSEAU ✪ **POPULATION** 68,910
✪ **AREA** 754 SQ KM ✪ **OFFICIAL LANGUAGE** ENGLISH

Dubbed the 'Nature Island', Dominica lures lovers of the outdoors with its mist-shrouded rainforest, dramatic underwater topography and lack of major tourist development. Its jungle-clad peaks are the highest in the eastern Caribbean, and geothermally active Boiling Lake is an eerie reminder of what simmers beneath the surface of this otherwise lush island. Home to the region's last surviving Carib population, 47km-long Dominica remains blissfully undeveloped. Ecotourism and adventure travel fuel a fledgling tourist industry, but travellers who like their islands wild should get here fast: visitor arrivals were up 25% from the previous year in early 2006, largely because of an increase in cruise ship visitors. Natural wonders aside, Dominica is also home to the World Creole Music Festival and Mas Domnik, a unique carnival celebration replete with street parades, calypso competitions and a Miss Dominica contest known as the 'Queen Show'.

DOMINICAN REPUBLIC

 CAPITAL SANTO DOMINGO ✪ **POPULATION** 9.2 MILLION
✪ **AREA** 48,730 SQ KM ✪ **OFFICIAL LANGUAGE** SPANISH

Fast emerging as a multitiered getaway destination, the Dominican Republic (DR) is equally family-friendly (north coast resorts cater activities for all ages) and adventurous (heaps of kiteboarding, windsurfing and whale-watching options abound). It stands out among the booming Caribbean tourism economies with a whopping 19% annual growth rate. But the rise of the Dominican peso in response to the growth spurt has undercut visitor spending by a reported 30%; keep your eyes peeled for price fluctuations in 2007. The nation displayed its sporting prowess during the 2006 Baseball World Cup, advancing to the semifinals before bowing to archrival Cuba. With increased hurricane activity, the DR needs to balance resort development with sustainability, to minimise the effects of wild weather like Tropical Storm Jeanne in 2004.

ECUADOR & THE GALÁPAGOS ISLANDS

 CAPITAL QUITO ✪ **POPULATION** 13.5 MILLION
✪ **AREA** 283,560 SQ KM ✪ **OFFICIAL LANGUAGE** SPANISH

Everyone talks about sustainable tourism, but Ecuador's been on the cutting edge of planet-friendly travel for years. Ecuadorian ecolodges have earned high praise and the country's indigenous tribes, especially in the remote Amazon Basin, are embracing ecotourism as a way to sustain their environment and culture. Unfortunately, not all parties are so » enlightened. Oil companies continue to wreak ecological havoc, and 2005 and 2006 saw indigenous communities fighting back by attacking pipelines. For travellers, supporting community-based travel initiatives is a great way to help Ecuador's people extricate themselves from poverty while sharing the richness of their culture. Canoe through lush rainforests filled with chattering monkeys, stroll among the colourful chaos of native craft markets in the Andean highlands or soak in the sun on a stunning coastal beach – and of course see the Galápagos Islands' mind-blowing wildlife – and you'll realise why these treasures must be preserved.

EL SALVADOR

⊙ **CAPITAL** SAN SALVADOR ⊙ **POPULATION** 6.8 MILLION
⊙ **AREA** 21,040 SQ KM ⊙ **OFFICIAL LANGUAGE** SPANISH

Many folks still associate El Salvador with civil war, CIA covert ops and braver-than-Braveheart Jesuits. But the war is over, and the country is becoming relatively stable. OK, there are still a lot of guns on the streets, and there is a rising gangland-style crime wave, but that doesn't mean that people aren't visiting. And it doesn't mean you can't have a great time exploring the nation's past along the Ruta de la Paz or simply smelling the flowers along the Ruta de las Flores. There are also volcanoes, rainforests and some of Central America's best- and least-known surf spots.

FALKLAND ISLANDS (ISLAS MALVINAS)

⊙ **CAPITAL** STANLEY ⊙ **POPULATION** 2970
⊙ **AREA** 12,173 SQ KM ⊙ **OFFICIAL LANGUAGE** ENGLISH

A 4WD trek to the penguin colony at Volunteer Point followed by a pint of beer in a British pub has become a classic excursion in this part of the south Atlantic. But, with around 700 islands in the archipelago, there's more to the Falklands than Stanley and sheep. The most breathtaking islands, such as Steeple Jason with its black-browed albatrosses or grass-covered Kidney Island, are accessible via visiting expedition cruise ships or local boats. Cruise-ship 'day-trippers' account for more than 30,000 tourists per year, and short bursts of frenzied bird-watching. Slower-paced visitors can catch the Saturday-only LanChile flights from Santiago.

FRENCH GUIANA

⊙ **CAPITAL** CAYENNE ⊙ **POPULATION** 199,510
⊙ **AREA** 91,000 SQ KM ⊙ **OFFICIAL LANGUAGE** FRENCH

Cross the border from any of French Guiana's dusty neighbours and you'll find a twilight zone of well-kept roads, fine cuisine and wild jungles – then pay in euros. France keeps a tight grip on this remote corner of its territory, precisely because it's a remote corner, perfect for launching satellites. From 2007 to 2008 two additional satellite launchers will begin servicing Kourou, where an estimated two-thirds of the world's satellites have been launched since 1980. If technology isn't your thing, head out to the Îles du Salut, the now-crumbling, defunct prison camps that Alfred Dreyfus and Papillon made legendary.

GRENADA

⊙ **CAPITAL** ST GEORGE'S ⊙ **POPULATION** 89,700
⊙ **AREA** 344 SQ KM ⊙ **OFFICIAL LANGUAGE** ENGLISH

Little Grenada went for nearly half a century without a hurricane, but was then devastated by storms one after another in 2004 and 2005. The three-island nation is battling back. Tourism to the country is not the well-oiled machine that it once was, but now there is a down-to-earth feel and more direct contact with locals. Grenada is in the process of constructing a 17,000-seat cricket stadium for use as co-host of the 2007 Cricket World Cup, and has a full schedule of home-grown festivities including Fisherman's Birthday Celebrations, and the Carnivals of Carriacou and Grenada.

GUADELOUPE

⊙ **CAPITAL** BASSE-TERRE ⊙ **POPULATION** 452,780
⊙ **AREA** 1780 SQ KM ⊙ **OFFICIAL LANGUAGE** FRENCH

One can easily see how present-day Guadeloupe, which tips out from the tranquil waters of the Caribbean into the tumultuous currents of the Atlantic Ocean, got its name: Karukera (Island of Beautiful Waters). A French colony, the mountainous archipelago remains heavily dependent on aid from across the Atlantic. However, tourism is beginning to replace sugar cane and banana production as a major revenue stream, especially on Grande-Terre, which sees its fair share of cruise-ship visitors. Every once in a while residents will call for independence from France, but with great music and a laid-back beach scene, most people seem content to continue to receive aid from France, relax and just enjoy the beautiful waters that first made Guadeloupe special.

GUATEMALA

 CAPITAL GUATEMALA CITY **POPULATION** 12.3 MILLION **AREA** 108,890 SQ KM **OFFICIAL LANGUAGE** SPANISH

It's been a rough year for Guatemala. Hurricane Stan walloped the country, burying entire villages beneath mud, washing away roads, and leaving subsistence farmers without crops or food. But Guatemalans are tough – 30 years of civil war will do that to you – and the country is bouncing back. And the big tourist draws like Antigua and Tikal survived the hurricane, ensuring continued growth for tourism in the years to come. Central America's number-two tourist destination, Guatemala attracts more than a million visitors annually. With the country still recovering, now is a perfect time to go on a volunteer vacation, spend a couple weeks learning Spanish or head out to explore mysterious Maya ruins.

GUYANA

 CAPITAL GEORGETOWN **POPULATION** 767,240 **AREA** 214,970 SQ KM **OFFICIAL LANGUAGE** ENGLISH

In 2007 Guyana will host the semiquarter matches of the Cricket World Cup, which sceptics decree will be a catastrophe. For the moment, there isn't even an ATM that accepts foreign credit cards, but if this chaotic little country can properly welcome the estimated 100,000 visitors, it can perhaps launch itself into a brighter era for tourism. Plagued with violent crime and instability, this English-speaking country of great character and unparalleled wildlife viewing has the potential to become the next Costa Rica or better. Until then, travelling in Guyana is as rough and off-the-beaten-track as you'll find anywhere.

HAITI

 CAPITAL PORT-AU-PRINCE **POPULATION** 8.3 MILLION **AREA** 27,750 SQ KM **OFFICIAL LANGUAGES** FRENCH, CREOLE

Under heavy UN security, Haiti re-inaugurated President Rene Preval in May 2006. The only president in Haitian history to previously finish a five-year term, Preval was tasked with rebuilding this highly troubled nation, the poorest in the western hemisphere, and plagued by factional violence and warfare since the 2004 coup ousting then-President Jean-Bertrande Aristide. Preval hit the ground running, reaching out across the Americas for international investment in the world's first black republic. Worth watching in 2007 will be Washington's response to Preval's ongoing dialogues with Venezuela, Cuba and the Latin American anti-neoliberal block. Two successes: joint Haiti and Dominican Republic ecological exhibits highlighting sustainability of frontier rivers; and a slight reduction in Haiti's once-unchartable HIV rates.

HONDURAS

 CAPITAL TEGUCIGALPA **POPULATION** 7.3 MILLION **AREA** 112,090 SQ KM **OFFICIAL LANGUAGE** SPANISH

Like every other Central American country, Honduras is on the hunt for tourists. And while the country will probably never match Costa Rica's mass-market appeal, it is seeing increased visitation. As more people come here to check out the azure waters around the Bay Islands, the unexplored Mosquito Coast and the towering Copán ruins, it is becoming more and more clear that tourism may truly be the 'most dangerous game'. Let's just hope Honduras can find a way to preserve the varied and intricate cultures that are drawing tourists here in the first place.

JAMAICA

 CAPITAL KINGSTON **POPULATION** 2.7 MILLION **AREA** 10,991 SQ KM **OFFICIAL LANGUAGE** ENGLISH

With anticipation building for the 2007 Cricket World Cup, times in Jamaica are irie, mon. In 2006 Jamaica elected Portia Simpson Miller the first female prime minister in its history; combating crime tops her mandate. More direct flights from the US and UK and 3000 new hotel rooms since 2005 have fuelled Jamaica's tourism industry, which is wisely targeting Latin American travellers in 2007. For off-track travel, angle south to unhurried Treasure Beach, or hike the Blue Mountains by moonlight, reaching the summit for sunrise (and eponymous coffee). Negril sunsets, long discovered, still inspire. Bob Marley Day is 6 February, and August welcomes the Red Stripe Reggae Sumfest. Seeking the ganja? Don't forget that marijuana is illegal in Jamaica. So if you want to stay high, stay low.

SNAPSHOTS.

MARTINIQUE

 ⚙ **CAPITAL** FORT-DE-FRANCE ⚙ **POPULATION** 436,130
⚙ **AREA** 1100 SQ KM ⚙ **OFFICIAL LANGUAGE** FRENCH

Martinique is a slice of France in the tropics. Although islanders occasionally clamour for independence from their status as a French overseas department, the prospect of losing economic aid from Paris generally tempers public support for nationalist ideals. A history of resisting mainland authority doesn't seem to deter the French from supporting Martinique's flourishing tourism industry, however: 80% of visitors hail from the mainland. Like Marseilles but with palm trees, cosmopolitan Fort-de-France is the island's busy capital. Locals don Paris fashions and nibble on croissants, but the zouk music pouring out of bars suggests a culture strongly rooted in West Indian Creole traditions. Elsewhere on the island, travellers still find forested mountains, laid-back fishing villages and fields of pineapples and sugar cane. Beach-lovers head for Les Salines, while others prefer the grim ruins of former capital Saint-Pierre, razed by erupting Mont Pelée in 1902.

MEXICO

 ⚙ **CAPITAL** MEXICO CITY ⚙ **POPULATION** 107.4 MILLION
⚙ **AREA** 1,972,550 SQ KM ⚙ **OFFICIAL LANGUAGE** SPANISH

Beyond the all-inclusives and vomiting spring-breakers, Mexico abides. The Yucatán is fast recovering after a devastating hurricane season, and the rest of the country continues to do what is seems to do best, just be Mexican: unique, fearless, exotic, playful, and just a bit cheesy. The country's rich past continues to be unearthed (literally). In April 2005, archaeologists announced the discovery of a 6th-century Indian pyramid in Iztapalapa, just outside Mexico City. Maybe you'll find the traces of ancient civilisations, too.

NICARAGUA

 ⚙ **CAPITAL** MANAGUA ⚙ **POPULATION** 5.6 MILLION
⚙ **AREA** 129,494 SQ KM ⚙ **OFFICIAL LANGUAGE** SPANISH

'Nicaragua's gonna pop! The war's over. The beaches are great. There are colonial cities; there are volcanoes. And it's cheap, really cheap.' Well, commentators have been saying that for years now, and the country continues to just not 'pop'. All the ingredients are there – it's pretty damned secure, it's scenic, it's the road less travelled. But Nicaragua is still considered a 'hard' travel destination, and some travellers just aren't ready to shift their paradigms and realise that 'hard' just ain't that hard anymore. Check it out before they go soft.

PANAMA

 ⚙ **CAPITAL** PANAMA CITY ⚙ **POPULATION** 3.2 MILLION
⚙ **AREA** 78,200 SQ KM ⚙ **OFFICIAL LANGUAGE** SPANISH

The next Costa Rica? Whatever. Tourist boards and punter mags can spin and crow, but the fact remains that Panama stands apart from its northern neighbour. For starters, it's pricier, as all those Panama City banks bump up the costs. It's also far less touristed, drawing less than half the visitor numbers of Costa Rica yet still growing its travel trade by 9% year on year, with Latin American travellers predominating. Visitors find ample wildlife in Panama – 30% of the land is protected parkland, and pristine beaches draw rave reviews – and wild nightlife in Panama City, the Miamiesque cosmopolis. In 2007, the multi-year Panama Canal widening continues, so anticipate protests and delays.

PARAGUAY

⚙ **CAPITAL** ASUNCIÓN ⚙ **POPULATION** 6.5 MILLION ⚙ **AREA**
406,750 SQ KM ⚙ **OFFICIAL LANGUAGES** SPANISH, GUARANÍ

Despite the title of Lily Tuck's bestseller, news from Paraguay is hard to come by. It seems like nobody visits this landlocked frontier country. This is a shame, because despite its poverty, legendary corruption and relative isolation, Paraguay has a lot to offer those looking for off-the-beaten-track adventures. Its subtropical rainforests are decorated with blue butterflies, dreamlike waterfalls and jaguars racing through the scrub, and from the hammock of a river boat you can spy macaws, herons, monkeys and other wildlife. The locals are legendary for their friendliness, probably because tourists are still a novelty rather than a nuisance. Paraguay launched a major marketing campaign in Europe in 2005, with the ambitious goal of increasing visitation by 20%. But even if that campaign reaches its lofty goal, visitation will still be one of the lowest in South America.

PERU

 ⚬ **CAPITAL** LIMA ⚬ **POPULATION** 28.3 MILLION ⚬ **AREA** 1,285,220 SQ KM ⚬ **OFFICIAL LANGUAGES** SPANISH, QUECHUA

Everybody in Peru has an opinion on ex-President Alberto Fujimori. Love him or hate him, one thing's for certain, the man made an impact on the country. After months of jail time, he's out of the picture, perhaps signalling the end of the strongman era of Latin American politics. All politicking aside, Peru is one of South America's biggest draws. And beyond the Gringo Trail of Cuzco–Arequipa–Puno, there are exploration opportunities that you won't have to share with thousands of other people. Try hitting the backwoods of the Cordillera Blanca, exploring the deceit and treachery that ended the Inca Empire in Cajamarca, or simply floating down the Amazon River, Bungalow Bill–style.

PUERTO RICO

 ⚬ **CAPITAL** SAN JUAN ⚬ **POPULATION** 3.9 MILLION ⚬ **AREA** 9104 SQ KM ⚬ **OFFICIAL LANGUAGE** SPANISH

Facing a US$740 million budget shortfall, the Puerto Rican government had to shut down for 10 days in May 2006. Schools and offices closed and commerce barely trickled, but the crisis was resolved by a compromise that included the island's first sales tax. The shutdown sideswiped tourism in Puerto Rico (PR): 20% of reservations island-wide were cancelled during the strife, causing the largest spike in new US jobless claims since Hurricane Katrina. Puerto Rico is an American commonwealth, though many deem it the 51st state. Others are just glad the US navy is not bombing Vieques anymore. With sustainable tourism initiatives and cultural assets like salsa, El Yunque rainforest and Old San Juan, PR should quickly rebound.

SABA

 ⚬ **CAPITAL** THE BOTTOM ⚬ **POPULATION** 1600 ⚬ **AREA** 13 SQ KM ⚬ **OFFICIAL LANGUAGE** DUTCH

The second most thrilling activity undertaken on Saba is taking off from its airport. The first is landing there. Saba's airport is just slightly larger than an aircraft carrier's flight deck, and the uneven terrain required some levelling to build the airport. The island is nothing more than one volcanic peak rising straight out of the Caribbean Sea like the tip of an iceberg, and it still has only one road (named 'the Road'). The least-visited island in the Caribbean, Saba might not have a single beach, but for those very, very few who make the trek, its ecolodges and world-class diving and hiking are reward enough.

SAINT BARTHÉLEMY

 ⚬ **CAPITAL** GUSTAVIA ⚬ **POPULATION** 8000 ⚬ **AREA** 21 SQ KM ⚬ **OFFICIAL LANGUAGE** FRENCH

Everyone knows St Barthélemy (St Barth) is nothing more than a jet-setting hot spot for the rich and famous, where all visitors arrive by private yacht or with at least one Oscar nomination. There's no doubt that St Barth is an expensive destination with high-end boutiques and pricy hotel rooms. But there's an actual culture behind the Gucci sunglasses that includes 350 years of hardscrabble pioneering history, resulting in the hardy attitude you'll find in modern-day residents. Many well-to-do families come back here year after year, giving the island a summer-camp feel. Except that at this camp, you might be roasting marshmallows alongside Woody Allen and Diddy.

SAINT EUSTATIUS

 ⚬ **CAPITAL** ORANJESTAD ⚬ **POPULATION** 2800 ⚬ **AREA** 30.5 SQ KM ⚬ **OFFICIAL LANGUAGE** DUTCH

It's a good thing the diving on St Eustatius (Statia, as it's commonly known) is legendary, as there's not much else to do here. The tiny island sees just a few thousand visitors per year, most of whom come here to scuba through sunken shipwrecks in the protected marine park and, since 2003, to volunteer for its nascent national-park system. Lucky divers might even come across blue beads from the days of slavery, underwater relics of the island's New World way-station past. Above the water line, Statia offers little else other than hiking trails and a few colonial buildings, but for some, this is its charm.

SAINT KITTS & NEVIS

⚬ **CAPITAL** BASSETERRE ⚬ **POPULATION** 39,130 ⚬ **AREA** 261 SQ KM ⚬ **OFFICIAL LANGUAGE** ENGLISH

St Kitts and its nation-mate Nevis are the sorts of islands where you might find yourself sipping from a coconut on a palm-fringed beach. Over the past » decade, the islands have thrown down the tourism gauntlet to battle for the Eastern Caribbean dollar and, besides resort and diving packages, beach weddings and wistful plantation inns have given birth to 'romance tourism'. A host of casinos on St Kitts and a Four Seasons mega-resort on Nevis haven't ruined the groovy Caribbean atmosphere, and the brand-new Warner Park Stadium will show off Kittitians' proud culture when the island hosts the Cricket World Cup in 2007. Remember to plan your trip around heavy cruise-ship traffic.

SAINT LUCIA

 ✪ **CAPITAL** CASTRIES ✪ **POPULATION** 168,460 ✪ **AREA** 616 SQ KM ✪ **OFFICIAL LANGUAGE** ENGLISH

It used to be that all St Lucia had to offer was bananas, bananas and more bananas. But these days people are looking beyond bananas, and the country is taking off as a tourist hot spot. Visitors come here to check out the exotic plants, sugary-sweet beaches, ephemeral sulphur springs and the Qualibou volcano. They also come to tie the knot, at least according to a report published by American Express, which named the island the top marriage destination for Britons in 2005. St Lucia beat out heavyweights like Las Vegas and the Maldives to win the honours. Unfortunately, word has it that it's nearly impossible to find an Elvis impersonator to preside over your wedding on the tiny island nation. But who needs Elvis when you have a volcano looming overhead and crystalline Caribbean waters?

SAINT MARTIN/SINT MAARTEN

 ✪ **CAPITAL** MARIGOT (ST MARTIN), PHILIPSBURG (SINT MAARTEN) ✪ **POPULATION** 35,000 (ST MARTIN), 34,000 (SINT MAARTEN) ✪ **AREA** 96 SQ KM ✪ **OFFICIAL LANGUAGES** FRENCH (ST MARTIN), DUTCH (SINT MAARTEN)

The hub in the Leeward Islands for almost one million cruise-ship visitors a year, Dutch Sint Maarten crowds tourists into flashy casinos, duty-free shops and theme restaurants. Those staying longer can linger on the French St Martin side, which classes up the island's northern half with gourmet dining and relaxed beaches. Bending to mass tourism by overdeveloping means that no visitor to St Martin/Sint Maarten will ever be bored and a Caribbean vacation can be affordable. Quick fact: the island is the world's smallest land mass shared by two countries, France and the Netherlands Antilles.

SAINT VINCENT & THE GRENADINES

 ✪ **CAPITAL** KINGSTOWN ✪ **POPULATION** 117,850 ✪ **AREA** 389 SQ KM ✪ **OFFICIAL LANGUAGE** ENGLISH

Once a trolling ground for pirates and now perennially popular with yachties, wealthy recluses and scuba divers, the islands of St Vincent & the Grenadines (SVG) are one of the most desirable destinations in the Caribbean. With 32 islands, there's something for everyone: Mick Jagger still hides out part of the year in Mustique, while bustling St Vincent is known for its no-frills fish market. *Pirates of the Caribbean: Dead Man's Chest* (2006), like its prequel, was filmed in SVG and has brought a greater degree of publicity and attention to the natural beauty of the islands.

SURINAME

 ✪ **CAPITAL** PARAMARIBO ✪ **POPULATION** 439,120 ✪ **AREA** 163,270 SQ KM ✪ **OFFICIAL LANGUAGE** DUTCH

Even cultivated travellers have a hard time placing Suriname on a world map. This oddball of the Atlantic South American coast speaks Dutch, considers itself Caribbean and has one of the most diverse ethnic compositions on the continent. Paramaribo, the capital, is a vibrant, Wild West–feeling place of colonial Dutch architecture, fabulous restaurants and mosques and synagogues as happy neighbours. Suriname's few visitors are primarily Dutch or international business people; if this seems like a crowd, head into the 1.6-million-hectare Central Suriname Nature Reserve to experience some of the world's most pristine rainforests.

TRINIDAD & TOBAGO

 ✪ **CAPITAL** PORT-OF-SPAIN ✪ **POPULATION** 1.1 MILLION ✪ **AREA** 5128 SQ KM ✪ **OFFICIAL LANGUAGE** ENGLISH

Trinidad & Tobago has had its tourism ups and downs, but there is no mistaking that this island-nation is lively and popular. The tourism authorities are working hard to draw in visitors, and initiatives are underway to make booking tours to top sights easier. Safety issues on the islands are important to note but so too are the positive travel stories. Trinidad's king of carnivals is set to mix calypso, soca and steel pans again in February 2007. Tobago is still one of the most overlooked and best-value destinations in the Caribbean; the word is to get here while it lasts.

TURKS & CAICOS ISLANDS

 ⚙ **CAPITAL** COCKBURN TOWN ⚙ **POPULATION** 21,150 ⚙ **AREA** 430 SQ KM ⚙ **OFFICIAL LANGUAGE** ENGLISH

Diving is the thing on Turks & Caicos, a 30-plus island cluster abutting the Bahamas and a 370km coral reef. Short-listed on *Scuba Diving* magazine's best lists, Turks & Caicos boasts resort diving (Providenciales), vertical drops and coral arches (Grand Turk) and shipwrecks and humpback whales (Salt Cay). The islands' bounty extends onshore, with locals and expats forging an impulsive arts scene, and Turks & Caicos winning awards for world's best beach and the Caribbean's best boutique hotel at the 2005 World Travel Awards. Economic good times have spurred murmurings of an independence push, but expect stable prosperity in 2007.

UNITED STATES OF AMERICA

See p22.

UNITED STATES VIRGIN ISLANDS

 ⚙ **CAPITAL** CHARLOTTE AMALIE ⚙ **POPULATION** 124,778 ⚙ **AREA** 352 SQ KM ⚙ **OFFICIAL LANGUAGE** ENGLISH

Flush with cash amid an economic boom, the United States Virgin Islands (USVI) is itching to upgrade. Not that the islands comprising 'America's Caribbean' – St Thomas, St John, St Croix most prominently – lack for amenities and fineries. This unincorporated territory of the US draws mass tourism with duty-free and tax-free shopping, noticeably in the St Thomas port town of Charlotte Amalie. It's not all trinkets and flip-flops here though. St John boasts 3845 hectares of untrammelled national parkland, and St Croix is distant enough (64km) from the other two islands to deter corporate tourism. What's worth watching? How the new year-round interisland ferry service may alter this landscape in 2007 and beyond.

URUGUAY

 ⚙ **CAPITAL** MONTEVIDEO ⚙ **POPULATION** 3.4 MILLION ⚙ **AREA** 176,220 SQ KM ⚙ **OFFICIAL LANGUAGE** SPANISH

If you like to be ahead of the pack, go to Uruguay now. That way, in 20 years, when now-crumbling colonial Montevideo is restored and filled with boutique hotels and chichi restaurants, you can brag, 'I was there when...' Now, it looks a combination of Old Havana and Romania before the fall of Ceauşescu: hauntingly decrepit mansions, quasi-Stalinist architecture, ancient cars, even horse-drawn carriages. But Uruguay's not all faded. Postcard-pretty Colonia del Sacramento is filled with day-trippers, and Eastern Uruguay's stunning beach resorts are mobbed with beautiful people. Venture inland to find hilly grassland where perhaps the world's finest beef has been raised organically since before anyone knew what that was. Tourism is on the upswing, with a 25% increase from 2003 to 2004; a whopping 88% of visitors are from elsewhere in South America, so avoiding the backpacker hordes is not a problem.

VENEZUELA

 ⚙ **CAPITAL** CARACAS ⚙ **POPULATION** 25.7 MILLION ⚙ **AREA** 912,050 SQ KM ⚙ **OFFICIAL LANGUAGE** SPANISH

Known for oil and sharp-tongued Hugo Chávez, many don't realise that Venezuela has gorgeous savannah, Amazon rainforest, the Andes, and the most Caribbean coastline of any single country. The Andean region is starting to attract more adventurous travellers who come to hike, mountain bike and paraglide. Isla de Margarita and the small town of Adícora are famed for windsurfing and kitesurfing. The 2006 World Social Forum in Caracas helped to put the city and country firmly on the leftist political map. Many are now coming to witness or try to volunteer in Chávez' Socialist 'Bolivarian Revolution'.

MONGOLIA

Sea of
Okhotsk

NORTH
KOREA

Sea of
Japan

SOUTH
KOREA

JAPAN

Yellow
Sea

CHINA

TAIWAN

NORTH PACIFIC OCEAN

MACAU

HONG KONG

LAOS

AILAND

VIETNAM

South
China
Sea

PHILIPPINES

CAMBODIA

BRUNEI

» ASIA

MALAYSIA

SINGAPORE

INDONESIA

» ASIA

AFGHANISTAN

⊙ **CAPITAL** KABUL ⊙ **POPULATION** 3.1 MILLION
⊙ **AREA** 647,500 SQ KM ⊙ **OFFICIAL LANGUAGE** AFGHAN PERSIAN

It seems like a long time since we featured Afghanistan in our very first guidebook in the 1970s. This war-ravaged country was once called the 'Crossroads of Asia', and travellers flocked here for the sublime scenery and the proud hospitality of its people. The much-hyped reconstruction after the Taliban's ouster continues fitfully along a difficult path. With the opium poppies still growing high and a tricky NATO expansion unfolding in the dangerous southern badlands, Kabul's carpet sellers will have to wait a little longer yet before the tourist dollars start flooding in again.

BANGLADESH

⊙ **CAPITAL** DHAKA ⊙ **POPULATION** 147.4 MILLION
⊙ **AREA** 144,000 SQ KM ⊙ **OFFICIAL LANGUAGE** BENGALI

Travellers are starting to talk about the archaeological attractions, throbbing cities and varying landscapes of Bangladesh, one of the poorest, most populated and most hospitable countries in the world. The tourism authority advises you to 'come to Bangladesh before the tourists', which is advice worth listening to, but perhaps only after the national elections in early 2007. This country takes its future seriously: political activism ranges from intellectual debate to violent street protests and the occasional bombing. The only thing that can overshadow this political climax is the Cricket World Cup, which will temporarily divert all fervour to the West Indies over March and April 2007.

BHUTAN

⊙ **CAPITAL** THIMPHU ⊙ **POPULATION** 2.3 MILLION
⊙ **AREA** 47,000 SQ KM ⊙ **OFFICIAL LANGUAGE** DZONGKHA

Bhutan's strong restrictions on foreign visitors attempt to preserve a unique cultural heritage, though some nationals may wonder whether cultural preservation amounts to cultural imposition. Despite the recent emergence of luxury hotels, the high-quality, low-impact approach to tourism shows in earthy and authentic organised tours, albeit for a cost of around US$200 per day. But then, who wouldn't pay to visit a country that was the last in the world to introduce television but the first to introduce a 'Gross National Happiness' indicator. Celebrations to mark the 2007 centenary of the monarchy have been postponed to 2008, as 2007 is an inauspicious lunar year.

BRUNEI

⊙ **CAPITAL** BANDAR SERI BEGAWAN ⊙ **POPULATION** 349,440
⊙ **AREA** 5770 SQ KM ⊙ **OFFICIAL LANGUAGE** MALAY

While a heady love affair with tourism has spun for decades around it, Brunei remains removed from the beaten track for most explorers. This looks set to change over the next few years due to a government plan to finally jump on the Southeast Asian tourist bandwagon. Angling for Brunei to become the next destination for adventurers with middle-aged incomes, the government is exploiting untouched hectares of wilderness, particularly the 50,000-hectare Ulu Temburong National Park. Here, nature-lovers will be able to make the most of multistage development, culminating in camping sites, suspension bridges and a low-impact rail system.

CAMBODIA

CAPITAL PHNOM PENH **POPULATION** 13.9 MILLION
AREA 181,040 SQ KM **OFFICIAL LANGUAGE** KHMER

Angkor's awe-inspiring temples attracted more people than ever in 2006 and numbers are expected to keep climbing in 2007. But Cambodia's charms go beyond Angkor Wat. The capital Phnom Penh is becoming a destination in itself, with hip restaurants, bars and floating nightclubs popping up like mushrooms. It's attracting artists, with the Phnom Penh Arts Festival in March and the Refugee Film Festival in July drawing crowds. Elsewhere, adventurers are finding new routes into the jungles of Ratanakiri and Mondulkiri or onto little-known islands in the Gulf of Thailand.

CHINA

See p34.

EAST TIMOR

CAPITAL DILI **POPULATION** 1.1 MILLION **AREA** 15,007 SQ KM **OFFICIAL LANGUAGES** TETUN, PORTUGUESE

East Timor remains an off-the-beaten-track, low on infrastructure, high on tick-list cachet destination. Tourism proper (as opposed to aid- or development-related travel) constitutes a smattering of enthusiastic souls rattling slowly around this mountainous half-island. Dili remains the hub for visitors, with its post-UN relative abundance of comfortable hotels and international food. Other hot spots include the ecoresort at tranquil Atauro Island, spectacular diving in Metinaro's pristine waters, elegant Portuguese-era *pousadas* (traditional inns) at Baucau and Maubisse and the chilly Mt Ramelau dawn climb. Tricky access, minimal infrastructure, political instability and security problems (in 2006 international troops were brought in to help quell internal violence) could prove a dampening influence on visitor numbers in 2007.

HONG KONG

CAPITAL VICTORIA **POPULATION** 6.9 MILLION **AREA** 1092 SQ KM **OFFICIAL LANGUAGES** ENGLISH, CANTONESE

Hong Kong locals have always viewed their city as international. But some say it only became truly international once the British left. Today you'll find a booming food scene: think innovative modern Chinese (Chinese sausage ice-cream is surprisingly good), a passion for regional fare, and some of the best chefs from around the world. Hong Kong still delivers the longtime favourites such as the awe-inspiring Tian Tan Buddha, world-class shopping, tropical hikes on Lantau Island, and the ever-romantic Peak. You could

say Hong Kong has finally come into its own, and increasing numbers of travellers obviously think so.

INDIA

See p38.

INDONESIA

CAPITAL JAKARTA **POPULATION** 245.4 MILLION **AREA** 1,919,440 SQ KM **OFFICIAL LANGUAGE** BAHASA INDONESIA

Indonesia has been a bit of a sleeper on the Southeast Asia tourist map in recent years. However, the portents for travel there in 2007 are good. The big-ticket attractions of Java's ancient wonders (Borobudur and Prambanan), Sumatra's orang-utans, and Bali's fine hotels, delicious food, pampering and 'easy' travel opportunities in this otherwise toughish region will continue to draw the lion's (relative cub though it is) share of travellers. More interesting still are the 'phoenix' destinations rising from the ashes of natural disaster and conflict (Aceh) and yet more civil unrest (Maluku). Both offer endless beaches washed by crystal-clear seas that reveal magical underwater worlds to divers and snorkellers.

JAPAN

CAPITAL TOKYO **POPULATION** 127.5 MILLION **AREA** 377,835 SQ KM **OFFICIAL LANGUAGE** JAPANESE

Forgotten about Japan lately? You're not alone. There were around six million visitors in 2006, a figure tipped to rise by another million by 2009. Compare this to China, which enjoyed six times as many visitors in 2005. Yet regional instability such as the tsunami and bird flu cast Japan's boons into sharp relief: here is an efficient, safe, and clean country with a captivating traditional arts heritage and world-famous hospitality. And there are always new discoveries to be made. Get off the beaten track in Tōhoku, don your snorkel in tropical Okinawa, and gorge on fine beef in Kōbe.

KAZAKHSTAN

CAPITAL ASTANA **POPULATION** 15.2 MILLION **AREA** 2,717,300 SQ KM **OFFICIAL LANGUAGES** KAZAKH, RUSSIAN

A few years back Kazakhstan was one of the more difficult counties to access in Central Asia, but now most European visitors can get visas without letters of invitation. With a healthy economy growing at 8% on the back of oil, Kazakhstan's infrastructure and facilities are also improving, particularly in the new capital, Astana. But this also means soaring hotel costs. The main areas of interest for travellers remain in the south, highlighted by beautiful Almaty, from »

SNAPSHOTS.

where you can trek over the mountains to Kyrgyzstan. For some real 'end of the earth' travel, try the desert scenery between the Caspian Sea and Uzbekistan.

KOREA, NORTH

⚬ **CAPITAL** PYONGYANG ⚬ **POPULATION** 23.1 MILLION
⚬ **AREA** 120,540 SQ KM ⚬ **OFFICIAL LANGUAGE** KOREAN

Sadly North Korea remains a destination for people with money. It's one of the most remote, isolated and down-right nutty countries on the planet; you can only come here on an organised tour and those don't come cheap. A highlight is the Mass Games in Pyongyang, a vast gymnastic spectacle featuring thousands of locals holding up placards to form mosaics praising the regime, to be held from August to October 2007. During this time American citizens, normally barred from travel in North Korea, will be granted visas. This will be a remarkable chance to visit a fascinating country frozen in time.

KOREA, SOUTH

⚬ **CAPITAL** SEOUL ⚬ **POPULATION** 48.8 MILLION
⚬ **AREA** 98,480 SQ KM ⚬ **OFFICIAL LANGUAGE** KOREAN

Previously a less popular Asian destination, South Korea has become something of a hot spot, attracting seasoned travellers in search of unique experiences. A series of outlandishly popular Korean soap operas inspires travellers with romance on their minds. You too can have your wedding photos taken in breath-taking Gangwon-do, then head to Jeju-do for a subtropical honeymoon Korean-style. Skiing has always been the big winter attraction, but in 2007 winter sports will be hotter than ever, particularly if Pyeongchang succeeds in its bid for the 2014 Winter Olympics.

KYRGYZSTAN

⚬ **CAPITAL** BISHKEK ⚬ **POPULATION** 5.2 MILLION ⚬ **AREA** 198,500 SQ KM ⚬ **OFFICIAL LANGUAGES** KYRGYZ, RUSSIAN

Long regarded as a paradise for independent travellers and mountaineers, Kyrgyzstan has begun a push to draw more mainstream tourists to its crown jewel, Lake Issyk-Kul. Expect several new resorts to spring up around the lake in 2007, while traffic to the region's newly improved airport will increase. Nationwide, ongoing political unrest in the wake of the 2005 'Tulip Revolution' continues to crimp tourism. Despite this, the country is

safer than ever and facilities exist to suit all budgets. Plan that exotic ski vacation, horseback trek or hiking excursion in the majestic Tien Shan mountains now – before the inevitable tourism boom arrives.

LAOS

⚬ **CAPITAL** VIENTIANE ⚬ **POPULATION** 6.4 MILLION
⚬ **AREA** 236,800 SQ KM ⚬ **OFFICIAL LANGUAGE** LAO

It's little wonder that a country described as 'the most laid-back on earth' is attracting ever more travellers. Ecotourism projects are all the rage, and in 2007 sustainable trekking will be possible in almost every province in Laos – just choose your level of remoteness. A high-flying alternative is the Gibbon Experience in Bokeo Province, where you can live in a tree house 23m above the ground and zip between the trees on flying foxes. Also expect to see more *falangs* (foreigners) poking around the stone jars and cluster-bomb casings on the mysterious Plain of Jars, which should become a Unesco World Heritage site soon.

MACAU

⚬ **POPULATION** 4653,120 ⚬ **AREA** 28.2 SQ KM
⚬ **OFFICIAL LANGUAGES** PORTUGUESE, CANTONESE

On the Pearl River Delta, Macau gets all the hype, and with good reason. The casino scene is booming and unprecedented numbers of Chinese are flocking in for some old-fashioned hedonism. But there's another side to Macau: awesome fare, classic colonial buildings, luxurious accommodation and a unique Macanese culture. Satisfy your curiosity at the newly opened American giant, Sands Macau, a casino with 300 gaming tables and hundreds of top-notch poker machines. For a room at the Sands Casino Hotel, you'll be gambling in the high-rollers room where it costs about US$75,000 for a seat, and the minimum bet is US$10,000.

MALAYSIA

⚬ **CAPITAL** KUALA LUMPUR ⚬ **POPULATION** 24.4 MILLION
⚬ **AREA** 329,750 SQ KM ⚬ **OFFICIAL LANGUAGE** BAHASA MALAY

The year 2007 promises to be huge for Malaysia. Celebrating its Golden Jubilee of independence, the country will be a hurly-burly of parades, street performances, carnivals and cultural events. The government has declared 2007 the year of 'Visit Malaysia', and more than

20 million visitors are expected to join the party. Daunted by the crowds? Skip the mainland and enjoy a bout of ecotourism in Kinabatangan, where the Tungog Rainforest Ecocamp is set to welcome tourists for the first time. Snorkel or dive world-renowned sites in Sabah, climb Mt Kinabalu, fly gargantuan kites in Kelantan or find a patch of idyllic beach in Terengganu.

MALDIVES

⊙ **CAPITAL** MALÉ ⊙ **POPULATION** 301,475
⊙ **AREA** 300 SQ KM ⊙ **OFFICIAL LANGUAGE** DIVEHI

Maldives is paradise on earth, but only if you're a tourist. Behind the powder-white beaches and the glamorous resorts lurks a nasty regime clinging to power despite a growing pro-democracy movement. A very good, carefully targeted campaign boycotting resorts that are owned by government ministers is being run by Friends of Maldives (www.friendsofmaldives.org). It's already seeing some success as the government is terrified of losing its main source of income. Recovery from the tsunami is almost complete, with a slew of luxury hotels arriving in 2007. Diving, snorkelling, water sports and sun worship don't come much better than this.

MONGOLIA

⊙ **CAPITAL** ULAANBAATAR ⊙ **POPULATION** 2.8 MILLION
⊙ **AREA** 1,564,116 SQ KM ⊙ **OFFICIAL LANGUAGE** MONGOLIAN

Untouched and underhyped, the Land of Blue Sky has attracted interest slowly but steadily. A trip to Mongolia is still a historical journey as well as an outdoor adventure, and outside Ulaanbaatar, life remains traditional. A horseback trek at Khövsgöl Nuur, a 2760-sq-km alpine lake backed by pristine mountains, never fails to impress. For a taste of Central Asia, head west to the ethnically Kazakh city of Ölgii, an interesting stop on the way to spectacular Altai Tavan Bogd National Park. Given the region's stability and timeless draws, there's no doubt that more and more travellers will be searching out this country's undiscovered pockets.

MYANMAR (BURMA)

⊙ **CAPITAL** YANGON (RANGOON) ⊙ **POPULATION** 47.4 MILLION
⊙ **AREA** 678,500 SQ KM ⊙ **OFFICIAL LANGUAGE** BURMESE

Cloaked in human rights controversy and political turmoil, Myanmar (Burma) is ruled by a brutal illegiti-mate military regime whose human rights abuses and refusal to acknowledge the democratically elected leader, Aung San Suu Kyi, make the independent traveller's decision to visit the country a difficult one. But once an informed decision has been made, it's possible to travel responsibly and to have one of the most satisfying, exhilarating and stimulating experiences that Southeast Asia has to offer. Soak up the cosmopolitan vibe in bustling Yangon (Rangoon), then head off on a clockwise loop around the country, visiting the spectacular ancient site of Bagan (free from Angkor's crowds) and dropping in on laid-back Mandalay, before jumping aboard a canoe and floating around the markets on Inle Lake.

NEPAL

⊙ **CAPITAL** KATHMANDU ⊙ **POPULATION** 28.3 MILLION
⊙ **AREA** 140,800 SQ KM ⊙ **OFFICIAL LANGUAGE** NEPALI

Nepal is emerging with newfound optimism from a decade of political wrangling and episodic violence. The streets are still chaotic and dirty, but the handover of power to the government by King Gyanendra in April 2006 has kick-started a transformation. Since 1996, the Maoist insurgency and the massacre of most of the royal family has caused steep downturns in tourist visits; many Nepalis dependent on tourism have turned to more sustainable industries. It will be interesting to watch the progress of this superb country, and how its people deal with its inevitable return to popularity.

PAKISTAN

⊙ **CAPITAL** ISLAMABAD ⊙ **POPULATION** 165.8 MILLION
⊙ **AREA** 803,940 SQ KM ⊙ **OFFICIAL LANGUAGE** URDU

Visitors remain wary of Pakistan, and the repercussions of the tragic earthquake of October 2005 will be felt for a long time. But intrepid travellers still enjoy Lahore's exquisite Islamic architecture and modern Islamabad as well as northern Pakistan's uncrowded trails, unrivalled scenery and friendly hosts. Although parts of the North-West Frontier Province and Kashmir were devastated by the earthquake, neighbouring regions were relatively unscathed, such as the adventurers' paradise along the fabled Karakoram Highway. Gilgit is the highway's staging post for detours to the spectacular Karakoram and Hindukush Mountains. In July 2007, Gilgit and Chitral's finest horses and riders will again compete at the high Shandur Pass polo ground.

SNAPSHOTS.

PAPUA NEW GUINEA

 ✪ **CAPITAL** PORT MORESBY ✪ **POPULATION** 5.7 MILLION ✪ **AREA** 462,840 SQ KM ✪ **OFFICIAL LANGUAGE** ENGLISH

Papua New Guinea (PNG) has an embarrassment of mind-blowing riches to divide among a paltry allocation of tourists. Most visitors concentrate on the rugged stretches of the historic Kokoda Track, the cultural maelstrom of the highland shows (Goroka, in mid-September, is the highlight) or the underwater splendour of Milne Bay. Equally remarkable are the spectacular topography (Mt Wilhelm tops out at 4509m and can be climbed in four days) and unique wildlife, including tree kangaroos and the fabled bird of paradise. PNG is also attracting attention as a surfing destination, with the best waves around Vanimo. Keeping all this as one of the world's great tourism secrets are PNG's entrenched security problems, which, despite Australian aid initiatives, do not look likely to abate in 2007.

PHILIPPINES

 ✪ **CAPITAL** MANILA ✪ **POPULATION** 89.5 MILLION ✪ **AREA** 300,000 SQ KM ✪ **OFFICIAL LANGUAGES** FILIPINO, ENGLISH

The Philippines faces familiar questions in 2007. Will Manila's new international airport terminal, gathering dust since 2002, finally open? Will unchecked development continue to jeopardise the environmental sustainability of tiny top tourist draw Boracay Island? Will Malapascua Island finally arrive as a marquee destination? The controversial airport was set to open in 2006 before a roof suspiciously collapsed. Until it opens, expect tourism to remain flat, and expect more visitors to bypass Manila in favour of up-and-coming second city of Cebu. Off-the-beaten-track destinations to enjoy the sparse crowds in 2007 include the Cordillera Mountains and the island of Samar.

SINGAPORE

 ✪ **CAPITAL** SINGAPORE ✪ **POPULATION** 4.5 MILLION ✪ **AREA** 693 SQ KM ✪ **OFFICIAL LANGUAGES** MALAY, TAMIL, MANDARIN CHINESE, ENGLISH

Singapore is packing in more travellers than ever before, with already impressive visitor numbers having increased this year by double digits. Large-scale remodelling of Clarke Quay and ongoing development of Marina Bay have added to the roar of the Lion City, and shopping and an unrivalled opportunity for culinary indulgence remain mainstays. Singapore's bid to establish itself as the arts hub of Asia has been incredibly successful: be sure to catch a show at Esplanade – Theatres on the Bay. The year 2007 will see a rise in medical tourism (top-notch facilities at bargain prices), consolidation of the boom in health and wellness centres, and more festivals than you can shake a stick at.

SOLOMON ISLANDS

 ✪ **CAPITAL** HONIARA ✪ **POPULATION** 552,440 ✪ **AREA** 28,450 SQ KM ✪ **OFFICIAL LANGUAGE** ENGLISH

The Solomons' tourism industry was on a slow path towards recovery, following the coup of 2000, until more political unrest in early 2006 brought the islands to international attention again for all the wrong reasons. However, there's never been any violence directed towards travellers, and with politics once more under control, it's again a safe destination to visit. That's not helping the tourism industry though; you certainly won't be competing with hordes of other travellers when you visit those amazing WWII dive sites or experience the unique Solomons culture. All that aside, travellers to the Solomons should always exercise a little caution, and if there's any political unrest you might feel safer bailing out.

SRI LANKA

 ✪ **CAPITAL** COLOMBO ✪ **POPULATION** 20.2 MILLION ✪ **AREA** 65,640 SQ KM ✪ **OFFICIAL LANGUAGES** SINHALA, TAMIL

Sri Lanka is hitting its stride post-tsunami with stunning coastal hot spots like Galle, Hikkaduwa and Mirissa looking more resplendent than ever. The mysterious teardrop island's attractions don't disappoint: lush forests, ancient cities, pristine beaches and dramatic tea-growing hill-country scenery. Now is a great time to visit Sri Lanka to experience a well-equipped uncrowded travel infrastructure offering amazing value for money. As the majority Sinhalese and minority Tamils have been involved in an on-and-off civil war for 25 years, avoid parts of the north; but otherwise daily life goes on as normal.

TAIWAN

⚙ **CAPITAL** TAIPEI ⚙ **POPULATION** 22.9 MILLION ⚙ **AREA** 35,563 SQ KM ⚙ **OFFICIAL LANGUAGE** MANDARIN CHINESE

Since 2002 the Taiwanese government has been throwing billions of New Taiwan dollars into an island-wide facelift and simultaneous PR campaign. The goal is to boost tourist numbers from 2005's one million to five million per year (including mainlanders), in time for Taiwan Expo 2008, a massive celebratory self-feting. Every year, the island has become more tourist-friendly, and best of all is the focus on independent travel. The Siraya National Scenic Area lures travellers looking for classic mountain-water vistas to the criminally underappreciated jewel of Tainan County in the south. Other developments include extensive bike and hiking trails, new museums, and improved transport and accommodation infrastructure.

TAJIKISTAN

⚙ **CAPITAL** DUSHANBE ⚙ **POPULATION** 7.3 MILLION ⚙ **AREA** 143,100 SQ KM ⚙ **OFFICIAL LANGUAGE** TAJIK

Tajikistan remains a mecca for independent travellers. President Emomali Rahmonov, expected to be re-elected in November 2006, is no friend to democracy but his continued reign will keep things peaceful and relatively safe. The country's paltry tourist infrastructure may improve if any of the four top-end hotels currently under construction in Dushanbe opens in 2007. Expect a small spike in tourism, most of it going through a handful of private adventure-travel companies. Improvements to the rugged Dushanbe–Khorog road will make the spectacular Pamir Mountains in the east more accessible than ever.

THAILAND

See p26.

TIBET

⚙ **CAPITAL** LHASA ⚙ **POPULATION** 13.5 MILLION ⚙ **AREA** 1,221,601 SQ KM ⚙ **OFFICIAL LANGUAGE** MANDARIN CHINESE

The hot topic of whether to travel to Tibet hit boiling point when the Qinghai–Tibet Railway became fully operational after its maiden journey in July 2006. If tourists don't heed activists' pleas to boycott this ultraslick tourist train (complete with extra oxygen to combat altitude sickness) it could not only boost the economy of Tibet, but also China's stronghold over it. Travellers who venture to the rooftop of the world discover that the fragile cultural heritage of Tibet remains resolutely unique. The Potala Palace, the traditional home of the Dalai Lama, sits in the world's highest city and on the Unesco World Heritage list.

TURKMENISTAN

See p196.

UZBEKISTAN

⚙ **CAPITAL** TASHKENT ⚙ **POPULATION** 27.3 MILLION ⚙ **AREA** 447,400 SQ KM ⚙ **OFFICIAL LANGUAGE** UZBEK

Following the May 2005 massacre in Andijan that left more than 200 people dead, Uzbekistan was suddenly considered a flash point for violence, but President Karimov has managed to keep a lid on the public unrest. While life on the ground for locals has deteriorated under Karimov's regime, travel conditions for tourists are still secure and easy along the main Silk Road cities of Samarkand, Bukhara and Khiva. For some real off-road adventure, head up to Nukus from where you can make a day trip to Moynaq, a former fishing village that once stood on the shores of the shrinking Aral Sea.

VIETNAM

⚙ **CAPITAL** HANOI ⚙ **POPULATION** 84.4 MILLION ⚙ **AREA** 329,560 SQ KM ⚙ **OFFICIAL LANGUAGE** VIETNAMESE

Vietnam's growth as a destination continues apace and, if bird flu stays away, record numbers of visitors are expected in 2007. To meet the demand, hotels and resorts are springing up in Hanoi, Nha Trang, Mui Ne and Ho Chi Minh City, many offering a truly world-class stay. But the tourists haven't fully arrived on Phu Quoc…yet. The island that Vietnam appropriated from Cambodia a few decades back is a little like the Thai islands 20 years ago; head there before everyone else does. For something more vociferous, get thee to Hanoi in July 2007 for the Asian Cup football finals.

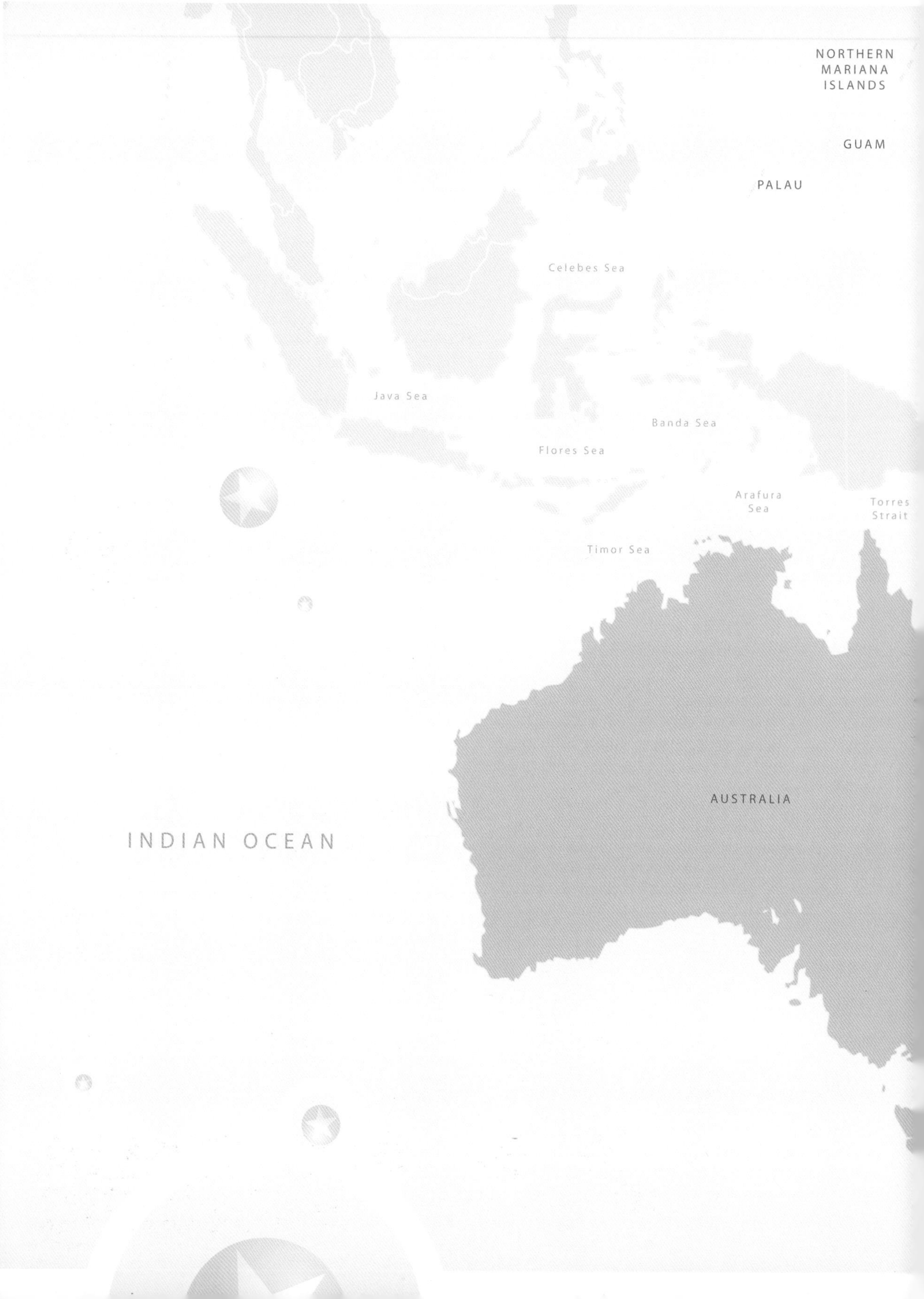

NORTHERN MARIANA ISLANDS
GUAM
PALAU
Celebes Sea
Java Sea
Banda Sea
Flores Sea
Arafura Sea
Torres Strait
Timor Sea
AUSTRALIA
INDIAN OCEAN

RONESIA

MARSHALL
ISLANDS

KIRIBATI

NAURU

Solomon
Sea

TUVALU

SAMOAN
ISLANDS

COOK
ISLANDS

TAHITI &
FRENCH
POLYNESIA

Coral
Sea

VANUATU

FIJI

TONGA

NEW
CALEDONIA

PITCAIRN
ISLAND

SOUTH

PACIFIC

OCEAN

Tasman
Sea

NEW
ZEALAND

» **AUSTRALIA
+ PACIFIC**

» AUSTRALIA + PACIFIC

AUSTRALIA

See p18.

COOK ISLANDS

 ✪ **CAPITAL** AVARUA ✪ **POPULATION** 21,380 ✪ **AREA** 240 SQ KM ✪ **OFFICIAL LANGUAGES** ENGLISH, COOK ISLANDS MAORI

The majority of travellers to the Cooks still don't leave Rarotonga at all – fools! Don't get us wrong: Rarotonga is great, with terrific snorkelling, a party atmosphere, excellent fresh seafood, mist-shrouded mountains, lots of kid-friendly activities…but the outer islands offer many more unique experiences. The beautiful atoll of Aitutaki, with its lagoon cruises and white-sand islets, has always been the most popular of excursions, but now the tiny proud island of 'Atiu, with its ancient stone *maraes* (meeting grounds) and secret *tumunus* (bush-beer sessions), is also better prepared to welcome travellers. The best event to plan your trip around is the Tiare Festival each November, with parades, dance and drum competitions and plenty (plenty!) of food.

FIJI

 ✪ **CAPITAL** SUVA ✪ **POPULATION** 905,950 ✪ **AREA** 18,270 SQ KM ✪ **OFFICIAL LANGUAGE** ENGLISH

Fiji is once more the Pacific destination on everyone's minds. There's been a significant increase in tourism, with the country's occasional political grumpiness now rightly seen as no threat to travellers, and low-cost flights also fuelling an increase in tourism. However, despite new hotels and resorts sprouting like frangipanis, the growth is largely confined to the tourism hot spots of Denarau, the Mamanucas, the Yasawas and the Coral Coast. Head north or east from Nadi, or, even better, offshore to Vanua Levu, Taveuni or Kadavu, and you'll find plenty of room to yourself. Nowhere else in the Pacific are there as many options, as pampered or as intrepid as you choose.

GUAM & NORTHERN MARIANA ISLANDS

 ✪ **CAPITAL** AGANA (G), SAIPAN (NMI) ✪ **POPULATION** 117,020 (G), 82,460 (NMI) ✪ **AREA** 549 SQ KM (G), 477 SQ KM (NMI) ✪ **OFFICIAL LANGUAGE** ENGLISH

Guam and the Northern Marianas are two separate political identities and offer two very different experiences for the traveller. Guam has the largest air traffic in the Pacific Islands, with around a million tourists per year, largely hailing from northeast Asia. Cosmopolitan and sometimes beautiful it might be, but Guam and its crowds of package shoppers still leave many travellers cold. On the other hand, with Japanese airlines having pulled out of the Northern Marianas, any tourism trail here has all but vanished, and you'll have entire islands to yourself. If you arrange your visit to coincide with a cultural event such as April's Flame Tree Festival, you'll see arts, music and dancing in the company of thousands of Pacific Islanders and relatively few other travellers.

KIRIBATI

 ✪ **CAPITAL** TARAWA ✪ **POPULATION** 105,430 ✪ **AREA** 811 SQ KM ✪ **OFFICIAL LANGUAGES** ENGLISH, GILBERTESE

Kiri where? Although there's a slow increase in the trickle of travellers coming to these tiny islands in the centre of the Pacific Ocean, Kiribati is still well and truly off the map for the bulk of travellers. Recent changes in air routes have bought it closer to Fiji and Hawaii, raising hopes in Kiribati for more visitors in the near future. With an eye to independent travel, the Otintaai Hotel has recently converted 10 rooms to cater to the backpacker market. Most travellers still head to Tarawa or Christmas Island, but improved transport options should see more travellers heading to Abemama, Abaiang and North Tarawa. Independence celebrations in mid-July remain the event of the year, with week-long parades, games and dancing.

MARSHALL ISLANDS

 ✪ **CAPITAL** MAJURO ✪ **POPULATION** 60,420 ✪ **AREA** 181 SQ KM ✪ **OFFICIAL LANGUAGES** ENGLISH, MARSHALLESE

The number of travellers visiting these stunningly beautiful islands remains small, and over half of them come for business rather than for pleasure. Their loss! There are so many better things to do in the Marshalls than work for the massive US military industry on Kwajalein Atoll. Scuba diving remains the pursuit of choice, with some visitors dodging the laid-back main atoll of Majuro altogether to head straight for Bikini's underwater wrecks or Rongelap's amazing sea life. Fishing enthusiasts too have been discovering the Marshalls, with many of them timing their visits for the week-long Alele festivities and fishing competitions in September. A final note: when US missile tests are scheduled on Kwajalein, flights will not land. Safety first.

MICRONESIA

 ✪ **CAPITAL** PALIKIR ✪ **POPULATION** 108,000 ✪ **AREA** 702 SQ KM ✪ **OFFICIAL LANGUAGE** ENGLISH

Pohnpei's justly famous Nan Madol, a Pacific Islands cross between Stonehenge and Venice, is still the single major attraction of the Federated States of Micronesia (FSM). Activities in the FSM are largely scuba-diving based, with the renowned (and much photographed) WWII wrecks of Chuuk Lagoon, but it can't be long before the world's surfing fraternity hears about Pohnpei and Kosrae's awesome breaks. Niche travellers increasingly want to round their trip out: not content with scuba diving, they also seek hiking, kayaking and cultural experiences. Traditional culture, such as on the island of Yap, is an attraction that the world has slowly started to discover, usually as a supplement to a diving trip. A trip to Kosrae in September can be timed around Festival Week, which includes singing, dancing and sports.

NAURU

 ✪ **POPULATION** 13,290 ✪ **AREA** 21 SQ KM ✪ **OFFICIAL LANGUAGE** NAURUAN

Nauru, via its national airline, the financially troubled Air Nauru, offers unusual and easy Pacific connections from Australia and Fiji to hard-to-reach destinations such as the Solomons, the Marshalls and Kiribati. Nauru itself is a pretty sobering place to visit, with tourist activities such as inspecting the devastation from a century of mining bird poo, and visiting Australia's grim detention centre for unfortunate asylum-seekers. Nonstop fun it ain't. With the country's finances perpetually teetering on the brink of ruin, there's always some doubt that Nauru will continue to be a viable home for its people for a great deal longer. Perhaps the best reason to visit is to see the place while there's still anyone there other than refugees and their guards.

NEW CALEDONIA

 ✪ **CAPITAL** NOUMEA ✪ **POPULATION** 219,250 ✪ **AREA** 19,060 SQ KM ✪ **OFFICIAL LANGUAGE** FRENCH

What sets New Caledonia apart as a travel destination from its Melanesian neighbours is the culture: a blend of transplanted French and indigenous Kanak. Even for those just here to relax beachside at their flash resort (still the vast majority of visitors to these islands), it's a blend of cultures that provides *bonne cuisine* (good cooking) and fantastic dance performances. Lately, many travellers are opting for a deeper cultural experience such as Kanak homestays in Hienghène or on the Loyalty Islands. A few younger, more independent travellers are starting to forge new trails away from the resort areas, and ecotourism and adventure tourism are taking off with activities such as kayaking and nature walks. This is prompting the government to spend a few francs on developing parks and reserves.

NEW ZEALAND

See p20.

PALAU

 ✪ **CAPITAL** KOROR ✪ **POPULATION** 20,580 ✪ **AREA** 458 SQ KM ✪ **OFFICIAL LANGUAGES** ENGLISH, PALAUAN

More often viewed in photographic form than in real life, Palau remains a little aloof from the mainstream travel industry. It's getting easier to reach the country from Asia but for now it's still mostly Asians themselves visiting these western Pacific islands, which for some reason are yet to be discovered by the rest of the world. Diving remains the main activity for travellers heading this way, and the startling Rock Islands are Palau's most photographed feature (with good reason). Wildlife, above and below the waterline, forms the basis of a still-nascent ecotourism industry. For now, cultural tourism, such as museums, is almost unknown. It takes some effort to tap into the Palauan vibe.

SNAPSHOTS.

PITCAIRN ISLAND

 ○ **CAPITAL** ADAMSTOWN ○ **POPULATION** 45
○ **AREA** 458 SQ KM ○ **OFFICIAL LANGUAGE** ENGLISH

You've probably heard of Pitcairn for all the wrong reasons: half the adult male population seems to be on trial, or already jailed, for sex crimes, and once more the island's viability as a long-term abode is being questioned. But this time, the British government seems to be making an effort to keep it viable, including investing in the type of infrastructure that might see the island receiving more travellers: some accommodation options, the possibility of more ships visiting from French Polynesia, and even the mention of an airstrip. If you're heading to Tahiti, ask around in advance to see whether you can make a side trip to the world's most isolated mutiny outpost.

SAMOA & AMERICAN SAMOA

 ○ **CAPITAL** APIA (S), PAGO PAGO (AS) ○ **POPULATION** 176,910 (S),
57,790 (AS) ○ **AREA** 2944 SQ KM (S), 199 SQ KM (AS)
○ **OFFICIAL LANGUAGE** ENGLISH

With cheaper flights more readily available, there's been a steady increase in the numbers of independent travellers, many discovering the quieter parts of Samoa, such as the more traditional island of Savai'i and the quiet beaches of southern 'Upolu. Experiences with Samoans themselves are increasingly sought by travellers – not just at the wonderful organised *fiafia* (dances), but with ordinary Samoans in the street too. Ecotourism and sustainable tourism is taking off, such as ecofriendly beach-*fale* (traditional thatched house) homestays and hiking in areas such as Sataoa, Sa'anapu and O Le Pupu-Pu'e National Park. Samoa will be hosting the South Pacific Games in August and September 2007: teams from 22 countries will participate in 30 different sports over 16 days, with games, dancing, feasts… This will be a Pacific Islands hot spot!

TAHITI & FRENCH POLYNESIA

 ○ **CAPITAL** PAPE'ETE ○ **POPULATION** 245,405 ○ **AREA** 4167 SQ KM
○ **OFFICIAL LANGUAGES** TAHITIAN, FRENCH

Low-cost airfares have seen a boost in visitors to this corner of the Pacific. Most of them still pause only briefly on Tahiti itself before heading *très rapidement*

offshore to the tourist hot spots of Bora Bora and Mo'orea, but a few linger on Tahiti to sample the big-city life. Others have been finding slightly more space for themselves on rather less visited isles such as Huahine or Ra'iatea, with a steady trickle also finding their way out to the remote Tuamotus. The Hawaiki Nui Canoe Race each November is worth planning your trip around. The Billabong Pro Tahiti surf fest in May also attracts a lot of attention – and some serious party action in downtown Pape'ete.

TONGA

 ○ **CAPITAL** NUKU'ALOFA ○ **POPULATION** 114,690 ○ **AREA**
748 SQ KM ○ **OFFICIAL LANGUAGES** TONGAN, ENGLISH

Whale-watching remains Tonga's boom industry, but scuba diving, hiking and (increasingly) surfing are drawing adherents too. Tongan culture is readily accessible and the pride in the country's history is palpable – kava ceremonies and dances serve to lure travellers away from the beach. Ancient stone relics draw a stream of reincarnated Lemurians. With lower-cost airfares there's been an increase in the number of independent travellers finding their way to Tonga. There have been a handful of demonstrations aiming to pin back the world's most autocratic monarchy, but even stroppy political Tongans are a polite lot, and there's no risk to travellers. July is a great time to visit, with the Heilala Festival and Miss Galaxy Pageant providing fun that's both traditional and flamboyant.

TUVALU

 ○ **CAPITAL** FUNAFUTI ○ **POPULATION** 11,810
○ **AREA** 26 SQ KM ○ **OFFICIAL LANGUAGE** TUVALUAN

Precious few travellers ever find their way to Tuvalu. In fact the country sometimes seems concerned with who's *leaving* rather than who's arriving. There have been negotiations with Australia, New Zealand, Fiji and Niue regarding resettling Tuvaluans when global warming sees these islands rendered unviable sometime in the next 50 years. It's a rather grim thought and hard to reconcile with the singing, dancing and seemingly untroubled people you see here. Perhaps you should visit while you have the chance. Tuvalu is relatively easy to get to as a side trip from Fiji. The few travellers who make it here tend to stay put in the 'big smoke', Funafuti, with cargo-ship travel to the outer islands still a time-consuming and fairly unreliable proposition.

VANUATU

 ⚙ **CAPITAL** PORT-VILA ⚙ **POPULATION** 208,870 ⚙ **AREA** 12,200 SQ KM ⚙ **OFFICIAL LANGUAGES** BISLAMA, ENGLISH, FRENCH

Vanuatu remains a destination visited mostly by sun-seeking holiday-makers, but a tiny stream of more intrepid and independent travellers has been slowly increasing, and with some effort they're discovering the far-flung outer islands. Cultural tourism has become more organised, with the famous *naghol* (land diving) ceremonies of Pentecost Island drawing a well-behaved and admiring crowd each April and May. *Kastom* (custom) ceremonies, kava drinking, traditional dancing and carving are also attracting attention. Apart from cultural tourists and beach-lovers, the most active travellers are those who don mask and tank to dive some of the world's most spectacular underwater wrecks.

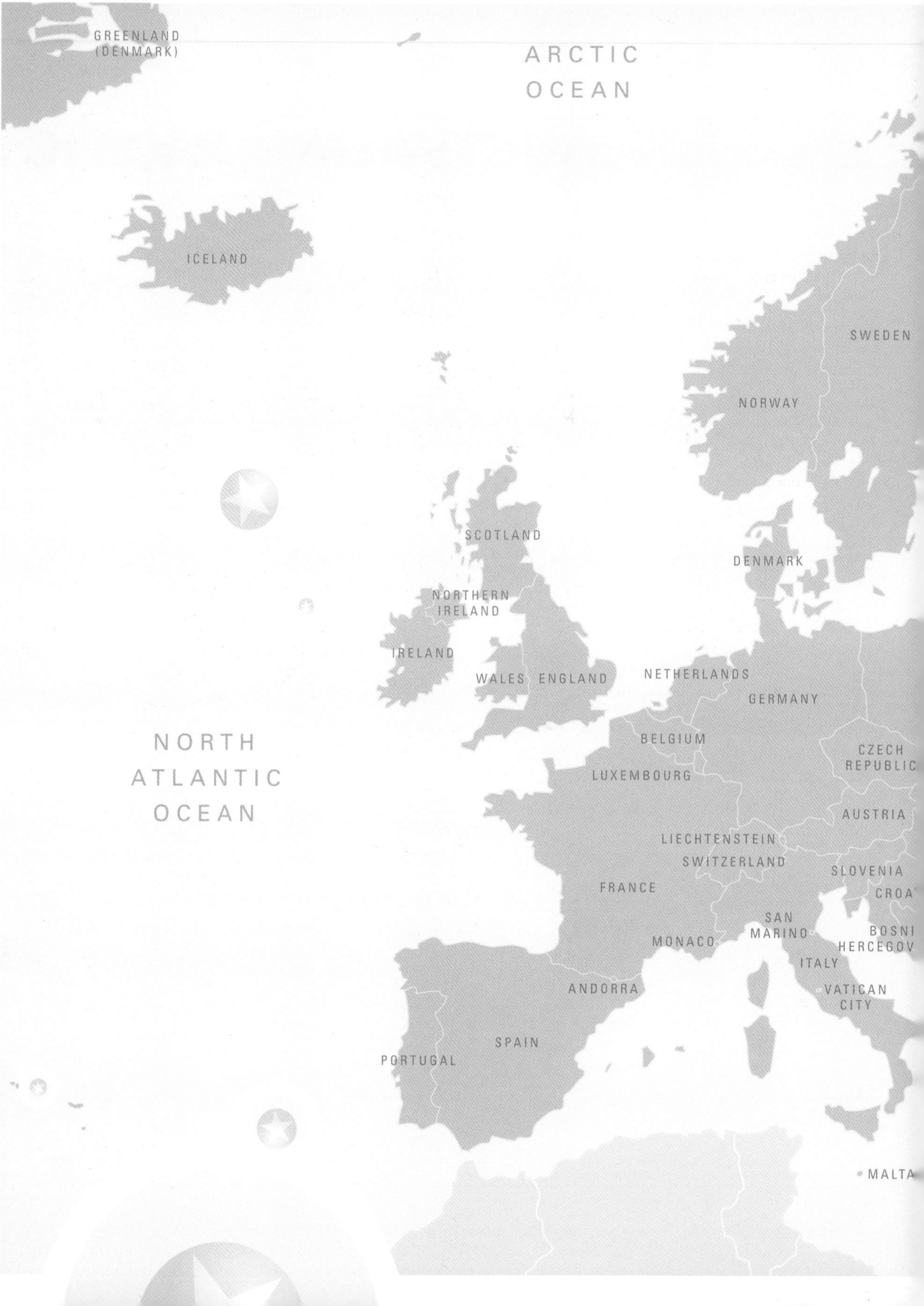
GREENLAND
(DENMARK)
ARCTIC
OCEAN
ICELAND
SWEDEN
NORWAY
SCOTLAND
DENMARK
NORTHERN
IRELAND
IRELAND
WALES
ENGLAND
NETHERLANDS
GERMANY
NORTH
ATLANTIC
OCEAN
BELGIUM
CZECH
REPUBLIC
LUXEMBOURG
AUSTRIA
LIECHTENSTEIN
SWITZERLAND
SLOVENIA
FRANCE
CROA
SAN
MARINO
BOSNI
HERCEGOV
MONACO
ITALY
ANDORRA
VATICAN
CITY
SPAIN
PORTUGAL
MALTA

» EUROPE

» EUROPE

ALBANIA

 ⊕ **CAPITAL** TIRANA ⊕ **POPULATION** 3.6 MILLION
⊕ **AREA** 28,748 SQ KM ⊕ **OFFICIAL LANGUAGE** ALBANIAN

Despite Albania being quite safe for tourists, there is little chance of foreign governments easing their travel advisories after a fatal shootout on a bus in the northern part of the country in February 2006. Much construction of tourist infrastructure is taking place along the coast, especially in Saranda and in Durrës where a new pier is being built. An outbreak of skin infections among swimmers in Durrës has raised concerns about the water quality. So far the campaign to prevent an oil pipeline being built through the Bay of Vlora has been successful, with locals fighting to preserve the area for tourism.

ANDORRA

 ⊕ **CAPITAL** ANDORRA LA VELLA ⊕ **POPULATION** 71,200
⊕ **AREA** 468 SQ KM ⊕ **OFFICIAL LANGUAGE** CATALAN

Andorra, the tiny 'parliamentary co-princedom' peeking up between the giants of France and Spain and long-famed for its bargain skiing, is moving upmarket. With some of the best skiing and snow-boarding in the Pyrenees, you can now take to the slopes in two newly amalgamated areas, Vallnord and Grandvalira. Top off a day in the snow with an upmarket meal or spend a day at Caldea, the country's enormous futuristic spa complex. When there's no snow, you can head to Soldeu or Ordino, in particular, for walking and mountain biking.

ARMENIA

 ✪ **CAPITAL** YEREVAN ✪ **POPULATION** 3 MILLION
✪ **AREA** 29,800 SQ KM ✪ **OFFICIAL LANGUAGE** ARMENIAN

Landlocked Armenia has had a traumatic history – and has the scars to show for it – but it remains the easiest and safest Caucasian country to travel in. This fact appears to be lost on locals, many of whom seem intent on emigrating, but is increasingly being recognised by canny travellers. Armenia offers the lively cultural life of capital city Yerevan, the turquoise beauty of Lake Sevan, a high-altitude climate and a tradition of overwhelming generosity (think lots of vodka toasts). And if the booming economy wasn't evidence enough of Armenia's re-emergence, its first ever appearance at the Eurovision Song Contest in 2006 surely is.

AUSTRIA

 ✪ **CAPITAL** VIENNA ✪ **POPULATION** 8.2 MILLION
✪ **AREA** 83,858 SQ KM ✪ **OFFICIAL LANGUAGE** GERMAN

With attractions that cater to both adrenaline junkies and culture fiends, Austria packs a big tourist punch. Mountain resorts in the Arlberg and Tirol (aka Tyrol) remain among Europe's favourite places to ski and snowboard in winter (despite the advent of competition ski-fields further east); and to hike, paraglide and otherwise adventure in summer. For those who don't care for such active pursuits, Austria, and particularly its grand imperial capital of Vienna, contains an abundance of artistic, architectural and historical sights. In 2007, Austria will capitalise further on the buzz from Mozart's birthday celebrations, and the charming smaller towns of Linz, Graz and Innsbruck will continue to exert a pull for city-breakers who are over the big-city thing.

AZERBAIJAN

 ✪ **CAPITAL** BAKU ✪ **POPULATION** 8 MILLION
✪ **AREA** 86,600 SQ KM ✪ **OFFICIAL LANGUAGE** AZERBAIJANI

Riding the fault line between Europe and Asia, Azerbaijan is the least visited and most pristine of the Caucasian countries, and a superb place to get off the beaten track. Travel here requires imagination, however, as there are few traditional sights and almost no tourism industry. The scenery in the Caucasus Mountains is the most obvious attractions, but there's also a wealth of quirkier draws: the fantastic mud volcanoes of Qobustan, the beautiful mountain villages of Xınalıq and Lahıc, and the bustling oil boom town of Baku, with its ancient walled city and modern skyscrapers. Travel in Azerbaijan remains a fascinating adventure.

BELARUS

 ✪ **CAPITAL** MINSK ✪ **POPULATION** 10.3 MILLION
✪ **AREA** 207,600 SQ KM ✪ **OFFICIAL LANGUAGE** BELARUSIAN

Tourism in Belarus continues to wait for the great leap forward. Despite an appetite for change on the streets of Minsk, President Lukashenko's suspiciously definite election victory leaves the country still stuck in its post-Soviet sulk. There are great reasons to go: the fast-changing capital's bars, clubs and cool hang-outs clash with a repressive regime to give Minsk a definite edge; and old-fashioned rural villages make for a fascinating window on old Europe. However, until political change arrives there's little prospect of Belarus being much more than a tantalisingly little-known and doggedly bureaucratic buffer between Russia and the EU.

BELGIUM

 ✪ **CAPITAL** BRUSSELS ✪ **POPULATION** 10.4 MILLION
✪ **AREA** 30,518 SQ KM ✪ **OFFICIAL LANGUAGES** DUTCH, FRENCH, GERMAN

Beer, chocolate and diamonds are only the beginning of what quirky Belgium has to recommend it. Brussels, the country's capital, offers the unique chance to watch puppet masters in action; the Toone family has been performing at their famous puppet theatre for more than a century and language barriers won't spoil your enjoyment of a marionette version of *Hamlet*. Some great events hit Belgium's cities in 2007: Ghent kicks off a nine-day festival of music and theatre in July; and in August 2007, Bruges' Pageant of the Golden Tree, which only occurs every four to five years, will see 2000 participants flood the streets in a sea of colour and floats.

BOSNIA & HERCEGOVINA

 ✪ **CAPITAL** SARAJEVO ✪ **POPULATION** 4.5 MILLION
✪ **AREA** 51,129 SQ KM ✪ **OFFICIAL LANGUAGES** BOSNIAN, CROATIAN, SERBIAN

After a particularly bloody and well-publicised birth during the 1990s, Bosnia & Hercegovina is embarking on a heady adolescence. The reconstruction of Mostar bridge linking Muslim and Croatian parts of the city in 2004 indicated that the country was intent on mending itself and on catching up with the rest of Europe. Contradictions and controversies remain, but they are unavoidable in a country with such a melange of cultures and influences – and therein lies Bosnia & Hercegovina's appeal. Come here for the Ottoman neighbourhoods of Sarajevo, tar-black Turkish coffee, bottled holy water from Međugorje and awe-inspiring mountain vistas.

SNAPSHOTS.

BULGARIA

 ✪ **CAPITAL** SOFIA ✪ **POPULATION** 7.4 MILLION
✪ **AREA** 110,910 SQ KM ✪ **OFFICIAL LANGUAGE** BULGARIAN

Bulgaria was originally slated for EU membership in 2007, however a post-Soviet hangover of persistent official corruption is proving distasteful to EU commissioners, so entry may well be pushed back. Corruption, however, is a hurdle best left to the Bulgarian judiciary. Visitors should instead aim to scale the country's seven mountain ranges, each with unique terrain, wildlife and countless opportunities for trekking and skiing. And if mountains aren't your thing consider hallowed Orthodox monasteries, festivals too many to mention, Roman and Thracian relics, revival-era architecture, rose oil by the bucketload and all that gorgeous, Black Sea coast.

CROATIA

 ✪ **CAPITAL** ZAGREB ✪ **POPULATION** 4.5 MILLION
✪ **AREA** 56,542 SQ KM ✪ **OFFICIAL LANGUAGE** CROATIAN

Set for entry into the EU in 2009, Croatia has well and truly shrugged off its recent traumatic past and is infused with optimism as it pursues the heady reform road. In the meantime, travellers have reclaimed the startlingly picturesque Dalmatian coast, and are now happily rediscovering Istria and the Gulf of Kvarner as well. Recently established no-frills flights to Zagreb mean that the country's interior and surprisingly hip capital are set to become hot destinations. Aside from to-die-for coastal towns, not-to-be-missed Croatian attractions include festivals in Dubrovnik, Zagreb and Pula, events indicative of a resurgent cultural and artistic life.

CYPRUS

 ✪ **CAPITAL** NICOSIA ✪ **POPULATION** 784,300
✪ **AREA** 9250 SQ KM ✪ **OFFICIAL LANGUAGES**
GREEK, TURKISH

Aphrodite's island is still a classic 'two weeks in the sun' destination for Brits abroad, but look beyond the overrun package-holiday resorts (and give it a miss in August) and you'll find a unique Mediterranean gem. Easing border restrictions mean you can now travel freely between the divided South and North, opening up the whole island to exploration, whether it's the spectacular Troödos and Kyrenia (Girne) Mountains or the remote Karpas (Kırpaşa) Peninsula, refuge of green and loggerhead turtles. Elsewhere, luxury spas are mushrooming in Cyprus; Aphrodite Hills in Pafos is the current toast of the detoxed, waxed and exfoliated elite.

CZECH REPUBLIC

 ✪ **CAPITAL** PRAGUE ✪ **POPULATION** 10.2 MILLION
✪ **AREA** 78,866 SQ KM ✪ **OFFICIAL LANGUAGE** CZECH

The Czech Republic is all about Prague, right? Wrong. Although Prague remains the country's top draw by a long shot (accounting for 70% of all tourism), we reckon that it's the lesser lights and humbler sights of the Republic that make it special. Cheap flights into Brno, in the country's east, have given travellers a taste for the non-Prague Czech Republic – just as fairy-tale, just as pristinely preserved, and with a mere fraction of the tourists. By 2007 surely everyone in the western world will have been to Prague, so it's time to go beyond it and discover the forests of 'Bohemian Switzerland' and picture-perfect towns of Moravia.

DENMARK

 ✪ **CAPITAL** COPENHAGEN ✪ **POPULATION** 5.5 MILLION
✪ **AREA** 43,094 SQ KM ✪ **OFFICIAL LANGUAGE** DANISH

Copenhagen still conjures up images of Lego and the Little Mermaid, but it's rapidly becoming the Barcelona of the north. Strøget, the world's longest pedestrianised shopping street, is more Helena Christensen than Hans Christian Andersen, and the Tivoli gardens with their roller coasters and Ferris wheels are the very antithesis of Disneyland. One of the most photographed statues in the world, the Little Mermaid remains the most popular attraction in the country, but the Museum of Erotica is proving just as popular. Probably best to leave the kids back at the hotel for the latter, even though Denmark was recently ranked the second-best place in the world to have children.

ENGLAND

⊙ **CAPITAL** LONDON ⊙ **POPULATION** 51 MILLION
⊙ **AREA** 129,720 SQ KM ⊙ **OFFICIAL LANGUAGE** ENGLISH

On one hand, there's never been a better time to come to England. London is revelling in its role as Olympic host for 2012, shrugging off the terror attack of July 2005 in a typically English manner. Resurgent cities, especially Manchester and Newcastle, are now boutique-hotel-filled destinations in themselves rather than somewhere to pass through to reach perennially beautiful countryside, which is itself more accessible than ever by foot or bicycle. Yet Bill Bryson isn't alone in branding litter a 'national disgrace', and public transport needs to keep improving. But when the sun's shining there are still few better places to be.

ESTONIA

⊙ **CAPITAL** TALLINN ⊙ **POPULATION** 1.3 MILLION
⊙ **AREA** 45,226 SQ KM ⊙ **OFFICIAL LANGUAGE** ESTONIAN

No longer Europe's best-kept secret, Estonia is thriving in the limelight. Change is happening apace in the capital city Tallinn where medieval cobbled streets sit alongside gleaming skyscrapers and historic buildings rub shoulders with stylish wine bars. But travel out into the countryside or to one of the islands, and the pace slows significantly. Here Estonia has been investing in spa treatments and you shouldn't visit without experiencing a traditional sauna. For the more adventurous there's even skiing and snowboard-ing – despite the vertically challenged landscape, Estonians are busy building up even the slightest bump to provide some downhill action.

FINLAND

See p156.

FRANCE

See p32.

GEORGIA

⊙ **CAPITAL** TBILISI ⊙ **POPULATION** 4.7 MILLION
⊙ **AREA** 69,700 SQ KM ⊙ **OFFICIAL LANGUAGE** GEORGIAN

Georgia has almost too much history to cram into its diminutive territory, a fact that accounts for much of its appeal and its ongoing internal strife. But this meant nothing to Jennifer Lopez. When she was offered an enormous sum to be the face of an international ad campaign for Georgian wines, Lopez was decidedly nonplussed. Frankly, we advise you to ignore J-Lo's scorn and head over to this, the most consistently beautiful country in the former Soviet Union. Quaff the wine (and the mineral water, which allegedly has hangover-defying powers), and take in cosmopolitan Tbilisi and the semitropical lushness of the southern Black Sea coast.

GERMANY

⊙ **CAPITAL** BERLIN ⊙ **POPULATION** 82.4 MILLION
⊙ **AREA** 357,021 SQ KM ⊙ **OFFICIAL LANGUAGE** GERMAN

Having hosted a minor world sporting event in 2006 (that's 'soccer', to the uninitiated), 2007 is set to be Germany's year. The World Cup's slogan, 'it's time to make friends', was a nice gesture, but it will be the opportunity the tournament gave the rest of the world to see how much the country has to offer that will catapult Germany into hot-spot status. Berlin is still a must-go for art buffs and committed clubbers, but smaller cities like Cologne and Hamburg are opening up with cheap flights, and wine and hiking tours are on the up among those who like a theme to their travel.

GREECE

See p36.

GREENLAND

⊙ **CAPITAL** NUUK ⊙ **POPULATION** 56,360
⊙ **AREA** 2,166,086 SQ KM ⊙ **OFFICIAL LANGUAGE** DANISH

Greenland is one of Europe's great travel frontiers, although the high cost of visiting puts off many potential visitors. However, with careful planning, it is possible to secure good value air fares with Air 	»

SNAPSHOTS.

Greenland – connections from Europe and, soon, the US have never been better – and advance booking brings ferries into the realm of the affordable. As well as surging Greenlandic national pride, the midnight sun and a boom in winter dog-sledding and northern-lights spotting visits, there's the chance that if you leave it too long there'll be a very different Arctic experience awaiting you. Go, because the icebergs may not wait forever.

HUNGARY

 ✪ **CAPITAL** BUDAPEST ✪ **POPULATION** 10 MILLION ✪ **AREA** 93,030 SQ KM ✪ **OFFICIAL LANGUAGE** HUNGARIAN

Now that hip, cosmopolitan Budapest has well and truly staked its claim as one of Europe's must-see cities, the rest of Hungary is emerging into the limelight. Exquisitely preserved Unesco World Heritage villages; health resorts and water sports on Europe's largest freshwater lake, Lake Balaton; canoe rides on some of the grandest stretches of the Danube; wine touring in Eger and Tokaj; horse riding across the Great Plain; hiking and caving in the Northern Uplands – 2007 will be the year the travelling masses start to see beyond the big 'B', into the multitude of possibilities in this beguiling country.

ICELAND

 ✪ **CAPITAL** REYKJAVÍK ✪ **POPULATION** 299,390 ✪ **AREA** 103,000 SQ KM ✪ **OFFICIAL LANGUAGE** ICELANDIC

Iceland continues its meteoric rise in popularity just as the unique Icelandic music scene blossoms further. Reykjavík, famed for nightlife as well as being home to the infamously cool Iceland Airwaves music festival, has added the Rite of Spring festival to its calendar. Though only three hours flying time from the UK, Iceland remains a remote uninhabited landscape punctuated by majestic waterfalls and glaciers. It's also the best place to try the newest extreme sport of snowkiting, and to spend 48 hours without ever seeing the sun set. Alternatively, try wandering in to watch proceedings at one of the oldest Parliaments in the world – there's no security on the door at all.

IRELAND & NORTHERN IRELAND

 ✪ **CAPITAL** DUBLIN (ROI), BELFAST (NI) ✪ **POPULATION** 4.1 MILLION (ROI), 1.7 MILLION (NI) ✪ **AREA** 70,280 SQ KM (ROI), 14,139 SQ KM (NI) ✪ **OFFICIAL LANGUAGES** ENGLISH, IRISH

A perennial favourite, Ireland continues to draw us in with its legendary good humour and good looks. Dublin will always lure visitors with its Gaelic charm and the rugged west coast has awed travellers for centuries, but it's in Northern Ireland that change is really afoot. The restoration of Belfast, set in motion by the Good Friday Agreement of 1998, has really taken off now that IRA arms have been decommissioned. For the first time it's possible to fly directly from New York to Belfast, and there are even plans to bring the *Titanic* home to her birthplace.

ITALY

See p24.

LATVIA

 ✪ **CAPITAL** RIGA ✪ **POPULATION** 2.3 MILLION ✪ **AREA** 64,589 SQ KM ✪ **OFFICIAL LANGUAGE** LATVIAN

The 'Ryanair effect' has impacted Latvia profoundly, and tourism numbers will continue to explode as the budget airline adds routes to Rīga in 2007. One legacy of the 2006 World Ice Hockey championships in Rīga is that there are about 1000 new hotel rooms to accommodate all those tourists. You should still book way ahead though. As rowdy stag parties continue to flood the streets of the Old Town on any given weekend, Rīga residents may soon demand that the city does more than pay lip service to the growing scourge of sex tourism. Beyond the capital, little Sigulda has big things planned for its 800-year anniversary celebration.

LIECHTENSTEIN

 ✪ **CAPITAL** VADUZ ✪ **POPULATION** 33,990 ✪ **AREA** 160 SQ KM ✪ **OFFICIAL LANGUAGE** GERMAN

The Alps in miniature. This Manhattan-sized principality offers most of the thrills of its bulkier neighbours, such as quaint villages and great skiing, plus royalty and low taxes. Liechtenstein's obscurity makes it special; come here so you can say that you've been. Stay at its one resort (inexpensive for this part of the world), ski the Liechtenstein Alps, send back a postcard with one of the country's stamps, and maybe open a bank account. As cheap flights make all of Europe easier to access, a trip to Liechtenstein is one holiday that will still buy you bragging rights.

LITHUANIA

 ✪ **CAPITAL** VILNIUS ✪ **POPULATION** 3.6 MILLION ✪ **AREA** 65,200 SQ KM ✪ **OFFICIAL LANGUAGE** LITHUANIAN

Lithuania's stupendous Unesco-honoured national song festival is the big event in 2007. Occurring every four years, it's the ultimate Lithuanian cultural experience. Aside from that, budget airlines Ryanair and Wizz Air will continue to add routes to the former capital of Kaunas. Most Kaunas traffic heads straight to Vilnius, but Lithuania's second city should also get more visitors, especially if it starts catering to stag parties. Vilnius is ill-equipped to handle a big tourism spike, so expect more accommodation to open, led by a planned offering from hotel chain Kempinski. Vilnius airport is getting a new terminal, but upon arrival you'll still have to exchange your euros, as Lithuania's plan to adopt the common currency in 2007 is dead.

LUXEMBOURG

 ✪ **CAPITAL** LUXEMBOURG ✪ **POPULATION** 474,410 ✪ **AREA** 2586 SQ KM ✪ **OFFICIAL LANGUAGE** LUXEMBOURGISH

The European Capital of Culture was initiated to bring the peoples of Europe together, and each year a different city in Europe is chosen to take on the title. In 2007 the honour falls to Luxembourg and the neighbouring areas of Lorraine, Rhineland-Palatinate, Saarland and Wallonia, when they will forget their respective borders and unite in exhibiting their cultural diversity and creative potential. Luxembourg will be alive and buzzing all year long with a fast-moving cultural programme capturing every artistic discipline. This will be a fantastic year to visit Luxembourg as the festivals and events bring the country alive.

MACEDONIA

 ✪ **CAPITAL** SKOPJE ✪ **POPULATION** 2.1 MILLION ✪ **AREA** 25,333 SQ KM ✪ **OFFICIAL LANGUAGE** MACEDONIAN

Don't forget your laptop when you are Macedonia-bound. It may not be immediately synonymous with technology, but Macedonia is set to become the world's first entirely wireless country through an international connectivity project. Otherwise, its attractions are decidedly more down-to-earth: mirror-smooth Lake Ohrid, the mountain-top monasteries of Treskavec and Sv Jovan Bigorski, the Ottoman jumble of Skopje bazaar and an increasingly buzzing nightlife and arts scenes. Recently designated a candidate for EU membership, Macedonia is only going to get more popular, so come now for cheap, high-altitude (wireless) fun and beat the rush.

MALTA

 ✪ **CAPITAL** VALLETTA ✪ **POPULATION** 400,220 ✪ **AREA** 316 SQ KM ✪ **OFFICIAL LANGUAGES** MALTESE, ENGLISH

Malta has long been one of the Mediterranean's most popular summer destinations. And why not, when the weather is hot and the hotels and restaurants are great value? Posh and Becks have holidayed on the island along with dozens of other families attracted by Malta's easy-going atmosphere and plethora of things to do. At only 316 sq km Malta certainly packs it in, from top-notch diving sites in the northwest of the island to the throbbing summer resorts of Sliema and St Julian's and the impressive historic cities of Valletta and Mdina. Looking to the future, the Maltese government plans to take tourism upscale. Let's just hope they don't overcook the golden goose.

MOLDOVA

 ✪ **CAPITAL** CHIŞINĂU ✪ **POPULATION** 4.5 MILLION ✪ **AREA** 33,843 SQ KM ✪ **OFFICIAL LANGUAGE** MOLDOVAN

Moldova remains an off-the-beaten-track locale. *Way* off. Being difficult to reach, elbowroom abounds at cliff-side monasteries, Chişinău has first-rate nightlife and you'll find the most superb, yet inexpensive, wine tours in the world (the October Wine Festival is already legendary). Visiting the breakaway »

Transdniestr region, a 3567-sq-km museum to Soviet times, is the stuff party stories are made of. After decades of ceaseless bad press – civil war, corruption, poverty, organised crime – Moldova has turned a corner, albeit slowly. In 2007, it has its eyes set on reducing bureaucracy, encouraging foreign investment and embracing tourism by dropping many of its visa requirements.

MONACO

 ✪ **CAPITAL** MONACO ✪ **POPULATION** 32,540
✪ **AREA** 1.95 SQ KM ✪ **OFFICIAL LANGUAGE** FRENCH

Monaco has always been synonymous with luxury, glamour, excitement and leisure. The glittering city of Monte Carlo is world renowned for its casinos and plush hotels, and for hosting the annual Formula One Grand Prix where people flock to the many hotels offering views of the track and the really wealthy look on from their yachts. The year 2007 looks to be an exciting one in Monaco, with new hotels and spas opening up and events lined up back-to-back throughout the year. The Monte Carlo Rally in January is followed by the International Circus Festival, then the World Music Awards, the Spring Arts Festival and the Tennis Master Series and we're only up to April!

MONTENEGRO

 ✪ **CAPITAL** PODGORICA ✪ **POPULATION** 616,260
✪ **AREA** 13,812 SQ KM ✪ **OFFICIAL LANGUAGE** SERBIAN

Once touted as 'the new Croatia', Montenegro can now legitimately sell itself as the newest country on earth. A referendum in May 2006 saw it bloodlessly detach itself from Serbia and set itself on the road to EU admission as a stand-alone proposition. Already coming onto the tourism radar, Montenegro's picture-postcard Adriatic coastline, peppered with rocky coves – and southern Europe's only fjord, at Kotor – is sure to get busier. But inland Montenegro offers lakes and mountains aplenty, including the high-altitude historical capital at Cetinje and the delights of Durmitor National Park. We suggest you drop in now and beat the rush.

NETHERLANDS

 ✪ **CAPITAL** AMSTERDAM ✪ **POPULATION** 16.5 MILLION
✪ **AREA** 41,526 SQ KM ✪ **OFFICIAL LANGUAGES** DUTCH, FRISIAN

When you think of the Netherlands you probably think canals, tulips, clogs and open-minded people. This is the country famed for its legalisation of soft-core drugs and its capital city's red-light district, but there is much more to this tiny country, we promise. Amsterdam will be bopping onto the scene in 2007 as the year of 'Amsterdam, feel the rhythm' kicks off. If you like music then Amsterdam is definitely the city for you. A large number of events from modern to classical music and dance will be taking place across the city. There are music festivals held annually in Amsterdam, including the Amsterdam Roots Festival, and the Amsterdam Dance Event, which is Europe's main electronic and dance music conference.

NORWAY

 ✪ **CAPITAL** OSLO ✪ **POPULATION** 4.6 MILLION
✪ **AREA** 324,220 SQ KM ✪ **OFFICIAL LANGUAGE** NORWEGIAN

In 2005 Norway celebrated the centenary of the dissolution of its union with Sweden and the country was in a jubilant mood, but the buzz now is all about Bergen. Norway's second-largest city may be a little more off the beaten track than Oslo but its bars and restaurants are bustling till the small hours. Bergen is also the gateway to the fjords and their spectacular scenery. Take the state-subsidised *Hurtigruten* steamer, which has sailed up and down the coast for more than a century delivering mail, cargo and passengers to inaccessible spots, and check out the Lofoten Islands where you can stay in a traditional stilted *rorbu* (fishermen's shanty) at the water's edge.

POLAND

 ✪ **CAPITAL** WARSAW ✪ **POPULATION** 38.5 MILLION
✪ **AREA** 312,685 SQ KM ✪ **OFFICIAL LANGUAGE** POLISH

Poland must be the low-cost flight capital of Eastern Europe. From here, you can fly to ten cities in the region, some better known than others. The number-one choice is Kraków. It's the only major Polish city to emerge unscathed from WWII, and its well-preserved medieval and Renaissance architecture is unrivalled. So what about the lesser-known cities? Bydgoszcz is great for visiting the Gothic city of Toruń; from Rzeszów the wonderfully remote Bieszczady region is a drive away or you can pop into the Ukraine; and Szczecin in the northwest is an interesting town in itself and gives great access to the Baltic coast and east Germany.

PORTUGAL

 ✪ **CAPITAL** LISBON ✪ **POPULATION** 10.6 MILLION ✪ **AREA** 92,391 SQ KM ✪ **OFFICIAL LANGUAGES** PORTUGUESE, MIRANDESE

Portugal, Western Europe's last remaining cheapie destination, is a real mixed bag. The long-frequented, package-deal Algarve region is now challenging independent travellers to find its hidden gems, and the vast Alentejo, to its north, is the place to lose yourself on the plains. A late-night hussy who still looks fresh in the morning, Lisbon has a reputation as a dynamic city destination that continues to grow, while Porto is dressing up its grittiness with a brand-spanking metro and a futuristic concert hall. The more adventurous visitors head into the hills of the north, or to Madeira and the Azores, now more easily accessible from both the UK and the US.

ROMANIA

 ✪ **CAPITAL** BUCHAREST ✪ **POPULATION** 22.3 MILLION ✪ **AREA** 237,500 SQ KM ✪ **OFFICIAL LANGUAGE** ROMANIAN

With mind-bending natural wonders, innumerable Unesco World Heritage sites and frighteningly quick urban development, the only thing holding Romania back since Ceauşescu's demise has been the country itself. Its anticipated 2007 entry into the EU has been the catalyst for the fastest-developing tourism infrastructure in Europe. Yet, while rural pensions build flashy websites, peasant colonies thrive. Indulge in Timişoara's friendly nightlife, then tour Maramureş by horse-drawn cart, and in between hike in the mountains and visit castles that have been immortalised in fiction. Alternatively, unwind on the Black Sea coast in the Danube Delta's enveloping nature or the busy beaches near Constanţa.

RUSSIAN FEDERATION

 ✪ **CAPITAL** MOSCOW ✪ **POPULATION** 142.9 MILLION ✪ **AREA** 17,075,200 SQ KM ✪ **OFFICIAL LANGUAGE** RUSSIAN

Remaining one of Europe's edgier travel destinations, Russia has complex visa requirements, notorious bureaucracy and a general air of Slavic mystery that keeps intrepid travellers coming, as well as catering to city-breakers who enjoy the sophisticated hotels and restaurants of Moscow and St Petersburg. Few people travel beyond either city, and those who do overwhelmingly follow the route of the magical Trans-Siberian Railway. Our advice is get off the beaten track: the Caucasus, the Volga Delta, Kamchatka and Arctic Russia are some of the most exciting destinations in the world and yet are virtually unknown to travellers.

SCOTLAND

 ✪ **CAPITAL** EDINBURGH ✪ **POPULATION** 5.1 MILLION ✪ **AREA** 78,772 SQ KM ✪ **OFFICIAL LANGUAGE** ENGLISH

The familiar continues to evolve in Scotland. As befits a city keen on hosting the Commonwealth Games, Glasgow is a confident, stylish and welcoming city. Top-notch new hotels like the Arthouse complement what's now the best dining and nightlife in the country. But natural Scotland still takes first prize in captivating visitors, with improved links to the Shetland Islands and even a controversial Sunday ferry sailing to the God-fearing Isle of Harris, making the outer islands the place to be.

SERBIA

 ✪ **CAPITAL** BELGRADE ✪ **POPULATION** 10 MILLION ✪ **AREA** 88,361 SQ KM ✪ **OFFICIAL LANGUAGE** SERBIAN

The nationalists' dream of 'Greater Serbia' has well and truly died, and with it the bloodshed and trauma of the 1990s. When Montenegro chose to go it alone in a May 2006 referendum, Serbia soldiered on without a backward glance. It seems the Serbs are too busy »

getting on with business and working hard towards EU admission. Touting Hapsburg and Ottoman relics, buzzing nightlife and sizzling *čevapčići* (grilled kebab of spiced minced meat), mountain villages and grand architecture, Orthodox Belgrade and Albanian Prizren, Serbia doesn't draw hordes of visitors, but for those in the know it offers another rich strand of the southern European tapestry.

SLOVAKIA

 ✪ **CAPITAL** BRATISLAVA ✪ **POPULATION** 5.4 MILLION ✪ **AREA** 48,845 SQ KM ✪ **OFFICIAL LANGUAGE** SLOVAK

Slovakia has long been in the shadow of its more glamorous cousin, the Czech Republic, but travellers are starting to discover that the country has a shine all its own. Its brightest light: the High Tatra Mountains, where outdoor enthusiasts flock to walk, climb, cycle or ski. This is a European mountain experience without the big crowds and the high prices, with charming resorts, majestic mountain scenery and beautifully preserved villages. With low-cost airlines now flying into the capital, Bratislava (itself becoming a hot destination for city-breakers looking for a less obvious Eastern European option), Slovakia's mountains look set to become the getaway of choice for discerning adventurers.

SLOVENIA

 ✪ **CAPITAL** LJUBLJANA ✪ **POPULATION** 2 MILLION ✪ **AREA** 20,273 SQ KM ✪ **OFFICIAL LANGUAGE** SLOVENIAN

This tiny nation continues to grow in confidence on the world stage. It will complete its entry into Europe in 2007 by adopting the euro, making it even more accessible to travellers. Trips to the capital, Ljubljana, a welcoming and very beautiful city, make a great short city break, but it's beyond that in the Julian Alps where outdoor enthusiasts can really enjoy the best of Slovenia. Quieter and cheaper than their namesake further west, the Julian Alps are just as stunning – if slightly lower.

SPAIN

 ✪ **CAPITAL** MADRID ✪ **POPULATION** 40.4 MILLION ✪ **AREA** 504,782 SQ KM ✪ **OFFICIAL LANGUAGE** SPANISH

Firm favourite, particularly with Brits, Spain has a popularity that endures. Burgeoning low-cost airlines have opened up lesser-known regions, and independent travel to the country has taken over from the package deal. Valencia, host to the America's Cup in 2007, is grabbing all the headlines, but Barcelona's must-see status remains intact. Boutique hotels and top-notch restaurants abound, from the Canary Islands all the way over to Mallorca, and Bilbao and San Sebastián continue to gain accolades for cuisine and culture. Surrounding these two and extending as far as the Atlantic, Green Spain has established itself as an outdoor enthusiasts' playground.

SWEDEN

 ✪ **CAPITAL** STOCKHOLM ✪ **POPULATION** 9 MILLION ✪ **AREA** 449,964 SQ KM ✪ **OFFICIAL LANGUAGE** SWEDISH

Still one of most beautiful cities in Europe, Stockholm and its island archipelago are attracting increased attention as a summer destination. You can sea kayak by day and camp on uninhabited islands by night, but with seven Michelin-starred restaurants (not bad for a city of less than 800,000), you may well prefer to kayak back to shore. Traditional Swedish delicacies such as reindeer stew and cloudberries are playing a big part in this resurgent cuisine, which has also gripped Göteborg (Gothenburg), where four restaurants are now Michelin-starred. Direct flights from London Stansted twice daily make Göteborg a lot more viable as a decadent lunch option.

SWITZERLAND

 ✪ **CAPITAL** BERN ✪ **POPULATION** 7.5 MILLION ✪ **AREA** 41,295 SQ KM ✪ **OFFICIAL LANGUAGES** GERMAN, FRENCH, ITALIAN

We hate that hackneyed tourist-bureau phrase, 'something for everyone', but with Switzerland, we have to make an exception. It's still Europe's number-one spot for winter sports and hiking, with the most breathtaking mountain scenery in the continent. And its cities are increasing in popularity as short breaks, giving travellers the chance to sample Zurich's heady nightlife, the vineyard-studded beauty of Lake Geneva, and festive Basel, the country's artistic centre. All eyes will be on Switzerland in 2007, as it gears up for the UEFA Euro 2008 football championship, which it's co-hosting with Austria. See? Something for everyone, including football fans.

UKRAINE

⊙ **CAPITAL** KYIV ⊙ **POPULATION** 46.7 MILLION ⊙ **AREA** 603,700 SQ KM ⊙ **OFFICIAL LANGUAGE** UKRAINIAN

In 2004 Ukraine rocketed into the international spotlight, winning the Eurovision Song Contest, then successfully (and peaceably) demonstrating for democracy in the Orange Revolution. Since then the euphoria has died down with the reality of everyday life on the edge of Europe sinking in. Nevertheless Ukraine has well and truly established itself in the popular consciousness as a place to visit. This is a surprising corner of Europe, where the ramshackle seaside charm of Odesa, the grandeur of Kyiv, the Tatar relics of Bakhchysaray, the beaches of Crimea and a post-Soviet greyness combine in an incongruous yet appealing composition.

WALES

 ⊙ **CAPITAL** CARDIFF ⊙ **POPULATION** 2.9 MILLION ⊙ **AREA** 20,764 SQ KM ⊙ **OFFICIAL LANGUAGES** ENGLISH, WELSH

Wales continues to thrive in an era of political devolution and regional pride. OK, there's been no repeat of the Six Nations Grand Slam of 2005, but Cardiff still hosts English sporting events with a warm welcome and a thumbed nose to endless delays at the new Wembley Stadium. Down the road and stealing Cardiff's thunder is Swansea, home to the new National Waterfront Museum and next door to the stunning Gower Peninsula. Further north, the green lifestyle pioneered by the thriving Centre for Alternative Technology is inspiring an ecoconscious young nation to treat their beautiful homeland that little bit better.

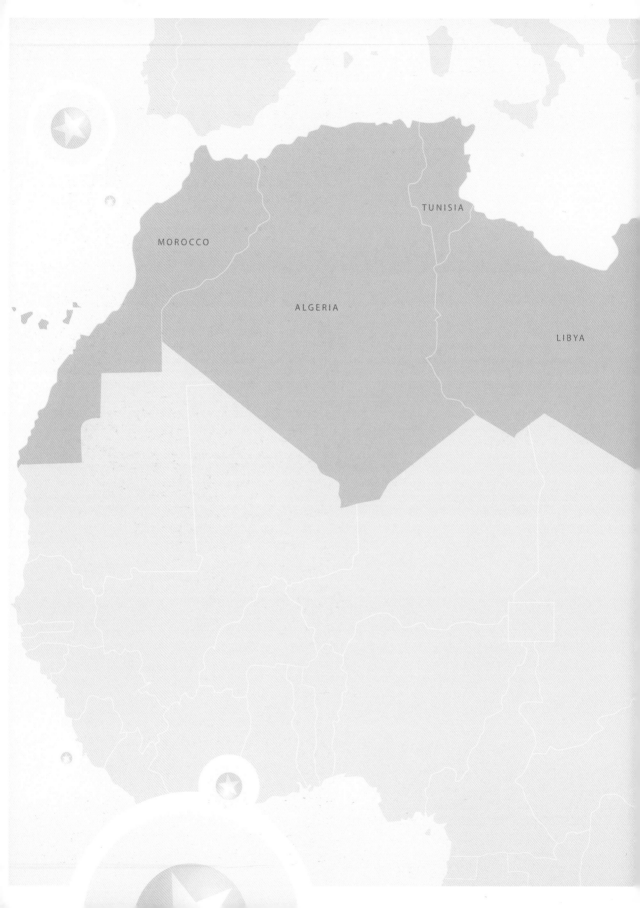

MOROCCO

ALGERIA

TUNISIA

LIBYA

TURKEY

SYRIA

LEBANON

Mediterranean
Sea

JORDAN

PALESTINIAN
TERRITORIES

ISRAEL

IRAQ

IRAN

KUWAIT

EGYPT

BAHRAIN

QATAR

UAE

Red Sea

SAUDI ARABIA

OMAN

Arabian
Sea

YEMEN

Gulf of Aden

INDIAN
OCEAN

**» MIDDLE EAST +
NORTH AFRICA**

MIDDLE EAST +
» NORTH AFRICA

ALGERIA

 ✪ **CAPITAL** ALGIERS ✪ **POPULATION** 32.9 MILLION
✪ **AREA** 2,381,740 SQ KM ✪ **OFFICIAL LANGUAGE** ARABIC

Algeria's ongoing political instabilities mean that it's not a destination that's high on the list for most travellers. However, should you choose to make the journey there are plenty of sights in safe areas to keep you entranced – and you certainly won't be competing with hordes of tourists for the pleasure. You'll be rewarded with gems such as moonlit views from the quintessential Saharan oasis town of Timimoun; incredible scenery at sunrise in the mountains at Assekrem (about 80km northeast of Tamanrasset); and the dramatic World Heritage–listed Tassili N'Ajjer and Hoggar regions. For a hassle-free trip, heed travel warnings, avoid the northeast and southwest of the country and consider joining a tour.

BAHRAIN

 ✪ **CAPITAL** MANAMA ✪ **POPULATION** 698,580
✪ **AREA** 665 SQ KM ✪ **OFFICIAL LANGUAGE** ARABIC

Already a runaway success, the Formula One Grand Prix in Bahrain is encouraging a resurgence of interest in this tiny Gulf island. The flood of new visitors that this international event has brought is resulting in some exciting new hotel projects, rebranding of tired malls and an ever-improving infrastructure.
So much for 'new world', but if it's 'old world' you're after, then the Bahrain National Museum is a good place to start to uncover the ancient treasures of Dilmun, scattered in various sites around this pearl-divers' island. The hunt for pearls both underwater and in the gold souk is timeless.

EGYPT

 ✪ **CAPITAL** CAIRO ✪ **POPULATION** 78.9 MILLION
✪ **AREA** 1,001,450 SQ KM ✪ **OFFICIAL LANGUAGE** ARABIC

The world's oldest tourism destination, Egypt deservedly tops must-see lists. Despite violence targeting foreigners, travellers eager to experience vibrant culture and the legacy of six millennia of continuous civilisation remain undeterred. A recently opened international airport at El Alamein should see more visitors exploring the Egypt that lies beyond 'the antiquities'. Red Sea diving and desert oasis safaris are popular alternatives to Luxor, although for most travellers the Nile Valley is unmissable. This year, time your trip to the Great Temple of Ramses II in Abu Simbel for February or October, when sunlight illuminates the inner sanctum of Ramses II's precisely engineered tomb.

IRAN

 ✪ **CAPITAL** TEHRAN ✪ **POPULATION** 68.7 MILLION
✪ **AREA** 1,648,000 SQ KM ✪ **OFFICIAL LANGUAGE** PERSIAN

Despite being one of the most hospitable countries on earth, Iran isn't exactly the darling of international politics right now and the country's much-speculated-about nuclear programme kept tourists away in 2006. Which means it's a great time to go. It's difficult to predict what will happen in 2007, but assuming there are no bombs, the tiny desert oasis of Garmeh, with its silence, date palms and warm welcome, will continue to enchant the adventurous. Iran's ski fields are also growing in popularity, with the slopes at Dizin and Shemshak north of Tehran boasting fine runs and an unexpectedly lively nightlife.

IRAQ

 ✪ **CAPITAL** BAGHDAD ✪ **POPULATION** 26.8 MILLION ✪ **AREA** 437,072 SQ KM ✪ **OFFICIAL LANGUAGES** ARABIC, KURDISH

A tragic recent history and ongoing bloodshed make Iraq a no-go area for the casual traveller. Should stability return and the American-led occupation end, the ancient sights, cultural festivals and unheralded diversity of this country will fascinate those intrepid enough to travel here. While countless treasures were lost to looters during the fall of Saddam, the 'cradle of civilisation' still has much to explore when you next get the chance, including 10,000 archaeological sites ranging from the reported birthplace of Abraham at Erbil, to the ziggurat and temples of Ur, and the ruins of Babylon. Meanwhile, pray for peace.

ISRAEL

 ✪ **CAPITAL** JERUSALEM ✪ **POPULATION** 6.3 MILLION ✪ **AREA** 20,770 SQ KM ✪ **OFFICIAL LANGUAGE** HEBREW

Israel is enjoying a boom in its tourist industry. In the wake of the 2001–05 *intifada* (uprising), visitor numbers are climbing back into the millions, which is filling up hotels to bursting point. If the good times continue, expect more crowds and higher prices. The positive news is that increased tourist dollars are adding infrastructure. A case in point is historical Jaffa, a windswept promontory south of Tel Aviv, where plans are afoot to redevelop the historical centre with new cafés, shops and traveller facilities. Security should still be a concern in Israel and the situation is always unpredictable.

JORDAN

See p164.

KUWAIT

 ✪ **CAPITAL** KUWAIT ✪ **POPULATION** 2.4 MILLION ✪ **AREA** 17,820 SQ KM ✪ **OFFICIAL LANGUAGE** ARABIC

It is hard to separate Kuwait's fortunes from that of its problematic neighbour, Iraq. It doesn't matter that this city-state has reinvented itself in the shape of a modern, sophisticated metropolis of gleaming new malls and waterside caffe-latte terraces; as far as most tourists are concerned, it neighbours Iraq and that's a problem. This blight by association may not be resolved any time soon. For those who dare to look beyond the media projection, however, Kuwait has some wonderful museums, souk and cultural activities, and the new resorts along its sandy coastline reward a visit.

LEBANON

 ✪ **CAPITAL** BEIRUT ✪ **POPULATION** 3.9 MILLION ✪ **AREA** 10,400 SQ KM ✪ **OFFICIAL LANGUAGE** ARABIC

How quickly things can change. Until mid-2006, Lebanon was fast returning to full health after its turbulent past. Beirut had a thumping pulse, with cool designer bars, funky boutiques and innovative galleries. Country-wide, 2007 would have seen the development of quality backpacker hostels, ecoresorts, and European-style mountain retreats. With the attacks from Israel that began in July 2006, these plans have taken a dramatic turn, and rebuilding infrastructure and repairing the emotional wounds from this man-made devastation will remain at the fore for a number of years. At the time of writing, it's difficult to predict what the recovery process will mean for travellers, but it seems likely that tourism to Lebanon in 2007 will be distinctly 'dark'.

LIBYA

 ✪ **CAPITAL** TRIPOLI ✪ **POPULATION** 5.9 MILLION ✪ **AREA** 1,759,540 SQ KM ✪ **OFFICIAL LANGUAGE** ARABIC

Libya suddenly seems a less remote travel destination, thanks to a thawing in US policy toward the country in May 2006, after 25 years of severed ties with its leader Muammar Gaddafi. Tripoli gets the thumbs up from many, with great shopping (pick up a Gaddafi watch in the medina); its clean beaches and sparkling sea; and the archaeological delights of the Roman ruins at Sabratha and Leptis Magna. Your liver will get a holiday too, as there's strictly no alcohol for sale here (although backyard-brewed *bokha* and Tunisian rosé are not too difficult to track down).

MOROCCO

 ✪ **CAPITAL** RABAT ✪ **POPULATION** 32.2 MILLION ✪ **AREA** 446,550 SQ KM ✪ **OFFICIAL LANGUAGE** ARABIC

Morocco has been playing host to foreign visitors ever since Bogart and Bergman played it again in *Casablanca*. But tourism is about to hit the big time, with the arrival of the low-cost airlines. Those looking for weekend sun are hitting Marrakesh in ever-increasing numbers, and the city's trendy *riad* hotels (traditional houses converted into hotels) are struggling to cope with demand. The beaches of Agadir are also booming, although the fashionable have long known that the charming port of Essaouira is the place to be. Get away from it all by trekking into the mountains, or just riding that camel into the Saharan sunset.

SNAPSHOTS.

OMAN

✪ **CAPITAL** MUSCAT ✪ **POPULATION** 3.1 MILLION
✪ **AREA** 212,460 SQ KM ✪ **OFFICIAL LANGUAGE** ARABIC

Few could miss the heightened interest in Oman this year. Having just celebrated the 35th year of its renaissance, Oman is accelerating the pace of change and promoting sensitive tourism. The much-vaunted Shangri-La complex is now open and is proving a success with visitors looking for luxury on the edge of the Arabian Sea. If you're worried you've missed the 'pristine moment' of Oman's integration into the modern world, then don't fret: the landscape is as wild and magnificent as ever. Chances are that you will have the 2000km coastline to yourself; and the mountain wadis remain wonderlands of natural beauty.

PALESTINIAN TERRITORIES

✪ **POPULATION** 3.6 MILLION ✪ **AREA** 7378 SQ KM
✪ **OFFICIAL LANGUAGE** ARABIC

Hardly a destination for tourists, the Palestinian Territories are filled with roadblocks, checkpoints and cities that always hover on the brink of violence. The troubles are no longer limited to conflict between Israel and the Palestinian militia, as rival Palestinian groups now slug it out on the streets of Gaza and elsewhere. There are a few reasonably safe places to visit, including Bethlehem and Jericho, but monitor the situation before you go. In good times, Hebron, Nablus and Ramallah are other options, but don't expect much in the way of tourist facilities. A good way to visit these places is on day trips from Jerusalem.

QATAR

✪ **CAPITAL** DOHA ✪ **POPULATION** 885,360
✪ **AREA** 11,437 SQ KM ✪ **OFFICIAL LANGUAGE** ARABIC

In a recent athletics grand prix in Doha, Justin Gatlin ran the 100m in 9.8 seconds, a world record and the kind of milestone that has helped Qatar build a reputation for hosting events of sporting excellence. This oil-rich state has been canny in its investment in sports and leisure facilities, and it now attracts a healthy number of tourists looking for winter sun, sea and sport. There's more to Qatar than the booming city of Doha, however. Dunes in the south of the country and some pleasant fishing villages in the north preserve the Bedouin heart of the country.

SAUDI ARABIA

✪ **CAPITAL** RIYADH ✪ **POPULATION** 27 MILLION
✪ **AREA** 1,960,582 SQ KM ✪ **OFFICIAL LANGUAGE** ARABIC

Cast aside clichés of oil-rich sheiks, date palms and expatriate workers, and visit one of the last frontiers of tourism. Wrangle a special visa and a healthy travel budget and join Saudi Arabia's 3.5 million annual visitors – most of these taking part in the hajj (pilgrimage to Mecca). Witness the ancient Bedouin *ardha* sword dance; taste the culinary delights of mezze feasts and see ancient rock-hewn Madain Saleh, a marvel akin to Petra in Jordan. Time your visit to coincide with Al Jenadriyah, the country's two-week culture and heritage festival held near Riyadh in late February or early March, to witness camel races and folkloric dances and join in one helluva party.

SYRIA

✪ **CAPITAL** DAMASCUS ✪ **POPULATION** 18.9 MILLION
✪ **AREA** 185,180 SQ KM ✪ **OFFICIAL LANGUAGE** ARABIC

While Syria's appealing second city, Aleppo, has always offered a more satisfying travel experience with its atmospheric boutique hotels and mazelike souks, the capital of Damascus is really starting to hit its stride. In a show of confidence in Damascus' future, hip Middle East clothing retailer Villa Moda has opened a branch here and the long-awaited luxury Four Seasons Damascus is finally taking bookings. However, the hit of the scene has been Beit Al Mamlouka, a boutique hotel in the Christian quarter of Damascus' Unesco-listed old city, which has garnered rave reviews since opening in 2005. With restoration work moving apace in the old city, dusty Damascus looks to be on the cusp of a renaissance.

TUNISIA

✪ **CAPITAL** TUNIS ✪ **POPULATION** 10.2 MILLION
✪ **AREA** 163,610 SQ KM ✪ **OFFICIAL LANGUAGE** ARABIC

While Tunisia continues to enchant with its traditional white architecture, sublime Sahara Desert, and spectacular ancient sites, the country is now taking a chic turn. Sure tourists still bake on Cap Bon's beaches and backpackers savour camping in the Sahara or shacking up at otherworldly Chenini (of *Star Wars* fame), but other travellers are gravitating to Tunisia's growing number of affordable boutique hotels. Carthage's minimalist Hotel Villa Didon (with restaurant Spoon Carthage by Alain Ducasse) and the luxurious Pansea Douar camp (complete with sandy swimming pool in the Ksar Ghilane oasis) have raised the bar significantly. The trend will continue in 2007, with stylish openings particularly in Tunis' medina. Wherever you stay, Tozeur's labyrinthine medina and lush *palmeraie* (the area around an oasis where date palms grow) along with the winter Festival of the Oases shouldn't be missed.

TURKEY

 ○ **CAPITAL** ANKARA ○ **POPULATION** 70.4 MILLION
○ **AREA** 780,580 SQ KM ○ **OFFICIAL LANGUAGE** TURKISH

Cliché has it that Turkey is the bridge between East and West, and endless debate rages as to whether it is European or not. It seems, however, that Turkey itself is finished with such uncertainty and is setting its own course as a Western, secular and determinedly modern nation. Yet the cliché is true to a degree, as Turkey *does* offer the delights of both hemispheres: the cosmopolitan neighbourhoods of Istanbul and remote vistas of the southeast, beach resorts on the Med and the underground monasteries of Kapadokya (Cappadocia). Who cares if it's East or West – visit and find out for yourself.

UNITED ARAB EMIRATES

 ○ **CAPITAL** ABU DHABI ○ **POPULATION** 2.6 MILLION
○ **AREA** 82,880 SQ KM ○ **OFFICIAL LANGUAGE** ARABIC

While many assume that the United Arab Emirates (UAE) capital is Dubai, the actual capital, Abu Dhabi, is making strides in the tourism stakes. With its laid-back, leafy charm, and its colossal Emirates Palace hotel, it offers a slice of slightly more 'authentic' Arabia. However, it is Dubai that's still the key UAE tourism destination with authorities predicting it will triple its five million annual visitors by 2010. With a busy roster of shopping festivals and international sporting events, Dubai is becoming a year-round tourism destination, despite summer temperatures often topping 45°C. No problem: new attractions such as the Ski Dubai indoor ski resort aim to keep visitors cool.

YEMEN

 ○ **CAPITAL** SAN'A ○ **POPULATION** 21.4 MILLION
○ **AREA** 527,970 SQ KM ○ **OFFICIAL LANGUAGE** ARABIC

Despite having mercifully slipped from the news recently, Yemen's image since 9/11 as a harbourer of gun-toting terrorists and kidnappers has barely changed. And this is hardly surprising when the kidnapping of tourists continues. With many Western governments issuing advice against unessential travel to Yemen, it is hard to recommend that travellers do otherwise. If the allure of one of the most stunning countries in Arabia is too hard to resist, however, then it's probably worth sticking to the main cities. San'a alone, with its medieval skyscrapers and labyrinthine souk, has more than enough adventure to keep a visitor occupied.

NORTH
ATLANTIC
OCEAN

MAURITANIA

MALI

NIGER

CH

CAPE
VERDE

SENEGAL

GAMBIA

GUINEA-
BISSAU

GUINEA

BURKINA
FASO

BENIN

TOGO

NIGERIA

SIERRA
LEONE

CÔTE
D'IVOIRE

GHANA

LIBERIA

CAMEROON

Gulf of Guinea

EQUATORIAL
GUINEA

SÃO TOMÉ
& PRÍNCIPE

GABON

REPUB
OF CON

ANGOLA

SOUTH
ATLANTIC
OCEAN

NAMI

Mediterranean Sea

Red Sea

SUDAN   ERITREA

DJIBOUTI   Gulf of Aden

ENTRAL
FRICAN
EPUBLIC

ETHIOPIA

UGANDA

1OCRATIC
UBLIC OF
ONGO

SOMALIA

KENYA

RWANDA

BURUNDI

INDIAN OCEAN

TANZANIA

SEYCHELLES

COMOROS

MALAWI

MAYOTTE
(FRANCE)

ZAMBIA

MOZAMBIQUE

ZIMBABWE

MADAGASCAR

MAURITIUS

Mozambique
Channel

RÉUNION
(FRANCE)

TSWANA

SWAZILAND

LESOTHO

OUTH
FRICA

» SUBSAHARAN
AFRICA

» SUBSAHARAN AFRICA

ANGOLA

✪ **CAPITAL** LUANDA ✪ **POPULATION** 12.1 MILLION
✪ **AREA** 1,246,700 SQ KM ✪ **OFFICIAL LANGUAGE** PORTUGUESE

Polish up your Portuguese and beat a path to Angola in 2007. Now a few years out of its 26-year civil war, it remains a true off-the-beaten-track destination for the adventurous traveller. There's a growing sense of prosperity in Angola, which is Africa's second-largest oil producer; with care, it's a relatively safe place to add to an African odyssey, but do check for travel warnings. Crush yourself into the overcrowded capital, Luanda, and experience the delirium of colour and activity in its streets and markets, then head down to nearby Parque Nacional da Kissama for some budding wildlife watching.

BENIN

✪ **CAPITAL** PORTO NOVO ✪ **POPULATION** 7.9 MILLION
✪ **AREA** 110,620 SQ KM ✪ **OFFICIAL LANGUAGE** FRENCH

International observers applauded the smooth running of Benin's presidential elections in March 2006, when former West African Development Bank head Yayi Boni replaced 72-year-old Mathieu Kérékou, who had reigned for most of the previous 35 years. It was an impressive feat for a country that both had a communist government in the 1970s and was the centre of the West African slave trade under the mighty Dahomey kings. Traces of this rich heritage can be seen, albeit in crumbling form, in palace-filled Abomey and former slave port Ouidah. Being the birthplace of voodoo, Benin is also the ideal place to find a fetish market.

BOTSWANA

✪ **CAPITAL** GABORONE ✪ **POPULATION** 1.6 MILLION
✪ **AREA** 600,370 SQ KM ✪ **OFFICIAL LANGUAGE** ENGLISH

We don't need to hire the No 1 Ladies Detective Agency to find Botswana's secrets for tourism success in 2007. The allure of the Okavango Delta, which sees the Kalahari's sands swallow the massive Okavango River whole, will remain as undeniable as it is incredible. Sharing the spectacle with more African wildlife than you can shake a stick at, from your sweet seat in a *mokoro* (dugout canoe), is exhilarating. The wildlife of

Chobe National Park and Moremi Wildlife Reserve will also be a big draw. For loftier perspectives, climb the Tsodilo Hills and gawk at ancient rock paintings and panoramas over a desert sea.

BURKINA FASO

 ✪ **CAPITAL** OUAGADOUGOU ✪ **POPULATION** 13.9 MILLION ✪ **AREA** 274,200 SQ KM ✪ **OFFICIAL LANGUAGE** FRENCH

Landlocked Burkina Faso is one of the world's poorest countries – a fact that belies the riches on offer here for travellers. Head to the 'Country of Honest Men' (as its name translates into English) for the spectacular waterfalls of Karfiguéla, Gorom-Gorom's humming Thursday market, and the out-of-this-world landscapes of the Pics de Sindou. Movie buffs should make a beeline for Africa's largest film fest, the Pan-African Film Festival to be held in February 2007 in the laid-back capital of Ouagadougou. Those with a thing for the Muppets will have to wait until 2008 for the International Theatre & Puppetry Festival, also to be held in the capital.

BURUNDI

 ✪ **CAPITAL** BUJUMBURA ✪ **POPULATION** 8.1 MILLION ✪ **AREA** 27,834 SQ KM ✪ **OFFICIAL LANGUAGES** KIRUNDI, FRENCH

Plagued by intertribal tensions and violence since its independence in 1962, Burundi may finally be on the brink of peace. After a peaceful conclusion to the political transition process in 2005, which included a constitutional referendum and series of national elections, the government spent 2006 implementing a programme to shift resources away from humanitarian programmes and refocus them on development and a poverty reduction strategy. However, despite all the progress, it's still not wise to pack your bags just yet. Sudden outbreaks of violence still occur throughout the country, including attacks and ambushes by rebel forces.

CAMEROON

 ✪ **CAPITAL** YAOUNDÉ ✪ **POPULATION** 17.3 MILLION ✪ **AREA** 475,440 SQ KM ✪ **OFFICIAL LANGUAGES** FRENCH, ENGLISH

Cameroon's tourist industry is a victim of geography. It sits in a bad neighbourhood, bordered by some very problematic countries. But this shouldn't put you off, as Cameroon has just about everything a traveller could want. You can trek West Africa's highest peak, Mt Cameroon, near the coast or hike in the rolling Mandara Mountains. Wildlife fans are catered for at Parc National de Waza and at Korup, the continent's oldest rainforest. Good beaches and cold beer are plentiful, and the bars are full of lively *makossa* music, a fusion of highlife and soul. What more could you ask for?

CAPE VERDE

 ✪ **CAPITAL** PRAIA ✪ **POPULATION** 420,980 ✪ **AREA** 4033 SQ KM ✪ **OFFICIAL LANGUAGES** PORTUGUESE, CRIOULO

Sunny, warm Cape Verde is an increasingly popular winter getaway for Europeans, especially the desert-like resort islands of Sal and Boa Vista. For better or worse, construction of hotels, all-inclusive resorts and time-share apartments will continue at a rapid pace on both islands in 2007. Developers also have their eyes set on the nearly deserted Maio – the next Sal? In addition, ramblers continue to discover the greener, more mountainous islands of Santo Antão, Fogo and São Nicolau, which possess unexpected pleasures. Dodgy ferry schedules still make island-hopping difficult, but a dependable new service linking Praia, Mindelo and the island of São Nicolau definitely helps.

CENTRAL AFRICAN REPUBLIC

 ✪ **CAPITAL** BANGUI ✪ **POPULATION** 4.3 MILLION ✪ **AREA** 622,984 SQ KM ✪ **OFFICIAL LANGUAGE** FRENCH

Ever have those days when you think life just isn't fair? Now imagine a life of those days, one after another… Welcome to the Central African Republic. It's blessed with mineral wealth, impenetrable natural beauty and wildlife galore, yet it's undeveloped and its population is one of the world's poorest. Why? Easy answer: the greed of its ruthless leaders and the insatiability of the West who wanted its resources. What's most shocking of all is the continued warmth and generosity of its people. The violent fallout of the 2003 military coup is still widespread and travel here is sadly still not wise.

CHAD

 ✪ **CAPITAL** N'DJAMÉNA ✪ **POPULATION** 9.9 MILLION ✪ **AREA** 1,284,000 SQ KM ✪ **OFFICIAL LANGUAGES** FRENCH, ARABIC

Long dominated by slave-trading Arabs, then left to wither by the French, Chad has every right in the world to cry. Sadly, it's too parched to shed even one tear. The Sahara's southern march continues to consume Lake Chad, leaving striking seashells swimming in a sea of sand. Chad has long been a key link in the east–west trans-Saharan route, although recent violent rebel attacks at André near the Sudan border may jeopardise that. The same rebels, who Chad claims the Sudan government supports, attacked N'Djaména in April 2006 in an attempt to overthrow the president.

SNAPSHOTS.

COMOROS & MAYOTTE

 ✪ **CAPITAL** MORONI (C), MAMOUTZOU (M) ✪ **POPULATION** 690,950 (C), 201,230 (M) ✪ **AREA** 2170 SQ KM (C), 374 SQ KM (M) ✪ **OFFICIAL LANGUAGES** ARABIC (C), FRENCH (C & M)

The year 2006 witnessed Comoros' first peaceful change of power in its 30 years of independence. The unique new constitution sees the presidency rotated every four years between the three major islands, Grande Comore, Anjouan and Mohéli. Though there are still rumblings from those in Mayotte who want to say goodbye to French rule and join Comoros, politics in these two nations have never been calmer. Now if Mt Karthala (one of the world's largest active volcanoes) just behaves, all you'll have to worry about is enjoying the islands' cobblestone medinas, virgin rainforests, sun-soaked beaches, ports swimming with dhows, and blazing ocean sunsets that set the sky on fire.

CONGO, DEMOCRATIC REPUBLIC OF THE

 ✪ **CAPITAL** KINSHASA ✪ **POPULATION** 62.6 MILLION ✪ **AREA** 2,345,410 SQ KM ✪ **OFFICIAL LANGUAGE** FRENCH

The Democratic Republic of the Congo (DR Congo; formerly Zaïre) is truly a behemoth in both size and in the scale of its problems. Despite the civil war officially ending and an interim government taking control in mid-2003, serious outbreaks of violence continue, particularly in the provinces of North Kivu, South Kivu, Maniema and Orientale. In early 2006, eight UN peacekeepers were killed in an ambush, and soon after Kinshasa was the site of opposition party members clashing with riot police. Whether or not the July 2006 elections have made a significant impression on the peace process remains to be seen. Check the latest before contemplating a visit.

CONGO, REPUBLIC OF

 ✪ **CAPITAL** BRAZZAVILLE ✪ **POPULATION** 3.7 MILLION ✪ **AREA** 342,000 SQ KM ✪ **OFFICIAL LANGUAGE** FRENCH

With a finger in the Atlantic and its body squeezed between the Democratic Republic of the Congo and Gabon, the Republic of Congo is at a crucial point in its history. A tenuous 2003 ceasefire accord between the Ninja rebels and President Sassou-Nguesso's government still hangs in the balance, due to outbreaks of violence that continue to throw the certainty of a peaceful and fruitful future into question. Due to strong safety concerns, travel outside of Brazzaville and Point-Noire is still not recommended. If you don't mind being holed up in these cities, buy a Ngok beer and settle in for some *babyfoot* (table football) with the locals.

CÔTE D'IVOIRE

 ✪ **CAPITAL** YAMOUSSOUKRO ✪ **POPULATION** 17.6 MILLION ✪ **AREA** 322,460 SQ KM ✪ **OFFICIAL LANGUAGE** FRENCH

If all goes according to plan, 2007 will see a reunited Côte d'Ivoire…but don't bet on it. Agreements have been made on disarmament and voter-registration plans, but there have been numerous false starts before and many leaders on both sides have grown wealthy under the status quo. Even if the best-case scenario comes through, the high crime rate isn't going to just vanish. Expats, wealthy Ivoirians, and the occasional intrepid traveller still hit the country's beaches, which are some of the best in Africa. Sassandra, Dagbego and Assinie offer safe sands with a mix of luxury and budget lodging. Parc National de Taï, where international environmental groups have kept antipoaching patrols on guard since the troubles began, isn't fully operational, but it's again possible to visit.

DJIBOUTI

 ✪ **CAPITAL** DJIBOUTI CITY ✪ **POPULATION** 486,530 ✪ **AREA** 23,000 SQ KM ✪ **OFFICIAL LANGUAGES** ARABIC, FRENCH

Diminutive Djibouti continues to be East Africa's least-known country and as a result attracts few travellers. While its lunar landscapes, harsh conditions and almost absolute absence of tourists scream intrepid backpackers' dream, the costs here are prohibitive. Currently the majority of travellers who visit Djibouti are simply using it to transit between Eritrea and Ethiopia (no direct route currently exists) and only spend a day or two. However, thanks to *National Geographic*'s hyping of the Danakil Depression, Djibouti will likely attract more visitors in 2007 with the means to fund 4WD descents into the depths of Lac Assal (Africa's lowest point) and Lac Abbé.

EQUATORIAL GUINEA

 ✪ **CAPITAL** MALABO ✪ **POPULATION** 540,110 ✪ **AREA** 28,051 SQ KM ✪ **OFFICIAL LANGUAGES** SPANISH, FRENCH

The discovery of oil offshore has reshaped Bioko Island, home to Equatorial Guinea's capital Malabo. Locals have all but abandoned some smaller cities, such as Luba, and flooded into Malabo along with expat oil workers. While oil platforms fill the capital's harbour and tankers patrol its waters, the opposite end of the island is almost vacant – except for the masses of turtles who come ashore annually to lay eggs on Ureca's beaches. The mainland (Rio Muni) is another world at another time. It can still reward you with beaches, rainforest, traditional African villages and even the odd gorilla at Monte Alen National Park.

ERITREA

 ✪ **CAPITAL** ASMARA ✪ **POPULATION** 4.8 MILLION ✪ **AREA** 121,320 SQ KM ✪ **OFFICIAL LANGUAGE** TIGRINYA

Eritrea was once heralded as a great place for travelling and, with a bit of luck and following wind, this could soon be the case again. But as long as it remains at odds with Ethiopia, tourism development won't be a priority. The state's recent programmes of nationalisation and mass conscription have devastated the economy, leading to regular power cuts, food shortages and skyrocketing prices. If poor infrastructure and Eritreans' plaintive whispers inspire you to understand more, then consider travel to this peaceful place that's yearning to be explored. Intrepid travellers will be drawn to Eritrea's apocalyptic wasteland of Dankalia and the Danakil Depression.

ETHIOPIA

 ✪ **CAPITAL** ADDIS ABABA ✪ **POPULATION** 74.8 MILLION ✪ **AREA** 1,127,127 SQ KM ✪ **OFFICIAL LANGUAGE** AMHARIC

Ethiopia, arguably one of Africa's most beautiful, intriguing and well-known countries, will unfortunately continue to be the continent's most misunderstood nation. The momentum gained by Ethopia's burgeoning tourism industry after the 1998–2000 Ethiopia–Eritrea war was destroyed by election-related riots in late 2005 and simultaneous border tensions with Eritrea. Although Ethiopia is quiet again, tourist numbers will likely remain low in 2007. As the world wakes to the astounding and inhospitable attributes of the Danakil Depression, more visitors will jump off northern Ethiopia's inspiring 'Historical Circuit' and dive into the country's baking depths. New ecolodges in the Rift Valley, along with the Omo Valley's vivid tribes, will also shift more interest to southern Ethiopia.

GABON

See p158.

GAMBIA

 ✪ **CAPITAL** BANJUL ✪ **POPULATION** 1.6 MILLION ✪ **AREA** 11,300 SQ KM ✪ **OFFICIAL LANGUAGE** ENGLISH

Tourism in tiny Gambia is almost entirely concentrated along the country's 80km Atlantic shoreline. This situation is likely to remain unchanged, as the government, heavily involved in the tourist industry, continues to invest and encourage investment along the coast. With areas around Bakau, Fajara, Kololi and Kotu being almost entirely built up, and a new sealed road extending southwards along the coast, the existing zone of mass tourism is likely to spread further south, towards the Casamance border. Several luxury hotels are already under construction there, notably in Brufut and Kartong. Although a few new tourist camps have opened upcountry, these still attract mainly bird-watchers; terrible road conditions keep all but the most intrepid travellers away.

GHANA

 ✪ **CAPITAL** ACCRA ✪ **POPULATION** 22.4 MILLION ✪ **AREA** 239,460 SQ KM ✪ **OFFICIAL LANGUAGE** ENGLISH

Ghana's coastal capital Accra is competing with the Gambia to become the top West African destination for British sun-seekers. Work has begun on a new five-star hotel, the Movenpick Ambassador Hotel, following a US$100 million investment by the government and Saudi Arabian business colossus Prince Al-Saud. The hotel is due to be completed in time for Ghana's stint as host of the African Cup of Nations in 2008, along with two new football stadiums in Accra; the capital already boasts swish resorts such as the Labadi Beach Hotel. This laid-back country's charms include Lake Volta, Ashanti culture, and legions of Guinness-drinking reggae fans.

SNAPSHOTS.

GUINEA

 ⊙ **CAPITAL** CONAKRY ⊙ **POPULATION** 9.7 MILLION
⊙ **AREA** 245,857 SQ KM ⊙ **OFFICIAL LANGUAGE** FRENCH

Guinea has long been a bastion of stability in an unsettled region, but there is much concern that these days of peace – which come, unfortunately, without the allied prosperity – are numbered. President Lansana Conté, a chain-smoking diabetic who has repeatedly been on his deathbed over the past five years, appears to have made few plans for his succession, and many observers fear the worst when he runs out of recoveries. New hotels and trained trekking guides keep coming to the waterfall-rich Fouta Djalon; assuming there is no descent into anarchy, travellers will too. In addition, expect a budget beach resort or two somewhere on the northern coast to start attracting those who used to chill on the beach at Bel Air before the building boom.

GUINEA-BISSAU

 ⊙ **CAPITAL** BISSAU ⊙ **POPULATION** 1.4 MILLION
⊙ **AREA** 36,120 SQ KM ⊙ **OFFICIAL LANGUAGE** PORTUGUESE

Peaceful, multiparty elections in 2005 and resolution of a constitutional crisis in 2006 are cause for cautious optimism for Guinea-Bissau. Still, the country's infrastructure is reeling from the 1998 civil war, making internal travel difficult and prices high, especially in Bissau, a capital city that is tranquil but of modest charms. Except for some hunting lodges on the mainland, tourism is relegated to the Arquipélago dos Bijagós and its powdery beaches. Sports fishers with means swear by its turquoise waters, and a number of luxurious lodges have recently opened or are in the works, alongside current, more rustic options.

KENYA

 ⊙ **CAPITAL** NAIROBI ⊙ **POPULATION** 34.7 MILLION
⊙ **AREA** 582,650 SQ KM ⊙ **OFFICIAL LANGUAGES**
KASWAHILI, ENGLISH

Kenya, a perennial powerhouse in everything East African, continues to inspire a legion of travellers with its wildlife, landscapes and people. Although the renowned safari havens of Masai Mara and Amboseli continue to flourish, it's central Kenya's Laikipia Plateau that is starting to steal some of the thunder. There, following in the footsteps of the Lewa Wildlife Conservancy, local Maasai and Samburu communities have created several exclusive reserves that host great wildlife and inspired ecolodges. The projects' proceeds then fund education, health care and sustainable projects within the community. For a taste of Kenya few are lucky enough to see, venture up to the Jade Sea (Lake Turkana).

LESOTHO

 ⊙ **CAPITAL** MASERU ⊙ **POPULATION** 2 MILLION
⊙ **AREA** 30,355 SQ KM ⊙ **OFFICIAL LANGUAGES**
SESOTHO, ENGLISH

This mountainous kingdom, afloat in the sea of South Africa, remains an entrancing escape from the clamour and underlying tensions of its all-encompassing neighbour. Both Bono and Prince Harry made high-profile visits to Lesotho in 2006: Bono checking the fruits of Live8 and visiting the textile factory producing his fair trade Product Red T-shirts; Harry starting his AIDS orphan charity. How these media events will change travel trends in 2007 remains unclear. However, pony trekking around mountainous Malealea and exploring San rock paintings and dinosaur footsteps at Quthing will always be great options. If crowds do seep in, explore Mokhotlong, Lesotho's remotest corner.

LIBERIA

 ⊙ **CAPITAL** MONROVIA ⊙ **POPULATION** 3 MILLION
⊙ **AREA** 111,370 SQ KM ⊙ **OFFICIAL LANGUAGE** ENGLISH

Despite the relative stability in Liberia since the elections of January 2006, now is probably not the best time to holiday in this West African nation. The devastating civil war that ended in August 2003 has left the country scarred and unpredictable. UN peacekeepers and police advisers are still in place in the capital Monrovia, where there's little remaining infrastructure, food or housing. When the situation eventually normalises, travellers will at last be able to explore the 1308-sq-km Sapo National Park with its rare West African primary rainforest, and the pristine beaches of the country's Atlantic coast.

» SUBSAHARAN AFRICA

MADAGASCAR

See p168.

MALAWI

 CAPITAL LILONGWE **POPULATION** 13 MILLION **AREA** 118,480 SQ KM **OFFICIAL LANGUAGES** ENGLISH, CHICHEWA

Malawi continues to have a little of everything for your African adventure: beaches, mountains, wildlife and welcoming smiles. While Lake Malawi will undoubtedly still be on top of most travellers' must-see lists in 2007, fewer travellers will be visiting the old south-shore haunt of Cape Maclear. Nkhata Bay is now a more rewarding spot on the lake's shore, although new, beautiful and remote lodges at Usisya and Ruarwe may shift people further north still. Camp at Chitimba and you'll enjoy the sweet isolated sounds of fishermen singing in the evenings as the moon rises over the lake. Likoma Island is a remote joy too.

MALI

 CAPITAL BAMAKO **POPULATION** 11.7 MILLION **AREA** 1,240,140 SQ KM **OFFICIAL LANGUAGE** FRENCH

West Africa's largest country is starting to make its way onto the tourist map. With visitor numbers growing sharply, Mali is a great place to practise your responsible travel skills. Look for ways to preserve the country's unique culture and fragile environmental heritage when you encounter the extraordinary Mars-like landscape and mind-blowing culture of the Dogon Country; or as you follow the Niger River, skirting the southern edge of the Sahara from Moti to Timbuktu. And don't forget to pack your sense of humour and a few rib-ticklers – the people of Mali love a good joke.

MAURITANIA

 CAPITAL NOUAKCHOTT **POPULATION** 3.2 MILLION **AREA** 1,030,700 SQ KM **OFFICIAL LANGUAGE** ARABIC

Mauritania remains one of West Africa's most popular countries, attracting thousands of desert buffs each year. But what could really give new impetus to tourism in Mauritania is the oil boom that began in 2006; as a result of investment and expats, there's a growing need for more varied infrastructure and a greater choice of activities, both in the capital and in the desert. A reputable outfit has started hot-air ballooning trips over the Adrar's sand dunes, and there are already well-established camel treks and 4WD expeditions. Real pioneers should head for Oualâta, an ancient Saharan town in the southeast and possibly one of Mauritania's best-kept secrets. An airport may open in nearby Néma in 2007, translating into a tourist influx – get there before it becomes trendy.

MAURITIUS

 CAPITAL PORT LOUIS **POPULATION** 1.2 MILLION **AREA** 2040 SQ KM **OFFICIAL LANGUAGE** ENGLISH

Mauritius is hot in so many ways. It's got sun-drenched beaches, fiery curries, a pumping tourist industry – and it's also the world's first coast-to-coast Internet hot spot. This little 'cyberisland', nestled in the Indian Ocean, is expected to lead the region in wireless connectivity, thanks to a bold government initiative. Tech credentials aside, Mauritius is memorable for its distinctive melange of Indian, Chinese and Creole cultures; vibrant markets awash with fake Ralph Lauren T-shirts and dodo fridge magnets; and festivals practically every week. Come dinnertime, set your taste buds alight with fish vindaloo and cool them off with a Phoenix beer. You can check your emails later.

MOZAMBIQUE

 CAPITAL MAPUTO **POPULATION** 19.7 MILLION **AREA** 801,590 SQ KM **OFFICIAL LANGUAGE** PORTUGUESE

Mozambicans continue to strive forward, letting their dark and only too recent past sink deep into yesterday's shadows. They're rebuilding their country at an incredible pace, and its allure is starting to gain international attention. Creating a wave of late is the Quirimbas Archipelago, with 32 coral islands that are home to world-class diving, superb beaches and a new national park. Several lodges now call the area home and are associated with conservation projects. The Manda Wilderness Community Trust on the Mozambique shore of Lake Niassa (aka Lake Malawi) is another ecotourism project gaining momentum. It supports sustainable development in local communities as well as a nature reserve.

SNAPSHOTS.

NAMIBIA

 ✪ **CAPITAL** WINDHOEK ✪ **POPULATION** 2 MILLION
✪ **AREA** 825,418 SQ KM ✪ **OFFICIAL LANGUAGE** ENGLISH

Although always one of the world's most beautiful countries, it wasn't until 2006 that Namibia was truly thrust into the international spotlight and onto supermarket checkout stands. What happened? Brangelina arrived. If you're wholeheartedly confused, you're one lucky soul (please send us the coordinates of your tabloid-free world!). Joking aside, the endless press about Angelina Jolie and Brad Pitt's 'secluded' escape to await their love child may have just outed southern Africa's best-kept secret. Despite this, you'll still be able to find peace among Sossusvlei's earth-shattering dunes, along the Skeleton Coast's sands and on Etosha's never-ending and wildlife-laden plains. For sublime solitude, climb to the summit of Spitzkoppe.

NIGER

 ✪ **CAPITAL** NIAMEY ✪ **POPULATION** 12.5 MILLION
✪ **AREA** 1,267,000 SQ KM ✪ **OFFICIAL LANGUAGE** FRENCH

Who says all publicity is good publicity? Dramatic news reports in 2005 told the world that locusts and drought had all but destroyed Niger's food supply, while in reality crop production was only 10% below average and food was still in markets. Although complicated, the crisis resulted from nomadic herders being unable to access or afford the available food. Fallout from the publicity continues to haunt Niger's tourism industry, despite its epicentre (Agadez) being unaffected by the crisis. Hopefully the new direct flights from Europe to Agadez will rejuvenate things by 2007. Agadez is the Sahara's mystical gateway to the Aïr Mountains and Ténéré Desert.

NIGERIA

 ✪ **CAPITAL** ABUJA ✪ **POPULATION** 131.8 MILLION
✪ **AREA** 923,768 SQ KM ✪ **OFFICIAL LANGUAGE** ENGLISH

Let's face it, Nigeria has an image problem when it comes to attracting tourists. Communal violence and email scams just aren't the country's best adverts. But for all Nigeria's problems, a recent international poll announced that Nigerians were the happiest people on the planet. The crazy urban sprawl of Lagos has a buzz like no other city in Africa, and you'll be welcomed with a smile, from the desert mosques of the north to the lush green south. Keep your ear to the ground (giving a wide berth to 2007's presidential election), and you might be pleasantly surprised.

RÉUNION

 ✪ **CAPITAL** ST-DENIS ✪ **POPULATION** 787,580
✪ **AREA** 2517 SQ KM ✪ **OFFICIAL LANGUAGE** FRENCH

The mosquito-borne chikungunya virus had a negative impact on travel in Réunion in 2005 and 2006. However, it's no worse than malaria, and it's easy to travel safely if you stock up on mosquito repellent. In any case, don't let it deter you from exploring the spectacular natural wonders of this island and its wildly dramatic mountain terrain. In 2007, part of the rugged interior is due to be classified as national park, which will mean increased infrastructure (refuges, paths, camp sites) and more outdoor options on offer, including treks, rappelling and canyoning.

RWANDA

 ✪ **CAPITAL** KIGALI ✪ **POPULATION** 8.6 MILLION
✪ **AREA** 26,338 SQ KM ✪ **OFFICIAL LANGUAGES**
KINYARWANDA, FRENCH, ENGLISH

Blanketed in a patchwork of greens that would rival those of Ireland, Rwanda is easily one of East Africa's most beautiful sights. Amazingly, it wasn't long ago that the country was red from head to toe, drowning in a sea of spilled blood. And if it wasn't for the allure of tracking gorillas in the mist, the horrors of the 1994 genocide may have scared off a generation of travellers. Yet with another year of impressive peace under its belt, Rwanda in 2007 should see more than a trickle of travellers venturing into the Virunga volcanoes searching for silver backs. You'll burst with joy. You'll weep in anguish. Rwanda will touch your soul.

SÃO TOMÉ & PRÍNCIPE

 ✪ **CAPITAL** SÃO TOMÉ ✪ **POPULATION** 193,410 ✪ **AREA**
1001 SQ KM ✪ **OFFICIAL LANGUAGE** PORTUGUESE

Swimming in the Gulf of Guinea, these sleepy islands with miles of deserted beaches, translucent waters, divine diving, jagged rock formations, lush rainforests and unique Portuguese-Creole culture are slowly being roused by the discovery of liquid gold (oil) off shore.

The gargantuan sums of potential oil income have already rung cash registers behind the eyes of some, leading to political corruption and turmoil. While it's clear (so far at least) that the oil industry's wealth hasn't reached the general population, it's uncertain how the industry will affect the islands' great natural attractions. Our advice? Put São Tomé and Príncipe on your 'sooner rather than later' list.

SENEGAL

◊ **CAPITAL** DAKAR ◊ **POPULATION** 12 MILLION
◊ **AREA** 196,190 SQ KM ◊ **OFFICIAL LANGUAGE** FRENCH

Senegal is a favourite tourist destination in West Africa, particularly popular with French and Spanish travellers. The beaches around Dakar and south of the capital, along the sheltered Petite Côte, are still the main attraction, though the resort zone of Saly-Portugal might lose in tourist favour. This is because the stunning beaches of Cap Skiring in the Casamance are becoming once again accessible through road-works, an excellent Dakar–Ziguinchor boat connection and, most importantly, signs of lasting peace in the Casamance. Northern Senegal is still the preferred destination of the most intrepid travellers, though the restoration of the ancient Podor fort and the cruise-tour of the classic boat *Bou El Mogdad* are likely to attract more tourists to this arid region.

SEYCHELLES

◊ **CAPITAL** VICTORIA ◊ **POPULATION** 81,540
◊ **AREA** 455 SQ KM ◊ **OFFICIAL LANGUAGES**
ENGLISH, FRENCH, CREOLE

According to the country's tourism marketing author-ity, the Seychelles is 'as pure as it gets'. With dazzling tropical-paradise beauty and breathtaking diving on offer, these 115 coral islands scattered across one million square kilometres of the Indian Ocean make an idyllic getaway…if you've got the cash. To fund your travels, try searching the Bel Ombre district on the island of Mahé for the legendary treasure trove of pirate La Buse, or visit a *bonhomme* or *bonnefemme di bois* (medicine man or woman) for a good-luck potion. Having secured your finances, kick back and enjoy the vibrant Festival Kreol, an explosion of Creole culture and cuisine, which is held every October.

SIERRA LEONE

◊ **CAPITAL** FREETOWN ◊ **POPULATION** 6 MILLION
◊ **AREA** 71,740 SQ KM ◊ **OFFICIAL LANGUAGE** ENGLISH

Although the news has been slow to spread beyond West Africa, the war in Sierra Leone has been over – and the peace has held solid – for five years now. As people finally realise that Sierra Leone is one of West Africa's safest destinations, the beach bums and bird-watchers are trickling back in. Luxury resorts are opening amid the palm trees across the Freetown Peninsula, but they haven't pushed out all the budget bungalows…yet. The peace dividend hasn't flowed out as fast to the provinces, though new hotels and newly paved highways mean travel to upcountry parks and towns is becoming less the adventure it once was.

SOMALIA

◊ **CAPITAL** MOGADISHU ◊ **POPULATION** 8.9 MILLION
◊ **AREA** 637,657 SQ KM ◊ **OFFICIAL LANGUAGE** SOMALI

Draped over the Horn of Africa like a contortionist over a razor-sharp sword, Somalia remains one of the world's most dangerous destinations. Although still recognised internationally as a country, for all intents and purposes it has been three separate countries since 1991: Somaliland in the northwest on the Gulf of Aden; Puntland in the northeast; and Somalia in the south. Although a slow trickle of brave travellers have tiptoed around Somaliland (the most stable of the three) since the border recently opened with Ethiopia, it's still a destination to take some care with.

SOUTH AFRICA

◊ **CAPITAL** PRETORIA ◊ **POPULATION** 44.2 MILLION
◊ **AREA** 1,219,912 SQ KM ◊ **OFFICIAL LANGUAGES** ZULU,
XHOSA, AFRIKAANS, NORTH SOTHO, ENGLISH, TSWANA, SOUTH SOTHO,
TSONGA, SWATI, VENDA, NDEBELE

South Africa will continue to be southern Africa's most visited nation in 2007. Long the traditional haunts of travellers, Cape Town, the Garden Route and Kruger National Park will continue to be popular: they are simply too majestic to ignore. Those travellers with more time on their hands, or those coming back for seconds and thirds, will likely head to the emerging destinations of Transkei and the Wild Coast, the »

SNAPSHOTS.

Drakensberg mountains and our favourite, the Kgala-gadi Transfrontier Park. For a sublime seaside taste that few South Africans get to enjoy, contact the National Parks Board for a chance to hike the Otter Trail.

SUDAN

 ✪ **CAPITAL** KHARTOUM ✪ **POPULATION** 41.2 MILLION ✪ **AREA** 2,505,810 SQ KM ✪ **OFFICIAL LANGUAGE** ARABIC

Sudan's year for travellers was meant to be 2006. But the ink was barely dry on the peace deal that ended 20 years of civil war in the south, than the world's TV screens were full of the unfolding rebellion in Darfur. Despite endless peace talks, the chances of that story having a happy ending soon remain slim. But remember that this is a country the size of Western Europe, and calm elsewhere has led intrepid travellers to explore the Nile route to Khartoum and on towards Ethiopia. Who knew that this country had more pyramids than Egypt?

SWAZILAND

 ✪ **CAPITAL** MBABANE ✪ **POPULATION** 1.1 MILLION ✪ **AREA** 17,363 SQ KM ✪ **OFFICIAL LANGUAGES** SWATI, ENGLISH

While another tiny, mountainous, landlocked and impoverished kingdom is struggling with unrest (Nepal), the Kingdom of Swaziland continues to be one of Africa's most stable countries. Witnessing the annual Incwala and Umhlanga ceremonies of King Mswati III, who is Africa's last absolute monarch, are still great reasons to visit. The Mkhaya Game Reserve is another, as it provides one of your best chances on the continent to see the endangered black rhino in the wild. Although recently burdened with the news that it now possesses the world's highest AIDS rate, Swaziland continues to be an incredibly easy-going country and a pleasant place to travel.

TANZANIA

 ✪ **CAPITAL** DODOMA ✪ **POPULATION** 37.4 MILLION ✪ **AREA** 945,087 SQ KM ✪ **OFFICIAL LANGUAGES** SWAHILI, ENGLISH

Tanzania will continue to be a premier African destination in 2007. All the justifiable fuss can be explained in three words: Serengeti, Kilimanjaro and Zanzibar. Although the mighty three will still pull serious numbers, it's more remote destinations like Kilwa Kisiwani, Mafia Island and the Mahale Mountains that will finally become blips on travellers' radar. Kilwa Kisiwani, off the southeast coast, hosts the intriguing ruins of a famed Swahili trading centre, while Mafia Island, 120km south of Dar es Salaam, offers access to the underrated Mafia Island Marine Park. The isolated Mahale Mountains proffer chimpanzees and slices of white sand dipping into Lake Tanganyika's crystal-clear waters.

TOGO

 ✪ **CAPITAL** LOMÉ ✪ **POPULATION** 5.5 MILLION ✪ **AREA** 56,785 SQ KM ✪ **OFFICIAL LANGUAGE** FRENCH

Once a tourist hot spot, this troubled country must now concentrate on political progress before it will have many tourist developments to report. President Faure Gnassingbé, who succeeded his despotic father in 2005, is starting political dialogue in the country and persuading refugees to return from neighbouring Benin. If this continues along with the pint-sized nation's headline-grabbing sports performances – it competed in the 2006 FIFA World Cup, and won the African light middleweight boxing championship – perhaps tourists will rediscover Togo. Intrepid travellers already love the coastal capital Lomé, where ribald bars line the broad boulevards, and the forest-covered hills in the coffee triangle around Kpalimé.

UGANDA

 ✪ **CAPITAL** KAMPALA ✪ **POPULATION** 28.2 MILLION ✪ **AREA** 237,040 SQ KM ✪ **OFFICIAL LANGUAGE** ENGLISH

Today, Uganda is likely Africa's biggest success story. Its economy is roaring and its vigorous campaign against AIDS has dropped infection rates from more than 30% in the 1990s to below 10%. The only black mark hanging over Uganda has been the north's insecurity, due to the vicious Lord's Resistance Army (LRA). However, 2006 saw Joseph Kony (LRA's leader) call for an end to the 20-year war. If this comes to fruition, the north's gems like Murchison Falls may open up to travellers again. Until then, Bwindi National Park's mountain gorillas, Rwenzori Mountains' snowcapped peaks and Lake Victoria's Ssese Islands will continue to be big draws.

» SUBSAHARAN AFRICA

ZAMBIA

 ⊙ **CAPITAL** LUSAKA ⊙ **POPULATION** 11.5 MILLION
⊙ **AREA** 752,614 SQ KM ⊙ **OFFICIAL LANGUAGE** ENGLISH

With Zimbabwe's tourism down the plughole, Zambia is happily picking up the pieces. Its side of Victoria Falls is simply humming with activity, transforming nearby Livingstone from a backwater to a boomtown. The falls still speak for themselves – stand at Knife Edge Point and bathe in the view and swirling mist. Simply transcendent. For those who don't think standing on a slippery 100m precipice is enough, there's now white-water rafting, jetboating, bungee jumping, abseiling and flights in microlites. With more people in Zambia for the falls, other gems like South Luangwa National Park are likely to also see more visitors in 2007.

ZIMBABWE

 ⊙ **CAPITAL** HARARE ⊙ **POPULATION** 12.2 MILLION
⊙ **AREA** 390,580 SQ KM ⊙ **OFFICIAL LANGUAGE** ENGLISH

While Zimbabwe's current economic and humanitarian crisis has played a part in devastating the once-booming tourism industry, it's safe to say the hostile political climate of land reforms, forced evictions and absence of personal freedoms is the main culprit. Annual inflation has surpassed 1000% and one quarter of Zimbabweans have now left Zimbabwe. The money they send back to family is now the nation's largest source of income, surpassing tobacco, maize, mining and tourism. If 2007 is like 2006, only a few intrepid travellers will visit Zimbabwe's former hallowed highlights of Victoria Falls, Great Zimbabwe and the national parks of Hwange and Mana Pools.

AVIA

Barents
Sea

Laptev
Sea

East
Siberian
Sea

EASTERN
EUROPE

RUSSIA

Bering
Sea

Sea Of
Okhotsk

CAUCASUS

CENTRAL
ASIA

NORTHEAST
ASIA

Sea Of
Japan

NORTH
PACIFIC
OCEAN

RANEAN
PE

Mediterranean
Sea

MIDDLE
EAST

CA

East
China
Sea

Red Sea

ARABIAN
PENINSULA

INDIAN
SUBCONTINENT

SOUTHEAST
ASIA

TRAL
RICA

EAST
AFRICA

INDIAN
OCEAN

INDONESIAN
ARCHIPELAGO

MELANESIA

Coral
Sea

UTHERN
AFRICA

AUSTRALIA

Tasman
Sea

NEW
ZEALAND

SOUTHERN
OCEAN

» WORLD MAP

ANTARCTICA

ACKNOWLEDGEMENTS.

Publisher **Roz Hopkins**

Publishing Manager **Chris Rennie**

Commissioning Editors **Ben Handicott, Bridget Blair**

Editorial & Production Manager **Jenny Bilos**

Project Manager **Adam McCrow**

Publishing Planning Manager **Jo Vraca**

Image Coordinator **Rebecca Dandens**

Image Research **Pepi Bluck**

Designer **Mark Adams**

Layout Designer **Mik Ruff**

Design Manager **Brendan Dempsey**

Cartographer **Wayne Murphy**

Coordinating Editor **Liz Heynes**

Assisting Editors **Kate Cody, Laura Gibb, Yvonne Byron**

Managing Editors **Annelies Mertens, Suzannah Shwer**

Publishing Administrator **Fiona Siseman**

Pre-press Production **Ryan Evans**

Print Production Manager **Graham Imeson**

Text: Part 1 Intro **Jason Shugg**

Text: Part 2 **Andrew Bain, Craig Scutt,
Meg Worby, Paul Smitz, Tony Wheeler**

With many thanks to **Alex Fenby, Amanda Canning,
Andrea Frost, Brice Gosnell, Carol Chandler, Clifton
Wilkinson, David Zingarelli, Ella O'Donnell, Emily
Wolman, Errol Hunt, Fayette Fox, Fiona Buchan,
Greg Benchwick, Heather Carswell, Heather Dickson,
Imogen Hall, Imogen Young, Indra Kilfoyle, Jane
Thompson, Janine Eberle, Jay Cooke, Jennye Garibaldi,
Jessa Boanas-Dewes, Judith Bamber, Kalya Ryan,
Kathleen Munnelly, Kerryn Burgess, Lucy Monie,
Marg Toohey, Michaela Klink, Michala Green, Myriam
Cotterell, Paula Hardy, Piers Pickard, Rachel Williams,
Rebecca Chau, Sally Schafer, Sam Trafford, Shauna
Burford, Simone McNamara, Stefanie Di Trocchio,
Stephanie Pearson, Suki Gear, Vivek Wagle, Wendy
Wright, Wibowo Rusli, William Gourlay**

COUNTRY INDEX.

LONELY PLANET BLUELIST.
The Best in Travel 2007
November 2007

PUBLISHED BY
Lonely Planet Publications Pty Ltd
ABN 36 005 607 983
90 Maribyrnong St, Footscray,
Victoria, 3011, Australia

www.lonelyplanet.com

Printed by SNP Security Printing Pte Ltd, Singapore

PHOTOGRAPHS
Many of the images in this book are available for
licensing from Lonely Planet Images.
www.lonelyplanetimages.com

ISBN 1741047358

LONELY PLANET OFFICES
AUSTRALIA
Locked Bag 1, Footscray, Victoria, 3011
Phone 03 8379 8000 **Fax** 03 8379 8111
Email talk2us@lonelyplanet.com.au
USA
150 Linden St, Oakland, CA 94607
Phone 510 893 8555 **Toll free** 800 275 8555
Fax 510 893 8572 **Email** info@lonelyplanet.com
UK
72-82 Rosebery Ave London EC1R 4RW
Phone 020 7841 9000 **Fax** 020 7841 9001
Email go@lonelyplanet.co.uk